The Sea Is Not Full

Ocean Sailing Revelations & Misadventures

All rivers run into the sea; yet the sea is not full;
unto the place from whence the rivers come,
thither they return again.

—Ecclesiastes, 1:7

The Sea Is Not Full

Ocean Sailing Revelations & Misadventures

Charles J. Doane

The Sea Is Not Full
Ocean Sailing Revelations & Misadventures

Design by Claire MacMaster, barefoot art graphic design

Cover illustration by JT Morrow, represented by DEBORAH WOLFE LTD
Watercolor illustrations by Scott Kennedy
Technical illustrations by Kim Downing

Printed by Printworks Global Ltd., London & Hong Kong

First Edition

ISBN 13: 978-0-9973920-3-6
ISBN 10: 0-9973920-3-7

As always, this is for

Clare and the *Lunacy* sisters,

but also for

Gunther Rodatz, a calm and stalwart shipmate,

and for

Doris Rodatz, a brave woman indeed,

and for those who came to us:

Lt. David Birky USCG

Lt. John Poley USCG

AST2 John Knight USCG

AMT2 Brian Light USCG

PRELUDE: A Delivery Gone Wrong

U.S. East Coast

January 2014

THE FIRST HINT I HAVE that this voyage will be more troublesome than most comes not long before it begins, when Gregor, who I consider a friend, calls to tell me he is nervous about my going. He is the man who runs the new company that has designed and constructed this boat we are about to deliver south—a brand-new 42-foot fiberglass catamaran. It is the very first boat he has built, the culmination of a lifelong ambition. He has always been passionate about catamarans, has written a respected reference book on the subject, has long been a dealer for several top European brands in the United States, and has always wanted to create boats himself.

This dream-burdened vessel, named *Be Good Too* by its new owners, who of course have also packed it full of their own aspirations, was completed seven months late, which in itself is not surprising. Even for well-established builders, it is not unusual to be late delivering hull number one of a new design. Gunther and Doris had planned to move aboard last June and then spend the summer shaking down their new boat while cruising the New England coast. Now they are getting her in January, fresh out of the box with no chance to test her, and want only to sail out of this awful winter and down to the Caribbean as quickly as possible.

Gregor's anxiety about me signing on as crew on *Be Good*'s maiden voyage is also not surprising. As a sailing journalist I am bound ultimately to write a review of this boat, the first new yacht of any size built on Long Island in many decades, and he has confessed to me she is not as perfect as he had hoped.

The next hint comes not long after we cast off our lines at the Liberty Landing Marina in Jersey City, just across the Hudson River from lower Manhattan. Passing beneath the Verrazano Narrows Bridge on our way down New York Harbor we unroll our jib and keep both our engines running so as to move south into warmer water as quickly as possible. There is a moderate west wind blowing flat on our beam, so we should be fast. But the boat seems a little sluggish, sailing about a knot slower than I would normally expect, as though she is shy of her first encounter with the ocean ahead of us.

We take no special note of this. What we're focused on is the air temperature. At the height of that afternoon's sun, as the marina's pump-out boat came to break *Be Good Too* out of her ice-choked berth, it had been well below freezing, not more than 10 degrees Fahrenheit. Now, with the wind blowing over the open water of the lower harbor, it feels even colder than that.

It is so cold the salt spray is freezing on our deck. Every horizontal surface above *Be Good*'s waterline is slick as glass, shimmering in the pale sunlight. Which is why we don't do the most obvious thing to increase our speed. Hank Schmitt, an old friend of mine, the professional skipper Gunther and Doris have hired to ensure their voyage south is safe, has decreed we will not raise the mainsail until the deck is clear of ice. The jib we can control from the cockpit, but with the footing on deck so uncertain Hank doesn't want anyone going to the mast or, even worse, onto the coachroof under the boom, which is high above the water.

It is so cold the raw-water intake for the boat's reverse-cycle A/C system is also frozen solid. So for these first several hours as we clear Sandy Hook in the early darkness of a winter evening, we have no source of heat other than our own circulatory systems. Later that night, however, once we are out in the ocean where the water is a little warmer, the intake thaws out. With the heater running, the cabin becomes a refuge of warmth and security, and come morning the deck too has thawed. Still it is cold enough that when Gunther and I go outside to raise the mainsail we have to dodge huge chunks of ice that fall out of the folds of the sail as it goes up the mast.

Our first technical problem rears its head soon afterward. It too seems unremarkable, for this is how things go when you're sailing offshore. Stuff goes wrong, and you deal with it. You fix it, you jury-rig a solution, or you simply do without whatever it is that broke.

In this case it is the bilge pump in the engine compartment at the back of the starboard hull. Though we can see no water in there, the pump has cycled on and will not shut off again, even when we switch off its power supply at the main distribution panel. The pump is burning up both electricity and itself, running dry with no water coursing through it.

Hank and I soon figure out that if you tickle the switch on the panel just right, the pump will shut down. It's not such a big deal, but as soon as this seems to be resolved, Doris announces that the bilge in the port hull is almost overflowing with water. For some reason the pump there isn't running at all, and we have to bail the bilge by hand, passing the water by bucket to the head, where we pour it down the sink.

Where is the water coming from? The only probable source we can find is the port-hull bilge pump's exhaust hose, which runs very close to the boat's waterline and has no check valve or siphon loop in it. Perhaps, we guess, water from outside the boat is siphoning back through the hose and through the pump straight into the bilge. So we pull all the slack out of the hose run, loop and secure the hose as high above the waterline as we can, and pray this will solve the problem.

By the following morning, finally, there's enough wind that we can shut down the engines. It's blowing a steady 17-20 knots, we're on a wide close reach, and the water beneath us is nearly flat. Ideal conditions. But still the boat won't sail as fast as she should, and we're making only a little over six knots where we might normally expect eight.

Later that afternoon the wind lapses and shifts south against us, so we switch on one engine and resume motor-sailing. This time we tack back and forth periodically, working our way to windward with the main flying and the jib rolled up. And still our speed seems depressed, a mere three knots instead of four.

Shortly after sunset the wind comes back, blowing harder than before, and the boat at long last starts sailing fast. Hank has now decreed we have enough southing that we can start bearing away to the east, so again we're on a close reach, making nine knots or better in 22-26 knots of apparent wind. When Gunther relieves me at 2100 hours that evening, we work together to put one reef in the main and agree we are now both pleased with the boat's performance. Afterwards, as I nestle into my berth and fall asleep, it seems all is right with the world.

SOMETIME AFTER MIDNIGHT the wind starts blowing harder still. I can feel it in my berth, and the sensation wakes me. A catamaran may not heel like a monohull, but still it must react to the waves around it. *Be Good*'s motion now in this stronger weather is quick, jerky, and unpredictable. Periodically I can hear small explosions resounding through the boat's structure as waves slap hard at random intervals against her two hulls and the bridgedeck that connects them.

I lie fitfully, drifting in and out of sleep, and when finally I go up at 0400 hours to relieve Hank I find the wind-speed indicator is bouncing around over 30 knots true. The mainsail now is double-reefed. The jib has been roller-reefed to about half its size. It is too dark to see the waves around us, but I can hear them hissing sometimes—they sound like tearing paper—as we continue slashing southward into the gathering gale. The air is much warmer now, a sure sign we have reached the Gulf Stream. The huge temperature differential between the water here and the water to the north of us is sure to heighten the turbulence in the weather system that is now taking hold of us.

This isn't my first winter delivery. I remember one voyage in February, also on a brand-new boat, where we had two gales in one week. The first came as we were setting off from Rhode Island; the next came when we were right off Cape Hatteras, which has an awful reputation as the Graveyard of the North Atlantic. To make matters worse, that boat's cockpit was wrapped in sheets of clear plastic as protection against the weather. The smeary view of the ocean outside and the sickly-sweet smell of the fresh plastic both made me nauseous, and one of the things I learned on that voyage is that it is usually best to feel the weather in an undiluted state.

For this is how these things go. If you sail offshore in this part of the world at this time of year, you must resign yourself to enduring bad weather. If you cannot do that, you should not go out in the first place.

Sometimes now heavy bolts of spray from the biggest waves are crashing into the large windows that stretch across the front of *Be Good*'s bridgedeck saloon. If we were lying at anchor in daylight off some tropical island these windows would afford a panoramic view of the sumptuous scenery around us, but now we can see nothing through them but a black void full of angry wet noise. The windows are very strong and can easily stand up to these assaults, but the seams around their edges are not perfectly tight. When the waves hit directly, streams of water are squirting through and trickling down on to the ledge beneath the window frames.

Hank frowns, demonstrating his frustration as he shows me how vulnerable the electrical panel is. It is installed to starboard, the direction the waves are coming from, and is right below the leakiest window. He has spread out two bath towels to catch the water before it can trickle down on to the panel.

Hank goes below for some well-deserved sleep and I am left to babysit the leaks through the last dark hours of the night. Every half hour or so, I wring out the towels protecting the electrical panel. Soon I also notice there are two different bilge pumps that have cycled on and will not shut off. It is too noisy to hear if they are pumping water or sucking air, so I let them run a while, then shut them off by tickling their switches. Soon enough they switch on again, and the process is repeated, ad infinitum.

Suddenly, for no apparent reason, the autopilot switches off, and the boat starts slewing off course. I rush out of the sheltered saloon into the cockpit outside and up to the helm station on the port side to grab the wheel. The warmth of the air and the humidity in it on the one hand feels reassuring after the bitter dry cold of New York Harbor, but this growing cascade of small problems is starting to seem more than just annoying.

I steer for a while, feeling the boat and the tumultuous sea around it, and once *Be Good* is well established on her course again, I punch on the autopilot. I pray it will work, for if it doesn't I'll be stuck hand-steering and won't be able to mind the towels and the bilge-pump switches below. I stand for several minutes at the helm in the small vortex of accelerated wind created by the bimini canvas overhead. I watch the autopilot steering the boat, monitoring its accuracy and the rudder-angle indicator and notice, not the first time, that we are carrying more port helm than seems normal.

I am inside the saloon again—mopping up water from the leaking window frames, tickling pump switches, watching a dull mercury-gray sun rising over a vast plain of white-capped waves—when Gunther comes up to relieve me at 0700 hours. I am still briefing him on the current situation when an alarm goes off at the helm. I rush out into the wind again and up to the wheel and find the autopilot display is blinking the words *Low Power*. I clear the alarm, turn off the pilot, and start steering while shouting to Gunther over my shoulder.

I hear a gentle thrum from inside the boat as he starts the generator. Soon he appears beside me with a grim look on his face and tells me the generator is not charging the battery bank. So I start up the starboard engine and put it in gear, and Gunther disappears to check on the battery monitor. When he reappears his look is slightly grimmer: the engine alternator is also not charging the batteries.

Suddenly we hear a short report from somewhere forward, as if a gun has been fired off, followed by the insistent clatter of a madly flogging sail. The jib sheet has parted. Immediately I remember this was one of the flaws Gregor had confessed to me, that the sheet lead was bad. Inside my head I'm dope-slapping myself: given these conditions that sail should have already been furled up by now.

I punch the autopilot back on and jump outboard to the headsail furling line on the port side. I start heaving on the line while Gunther scrambles aft to check on the main circuit breaker in the starboard engine space. As soon as I have the sail rolled up, I slip back inside, jump down into the starboard hull, and poke Hank, who is fast asleep, curled up in a sleeping bag in the aft berth.

"We're starting to have adventures," I tell him. "You might want to be awake for this."

Hank has been sleeping fully dressed and in an instant surges up into the saloon. I take the wheel and shut down the autopilot again while Hank and Gunther swarm through the electrical system, looking for a break in the charging circuit. Soon enough Hank comes to the wheel with a smile on his face and tells me I can turn the pilot back on: the system is working again.

Hank and I stand by the helm and monitor the pilot's performance for a while. Soon we notice that the helm is always hard over to port. We don't need an autopilot to do that, so once again we shut it down and then screw on the wheel brake with the wheel turned all the way to the left.

This seems weird. Yes, we are more or less closehauled on starboard tack, motor-sailing in a strong breeze under a double-reefed mainsail with no head-sail on, so some strong weather helm is to be expected. But it is the starboard propeller we are turning, which should help keep the boat from wanting to round up to starboard into the wind, so it doesn't quite make sense that we need maximum port helm to stay on course.

But the most important thing is the situation now seems stable. The growing cascade of problems seems to have stopped. The boat is riding well enough, though its motion is still violent in the building seas, and small bits of water are still squirting in around the saloon windows when the waves hit them just right.

Hank asks how long I've been up, and when I tell him he says I should get some sleep. And I should feel free to use his berth, as the boat's motion is less violent back there.

I WAKE UP AGAIN at around 1100 hours, about three hours after I fell asleep in the strangely silent cocoon of Hank's berth. Once again I can tell from the boat's motion, though it is somewhat dampened in this aft stateroom, that the wind has increased some more. There seems to be a pattern: whenever I fall asleep and wake up again the wind is stronger.

Note to self: no more sleeping until this is over.

I pull myself up to the saloon and find Hank alone, reading a book as he stands watch. The seas outside look even angrier than before, and the windspeed indicator is often pumping over 40 knots. It's blowing hard enough now to be called a proper gale.

We chat for a while, and then, at about 1130 hours, we take an enormous direct hit all across the forward saloon windows. The wave that does this seems not only to have been much larger than the others, it seems also to have come in from a different angle—from directly ahead instead from off our starboard bow. Hank and I are standing right behind the windows when it happens. There is the massive concussive sound of the impact, nothing less than an explosion, and instantly a large upholstered piece of trim is blown off the central vertical window pillar into the middle of the saloon. A huge amount of water squirts into the saloon directly behind it, but the windows themselves, thankfully, do not buckle.

The blow from this wave stops us dead in the water and even seems to back us up a little. Immediately there is another wave answering the first that surges up and breaks rudely all across our stern. Later we'll notice this was strong enough to tear a large teak stern step right off its mounting bracket.

As soon the boat stops it starts spinning in the waves. It rounds up to windward, seeming to shrug off all its port helm and the thrust of the starboard engine, tacks through the eye of the wind, and keeps right on turning, bearing away to starboard, until the mainsail power-jibes with a thunderous crash back to the boat's port side.

Before this process is complete Hank has leapt outside and is standing at the helm. The wheel brake is off, the port engine has been started, the wheel is still hard over, and Hank is giving both propellers full throttle to get us moving forward again.

Will the boat now answer its helm?

It keeps spinning, and another pair of thunderous crashes overhead as the main tacks and then jibes again tells us the answer is no.

I have sailed many miles with Hank. I first met him in 1992 in the Canary Islands not long after he lost the mast on his own boat, a rugged Tayana 37 cutter. Working since then on other boats as a delivery skipper, he was once again dismasted and on seven different occasions lost steering due to rudder or quadrant problems. Every single time he managed to bring his charge home safely. Never once have I seen him rattled by weather or by any mishap occurring aboard a sailing vessel. But he seems rattled now, and his voice sounds uncertain as he shouts out a question over the keening wind.

"I can't control the boat! We should take down the main and just lie ahull, right?"

Gunther and I, standing now in the cockpit below the helm station, are for sure feeling more apprehensive than Hank and have nothing to say in response to this. Hank wrestles with the wheel some more, to no effect, and then his question becomes an order.

"We can't jibe like that again! Let's take down the mainsail!"

We let the main halyard fly, and Hank and I scramble on top of the coachroof to drag the big full-battened sail down the mast track into its boom bag. The wind tears at the sail without mercy, flogging it back and forth, and two battens near the top break loose from their cars on the track as we claw them down into the bag. In just a few moments the sail is secure and we are lying dead in the water, broadside to the seas. The wind is still howling and seems only to be growing stronger.

I have often sailed in gales, but I've never done this before. In fact, I have always believed this is a very bad idea, just lying to steep breaking waves and letting them do with you what they will. I've always believed it is best to stay active, to keep some canvas up and keep sailing somehow, or at least heave-to, with one sail working against the other to keep the boat heading slowly into the seas at an angle.

Now, however, it seems we must take our chances. We are at the mercy of the ocean. If we meet another wave like the one that has just crippled us, we just might be capsized. And if this boat flips over—as wide as it is, with no ballast down deep to bring it rolling back up again—it will stay flipped over, and we'll all be in serious trouble.

Scott Kennedy

PART I

A SEA OF DREAMS

And you, you will come too, young brother; for the days pass, and never return, and the South still waits for you. Take the Adventure, heed the call, now ere the irrevocable moment passes! 'Tis but a banging of the door behind you, a blithesome step forward, and you are out of the old life and into the new!

—Kenneth Grahame, *The Wind in the Willows*

FINDING A BERTH

Key West, Florida
March 1992

FOR ME, AS FOR SO MANY OTHERS, this all started as a dream. An inchoate desire to go to sea. Such dreams have long plagued the minds of young men, though in the past they had very material objectives to motivate them. Untold wealth, rape, pillage, plunder, unknown lands to discover and subjugate—these were the enticing rewards that once lured sailors out to sea.

In modern times the dream has been unraveled and undiluted. All lands have been discovered and are well charted; all pillaging and plundering is now conducted via telephone and computer. Where once an ocean voyage was an unpleasantness to be endured en route to a big pay-off, now the voyage itself is the locus of desire. The objective, the unknown place, is not the land on the other side, but the ocean in between.

By the spring of 1992 I had fulfilled the two other ambitions that had propelled me through my youth: I had worked for a daily newspaper; I had attended law school. Even worse, I had practiced law.

In school, which I found quite interesting, all the legal cases we studied involved fascinating questions touching on core concepts of justice in the various bailiwicks of human society. These were cases that had changed the law and in some instances society itself, which of course was why we read them.

In real life all the cases I worked on at my law firm in Boston involved self-centered people who were determined not to pay out money they owed to other self-centered people who were determined to get more than they deserved. There were no great principles involved, no great questions to answer. My job was either to defend the pile of wealth at stake or to go after the pile. In doing so I had to make arguments that were false and insincere, or I made arguments the other side knew were true and just, but refused to recognize as such.

It seemed an aggravating and pointless existence. At last, in desperation, I turned to a third ambition, nurtured since childhood, which seemed entirely frivolous. The one nice thing about my office in Boston was that it commanded a fine view of the harbor, and as the season wore on and more sailboats appeared upon it I found it harder and harder to concentrate on my work. I watched the silver light of the morning and afternoon sun playing across the water, watched the boats tacking back and forth, and let my mind drift east out toward the unseen sea.

In this modern age you'd think opportunities to travel across oceans in sailboats might be hard to come by, but in fact they are easy to find if you know where to look. In the back of sailing magazines I studied ads placed by people who owned boats and needed other people to help sail them places. Many of these people were making ocean passages. One ad I found even offered the prospect of payment, so of course I called that number first. I described my experience, which was quite limited, and the appropriately salty-sounding voice on the other end of the line immediately invited me down to Key West for a face-to-face interview.

When I told my parents I was quitting my job as an attorney and applying for a paid position on an ocean-going sailboat, they were not impressed.

"It's those damn magazines," growled my mother, who guessed at once where I'd found this improbable chance at employment. During my high school days, instead of *Playboy* and *Penthouse*, one end of my bedroom had been piled high with copies of *SAIL* and *Yachting*. Now at last, she feared, the seed of all this pornography was taking root.

I drove all the way down from Boston to Key West almost without stopping. There, in a white clapboard house on South Street, in an ill-kept yard filled with an alluring array of nautical debris, just a few blocks east of the mad scar of hype and immodesty that is Duval Street, I found a disheveled elf of a man who called himself Captain Frank. He seemed almost a parody of a sailor. He wore a hat, just like the skipper on *Gilligan's Island*, a sail tie for a belt, and smelled ripe, as though his access to fresh water was limited.

He also seemed restless. He roamed about his untidy sitting room, followed always by a floppy black basset-hound mix named Zoot, and told improbable stories of his youth. Of his beatnik days in Provincetown, out at the end of Cape Cod, where he lived with writers and artists and Portuguese fishermen and took the ferry each month to Boston to get dosed with LSD in experiments conducted by mad doctors at Harvard. Of his working days in San Francisco, fishing for salmon under sail, the last man on the bay ever to do so (he noted with great pride). Of his voyages skippering a three-masted schooner. Of the four hurricanes he had survived at sea.

And now, he confided, he had reached a crisis point in his life. He had been trapped here in Key West for far too long. It was time to get out and sail away.

"It's terrible," he complained. "Everyone here waits on tables for a living. There are no real people left anymore."

He had a panicked look in his eye, as though the police might at any moment burst through the door, tie an apron around his waist, and send him off to serve up margaritas to tourists in Jimmy Buffett's bar on Duval Street.

He took me across town to a dusty little boatyard tucked into a corner of Garrison Bight, where he introduced me to his boat, a 35-foot Tahiti ketch named *Zootie*. He was inordinately proud of her. She was built of cypress, he proclaimed, a very worthy species of wood, by a Michigan farmer who dreamed he would someday sail her across the Pacific Ocean. This farmer had worked very hard for many years building this boat in his backyard, taking great care in her construction, and finally succeeded in launching her. He sailed her down the Mississippi River, and then, just as he at last reached open water on the Gulf of Mexico, had died of a heart attack.

"Fortunately for me," said Captain Frank with a wink. "It's very hard to find boats like this, and she was in perfect condition when I bought her."

But that was then. The problem now was that the boat, standing propped up somewhat crookedly on jack-stands in one corner of the yard, seemed utterly derelict. Most of her deck hardware and galvanized steel rigging was covered in rust, and her interior had been gutted.

"Looks like she needs some work," I observed.

"She needs a bit," conceded the captain. He explained that the boat had been moored over at the U.S. Navy's Truman Annex, courtesy of a special deal he worked out with his good friend the commanding officer (wink, wink) and that during the winter there had been an awful storm. One of the big Navy launches had pulled free of its mooring, blew down on *Zootie*, beat the hell out of her port side, popped open several seams, and sank her.

"I refloated her in less than a day, and most of the hard work has already been done. I've repaired the hull. The engine has been rebuilt, and it's all ready to go right back in. All we have left to do is re-wire her, re-rig her, and put in new furniture."

Once these few simple chores had been seen to, the plan was to sail *Zootie* across the Gulf of Mexico, down the east coast of Central America, through the Panama Canal, then up to the west coast of Costa Rica. There Captain Frank had a business partner who owned some property and led tours on horseback through the rain forest.

"We're teaming up," he explained. "I'll do charters on the boat, and he'll keep doing horseback tours. We're calling the business Narwhal/Unicorn Adventures. What I need is a first mate to help me get the boat south and

The Tahiti ketch, designed by John Hanna in 1923, was based on work boats sailed by Greek sponge fishermen and for a generation or more was considered by many to be an ideal craft for ocean voyaging.

then help run it once we're down there."

He described at some length what a paradise Costa Rica was. "They have no military," he exclaimed, as though this were proof in itself that there could be no finer place on the planet.

I stayed three days in the house on South Street, sharing a spare bedroom with Buck, a shipwrecked fisherman who supposedly was helping fix up *Zootie* in exchange for room and board. He had hooked up with Captain Frank after the snapper boat he was working on broke up in heavy seas about 100 miles off Jacksonville. He spent six hours treading water, he told me, holding on to a shipmate who was unconscious, in a state of shock, with both legs broken, before they were both finally rescued and taken to shore.

This seemed very impressive, of course, and compared to Buck I felt acutely unqualified as a seafarer. I was also taken aback when, on our second night together as roommates, he suddenly burst into the room drunk out of his mind.

"Hey, Buck," I called. "Are you alright?"

He paid me no mind and circled unsteadily around and around like an arthritic dog looking for a place to lie down. With a great groan, he then pulled out his member and pissed all over the carpet. When he was done, he heaved a sigh of relief and collapsed in a heap next to the great pool of urine he had emitted.

Later that same night I was woken by howling cries of pain that seemed to be coming from somewhere nearby. It was a woman's voice, rising in a crescendo again and again: "Oh, God. Oh, God. Oh, GOD!" Until finally it subsided and trailed away into silence like the wailing of an evaporated phantom.

In the morning I mentioned this to the captain, and he explained that the howling woman was Mary, who lived in the room over the carport and actually owned the house we were staying in.

"You don't have to worry about her. She's very sick now, but I have people who come in to look after her. She's the beneficiary of a trust I administer. Maybe you can put on your lawyer hat and help me with that once we start working together."

His eyes twinkled a bit as he said this, hinting that this perhaps was the real reason he might be interested in taking me on.

Everything about the man seemed sketchy, but he was certainly entertaining, and if he was willing to believe I knew enough about sailing and boats to be useful to him, I was willing to believe he was more or less honest and competent and would somehow get his boat sailing south toward the Panama Canal in the next three months before hurricane season started. We shook hands on this, our misguided faith in each other, and I at once drove back to Boston, where I began disassembling my life on shore.

This was both a painful and liberating process. I'd never thought of myself as a material person, but as I examined the possessions I'd accumulated in the years since graduating from college, I realized how attached I was to many of them. Few of these things were valuable, but most were closely associated in my mind with some part of my identity. Clothes, books, furniture, a vast collection of records and tapes, paintings, prints, posters, a bicycle, a motorcycle, pots, pans, plates, and piles and piles of paper—all this and more represented mnemonic links to my past, manifestations of the ideal self I aspired to present to the world, the architecture of my intelligence, my sources of fun and amusement, the tools of my survival in civilized society.

I forced myself to be as ruthless as possible. I sold the few things that could be easily converted to cash and packed a few more I could not conceive of giving up into boxes that I stored in my parents' attic. Most of it, however, I put out on the street one night before the weekly morning trash pick-up. I sat in my dark apartment window one story over the curb, drinking beer and smoking cigarettes as I watched passers-by pore through the heaping pile of stuff that was my past existence. Bit by bit they bore me away. First the nice suits I had worn to work each day, then the music and books I had hoarded for decades, perfectly good tables and chairs, and various other odds and ends, all of it dissipating before my eyes.

Initially this seemed something like dying, but as my pile gradually grew smaller and smaller, it felt more and more as though I was being relieved of burdens. Off of me... and on to all these strangers. When at last the tide receded there was little left for the trash men to take away, and I felt I'd been reborn. Washed clean. My past was gone, and there was nothing left to inhibit the future.

I ARRIVED BACK IN KEY WEST nearly a month after I left with just one bag of clothes and a couple of small boxes of other random possessions that fit easily in the back of my car. Captain Frank was gone, but only temporarily, as he had flown down to Costa Rica to sign papers with his partner to create the corporation that would own the boat once we got it there. Zoot the dog was still in residence, and in the yard I found another sailor, Ryan, who was building himself a dinghy out of plywood. He explained that the captain was due to return the following day. Meanwhile, it turned out, Buck had disappeared. According to Ryan, he had stolen $500 from the captain and then ran off with the young woman who'd been taking care of Mary.

That evening I borrowed an old bicycle I found in the carport and rode over to Garrison Bight to inspect the boat. I was anxious to see how much progress had been made refitting her, and my heart sank when I found she was in exactly the same state as before. I fought back a dark wave of pessimism and examined the boat in detail, making a list of everything I thought needed to be done to get her sailing again. Then I sat on her coachroof and watched the sunset as I imagined her floating beneath me.

All the next day I loitered around the house waiting for Captain Frank to arrive. Finally, in the early evening, a lively young man with red hair and freckles appeared in a car. This was Sean, who was good friends with Jesse, the captain's Costa Rican partner. He was supposed to meet Jesse and the captain at the airport in Miami and drive them down to Key West and had waited around there for hours after their plane arrived without them. Finally, as he could think of nothing better to do, he decided to drive down on his own.

Together we paced around the captain's sitting room, speculating about what might have happened, and then, at my urging, Sean started making phone calls.

Soon we had some facts. The most important one was that Captain Frank had been found unconscious that afternoon in his bedroom at Jesse's house in Costa Rica. He nearly died on the way to the hospital, where the doctors at once operated on him to remove a blood clot from his brain. This evidently had been a historic moment, as this purportedly was the first major brain surgery ever performed in Costa Rica. The necessary equipment had just arrived that week, and everyone was eager to try it out.

The good captain fortunately survived his ground-breaking surgery and was expected to recover, but first he had to spend several weeks in Costa Rica recuperating. Meanwhile, I had little choice but to sit tight and mind the house on South Street while awaiting his return.

Was there any chance we might still sail south before the start of hurricane season? I really had no idea. I remembered what the captain had told me about the poor farmer who built *Zootie*, and I wondered now if she was a cursed vessel.

I was saved from my introspection by the advent of "Rocking" Robin, who came by the house one evening with a cold beer and the offer of a job. He was a good friend of the captain's and had once worked on shrimp boats, which in Key West, I gathered, was something like being in an outlaw biker gang. Now Robin was married and respectable and was hanging sheetrock for a living. He and his partner Rick had as much work as they could handle and would be happy, he said, to have an assistant help them out for a while.

I became particular friends with Rick, who was endlessly amused by the fact that he now had an attorney working as his apprentice. He was a third-generation drywaller, originally from Kansas City, a somewhat heavy, once lean man, with skinny arms and legs sprouting out from a great belly that hung way out over the top of his pants. He had long curly hair and a face that was always laughing or smiling. When he was young he'd served in the Navy, in Asia during the war in Vietnam, where he developed a taste for warm weather.

"I came down here because you can't go any further south than this," he told me. "Seriously, if the road went out another 50 miles, that's where I'd be. And if Castro died tomorrow and Cuba opened up, I'd be the first guy hanging sheetrock in Havana."

At work, while I dangled from ladders holding huge slabs of sheetrock in place as Rick stamped around on stilts driving home screws, he warned me about Captain Frank.

"Not that I don't like the man," he insisted. "But I'm telling you, he is a major A-number-one bullshit artist."

According to Rick, *Zootie* wasn't on a mooring in a storm when she sank, but was tied up at a dock in perfectly calm weather. She was always taking on water, he said, and one day the captain left a bilge pump running with an unsecured discharge hose that slipped back aboard and flooded the boat.

"You absolutely do not want to sail anywhere on that boat," he proclaimed. "She is nothing but a collection of leaks loosely organized as a hull."

Perhaps, but she was still a boat and still the only focal point for the dreams that swirled about my brain. I did not have the skill required to start refitting her myself, but I at least pretended to take care of her. Every morning, before going off to meet Rick and Robin, I rode my borrowed bicycle over to

Garrison Bight and opened up the boat to keep fresh air circulating through her interior. And in the evenings, hot and sticky from the day's labor, I rode back and closed her up again.

FINALLY, AFTER WEEKS OF WAITING, one evening I was riding back from the boatyard and from halfway down South Street spied a great mound of luggage heaped up on the front stoop of the house. I gave a great shout as I zoomed up on the bike, and sure enough, there was Captain Frank playing with Zoot the dog in the yard. With him was a tall hulk of a young man, quiet and resolute, with long black hair parted down the middle and a trim goatee beard—Jesse, the famous partner from Costa Rica.

The captain obviously was very happy to be home again. In a matter of minutes, he had dragged his luggage into the house and unpacked it all. He then dove into a secret storage compartment under his bed and pulled out all the valuables he'd hidden away there—various firearms, a fancy pair of binoculars, two sextants, a high-frequency radio, and an exotic paper-graph barometer. He settled down in the midst of this treasure with Zoot on his lap, smiling and laughing like a child on Christmas morning.

Superficially he seemed much like his old self, but I could tell it took some effort. He was but a wisp of a man in the first place, and now he seemed so frail as to be on the verge of collapse. Most disturbing of all was his head, which was shaved, with a huge horseshoe-shaped scar on top, as though he'd endured some awful Planet-of-the-Apes lobotomy.

Over the next few days I tried several times to talk with him about the future, and he assured me, in a dismissive tone, as though it were silly of me to ask, that he most certainly would sail south as planned. I also had some conversations with Jesse, and he was much more circumspect. He doubted the captain was going anywhere this year and explained they'd agreed the captain's doctor in Key West would ultimately decide when he could leave.

Jesse also told me how scared he was when he found the captain laid out cold on the floor of his guest bedroom back in Costa Rica—no pulse, no breathing—and how he'd pounded on his chest to keep him alive long enough to get him to the hospital. And all I could think of the whole time I was hearing this was how that could have been me doing the pounding, miles out at sea in a leaky wooden boat, far from any hospital.

Even before the captain's return I'd started a desultory search for another boat to sail on, and now I began looking in earnest. I bought a clutch of sailing magazines and also studied the local newspaper, where I found an announcement that a local schooner, *Constellation*, would soon be leaving on a transatlantic voyage to Spain. I knew the boat, as I'd often seen her tied up stern to the wall at the seaport right across from the Schooner Wharf bar—a classic John Alden design, easily over 90 feet long, if you measured from the tip of her bowsprit to the end of her boomkin aft, with a deft spring to her sheerline and an elegant staysail rig.

I marched down to the seaport and studied the boat silently for a while. Finally I screwed up my courage and hailed one of the crew working on deck, a piratical-looking fellow wearing a bandana and ponytail.

"You're going to Spain," I called out. Not a question, but a statement.

The pirate stopped what he was doing and glared at me.

"Yes, we are. We're leaving this week."

"Are you looking for crew?"

The pirate smirked a bit, gave me a quick look up and down, then motioned aft with his thumb.

"You can talk to the skipper about it. He's down below."

And so I met Cliff, the owner and skipper of the boat, and his wife, Ruth Ann, enthroned in the main saloon, presiding serenely over the mayhem of their final preparations for sea. Compared to Captain Frank, they seemed a picture of sanity and composure. Cliff with a bushy gray Quaker beard, no mustache, eyes blinking moistly behind a pair of thick glasses; Ruth Ann with a look of quiet determination, smiling gently in between drags on a discount cigarette.

They talked at length about the boat and described how they'd found her a derelict hulk in Fort Lauderdale four years earlier. Since then they had worked ceaselessly to restore her while taking tourists out on day-trips. Now they intended to sail to Spain in a cruising rally called the TransARC that was scheduled to start out of St. Augustine during the first week of May. Summer would be spent cruising the western Mediterranean, then they would sail west again to the Bahamas in another rally, the America 500, celebrating the quincentennial anniversary of Columbus's first voyage to the New World. First, however, they were leaving Key West in just three days and going up to South Carolina for some fund-raising and publicity events.

As for crew, this was being handled on a share-expense basis. Five thousand dollars to do the whole trip, Spain and back, with room and board included from now until December, and there was just one berth left. I had to decide by the end of the day if I wanted it, as the deadline for submitting TransARC crew lists was the next morning.

For appearance's sake, I said I had to think about it, but the truth was I could scarcely conceive of not signing on. I stood for a while after our interview on the seawall looking down on *Constellation*'s deck, admiring her lines, her gleaming white hull, the graceful symmetry of her rig, and soon realized my casual gaze had degenerated into a lover's myopic stare.

I wrenched myself away and wandered around town for a few hours, trying hard to focus on whether joining *Constellation* might somehow be a bad move. It seemed something of a come-down, of course, to go from a paying gig to one I had to pay for, but in fact I'd long ago realized that Captain Frank was unlikely to ever deliver on his promise of a salary. And even if I discounted all the sailing I'd get to do, all the way across the Atlantic and back, paying $5,000 for a place to sleep with all meals included for the next nine months seemed like a pretty good deal.

In the end, I knew that if I really wanted to go to sea that spring, this would likely be my only opportunity. So later that evening, with a glad heart, I stopped by the boat again and sealed my fate by handing Cliff a check.

Over the following two days I focused on rearranging my affairs and used a Cuban laundromat on White Street, a few blocks down from the house, as my transition headquarters. There was a pay phone there, plus they served tasty bocadillas and kick-ass coffee. I changed my forwarding addresses, saw to the filing of that year's tax return, concentrated what wealth I had in a single easy-to-access account, and made arrangements to stash my car and spare belongings at a self-storage facility on Big Coppitt Key.

Back at the house, meanwhile, I noticed the captain had recently moved a desk into my bedroom and had placed upon it great piles of paper. These, I saw, pertained not only to Mary's trust, but also to a lawsuit involving the Key West Historical Society and the wreck of an old Spanish galleon, in which the captain had been accused of committing fraud and forgery.

I put off the inevitable as long as I could. Finally, when the captain came in and found me stuffing my clothes and last few belongings into my backpack, there could be no denying the obvious.

"You're leaving town," he said in a thin wounded voice.

"I'm running away to sea," I answered and told him I'd found a berth aboard *Constellation*.

"So... you're going off on *Constellation*," he mused with a tone of inevitability, as though he had long guessed this was the boat that would steal me away from him.

I tried to explain myself, about what Jesse had told me, and how I couldn't wait around for a year to help him sail south on *Zootie*, but he quickly cut me off.

"What Jesse doesn't understand, what no one understands, is how badly I need to get out of here."

And with that he scooped up all the papers on the desk, clutched them in his arms, and stalked angrily from the room.

I moved on to *Constellation* that evening and spent all the next day working with the crew to prepare for our departure the following afternoon. At this point, aside from Cliff and Ruth Ann, there were just three others onboard.

Jack, the young pirate I first spoke with, fortunately turned out to be quite gregarious and was very willing to take a moment to explain things to me. Then there was Henry, a middle-aged fellow with a wan demeanor, who seemed to know little about boats and mostly stood around watching other people do things. The one who worried me was Tim, the first mate, a tall, wiry young man with a perpetual scowl on his face. He was openly hostile to both Henry and me and made it very clear that he did not suffer fools gladly.

After we finally finished working for the day, Jack and Tim, who were obviously close, were preparing to go out for beers together, and Jack, bless him, asked if I wanted to come along. Tim frowned, but did not object, and together we sallied forth to the Green Parrot bar on Whitehead Street.

This was the funkiest, least touristy bar in downtown Key West. It was a Friday night, and the place was packed with blue-collar types who had just knocked off work, including Rick, my drywall buddy. He shrieked out my name the moment he saw me walk through the door.

Tim, who apparently knew Rick pretty well, was incredulous.

"You mean you *know* this guy???"

"Are you kidding?" answered Rick as he threw an arm around me. "This is my attorney!"

Tim raised an eyebrow, but said nothing. Rick, meanwhile, at once started telling me how he'd heard all about how Captain Frank caught me like a thief trying to sneak out of the house.

I tried to deny this and started explaining exactly what had happened.

"Never mind that," exclaimed Rick as he handed me a beer and offered up a toast. "The important thing is you're not going to sea with Captain Wrongway Peachfuzz!"

BUZZARD'S ROWBOAT

Southeast U.S. Coast
April–May 1992

THE PROCESS OF FALLING IN LOVE inevitably involves a period during which the object of one's desire is highly idealized. This is eventually followed by a reactionary period, during which the flaws of the loved one become obvious and are even magnified. If the relationship is to endure, these two tendencies must ultimately achieve an equilibrium. The loved one's deficits, however egregious, must be acknowledged and accepted, and some fragment of the rapture inspired by those idealized virtues must survive and be nurtured.

In my relationship with *Constellation*, it seemed this evolution was accelerated. As to the first half of the process, her virtues were self-evident. Anyone who has ever admired sailing vessels must readily acknowledge that the old so-called "fisherman" schooners designed by John Alden are among the most beautiful boats ever conceived, and *Constellation* was undeniably an exemplar of the breed.

Originally, in the once-upon-a-time, she had been a rich man's plaything, christened *La Reine* after her launching in East Boothbay, Maine, in 1932. During World War II she was commandeered into the U.S. Navy's Corsair fleet and hunted for German submarines on the East Coast. Afterwards she was reconfigured as a more modern private yacht and eventually made her way to the West Coast. Her workmanlike gaff mainsail was replaced with a taller Marconi mainsail, a useful doghouse was added to her main cabinhouse aft, and in this garb, as *Constellation*, she was competitive in the Transpac, racing from California to Hawaii during the 1950s. The changes to her rig and deck were carefully made and in no way detracted from her appearance. They certainly improved her functionality and if anything, even to the discerning eye of a grumbling traditionalist, they made her seem all the more graceful.

I had spent a good part of my youth ogling photos and drawings of traditional ships and sailboats, and in joining *Constellation* it seemed as though I had stepped through some dimensional boundary into a storybook dream. But I could also see that *Constellation* was a very old boat, with a sometimes fractious crew, and it soon became apparent that all was not in perfect order.

Our departure from Key West, just two days after I moved aboard, was less than auspicious. The night before we sailed a woman named Veronica, who lived on the barely floating hulk of another schooner tied up next to us, suddenly decided she needed to evict her boyfriend Jeff. Her screaming tore me awake and out of my new berth, and with the others I rushed on deck to see what the emergency was.

From onboard *Constellation* we could see clumps of clothing and odd bits of luggage flying through the rigging of Veronica's boat. Waves of cursing punctuated by loud accusations of infidelity, insobriety, and low morality echoed down the waterfront. It seemed Jeff might at any moment strike Veronica, so we did not feel we could ignore the fight. Unfortunately, it went on for nearly an hour. Finally we saw flashing blue lights stuttering down William Street, and at last the sheriff arrived and dragged Jeff away.

The next morning the five of us on *Constellation* rushed about in a torpor attending to last-minute chores. In the middle of this, Jack's fiancé Jennifer suddenly appeared, unfolded a lawn chair, and installed herself on the seawall, where she sat watching us while sobbing intermittently. Jack stood by her much of the time, trying to soothe her, which annoyed Tim no end. To make sure everyone knew this, he frequently made loud remarks about the help we weren't receiving. The evening before, deep in their cups in the Green Parrot,

Alden design no. 498, *La Reine*, later renamed *Constellation*, was originally built for C. V. Watson at the Hodgdon Brothers yard, which is still operating today.

he and Jack had seemed inseparable, but now it appeared Tim's loyalty had been exhausted.

Finally in the early afternoon we cast off, cheered on by a small crowd of well-wishers, including Jennifer, who rose up from her lawn chair and smiled bravely as she waved farewell. Veronica, with hollow eyes and a beer in one hand, handed over the last spring line from her boat as we pulled away from the wall.

There was a moderate wind blowing from the north. The first leg of our course, along the bottom of the westernmost arm of the Florida Keys, was nearly due east, so initially we had an easy time of it. Schooners, which carry lots of midship sails, always sail well on a beam reach. We bantered idly with a few people who followed us on boats of their own, and then one by one they fell away and retreated to the diminishing line of islands behind us. We sauntered along in open water, outside the protected but constrained waters of Hawk Channel, and enjoyed a huge boost in speed as the Gulf Stream swept us away from the sunset.

During the night, as our course trended more and more northward, and as the north wind grew stronger, life onboard became less comfortable. We still had the Stream sweeping us along, but with the current now cutting against the wind, the waves became much steeper and choppier. "Square waves" was what Tim called them, and it was an apt description. We were also now sailing closer to the wind, so we were bashing more directly into those slab-sided seas, and it felt as though the boat were repeatedly slamming her head against a wall. The slamming was rhythmic, with an accent on every fourth syllable.

Bam Bam Bam BAM Bam.

Bam Bam Bam BAM Bam.

By sunrise the wind was stronger still, the square waves had grown larger, and the boat's motion became increasingly violent. I had never before been susceptible to seasickness, but now I started feeling queasy. The day before we had taken on diesel fuel and accidentally spilled some on the floor of the main saloon, where the fuel fill was located. The odor of the fuel now permeated the boat and augmented my nausea.

Even worse, as soon as he realized I wasn't feeling well, like a bird dog alert to the distant thrum of wings, Jack plopped down beside me in the cockpit. He whispered in my ear, describing a greasy breakfast in pornographic detail. He then cackled gleefully as I lurched for the rail and puked my guts out.

The boat didn't like the motion either, and the stress of it soon opened up a slow, but steady leak somewhere deep in her hull. It is not unusual for a wooden boat to leak, particularly an older one. Every seam between each plank, stuffed with thick cotton caulking to keep the water out, is a potential weak spot. Cliff had owned *Constellation* now for three years, but he'd never really sailed her in rough water before, and he'd never seen her leak this much. To play it safe, just as the sun was setting that day, he decided we should put into Fort Lauderdale.

We spent all the next day at a marina there, working hard on the boat. Jack dove on the hull and inspected it closely, looking for weak seams while breathing through a hookah rig. This consisted of a tiny electric air compressor, normally used for pumping up fenders and inflatable boats, with a long thin hose about 25 feet long that had a scuba regulator installed at the end of it.

"You keep an eye on that compressor," Tim warned me. "Keep it cranked up full blast and if it stops running, yank that regulator out of his mouth."

We mixed up a big batch of underwater epoxy, and Jack used this to patch the spots that looked suspect. When that was done we pulled up the carpet in the main saloon, which still reeked of diesel fuel, threw it out on the dock, and scrubbed it clean. Afterwards we scrubbed the deck with fresh water, had dinner aboard, and cast off again not long after sunset.

We continued sailing north, following the current of the Gulf Stream. Cliff divided us into a series of staggered four-hour watches, so that we each spent our first two hours on deck with one shipmate and the next two hours with another. I shared the first half of my watch with Cliff and the second half with Tim, which was something like being caught between a rock and a hard place. I figured they either suspected I was incompetent and wanted to keep an eye on me, or they thought me a promising prospect and wanted to make sure I was properly trained.

Cliff was worried about my steering. *Constellation* had no self-steering apparatus, no autopilot or windvane, which meant she constantly wanted a hand on her wheel, and whenever it was mine, Cliff at first felt compelled to lecture me on what I was doing. *Constellation* was well balanced and wasn't hard to steer, and I had no trouble keeping her on course. As soon as he realized this, Cliff stopped coaching me and was happy to leave me alone on the wheel while he roamed the boat worrying about other things.

Tim was more of a hard case. He seemed to revel in acting like an asshole, as though he considered it part of his job as first mate, and always removed himself from the rest of us with an impervious hauteur. He was never patient, but he liked to laugh and was intelligent, and on this level I could engage with him. He had a fund of amusing and illuminating tales to tell, many involving sailing and the sea, and I was more than willing to listen to them.

During our watches together, at least at first, he mostly pontificated about himself. Originally, I learned, he was from Massachusetts and when he was younger had served in the Navy, working as an electrical engineer aboard aircraft carriers in the Pacific. After leaving the Navy, he lived on Guam for a while, where he started working on yachts. More recently he'd been based in Key West, working some construction, which was how he knew Rick, and delivering yachts, which was how he met Jack. Together he and Jack had delivered many boats into charter fleets all over the Caribbean.

In his spare time, working without pay, Tim had spent the last three years helping Cliff fix up *Constellation*. To hear him tell it, he was responsible for much of her restoration. Serving as mate on this voyage to Europe and back was supposed to be the pay-off. With this credential on his résumé, he hoped he could then take a step up and start working as a skipper on big private yachts.

Our second night out, east of Jacksonville, where my old roommate Buck had nearly drowned, the wind suddenly grew stronger and started howling out of the south at nearly gale strength. It was all hands on deck to shorten sail, our first time working together under pressure. I was on the foremast and suffered the supreme embarrassment of letting one of the halyards get away from me, so that it was waving about loose in the air well outboard of the gunwale.

My heart clinched tight, and I looked at Tim with something like panic in my eyes. This was a test, I realized. Either he would forgive me or forever think me worthless.

"Don't worry," he said with a grim smile. "It'll come back. Just don't pull on your end of the line." He braced himself and stood waiting by the gunwale. Sure enough the halyard soon swung inboard again, and he snagged it with a boathook.

Moments later, Tim himself took a huge flyer halfway across the deck and landed on his ass in the scuppers after the handle blew out of the winch he was grinding. It wasn't very pretty, but in the end we got the job done.

Soon afterwards, I was on deck alone steering. Off to the east, over the heart of the Gulf Stream, there was a long line of pitch-dark thunderheads alive with lightning, spitting and glowing like a distant artillery barrage. Directly overhead the sky was perfectly clear, studded with brilliant stars, as peaceful a prospect as one could hope for. To the west there was a gorgeous sliver of a young moon perched just above the horizon, glowing softly behind a thin veil of clouds.

The boat plunged onward, racing along under one lonely sail, the wind still raging behind us. I felt like a god, surrounded by all this, omnipotent, with my hand on the wheel of this enormous sailboat, but also diaphanous and ephemeral, like a moth, pressed between the opposing forces of the lightning and the moonlight.

TWO DAYS LATER WE REACHED Beaufort, South Carolina. In the very early morning before sunrise as we closed the coast, I marveled again at the stars overhead, shining in a crystal-clear sky, while the horizon all around us was shrouded in dense fog. We were motoring, as there was no wind, and the still water was alive with phosphorescence. Beneath the boat there appeared a meteor shower of dolphins drilling bright green tunnels of light through the water in all directions.

I had wondered about Henry, our fifth crew member, quiet and pale with flat gray hair, who did little or no work on the boat. He was treated with barely concealed contempt by Tim and Jack, was merely tolerated by Cliff, and only Ruth Ann afforded him any modicum of kindness or respect. The mystery of Henry and why he was aboard, I now learned, was tied up with the mystery of why we had come to South Carolina.

Apparently, Henry was our impresario, the ship's publicist and fundraiser, and had somehow arranged for *Constellation* to officially represent the state of South Carolina in the America 500 cruising rally we planned to join in Europe. Now we were to capitalize on that relationship, and our presence here, theoretically, would cause largesse to rain down on us.

Beaufort was not a very large town, not much more than a village really, buried in the labyrinth of islands and creeks of the Carolina coast south of Charleston. The appearance of a sailing vessel the size of *Constellation* was inevitably noteworthy, and as soon as we tied up at the town dock a small crowd gathered to greet us. The next morning Cliff ordered us to dress ship and produced a great tangled mess of Christmas lights and signal flags for us to hoist into the rig.

Tim would have none of it. "I don't do dog-and-pony shows," he announced. "My job is to sail the boat." And he packed up his duffel bag and moved ashore into a motel room.

Jack and I were left to solve the puzzle of the lights and flags, and Henry pretended to help. It took hours to sort them all out and replace the dead bulbs, but when we were done the boat looked magnificent, with lights twinkling and flags fluttering all the way from the end of her bowsprit, up and over both mastheads, and down again to the end of the long boomkin on her stern.

Like carnival barkers, we put up a sign, gave tours of the boat, sold T-shirts, and answered questions about our impending voyage. Pursuant to a deal made with the local Chamber of Commerce, we spent all of one day taking people on short harbor sails up to the highway bridge and back for $25 a head. The next morning there was a ceremony, and Cliff was officially presented with the state flag. The president of the Chamber of Commerce proudly announced how much money we'd raised, and thanked Cliff for helping to finance the town's new visitor center.

Cliff looked as though he'd been impaled with a spear. Afterwards he sat in the saloon and drank beer all through the afternoon, stroking his beard and grumbling about how much money he could be making doing day trips in Key West. From there he launched into a bitter tirade against Henry.

Finally he turned to me, eyes nearly full to overflowing. "Does it make any sense to you?" he pleaded. "Why shouldn't people want to help support a beautiful old schooner like *Constellation*?"

I shook my head no, but to me it made perfect sense. After all, how could we expect people to help pay for a trip to Europe they weren't going on?

Our last iron in the fire was a private charter, a catered dinner cruise sponsored by the most prominent family in Beaufort. Here at least we made some money we could keep, and I met an interesting woman, Elayne, who ran a folk-art gallery out on St. Helena Island. She once had been married to a shrimper, but he started using his boat to smuggle pot from Jamaica, then from Colombia, and then one day he disappeared entirely and was never heard from again.

"I have no idea what happened to him," she told me cheerfully. "I stopped worrying about it a long time ago."

Two days later I borrowed the ship's bicycle, a rusty old Key West "conch-mobile," and rode out to visit her.

Elayne's gallery was alive with voodoo spirits. Prior to the 1960s, I learned, when they built the first bridges and roads out to the Carolina sea islands, most people living out here were descended from slaves who once worked the island plantations. Many still spoke Gullah, the patois dialect spoken by their ancestors. Many also still worshipped, or at least acknowledged, the old spirits, who they enshrined in their art—mad riots of colorful house paint thrown across decrepit refrigerator doors, odd bits of corrugated tin, and detailed assemblies of stray lumber and popsicle sticks.

There was Whooping Boy, the lonely spirit of a murdered child whose cries of pain were once heard throughout the islands.

"The problem now," explained Elayne, "is that no one can hear him, because his moaning is drowned out by the sound of car tires hissing on paved roads."

Then there was Jack O'Lanton, a very powerful spirit, with fiery light streaming out the crack of his ass. His paintings were by far the most exciting, and evidently he was still a force to be reckoned with. According to Elayne, there was one notorious stretch of road on St. Helena where a strange light was known to appear at night and disable automobiles.

"I've seen it myself," she insisted. "And a friend of mine once crashed into a tree trying to outrun it."

Most importantly, there was Buzzard. He was an all-purpose malicious spirit who brought misfortune to all who crossed his path. If you suffered from a very long streak of bad luck, you were said to be Buz Ro'bo, or Buzzard's Rowboat. I noticed certain paintings and sculptures in the gallery depicted this—desperate characters trying to propel small boats through chaotic maelstroms of water.

"I really don't think he's evil," noted Elayne. "I just think he has a really warped sense of humor."

Afterwards, I rode back into Beaufort, with car tires hissing along beside me, and cruised around town inspecting the scenery. Lots of sleepy streets with great eruptions of flower beds lurking in front of houses and stores. I ended up in the middle of a small crowd downtown watching the Preacher People. These were young Christian evangelists who, I was told, often wandered about loudly reciting gospel.

"They're giving the Lord a bad name," muttered one woman standing next to me. "The police are starting to arrest some of them."

They thumped on their Bibles like wild animals. One stepped up to me, as though he saw there was something different about me, looked me right in the eye, and promised I would spend an eternity in hell if I did not join them.

THOUGH WE RAISED LITTLE MONEY in Beaufort, Cliff did learn about a boatyard further up the coast where we might get *Constellation* hauled out of the water on the cheap. He wanted to be sure we had sealed of our leak, and since our rallies back and forth across the Atlantic were theoretically competitive, he also wanted to swap the boat's three-bladed cruising propeller for its more svelte two-bladed racing propeller.

Tim returned at last from his motel room, looking much refreshed, bragging about some woman he had seduced. Henry, meanwhile, rented a car and temporarily retreated to Florida to tend to his failing steam-cleaning business and his increasingly estranged family in Orlando.

"My wife doesn't understand why I'm doing this," he told me just before he left. "I guess I don't understand it either. It's almost like a disease."

We sailed up to Charleston, spent two days there, and then moved on to another free berth Cliff caught wind of, on a floating dock in front of a restaurant at the head of a tidal estuary called Shem's Creek. The approach was very tight. The channel up the creek was choked so narrow with tied-up shrimp boats we had only a few feet of clearance on either side. The basin at the head of the creek, if anything, was not quite as wide as the boat was long.

To put the boat on the dock, Cliff literally had to spin her on a dime and turn her through a full 180 degrees within her own length. Doing this with a large full-keeled boat like *Constellation* to me seemed absurdly miraculous, like putting a tutu on an elephant and asking it to dance a pirouette. But Cliff never flinched. There was a great roar from the engine, a cloud of smoke belching up from under the transom, a mad spinning of the wheel back and forth. Our boomkin just nicked the hull of a shrimp boat on the opposite side, while our bowsprit passed right over the dock and nearly knocked over one restaurant table. Crowds had gathered in front of all four restaurants lining the basin to watch, and they gave out a great cheer as we finally came to a stop spot perfect on the dock and tossed our lines ashore.

"I can't believe we just did that!" I exclaimed to Jack as we secured the lines.

"You just wait," he cackled. "You haven't seen anything yet."

And indeed, I hadn't.

Two days later we moved on again, up the Wando River to a ramshackle backcountry boatyard called Halsey's. It was inhabited by decrepit shrimp boats and some old yachts rotted beyond repair, and the allegedly fresh water in the shower reeked of sulfur. But they did have a working marine railway and a large Travelift, so it seemed likely they'd be able to haul *Constellation* one way or the other.

The railway was occupied, so Cliff thought we might as well try the Travelift. This inspired some debate as to the true weight of the boat and whether the lift could handle it. The weight of any boat is always a mystery, until you actually pick it up and weigh it with a load cell, and in fact they are almost always heavier than you think. In *Constellation*'s case, we didn't even know what her original design weight was supposed to be, and there was so much stuff onboard she most certainly was much heavier than that.

Tim and Jack were very afraid we might drop the boat, but Cliff was sanguine. Bob, the owner of the yard, said he was game to try it, as long as we had insurance.

The following day we waited for the very top of the high tide, and then, with a bit of yelling from Cliff, a bit of gouged wood on either side of the hull, and much help from a skiff with a strong outboard pushing hard on our bow, we forced the boat through a tight dog-leg turn and got her lined up in the hole beneath the lift. Then came the moment of truth—and we found there wasn't quite enough water to float the boat into the slings.

"She draws 10 feet, right?" said Bob.

"Maybe a little more," conceded Cliff.

"Well, this is it, right here." Bob pulled a tide table from his back pocket. "This is the highest it gets all month."

We spent three more rainy days waiting for the shrimp boat on the railway to finish its bottom job. The time we were wasting gnawed on Cliff like a virus, and he became increasingly irritable. Henry returned from Orlando and was so anxious to stay clear of him, he actually helped the rest of us with the maintenance jobs we were working on.

The day the shrimp boat was launched was bright and sunny, but brought us no cheer. Again, even at the top of the tide, we didn't have quite enough water to get *Constellation* on to the railway. Cliff threw an ugly tantrum as we backed off the ways in defeat. He chewed us out over our handling of the lines and fenders, though we had done nothing wrong, and barely restrained himself from hitting Henry. As soon as we had the boat tied up again, Ruth Ann, looking pretty upset herself, grabbed him by the arm and told him it was time to take a walk.

A couple of hours later I emerged from the yard's shower, reeking of sulfur, toilet kit in hand, towel draped over my shoulder, and there was Cliff standing with Tim and Jack in the middle of the yard sharing a six-pack. I gave them a wave and made a beeline for the boat, but they called me over and thrust a beer into my hand.

Cliff was grinning now and was clearly a little drunk. Together the three of them tried to regale me with the story of *Constellation*'s last haul-out, the previous fall at a yard in Tarpon Springs, where Cliff had had the hull refastened.

"You remember those dogs?" asked Cliff, eyes bright.

Tim and Jack howled with laughter and told me how they'd had to crawl and leap over fences and rooftops to avoid the vicious watchdogs that roamed the yard at night.

Then Cliff moved in, thrust his face into mine, and told me a story about when he was a pilot in Vietnam during the war. He was flying a small reconnaissance plane, was taking fire from the ground in a foggy valley, and was very afraid he would not survive.

"I radioed the men down on the field and told them to fire off some parachute flares so I could judge the wind and see how deep the fog was. And I did it." He wriggled his shoulders and took a long drag on his cigarette. "Not exactly by the book, but I landed that fucking plane."

Then he slapped me on the back.

A little later Jack took me aside and told me this was intended as an apology. "It's Cliff's way of eating crow," he explained. "It means he really trusts you."

WE SAILED OUT THE WANDO RIVER the next evening, a Friday, bound for St. Augustine, Florida. From there in just over two weeks' time we were scheduled to leave for Europe with the TransARC rally. Cliff had spent the morning working the phone and found a yard there that said they could haul us out first thing Monday morning, so the mood onboard was again optimistic.

Traditionally it's considered bad luck to set sail on a Friday, and though we never thought of this at the time, we soon had reason to. All day Saturday we motor-sailed straight into a fierce headwind. Sheets of white water rushed over the bow and down the deck, the hull started leaking again, and the engine seemed to be straining. I thought the interior of the boat smelled faintly of its exhaust and said so.

"Don't you smell that?" I asked Cliff, but he only frowned, as though insulted I had impugned his engine.

I turned to Tim. "You don't smell anything?"

His eyes widened, as if to question my sanity, and he shook his head no.

Early that evening the wind veered into the west. We shut down the engine and raised more sail and all through the night screamed down our rhumbline route making eight knots or better. Thick bolts of lightning, planting themselves like trees of fire, drove straight down into the Gulf Stream off our leeward side. To windward there were scattered stars showing through the broken clouds, and our wake glowed faintly green as we surged through the phosphorescent sea.

I felt like God again for a while, alone at the wheel in the middle of that night. But later, after coming off watch, I experienced the flip side, trying to fall asleep in a place that felt something like hell. The boat's interior reverberated with the shrieking and groaning of wood under pressure, the hull next to me pulsing as the ocean roared by mere inches from my head, everything around me rolling madly to and fro as we plunged on toward the south.

Coming on deck in the morning, I saw we were approaching the coast and the inlet leading into St. Augustine. Cliff started up the engine again, then gave the order to douse the sails.

After we finished with the sails, Ruth Ann turned to me and smiled. "I left an omelette for you in the galley," she said.

Perfect. I suddenly realized I was ravenous and dove below to fetch it. But as soon as I stepped down the companionway into the saloon I found the boat's interior was thick with oily smoke.

"Hey! Hey!" I shouted. "Something's wrong down here!"

Cliff, Tim, and Jack all shouted back in unison, told me to shut my mouth, and to stop trying to scare them for no good reason.

Feeling wounded now and petulant, I darted through the smoke, retrieved the plate with my omelette, returned to the cockpit, and sat eating in silence. I had taken just a few bites when suddenly a huge pillar of jet-black smoke came pouring out the midship hatches.

"Holy fuck," muttered Jack. "I think we're on fire."

He and Tim plunged down the companionway. I put down my plate and followed right behind them. The smoke below now was as thick as ink, so dense we couldn't see through it.

"I'm shutting down the engine!" called Cliff.

And almost instantly the smoke dissipated.

So no, we weren't on fire. But we were adrift now, rolling in the sometimes breaking swell at the mouth of the inlet, with a hard stone breakwater less than 100 yards to leeward.

"Let's raise the main and forestaysail, please," said Cliff in an even voice. Then he wriggled his shoulders a bit.

We quickly raised the sails, and soon the boat was moving again and answered her helm. It turned out we had no charts for St. Augustine, which I'd noticed by now was somewhat routine. We'd had no chart for entering Fort Lauderdale, or for Charleston, which we entered at night, or for the Wando River.

"Tim, have you been here before?" asked Cliff.

Tim nodded. "I remember it well enough. There's a drawbridge. We need to stay in the channel approaching it, but on the other side there's good water all across the east side of the main harbor. There's probably room to anchor just before the bridge if you want, west of the channel, but we may be aground there at low tide."

"We're going through the bridge," said Cliff. "I want to get to that boatyard. We don't know when this engine will run again."

Tim nodded again and said nothing.

Cliff called the bridge tender from the wheel on a handheld radio and explained our situation—that we had no power and needed to transit the bridge under sail—and asked if the bridge could open on demand.

"Only in an emergency," he answered. "Otherwise we open on the half hour. The next opening is in 15 minutes."

Evidently it was up to us to declare an emergency if necessary, but Cliff was unwilling to do that. He wanted this to seem routine.

As far as the wind was concerned, we were fortunate. It was still blowing northwest, which meant we could clear the inlet and enter the harbor on a reach, then bear away and run through the bridge with the breeze large on our starboard quarter. The only problem was timing, for once inside it was clear we'd probably have only one shot at this. The approach channel was narrow, with little room for a vessel the size of *Constellation* to maneuver, and if we had to luff up or tack to wait for the bridge, there was a good chance we'd end up aground.

It was also obvious we'd never reach the bridge in time for the next opening, which meant we had to spend nearly 40 minutes sailing a distance of about a mile without losing control of the boat. Cliff ordered us to drop the staysail and reef the main, and the boat slowed to a crawl, moving just fast enough to answer her helm.

The next half hour seemed an eternity. We watched the bridge open and close once to let two sportfishing boats through and continued creeping forward in the increasingly fickle breeze. Finally, with five minutes to go to the next opening, Cliff thumbed the transmit button on the radio again.

"We'll raise more sail as soon as you open," he told the bridge tender. "We'll get through as quickly as we can."

"Just get as close to the bridge as possible," came the stern reply.

At one minute to go there was still no sign of the bridge opening—the gates on the roadway had not dropped, the yellow warning lights were not flashing. Cliff gave the order, and in an instant we had the staysail up and were shaking the reef out of the main. The boat picked up speed, then suddenly, almost instantaneously it seemed, the gates dropped, the lights were flashing, and bridge popped open.

It was exactly 11:30. Standing at the rail outside his booth far above us, the bridge tender looked down and gave us a big wave as we sailed through.

Next we needed a place to park. Tim explained the boatyard we were heading for lay just a short distance up a narrow river that branched off the main harbor to the right. The river mouth was just in front of yet another bridge, a fixed one we were too tall to pass under.

We sailed the length of the harbor on an easy broad reach, passing by the main anchorage and the red-tile rooftops of downtown St. Augustine. As we approached the bridge, Cliff pulled out a pair of binoculars and studied the river entrance. There was another sailboat coming out, and the angle at which its sails were trimmed seemed encouraging.

"Maybe we can do this," muttered Cliff.

So we sailed all the way down to the bridge, turned up to windward, and sheeted the sails in hard. It was immediately clear, however, that we could not lay the river mouth.

"Helm's a-lee!" called Cliff.

Fortunately, we were moving just fast enough to tack away from the bridge before we hit it.

"Over there," said Cliff. "We can land there."

He pointed across the harbor to where a brand-new pier and a long floating dock with not a single boat on it lay gleaming in the bright sunlight. We could not have asked for a more perfect place to land a 92-foot schooner under sail. We dropped the mainsail, turned the boat, jibed the staysail, and sailed gently up to the dock. As we tied off our lines, a small group of men came ambling down the pier and congratulated us on a job well done.

We spent the afternoon cleaning up, wiping away the thick layer of oily soot that covered the interior of the boat, while Cliff worked on the engine. Apparently, its exhaust manifold had blown itself to bits. Cliff somehow jury-rigged a temporary repair, whereupon we motored across the harbor and up the river to the yard where we expected to get hauled out in the morning.

It was a godforsaken piece of waterfront real estate if ever there was one, littered with crumbling sheds and the remains of ruined shrimp boats. And there, standing on its marine railway—its only railway—was an immense white sportfishing boat. As soon as we tied up at the dock out front, one of the yard's owners came down, the one Cliff had spoken to on the phone, and pointed at the sportfish on the ways.

"We can't haul you," he said. "Not for a week at least. While I was talking to you, my partner made a deal to haul that one there."

Soon afterwards the partner came down to see us.

"You gotta get your boat off our property," he said. "This ain't no goddamn marina."

And he stomped off with a scowl on his face, leaving Cliff standing speechless on the dock.

HAVING SO CALMLY HANDLED the crisis of our arrival in St. Augustine, having landed the plane in the foggy valley, as it were, Cliff now started unraveling as we prepared at last to set out across the Atlantic. We had an immense amount of work to do, complicated by the fact that the jobs we had planned to do with the boat hauled out now had to be done underwater.

But at least we had a pleasant environment in which to work. Having been chased away from the boatyard, we returned to the first dock we had landed on and were again well received. This was a part of a small private club—a fish camp, as they are called in Florida—run by an affable fellow named Harold, who told us we were welcome to stay as long as we liked.

It was an idyllic place—a collection of small open-air bungalows with jalousied windows, in the West Indian style, set at the end of a small peninsula in a grove of palm trees. Out front, beached in the reeds behind the dock where we were tied up, there was an old wooden ketch, Harold's first boat, in which he'd cruised the Bahamas singlehanded when he was just 17 years old.

In addition to our work list, we also had to cope with an influx of guests and new crew. There was Ron, a middle-aged Englishman, and his American wife Gail, who had admired *Constellation* while we were in Beaufort and had arranged with Cliff to join the boat for all or part of our voyage. There was also Bill, an old friend of Cliff's from the West Coast, and his fiancé Patricia. Bill was a large bearded man, forever pulling on a pipe. He had long dreamed of making an ocean voyage and originally planned to sail on *Constellation* all the way across the Atlantic. Tragically, he'd just been diagnosed with terminal bone cancer and now had decided to go only as far as Bermuda.

Lastly, there was Cliff and Ruth Ann's daughter, Jean, and her two-year-old son, Kale, who had come all the way from Iowa to see us off.

The boat was crowded with all these extra people aboard, and for the most part, like Henry, they did little work. Bill, an avid armchair navigator, spent much time studying charts and sailing directions, and Jean, a cheerful, energetic soul, was a great help to Ruth Ann, who was struggling to provision the boat for the long voyage ahead. But otherwise Cliff had to rely mostly on Jack, Tim, and me to help prepare the boat for sea.

Through it all, Cliff reeled uncontrollably from crisis to crisis. He threw a fit after the TransARC rally team came to inspect the boat and lengthened our job list considerably by decreeing that our running lights were out of position, that we needed backup kersosene lights, and that our batteries were not properly installed. He threw another fit when Jack temporarily lost the propeller shaft key while changing the propeller underwater. Then came a tremendous explosion, during which he actually hit Henry for mishandling a fender while we were turning the boat around on the dock so we could load a new anchor chain onboard.

Henry said nothing and cowered like a whipped dog. Bill, watching from the dock as he puffed on his pipe, remarked thoughtfully: "He handled that just right. Just stood there and took it." And then he added: "Cliff does have a temper, you know."

Later that evening Cliff flew into yet another rage after learning that some electronics he'd ordered had been lost in the mail and that the boat's insurance might be voided because of a missing survey form. First he yelled at Ruth Ann after she asked some innocent question about the provisions, then ended up in a vicious fight with Jean, who stepped in to defend Ruth Ann. In mid-fit, he then suddenly turned on Henry.

"Our contract is done!" he shouted. "You will never get a piece of this boat. You'll get your money back, and then I never want to see your face again!"

I was astounded by this and later asked Tim and Jack about it. They explained that Cliff hadn't had the money to pay the last yard bill, about $10,000, after the haul-out and refastening job in Tarpon Springs. Instead Henry had paid it, using his dead mother's credit card, and took from Cliff in return a promissory note backed by the boat itself.

"It drives Cliff over the edge every time he thinks about it," said Tim. "That he sold his soul and maybe the boat to Henry and his dead mother."

IN THE END we finally did make it. The TransARC inspectors were placated. The missing electronics and insurance survey showed up just in time. Jack packed more epoxy into various seams below the waterline. Our larder and tanks were full. Our various repairs to the engine exhaust and myriad bits of rigging and hardware were perfected, and at last we believed we were ready to sail to Spain.

There was a formal racing start just outside the St. Augustine inlet, with flags flying and cannons firing, and 30-odd TransARC rally boats turned east and sheeted home their sails as the last gun sounded. As soon as *Constellation* crossed the line, Cliff called us all amidships and in his capacity as captain performed a brief ceremony, uniting Bill and Patricia in matrimony. Immediately afterwards we hoisted a large banner—Just Married it read—and broadcast an announcement over the VHF radio. There was a joyous riot of noise as all the other boats in the fleet sounded their horns in response.

The boat still was crowded. Jean and Kale had stayed ashore, but they were replaced the day before the start by two new crew members. There was Tom, a cheerful freckled fellow with thin red hair, who somehow managed to mention having served in Vietnam in most every conversation I had with him, and Bud, an older man who looked like a cross between Captain Kangaroo and a gay pirate, with a taut round belly, spindly legs and arms, lemon-blond hair and a beard, and a shiny gold ring in one ear.

All told there were twelve of us aboard. Every berth was full, even the two foc'sle berths all the way forward where the anchor chain was stored, and two of the crew, Bud and Henry, had to share one berth, taking turns sleeping as they came on and off their different watches. But still, the mood onboard was congenial and the weather, for the first few days at least, was settled and easy.

At night I had vivid dreams. I couldn't say if it was the lulling motion of the boat, experienced now endlessly, day after day, or the release of having at last achieved my long-sought goal. When sleeping my consciousness seemed porous, and all of my memories flooded into and through each other, with past characters in my life mixed up in a jumble of improbable plots, dramatic crises, and wonderful denouements. All this to the tune of water, an entire sea of it, hushing past my berth as I slept. Even when I was awake, the seepage continued and those dreams, so intense, bled into my mind like stains on reality.

Then came our third night out, some 350 miles from shore, and it seemed the boundary between my dreams and reality was shattered. There was some clamor and commotion, a panic of activity on deck and in the main saloon. I felt the motion of the boat, and it was much stronger now. The water was hissing again, surging past the hull.

There was a voice. Cliff shouting, a familiar sound, but now he was more than just angry. He was afraid.

Tim shouting back: "Don't yell at me! I'm doing everything I can."

Must be a dream, I told myself. But I had to test it and cracked open one eyelid in the teeth of the night. Out in the saloon I could see flashlight beams swizzle-sticking through the darkness, saw bodies wrestling with some heavy piece of equipment.

Can't be a dream, I realized, and I tried to force myself awake. But I couldn't do it. I fought the sleep as hard as I could, but I couldn't overcome it, and finally surrendered.

They'll call if you they need you, I told myself, again and again. In my mind, as I fell back down the well of unconsciousness, I ran over the things I should grab in case we abandoned ship: my shoulder bag, jammed in a corner at the foot of my berth, with my passport and wallet inside; some warm clothing from the gear hammock swinging just over my head; my rigging knife, swinging on a hook by my side. And after that I remembered nothing.

In the morning I stumbled on deck in a daze and learned we had in fact come tolerably close to sinking during the night.

"The leaks," explained Tim. "They're much bigger now. Three or four at least, all along the port side and somewhere up forward, too. No one noticed until the water was way up over the floorboards, and then we had a real shit-fight dealing with it. Didn't you hear us?"

I nodded my head. "I thought I heard something," I answered.

"Well, it's a good thing you're rested. I've been up all night, and now you can mind this pump for a few hours while I get some sleep."

It was a big gasoline-driven trash pump, capable of moving over 500 gallons a minute. It sat on deck lashed to the mainmast pinrail, with one fat four-inch-diameter firehose snaking down through an open porthole into the main saloon and thence to the bilge. The exhaust hose, just as fat, ran overboard and was lashed to the caprail.

All morning and into the afternoon I sat there on the cabin coachroof beside the pump. Every 15 minutes, per Tim's orders, I yanked on the starter cord, heard the pump's angry snarl of combustion, and marveled at the quantity of water that gushed out the end of the exhaust hose. A couple of minutes later, when I heard the bilge sucking dry, I shut down the pump and started checking my watch again.

Meanwhile, I studied the sea and sky around us. The sun was bright and the wind was up, blowing hard from the northwest. We were running off before it on a shallow broad reach, heading straight back to Florida. The waves were steep and most were breaking, snarling a bit as they rushed at the boat's transom.

EATER OF SOULS

Florida and Beyond
May–June 1992

THAT FIRST AFTERNOON after nearly sinking we were visited by a vast pod of dolphins. Dozens upon dozens of them leaping across the disheveled gray water toward us. With their perpetual cetacean grins, they seemed oblivious to *Constellation*'s distress as they gamboled like children in our bow wave.

Soon afterward three whales appeared close off our port side. They lolled about, spouting lazily for 20 minutes or more, and this surfeit of attention from our fellow mammals seemed to us a good omen. By now the flow of water from our leaks had subsided enough that the small electric pumps in *Constellation*'s bilge could keep her afloat, so in fact there was cause for optimism. We shut down the trash pump and were relieved to hear the angry clatter of its two-stroke engine fade away into the hissing sound of the sea running along our hull.

Still, just in case, we kept the big pump lashed in place on deck, and with our metaphorical tails jammed firmly between our legs limped back toward the continent. Like an over-matched boxer leaning away from an opponent's punches, we tried to keep *Constellation*'s stronger starboard side to windward and sailed with the breeze abaft the beam as much as possible.

Soon, however, *Constellation* suffered more injuries. Suddenly one of her starboard mainmast shrouds broke loose, as the chainplate securing it snapped in two, and this gave rise to a fear that we might be dismasted. We lashed the shroud as tightly as we could to a big pad-eye on the caprail and prayed it would hold. The following day our generator and battery charger failed, so we had to keep the main engine running to assure a steady supply of power to our overworked bilge pumps. Not long afterward, during a hard 35-knot squall, the forestaysail, a well-stained piece of canvas, suddenly exploded into pieces and was shredded beyond repair.

The crew wasn't faring much better. Ron, Gail, and Patricia were perpetually seasick and lay huddled like refugees under blankets on the watch berths in the doghouse. Meanwhile, poor Bill, our armchair navigator and terminal cancer patient, had been lying motionless in his berth below ever since we left St. Augustine, and we weren't entirely sure if he was conscious or not.

The rest of us, those who were still functional, were thinking hard about the future. Cliff announced that our goal was to reach Palm Beach, back in Florida, but did not say what we would do there. Both Jack and Tim, but most particularly Jack, complained bitterly whenever Cliff was out of earshot and swore they would jump ship as soon as we reached shore. The only one who seemed happy was Bud, who liked nothing better than to steer the boat in poor weather.

Finally, on the evening of May 15, a Friday, six days after leaving St. Augustine, having sailed halfway to Bermuda and back, we entered the Palm Beach inlet and landed on a dock at a boatyard called Cracker Boys. As he'd promised, Jack took Cliff aside as soon as we were tied up and resigned his commission as second mate. Within an hour he'd rented a car and was loading his gear into it. Tim, meanwhile, had also packed a bag and announced he was driving down to Key West with Jack. He said nothing, however, about what his ultimate intentions were.

Before taking off Tim grabbed a towel and headed for the boatyard showers. I grabbed one, too, and immediately followed after him.

"Are you coming back, or not?" I asked straight out as we were drying off afterwards.

Tim looked annoyed, as he often did when confronted with questions posed by persons inferior to him, and for a moment was silent.

"You know, I may just be stupid enough to stick this out," he said finally. "I've never had a boat sink out from under me. I guess it won't hurt to try it at least once."

The next morning Cliff finally made a pronouncement: he wanted to fix up the boat as quickly as possible and strike out again for Spain. But over the next two days various other crew members also packed their bags and drifted away. Bill, Gail, and Patricia declared they would not be returning, but Tom, Bud, and Ron all said they'd be back as soon as the boat was repaired.

Poor Henry wasn't sure what to do. He too had rented a car and on Sunday morning invited me to go for a ride.

"What do you think?" he asked as he piloted the car through the neighborhood just behind the boatyard, a no-man's-land full of strip joints, raggedy beauty salons, storefront bail-bond offices, used car lots, and slit-trench bars. "Do you think I should stick this out?"

The streets were nearly empty, save for a handful of homeless men who pushed overloaded shopping carts along cratered sidewalks, eyes peeled for empty bottles and cans.

"I have no idea," I answered. "I don't know your circumstances as well as you do."

"Well, I think you know how much I want to do this. But like I told you, I have my family and business to think about." He sighed wearily, as though the burden he carried was too heavy for him, only it wasn't clear if the burden was his desire to go to sea aboard *Constellation*, or the family and business back in Orlando.

"It's a call only you can make," I told him. "This is your life, your priorities. No one else's."

Henry turned the wheel, the car lurched around a corner, and we suddenly emerged in a Florida that looked more familiar to me. Big four-lane roads bordered by big-box stores, generic chain restaurants, shiny clean gas stations, and parking lots the size of cornfields. There was more traffic, too, mostly bright white late-model sedans driven by hunchbacked senior citizens who wore wearing brightly colored clothing and peered over the tops of their steering wheels like gophers peeking out of their holes.

"Do you think the boat is safe?" Henry asked. "Can it even get to Bermuda? I'd really like to go at least that far."

Now it was my turn to sigh, for this was one of many questions I was asking myself. Was the boat sound? Could I endure sailing under Cliff? Was I willing to stay aboard with or without Tim? Was it too late in the season to find another boat to crew on?

"I guess it all depends," I said finally.

"On what?"

"On whether Cliff does right by the boat. On whether he's willing to spend the money to fix her up right."

"Well," sniffed Henry. "He's not getting any more from me."

We drove on in silence, and the road became even wider, six lanes instead of four, with perfectly square intersections every half-mile and byzantine shopping malls instead of individual stores on either side. I sat staring at all this, the soul-sapping ubiquity of it, thinking this was exactly what I needed to get away from. This was why I wanted to go to sea.

"This is all like a foreign country to me," remarked Henry, as though he sensed what I was thinking.

His statement mystified me. "But doesn't everything around Orlando look just like this?" I asked.

"Yes," he answered. "But up there I know my way around."

And by the end of that day Henry was gone, too, still undecided as to whether he'd return or not, and I was left alone with Cliff and Ruth Ann.

The next morning on waking, however, I stuck my head out the companionway and found Tim crashed out in one of the doghouse watch berths. He cracked open one eye, red-rimmed from a weekend's debauchery in Key West, and glared at me.

"You came back!" I exclaimed.

The eye stopped glaring and closed again.

"It's like a soap opera," he muttered. "I have to find out what happens next."

NOW AGAIN WE CONFRONTED the great question: was it possible to get *Constellation* out of the water? As soon as the Cracker Boys yard office opened for business that morning, Cliff disappeared into it and emerged soon afterward with a familiar look of frustration on his face.

"They won't do it," he told us. "They're not sure their lift can pick up the boat, and they don't want to chance it."

He went below, gathered a handful of quarters, and headed to the payphone booth just outside the office. Eventually he returned, smiling now, and announced we were moving the boat to the Rybovich-Spencer yard, a mile or so down the waterfront.

Tim assured me this was very good news. Rybovich was one of the best boatyards in the country, with three big marine railways and an expert service crew that routinely repaired and maintained sumptuous megayachts that made *Constellation* look like a backyard salvage project.

But still our fate was uncertain. We tried the next day to haul the boat on Rybovich's one empty railway, but found once again that draft was critical and that we'd missed the top of the tide by an hour or so.

The following day we tried again with a more careful eye on the clock, but still there were problems. We carefully maneuvered the boat into position over the cradle on the railway, and the yard crew then started hauling her up the ways, but her stern rose up well ahead of her bow, and they had to quickly back her down again. There ensued a mad scramble as we maneuvered the boat off the railway and the crew pulled the cradle clear of the water so they could nail down more bilge blocks up forward. Then came another attempt, and again the boat's bow was sagging as she was hauled up the railway.

There was a long pregnant pause. We were losing the tide and didn't have time now to maneuver the boat on and off the railway again for a third attempt.

"A diver could do it," said the crew foreman. "A diver could maybe get another block under there."

"You have a diver?" asked Cliff hopefully.

"He's on vacation, won't be back for a week. I'm afraid we'll have to try again tomorrow."

"No, wait!" declared Tim. "I'll do it."

There was another mad scramble as Tim climbed into his wetsuit and donned a mask and fins while I rushed to set up the hookah rig. Tim stuffed the regulator in his mouth as soon as I handed it to him and plunged under the water with a tape measure. He resurfaced just a moment later.

"Fourteen inches!" he called out.

After a brief but frantic search the yard crew produced a large wood block of appropriate dimensions. They nailed three lead pigs to it, and Tim meanwhile strapped on an extra weight belt.

"You got that compressor turned up full blast?" he asked me.

I nodded, and down he went again.

A furious maelstrom of bubbles and kicking swim-fins roiled the water's surface as Tim struggled to drag the extra bilge block down under the boat. Then for several long moments there was nothing but bubbles, more bubbles, and then suddenly Tim's head re-emerged.

He yanked the regulator from his mouth. "We're good! Let's do it!"

The railway's donkey engine roared back to life as Tim climbed out of the water, and then came the joyous moment. After nearly two months of wandering the coast from Florida to South Carolina in vain, after sailing halfway to Bermuda and nearly sinking, after five different attempts at four different yards, *Constellation* was at last hauled dripping from the water.

That same afternoon the yard's two wood-hull specialists, who both wore beards and were both named Don, started swarming over the boat's bottom with picks and hammers. When they quit work at the end of the day they looked a bit shell-shocked, as though they had seen something awful that defied nautical propriety, but to us they said nothing.

The following morning, after a couple more hours of picking and hammering, they came to Cliff and delivered their diagnosis.

"It's amazing," said the older, slightly taller Don. "On a big part of the port side, and on a smaller part of the starboard side up forward, the planks..." He paused here, as though he couldn't believe what he was about to say. "The planks aren't fastened to the frame. The only thing holding them in place is the caulking in the seams, and in lots of places that's coming loose."

Now it was Cliff's turn to look shell-shocked.

"It's a miracle you made it here," said the other Don. "I can't believe you went so far without having any planks fall out."

"Didn't you say you just had the hull refastened?" asked the first Don.

Cliff nodded numbly. "In Tarpon Springs, about six months ago."

"Well, those guys did a terrible job. I guess they must have gone to lunch when they were screwing down planks, had too many beers, came back, and forgot where they left off."

The younger, slightly shorter Don nodded in agreement. "Must have done that a few times."

"We got a lot of work to do," said the first Don, and together they picked up their tools and returned to work.

For the next nine days the four of us—Cliff, Ruth Ann, Tim, and I—

endured the strange purgatory of living on a boat hauled out in a yard. Each morning we were wakened by the ungodly hammering of the Dons, like an incoming tide pounding a wreck on a reef, as they labored to put our Humpty Dumpty of a boat back together again. We had some electricity aboard, courtesy of some very long extension cords, but no running water, and every time we wanted to wash anything, or use a toilet, or do anything off the boat, we had to climb up and down a wobbly 15-foot ladder.

And while the Dons worked on the hull, we did everything we could to make *Constellation* whole. Tim repainted her topsides. I refinished all of her caprail and various other bits of teak on deck. Cliff replaced chainplates, somehow repaired the battery charger, and installed a new alternator on the engine. Ruth Ann meanwhile found an old sailmaker's sewing machine and set to work patching up our many well-worn sails.

The boat itself looked like entropy personified. Huge sticky clumps of teak dust drifted around the deck like tumbleweeds. Great piles of filthy rags and paintbrushes, worn-out scraps of sandpaper, power tools and extension cords, loose sails and stray bits of gear lay everywhere akimbo. Meanwhile, those crew members who were still willing to sail on *Constellation*, but weren't willing to work on her, stopped by occasionally to monitor our progress.

The most interesting visit was from Tom, our perpetually disgruntled Vietnam veteran, who had run into Jack down in Key West.

"He is very angry," explained Tom. "I think that girlfriend of his has been whispering in his ear. He swears he's going to sue Cliff for wages, for all the work he's done on the boat."

"No way," said Tim. "He's just talking. No way would he ever do that."

"I don't know," shrugged Tom. "Seemed pretty serious to me."

Toward the end of our time in the yard I took half an afternoon off, appropriated the ship's bicycle again, and took a ride up the waterfront. I hadn't gone very far when I passed a big storage lot, a block behind the

Cracker Boys yard, that was filled with sailboats blocked up on jack-stands. At the back of the lot, peeking out from a crowd of generic fiberglass hulls, was the brightly varnished bow of a unique vessel I instantly recognized.

This was *Antje*, a 32-foot Dutch lemsterrak that once belonged to an old friend, Richard, who I knew from college. The gate to the lot was chained shut, so I couldn't take a closer look, and very little of the boat was visible, but there could be no mistaking her.

Richard, who knew little about boats, had purchased *Antje* on a whim while traveling through the Netherlands. She was essentially little more than a barge, fat and flat-bottomed, with leeboards on either side to hold her up to the wind while sailing, but was built entirely of wood, all of it finished bright, with many hand-carved details sprinkled about her deck and interior. Her spars were also varnished wood, with a delicate curved gaff atop her mainsail. Her most seductive feature was an exquisite stained-glass window on hinges that opened from her galley below directly into the cockpit. Convinced that such an unusual boat must be very valuable, Richard had shipped her by freighter to the States, where he hoped to sell her for a profit.

I came aboard as navigator. Richard and another friend, Dave, who knew even less about boats, had managed to sail *Antje* from Port Elizabeth, New Jersey, where she was off-loaded from her freighter, all the way to Sag Harbor, at the east end of Long Island. They wanted my help to sail across Block Island Sound, out of sight of land, to Newport, Rhode Island, where Richard thought he could find a buyer.

There was in fact very little to navigate with—no depthsounder or electronics of any sort, no tide tables, no parallel rules, not even a pair of dividers. The only useful tool aboard was a small compass, which was mounted a long way from the tiller.

"How do you read that compass while steering?" I asked Richard.

"I've never used that compass," he answered.

“Then how’d you get the boat here from New Jersey?”

He held up an index finger. “We just pointed at where we wanted to go. We could always see where we needed to go next.”

Fortunately, we did have a chart, so I did the best I could with what was available. I checked the compass for any major deviation, remounted it in a small bucket on the cockpit sole where the helmsman could see it, used a cardboard Kleenex box in place of a parallel rule, and laid out a course for Block Island, where we planned to stop for the night before heading on to Newport.

The sun was just setting as I took my last bearings on the Long Island shore behind us. I could only guess at what the tide would do to us as we crossed Block Island Sound, but was reassured when I thought I felt it suddenly grip our hull and start dragging us out to sea. I adjusted our course accordingly and crossed my fingers.

Just as the sky went black we raised a flashing red light on the horizon far ahead of us, and my heart leapt.

“Steer for that light,” I told Dave, who was on the tiller. “That’s got to be the entrance to Great Salt Pond, on Block Island.”

Then I went below to take a nap, as I suddenly felt tired as the relief of getting a visual fix on our destination swept through me. I awoke some hours later and came on deck to find the boat motoring quietly through the moonless pitch-black night. Visibility was extremely poor, due entirely to the lack of light, and the only thing I could see anywhere around us was the flashing red light straight ahead, which still seemed to be some ways off in the distance. Dave was still steering straight for it. Richard, our putative skipper, was meanwhile fast asleep below, having retired, Dave told me, right after I did.

Still yawning, I went forward to see if I could perceive things more clearly from the bow. I was up there peering ahead into the impenetrable gloom, when suddenly the flashing light in front of us disappeared, as though eclipsed by some unseen object. I started shuffling aft again to tell Dave maybe we should turn around, when suddenly the boat ran aground and slewed up sideways on to a beach.

Incredibly, though it was now after midnight and we seemed to be in the middle of nowhere, a small crowd of people quickly gathered to offer advice and bear witness to our stupidity. It turned out we were in fact on Block Island, about 50 yards south of the entrance to Great Salt Pond, where I could now see another flashing red light that I had somehow missed before.

Conditions were very calm. So calm it theoretically should have been possible to kedge the boat off the beach with an anchor, except we didn't really have a proper anchor. Up on the bow, where a proper anchor might normally be found, forward of a delightfully elaborate hand-cranked windlass, there was instead a large grappling hook, which was painted bright green to match the color of the boat's bottom paint. This looked well suited to dragging bodies of water for corpses and other lost objects, but promised to be of little use when it came to pulling a heavy boat off a sandy beach.

One member of our ersatz Grounding Committee, eager to be helpful, ran home and soon returned with a small Danforth anchor. It looked woefully undersized, but Richard was desperate to try anything. He grabbed the proffered hook, jumped gallantly into our dinghy, a mere slip of a pram, and started paddling vigorously out into the darkness with a length of line to set it. He wasn't more than 20 yards off the beach when the dinghy, which was quite unstable, suddenly capsized in the gentle one-foot swell. Richard swam back ashore, cursing under his breath, and dragged the little anchor up the beach after him.

"What about that dinghy?" asked one member of the Grounding Committee.

"I don't want it," declared Richard. "I've always hated that dinghy."

Whereupon the Grounding Committee made pointed remarks about hazards to navigation and our precious natural environment. Until at last Richard relented, swam back out, and reluctantly pulled the capsized dinghy to shore.

Our pride, of course, was sorely abused by all of this, but *Antje* was made of much sterner stuff. With her stout construction, broad flat bottom, and retractable leeboards, she was just as happy lying aground on a beach as she was afloat. We spent an uncomfortable night aboard, listening to waves slap resoundingly against her hull, and in the morning, with the help of a small towboat, had no trouble pulling her off on the next high tide. No harm was done, and we proceeded on to Newport that same afternoon.

And now here *Antje* had found me again, and at this early point in my ocean-voyaging career this in itself seemed miraculous. Soon enough I would learn that such coincidences are quite common, that the family of sailing vessels and the people who travel upon them is small and close-knit, however wide the canvas they wander across, and that their paths are constantly converging and reconverging in the most distant and unlikely places. But now, in this place and at this time, standing outside this neglected storage lot on this sun-blasted coast so far from New England, I thought surely there must be some purpose in this.

What it seemed, frankly, was ominous. My running *Antje* aground on that beach that dark night all those years ago had been the greatest, most egregious mistake I'd ever made aboard a boat. And now I had to wonder if I was in the midst of making an even greater one.

IT IS AN UNDENIABLE TRUTH that any sailing vessel you have helped to create, or have helped to maintain in any significant way, becomes to you an object of great worth and beauty, no matter how unworthy or ugly it may appear to an objective eye. So it was that I could not conceive of walking away from *Constellation* once she was launched again. Now her hull was supposedly tight, the menagerie in her engine room had been coaxed into some useful semblance of cooperation, her sails had been mended as much as possible, and as she eased back down the Rybovich railway into her element, with her gleaming white topsides and freshly finished teak, she seemed to me more attractive than ever.

Immediately after the launching Cliff produced a big cooler full of beer and invited all the boatyard staff who had helped us during the refit to an impromptu party down on the dock where the boat was now tied up. The two Dons, quite properly, drank a good deal more than anyone else.

"She's looking good," pronounced the older one, and we all beamed in the glow of his approval. "Where do you reckon you're headed from here?"

When we told him the appreciative look on his face suddenly evaporated.

"This boat isn't going to Spain," he said in a matter-of-fact tone. Then he reached into the cooler for another beer.

"No sir," agreed the younger one.

Cliff stood motionless for a moment, looking a bit like a fresh-caught fish that had just been stunned with a blow from a winch handle. Then suddenly we all heard his name booming through air as he was paged on the yard's PA system.

Cliff picked up the nearest dock phone, listened a moment, then turned to the rest of us: "There's a mailman up at the office with a registered letter for me."

Tim and I both froze, beer cans poised on our lips.

"Could be a summons," I warned, remembering Jack and the threatened lawsuit.

"Maybe," said Cliff.

"Don't accept it," I urged.

Cliff grumbled a bit, wriggled his shoulders, then stalked up the pontoon toward the yard office with Tim following anxiously in his wake. In a few moments they reappeared, grinning from ear to ear.

"I never even touched it!" boasted Cliff. "I asked the mailman to hold it up for me, and I saw the return address printed right there in the corner—Monroe County Courthouse. So I asked him if he'd have any heartburn over sending it back undelivered, and he said no problem. He just wrote out on the slip: Boat Already Sailed."

Everyone gave out a big cheer, all aspersions as to *Constellation*'s seaworthiness were instantly forgotten, as though Jack's lawsuit was the only bullet we might possibly have to dodge, and we all dove into the cooler for yet another beer.

We set sail two days later, on June 1, some 18 days after we first arrived in Palm Beach. Our crew was now smaller than before. Once our repairs were complete, Ron had promptly returned to us, as promised, as had Bud, but Henry, our indecisive Hamlet, was never seen again. Tom, meanwhile, seemed to be hedging his bet. He announced he couldn't make the leg to Bermuda and sent in his place—as a guinea pig, I suspected—a young friend of his, Brent, a broad, silent Canadian lad with long blond hair and a deep tan.

We had no wind that first day and motored through glass-flat water across the narrow pipe of the Gulf Stream. A few hours before sunset we skirted the northern edge of the Little Bahama Bank. To me, raised on the monochromatic depths of the Gulf of Maine, it seemed entirely surreal.

Suddenly there was a dramatic change in the color of the water, from a deep-sea blue, where our depthsounder showed hundreds of feet beneath us, to a much brighter, intense turquoise, where depths were less than 30 feet. Though we were 50 miles or more from the nearest land, we passed close by several boats anchored out like space stations in the middle of nowhere—a large dive boat, one sailboat, and four luxurious motoryachts. Then they were gone, and the water turned dark blue again.

By the end of the second day, after another 24 hours of interminable motoring, we had fallen into a steady shipboard routine. Cliff had divided the six active crew members (excepting Ruth Ann, our ever-busy cook) into a triad of two-man watches, and my mate was Bud, with whom I also shared a stateroom, midship on the port side.

When we were on watch together, I enjoyed getting to know Bud better. He was older than I thought, given his curly blond locks and boyish visage, nearly 70, bouncing back now from a recent tragedy. During World War II he had served in the merchant marine on the dreaded Murmansk run, running supplies to our Soviet allies in often deplorable conditions. He graduated from that into a successful career as an insurance salesman, with a wife and kids and a house, and retired early so as to spend time cruising with his wife on their 37-foot sailboat.

Bud actually broke down crying on deck beside me when he told me what happened next. He and his wife were out sailing together off the Florida Keys when suddenly she became ill. Bud did not take this as seriously as he might have and dawdled a bit getting back to shore. Next thing he knew he was alone, and his wife lay dead in a hospital.

Soon afterward Bud sold his house and moved onto the boat full-time down in Key West, where he spent a long time depressed, drinking too much, blaming himself for what had happened. But then he was saved when he met the new love of his life, the wonderful Lucille. I swear he looked as happy and as excited as an adolescent boy as he described to me, in almost unseemly detail, how he finally worked up the nerve to kiss her for the first time.

And now his plan was very simple: here on *Constellation* he would at last realize his lifelong dream of crossing the Atlantic under sail, then he would return to Florida, sell the boat, and move back ashore with Lucille.

All of which inclined me to feel sympathetic toward Bud, at least when he was awake. When he was asleep, however, in his bunk beneath me, I soon learned to loathe the man, as his snoring capabilities were extraordinary. This wasn't just an occasional phenomenon, but an incessant one, a snarling high-volume ejaculation that poured forth from his nose and mouth whenever he slipped into unconsciousness.

I tried everything I could think of to stifle him. Draped my leg over the side of my berth and prodded his tumescent belly as hard as I dared with the heel of my foot. Dropped hand towels from on high down upon his face. Reached down with my hand and pinched his nostrils shut. But nothing ever worked, and Bud roared on beneath me, and sometimes it seemed I might never sleep again. I understood at last I was confronting something exceptional when I was awakened one night by the awful sound of Bud snoring in stereo.

How was this even possible? I leaned my head down as far as I could, listened closely, and finally realized: he was snoring through both his face and his anus.

The next morning when we were on watch together, I felt I had to say something about this.

"You know, Bud, your snoring really is driving me crazy. Last night, I swear, you were doing it out both ends simultaneous."

"What do you mean?"

"I mean you were snoring out your ass."

"I was not!" he snapped defensively.

"And through your nose and mouth, at the same time."

"I was not."

"I swear, man, you were. You really have to do something about it. No way can Lucille tolerate something like that for very long."

Bud said nothing in response to this. Only scowled at me, a terrible facial contortion I would never have thought him capable of, and from that point forward relations between us were much cooler than before.

Meanwhile, as if in harmony with Bud's snoring, *Constellation*'s engine droned on incessantly, hour after hour, as we motored across the vast windless ocean. Finally, on our fourth day out, a breeze came up, a steady 15 knots from the southeast, which put us on an easy close reach for Bermuda. Cliff switched off the engine, and sweet peace prevailed as we happily surged onward under sail.

Only a few hours later, however, our mainstaysail suddenly burst a seam, just above the seam that Ruth Ann had laboriously re-stitched two weeks before, and had to be taken down. Two hours after that a squall came through and blew out our jib.

Tim and I pulled on some foul-weather gear and sallied forward on to the spray-drenched bow to pull it down.

"Just how old are these sails?" I asked.

Tim shrugged. "Most were built in the '70s, I think. Some go all the way back to the '50s, when the boat was rerigged."

"Cliff never thought of getting new ones?"

"Oh, he got an estimate once. For all new working sails, but it was way too high. Would have cost more than what he paid for the boat."

I'd assumed after our stay at Rybovich-Spencer that Cliff must have deeper pockets than he was willing to admit to, but now again I had to wonder just how much bubble gum and baling wire was holding *Constellation* together.

"How'd he pay that yard bill we ran up? It must have been enormous."

Tim laughed: "He didn't. He talked his brother into picking it up."

The following day the wind died again, and we were confronted with a different sort of predicament. Cliff calculated that we'd already burned some 200 gallons of diesel, and having learned during a VHF radio conversation with a passing boat just how expensive fuel was in Bermuda, he was unwilling to burn any more. So now we struggled under a blazing sun to keep the boat moving under sail alone in the fickle zephyrs and cat's-paws of breeze that came our way.

Fortunately, though *Constellation*'s sail inventory was frail, it was also large. We had an old used genoa off another boat to fly in place of our blown-out jib, a few other headsail-shaped bits of canvas that could serve as make-shift staysails, and also two big quadrilateral sails unique to schooners that I had never encountered before. The smaller of these, called the fisherman, or just "the fish," was bent on to a track on the back of the foremast, with its throat hoisted aloft as far as the foremast spreaders and its peak hoisted to the top of the mainmast. Its clew, which overlapped the top of the mainstaysail, reached back to the mainmast a good 20 feet or so above the deck. The other much larger sail, an almost imponderable beast called the gollywobbler, occupied the same position in the sail plan, but with its luff hoisted the full length of the foremast and its clew sheeted well abaft the mainmast almost at deck level. When hoisted it seemed like a giant stage curtain that had been draped across the middle of the boat.

Unfortunately, too little wind can be just as destructive as too much wind. To sail effectively in doldrum conditions you must carry maximum sail all of the time while watching your sails chew themselves to pieces most of the time. Accordingly, the fisherman was soon split in two beating itself up in the slack breeze. And when we hoisted the mighty gollywobbler in its place, it too was quickly damaged, but with much smaller tears closer to the deck, so that we could stitch them up by hand while the sail was still flying.

Finally, on our seventh night out of Palm Beach, with the wind at last a bit fresher and filling our sails nicely, we spied a dim glow on the dark horizon ahead of us. Gradually it grew brighter and larger and resolved itself into a constellation of many individual lights strung out along the surface of the water. By morning all those lights had disappeared and had morphed into solid land, with houses and buildings scattered all over it. We doused our sails, fired up the engine, squeezed through a narrow cliff-faced declivity known as Town Cut, and so arrived at last at St. Georges Harbor in Bermuda.

On completing formalities, we landed the boat on a sturdy-looking dock in front of the St. Georges Dinghy Club, which ranged down a steep hillside close by the harbor entrance. By the end of that day, having squared away the deck, Tim and I were celebrating our landfall by getting well and truly drunk.

In a rush of enthusiasm we assembled the ship's inflatable tender, mounted its outboard engine, and set off exploring. Bottles of beer in hand, we landed on a small island just south of Town Cut, scaled a steep cliff face, and surveyed the harbor beneath us as the sun eased toward the horizon in a bright pink-and-purple haze.

As the sky grew darker, we plunged back down the cliff and found the dinghy again. Puttering then along the island's shore, we discovered a deep trench of an inlet, a tiny secret canyon leading to some tiny secret place we could not see.

"There!" I urged Tim. "We must go in there!"

Tim obediently turned the boat down the narrow defile. The water in the inlet quickly became too shallow for the outboard's drive leg, so Tim pulled up the engine and I jumped overboard and waded the length of the canyon, pulling the dinghy after me.

Twenty yards later we emerged in a small basin of perfectly still water surrounded by a thicket of mangroves. And on one edge of the basin, beside the entrance where the mangroves had been cleared away, we found the ruined remains of an abandoned miniature boatyard. The wrecks of tiny plywood boats no bigger than our dinghy, but with tiny decks and cabinhouses, lay submerged in the water or pulled up into the weeds on shore. On one side there was a small cinder-block shed surrounded by various bits of miniature marine hardware, and leading down from the shed, running into the clear shallow water beneath us, there was a miniature marine railway.

Suddenly all the angst and tension of the past several weeks was shattered by our drunken hilarity.

"Cliff! Cliff!" we called out as we laughed uncontrollably. "We found a place to haul the boat!!!"

WE WERE NINE DAYS in Bermuda. During this time we repaired various sails, replaced our new alternator, which evidently was defective, and motored from one end of the island to the other looking for inexpensive diesel fuel. Brent, our large silent Canadian, boarded a plane for home and was replaced by his sponsor, Vietnam Tom, who apparently was satisfied that *Constellation* was now worthy of his presence. There came also another Canadian, smaller and more voluble than Brent, Dave, who was Ron's son and seemed a useful addition, as he had some experience sailing Alden schooners.

Lastly there came Curly, a good friend of Tom's who looked very much like Kenny Rogers, with white shoulder-length hair and a full beard, but with a blue watch cap rather than a Stetson perched atop his head. He was well known in Key West, as he had once owned a popular bar there and had also skippered a successful sportfishing boat, but had squandered all this in his insobriety. Cliff and Ruth Ann were reluctant to have him join us, but Tom had lobbied steadily on his behalf, and Curly had sworn he was mending his ways. He had just inherited some money from his mother, so could pay for his berth up front, and declared that his goal during this voyage was to give up drinking for good.

Within hours of arriving, however, Curly had embarked on an epic bender. Over the course of two days he was thrown out of, or declared an adopted son in, almost every bar in Bermuda as he toted his mother's ashes from pub to pub in search of a sympathetic ear. His wanderings finally ended at the Dinghy Club bar, just up the hill from where we were docked. After several hours there he was finally kicked out after he loudly proclaimed his desire to copulate with Queen Elizabeth.

Cursing incoherently, Curly stumbled down the club's stairway. With his urn of ashes clutched to his side with one hand, he formed a loose fist with the other and shook it at his persecutors. He then staggered down the hill to the dock, heaved himself aboard *Constellation*, and collapsed like a felled tree into one of the doghouse watch berths. A few hours later we cast off our lines, motored out Town Cut beneath a rising full moon, and set sail for the Azores.

Soon enough, as *Constellation*'s hull whispered through the night and into the light of the next day, the rest of us lapsed into a vaguely euphoric sense of removal from land. The cares of our lives on shore all fell away from us. Once again our whole society consisted of a very small number of individuals, and all other relationships were temporarily meaningless.

Tim and I were assigned to stand watch with Curly, who was the only one aboard who remained outside our society, as he continued to lie unconscious in his watch berth. On our second afternoon offshore, he did finally rouse himself, but only briefly. He lurched to the rail, vomited overboard, then lurched back to the berth and expired again. He was still there when Tim and I came up on watch that evening after dinner. We stood together for a while, just a few feet from Curly's horizontal form, and made sarcastic remarks about how helpful he was.

To our surprise, he suddenly lifted his head, cracked opened his eyes and fixed them upon us.

"Fuck you, assholes. I'll be up tomorrow."

And then he passed out again.

He was as good as his word. The following morning Curly got up, ate a bowl of breakfast cereal, drank some orange juice, and then took a sober keen-eyed tour of *Constellation*'s deck. He soon returned to the cockpit with a flying fish he'd picked out of the scuppers.

"Look at this. It's perfect," he pronounced and displayed his find in cupped hands, as though it were a sacrament.

He pulled a well-worn knife from his pocket, rumbled through the ditty bag of fishing gear he'd brought with him, and in a just a moment had fashioned the dead fish into a lure by slitting open its corpse and lashing it neatly around a large hook. He dropped this overboard at the end of a handline and stood patiently at the stern waiting for a strike while conversing amiably with anyone who wandered within range.

Constellation, meanwhile, surged over the sea like an animate creature. Our course trailed gently north as we sailed east toward the Azores, and soon we fell into a glorious seam of moderate westerly wind, the underside of a large low-pressure system that tumbled about in a counterclockwise swirl to the north of us. One day passed fluidly into and through the next—always with the consistent sound of the wind and the waves in our ears, always with the deck rolling gently beneath our feet, always with a great wall of crenellated clouds, like ragged bales of dirty wool, looming over the horizon off our port side.

Crew relations became much more congenial. Bud and I were now assigned to different watches, so I could be sure of catching some sleep when he was on deck. Ron seemed very pleased to be sharing a watch with Dave, who proved a very willing hand on deck. Curly, thank God, had assumed human form. Tom stopped complaining about his never-forgotten tour of duty, and Cliff, for the first time since I'd joined the boat, seemed oddly relaxed and at peace.

It seemed at last we had cohered into something like a family. Until one day Tim brought on deck a small plastic action figure he'd found in some forgotten corner of a cabinet underneath his berth. It was a little piece of nothing, a child's plaything about six inches tall—bare-chested with an exaggerated physique, gray skin, brown boots, yellow trousers, and jet black hair done up in a ludicrous top-knot ponytail. On its face was a lurid cartoon scowl.

"Anyone know who this is?" asked Tim as he held the figure aloft, hoping one of us might recognize this character from some comic-book or action-movie franchise.

"Aha!" I exclaimed, remembering a favorite H. P. Lovecraft story. "To me that looks like Yog-Sothoth!"

"Yog-so-who?" asked Tom.

"Yog Sothoth. He is the Eater of Souls. He knows all. He sees all, and to share in his knowledge you must become his eternal slave."

"Where the hell does *that* come from?" Tom again, eyebrows raised in mock alarm.

"Some story I read."

"Yes," pronounced Tim. "That's exactly who I think this is."

And like children we played with Yog. We placed him in various poses, lashed him for a time to one of the grabrails atop the doghouse with one fist raised in defiance to the heavens above, and eventually hung him upside down by one ankle on a length of twine from the boom gallows behind the steering wheel. And we were all greatly amused by this in an idle sort of juvenile way, save for Ron, who professed grave concern.

"I really don't think you should keep him tied up like that," he warned. "Nothing good can come of it."

We thought he was only kidding, but then the following day the skirts of the low-pressure cell that had eased us so effortlessly eastward shifted north away from us. The needle on our barometer inched upwards as high pressure to the south consumed us, the clouds to the north dissipated, and the wind gradually died.

Once again we had to work and suffer for every mile of progress we made, tending our ephemeral sails as they chafed and flogged against the rig. Eventually the awful banging and slamming became unendurable, so we doused the mainsail and forestaysail and left it to the gollywobbler and jib to drag us along as best they could. Finally, however, the whipsawing motion of the boat took its toll. Quite suddenly the gollywobbler split into two pieces, clean across, and we were left rolling madly back and forth under the jib alone.

"Enough!" declared Cliff.

And as he stumped below to start the engine, Tim and Curly went forward to raise the two staysails in hopes of easing the boat's motion. Whereupon the forestaysail block blew to pieces in mid-hoist, and the sail, block, and halyard came crashing down on top of Curly. Cliff meanwhile discovered he'd forgotten to close a certain important valve on the stern exhaust while we were sailing. Seawater consequently had backed all the way up the exhaust line and into the engine, rendering it inoperable.

By now the sun was setting, and as Tim and Cliff worked below in the airless engine room, I was left alone on the wheel. One hour passed, then two. Then a third and a fourth. Eventually I was reduced to a near-hallucinatory state of compass-card vertigo as I struggled in vain to maintain some semblance of a course. As I wrestled with the wheel, I glanced over my shoulder and saw the tiny form of Yog Sothoth swinging wildly by his ankle in the harsh glow of the stern light.

By the following morning things had improved somewhat, at least as far as wind and wave were concerned. The swell had died down and the wind was a bit stronger, still blowing from the northwest, so that we were emboldened to raise our big blue spinnaker for the first time. This greatly stabilized the boat's motion and pulled us eastward at a sedate but steady rate of speed. This continued all through the morning and into the afternoon until, for some inexplicable reason, we decided we had to mess with Yog Sothoth some more.

Perhaps it was revenge. Perhaps it was merely boredom. But in only a moment we cut Yog down from the boom gallows, lashed a big hook to his belly, and had him trailing astern on one of Curly's fishing lines. It turned out he made a pretty good lure and exhibited lively action, skipping and bouncing along the surface of the water behind us. Several hours later, however, shortly before sunset, we reeled in the line and found both Yog and the hook were gone.

Ron was horrified and pronounced this must be a very bad omen. The Eater of Souls, he assured us, would now wreak his vengeance upon us.

During the night it seemed his prediction was coming true. The wind started fading again, and the boat's motion again overwhelmed the sails. The spinnaker was the first to go—a relatively small tear, but in the fattest part of the sail, where it was sure to grow larger, so we quickly doused it and raised a jib in its place. The reduction of sail area only aggravated the boat's motion, and soon afterwards the mainstaysail let go, tearing all the way across its belly along the length of one seam.

By sunrise we were in a pitiful state. More than half our sail inventory was unusable, our engine was still inoperative, and we were rolling in a mean swell, with only two of our smaller sails, the yankee jib and forestaysail, working to pull us on toward land.

EASTERN LANDFALLS

Azores to Spain
July 1992

THE UNADULTERATED PSYCHOLOGY of the ocean sailor has always been both self-serving and schizophrenic. When the wind is favorable, blowing from the right direction, moderate and manageable in strength, we are convinced it will continue this way indefinitely. Wild extrapolations of the vessel's progress are gleefully calculated and celebrated. But when conditions are adverse—when there is too much wind, or too little, or it is blowing from the wrong direction—we pray crapulously for the change we know must come. We cling to this certainty, that the only constant is change, and hang every moment on tenterhooks awaiting its advent.

Aboard *Constellation*, becalmed now just a good day's sail west of her destination, it could not come soon enough. Crew morale had plunged to new lows. Everyone was having trouble sleeping due to the boat's wild motion, Tom started complaining about the food, Cliff started yelling at Tom, Ruth Ann started yelling at Cliff, Tim seemed as imperious than ever, and Bud's oppressive snoring, when he did manage to fall asleep, seemed even louder and snarlier. Ironically, the only person aboard who was both composed and cheerful was Curly, who was buoyed we suspected by our proximity to the bars of the Azores.

We spent nearly 48 hours in this purgatory, hanging on those hooks, and finally relief came not as a change in the weather but in a rumor from below that maybe Cliff had figured out a way to get the engine running again. Like expectant parents we loitered on deck, each lost in a reverie of hope, until at last a confirmatory rumble issued from the boat's bowels. There followed the respiratory splat-splat of exhaust water at the transom, and we were united again in our celebration of Cliff's success.

To me it seemed miraculous. I had supposed the engine's inhalation of seawater must inevitably prove fatal, but now we were told that the engine would run very nicely if only we poured a cup of fresh water into a certain magical orifice every half-hour or so. I could not understand how this was, or what was happening to the water and why we needed to keep replenishing it, but that didn't matter. All that mattered was that we were moving forward again.

Our first hint of landfall after some 17 days at sea came at night in the guise of dolphins. The water was alive with phosphorescence, and again we saw bright green tunnels of light unfolding beneath us. We could tell by their diameter that these dolphins came from a prosperous coastal tribe that fed in well-populated underwater terrain.

The next hint came after sunrise—a faint but unmistakable scent of land. I recognized it immediately. It was the same tangy, beachy odor that evokes the sea when one is ashore, a scent unique not to the sea nor to the land, but to the littoral shore where they meet.

By afternoon, however, we still had not seen any land, though our chart and GPS receiver told us that Pico, an 8,000-foot volcanic mountain, was now just a few miles in front of us. In all directions we could see nothing but thick low-lying clouds that seemed to mold themselves around us. Finally, at less than two miles out, the coast of the island of Faial emerged. The headland of Castelo Branco, a dark, suddenly large solid form in the gray vapor ahead. We passed it, and the rest of the coast was revealed as a parade of cliffs that led us ultimately to the harbor at Horta.

We tied up on the outer seawall and by early evening most us were in Peter's Café Sport, close by the waterfront in what is arguably the most famous sailor's bar in the world. Predictably, much beer was consumed. We also accidentally ordered (and happily consumed) massive quantities of toast.

One great treat of ocean sailing is that every place you put into seems somehow to have been created especially for you. This seemed particularly true in Horta. Most sailing vessels that transit the North Atlantic from west to east are likely to stop here, and for centuries all sailors who've come here—from the whalers of old to Joshua Slocum and the generations of bluewater yachtsmen who followed him—have been welcomed with open arms.

Each member of *Constellation*'s crew now sought to exploit this hospitality in his own way. Tom immediately packed his bag and checked into the fanciest hotel in town, in an old fort overlooking the harbor. Curly, as expected, launched into another supernatural drinking binge. Ron and Dave, meanwhile, went off for some quiet father-son walks through the surrounding hydrangea-studded countryside. And Cliff, of course, was very focused on finding someone who could fix our engine.

What I most wanted to do was make a painting. It is an old custom that every crew stopping at Horta should leave a painting commemorating their vessel and its visit somewhere on the harbor wall, and I at once threw myself into this project. Here at last was something in which I could direct Tim, rather than the other way around, and I quickly dragged him off to a hardware store, or *loja de ferragens*, to collect supplies. I also enlisted Dave, and in just a few hours we produced a vast colorful mural, easily the largest in the harbor, which featured a cartoon caricature of *Constellation* and of Cliff and Ruth Ann and a catalogue of our various mishaps.

We were immensely proud, and the rest of the crew were duly appreciative, save for Cliff, who said nothing and only wriggled his shoulders a bit after inspecting it.

The next day Tim and I went to visit Tom in his hotel room. He let us use the shower and afterwards showed us a big pile of photos he'd just had developed. These included several images of Yog Sothoth, including one I particularly admired of Yog dangling upside down from the boom gallows. I quickly palmed this photo and slipped it in my pocket when Tom wasn't looking.

He seemed in good spirits, but his mood soured as soon as we started talking about the boat.

"I'll tell you this right now," he warned. "If Cliff pushes me too far, I'm gonna smack him. No way am I taking crap from him."

And from there inevitably he somehow segued into the subject of Vietnam and how badly he felt about the war, because it had all been for nothing.

"Maybe it wasn't for nothing," I said and suggested maybe Tom should think of Vietnam as a battle we lost in a war we ultimately won, and that maybe he should feel proud of the part he played in winning that war.

Tom's eyes widened as he thought about this, but then quickly narrowed again.

"No, it still doesn't make any sense to me," he said firmly, with a hint of anger, as though he resented my trying to rearrange his view of himself.

Later that afternoon Tim and I revisited our painting on the harbor wall. I pulled the stolen photo from my pocket and knelt down by one corner of the mural where we had painted a pale white tombstone bearing the legend:

R.I.P.
YOG SOTHOTH
SACRIFICED AT SEA
6/28/92

"Got a light?" I asked.

"What are you going to do?"

"Time for a little exorcism." And I held the photo out in front of the tombstone.

Tim pulled a lighter from his pocket and knelt down beside me.

We were poised on the verge of this sacramental moment—my hand holding out the photo, Tim's hand touching the flame of the lighter to one corner of it—when suddenly there was Tom again standing right behind us.

"What the fuck is this voodoo?" he demanded and snatched the photo away from me. "Where the hell did you get this?"

He waved the photograph at me as an accusation.

I tried to explain myself, spouting assurances that I meant no harm, but Tom immediately cut me off: "No more voodoo! And you keep your hands off my stuff!"

And he stomped off in a cloud of confusion and bitterness.

WE STAYED ONLY A FEW DAYS in Horta, as Cliff soon learned there was no mechanic there who could help us, and when we left Tom was not onboard. We sailed first to the island of Pico, just across from Faial, and landed at a village on its north coast called São Roque.

It was a difficult approach, through a fierce blast of katabatic wind that fell howling down on us over the back of the island's great volcano. It took us by surprise, knocked us on our beam ends, and shredded the mainstaysail, which we had just finished repairing. We recovered and continued into the harbor, which was tiny with little protection and had a mean swell hooking into it. The boat slammed hard against the seawall as we landed on it, leaving some ugly scars, and one seam popped open above the waterline on our port side.

Cliff went ballistic and cursed us all as incompetent line-handlers, though none of this could properly be blamed on the crew. As soon as the boat was secure, Tim and I jumped off and stalked silently through the tiny community. It was a Sunday, some sort of saint's day, and we ended up perched atop an old stone wall watching a small parade of villagers shuffle past bearing a porcelain figurine on an altar covered with flowers. Three musicians brought up the rear, blowing a dirge on tarnished trumpets to the uneven beat of a big bass drum.

The next day we sailed again and soon arrived at the island of Terceira, at a small city called Angra do Heroismo, or the Bay of Heroes, after a 16th-century battle in which desperate Portuguese colonists drove an invading Spanish army into the sea with a herd of stampeding cattle. It is a gorgeous town, said to be the most beautiful in the Azores, but we were busy and had little time to explore. We had our damaged topsides to repair and sails to mend, as always, and also there was a U.S. air base nearby with a large commissary. Cliff was determined to take full advantage of his retired military status, and he and Ruth Ann loaded two taxicabs full of groceries, all of which had to be inventoried and stowed away.

We sailed due east from Terceira bound for São Miguel on a warm, clear night with a steady 20-knot breeze blowing from the south. We had repaired enough sails by now that we could fly full working canvas—the mainsail, a secondhand genoa in place of the recently shredded mainstaysail, the forestaysail, and the yankee jib—and with the wind full on her beam, her best point of sail, *Constellation* at last had a chance to remind us what she was capable of. She covered the 120 miles to Ponta Delgada, the main city on São Miguel and the capital of all the Azores, in just 12 hours.

Nothing went wrong, nothing broke, and I spent the entire night on deck reveling in the boat's performance. Ten knots in a car, not even 12 statute miles an hour, is little better than traffic-jam speed, but in a boat, particularly one as large as *Constellation*, weighing nearly as much as a small building, it feels something like light speed. I stood mesmerized, listening to the incessant roar of water rushing past the boat's hull, and my heart felt as big as the sails billowing in the night sky overhead.

Arriving at Ponta Delgada late the following morning, we all felt proud.

We stood on deck admiring the size of the city, which even had some high-rise buildings along its waterfront, and soon noticed Tom, who waved at us from the sun-splashed balcony of his deluxe room in the best hotel in town.

We picked up a mooring in the middle of the harbor, and Tom was waiting for us when we came ashore in the dinghy. He had decided to rejoin the boat, out of loyalty to Curly he claimed, and had flown over from Horta the day before. As a gesture of goodwill, he offered to host a poker game for the crew at his hotel that night.

This was attended by Dave, Tim, Curly, and myself and was at first perfectly civilized. Tom had reserved a formal drawing room, which came fully equipped with a crystal chandelier, fancy wallpaper and wainscoting, an antique felt-topped table to play on, and a butler with a silver tray to fetch refreshments. The mood, however, soon deteriorated. Tim and Curly had been drinking all afternoon, and Curly was having trouble with his etiquette. I was in the middle of dealing one hand when suddenly he grabbed the deck and started peeking at the cards on top.

"What the hell are you doing?" I demanded and snatched the deck away from him.

"Looking at the damn cards," he mumbled and grabbed the deck back.

"Aw, c'mon. That's not how you play cards."

"You saying I don't how to play cards?"

And at once Curly was on his feet, pumping his fists and challenging me to a fight.

I just got up from the table and left. Dave, who I don't think really knew how to play poker in the first place, got up and left with me. Together we walked down to what the locals called the yacht club, a rather ramshackle open-air bar at the head of the dinghy pontoon. We had little choice but to wait here for the others, as we couldn't in good faith take the dinghy back to the boat without them.

Eventually Tim appeared, and he described in animated detail how the game finally broke up after he got in a fight with Curly and punched him in the face.

"Not once, but twice," he exclaimed. "I had to punch him twice!"

Dave and I took Tim out to the boat, then returned to look for Curly, whom we eventually found coiled up on the ground outside the gate to the club. We propped him up and guided him down the wobbly pontoon, where he tripped on a loose line and fell crashing into the water. After a huge struggle, we managed to haul him out and into the dinghy, where he passed out cold. We took him out to *Constellation*, but could not revive him once we got there. Nor could we manhandle him out of the dinghy, over the caprail, and on to the deck.

I wanted to just leave him for the night, but Dave was worried he'd flop out of the dinghy and drown. So to be safe we lashed him down. We found some line and tied Curly's arms to the dinghy's gunwales and his legs to the thwart seat and in the morning were relieved to find he was still there. He made an awful fuss when he woke. Like Gulliver strapped to the beach in Lilliput, he yelled and thrashed furiously until finally he freed himself.

Our primary purpose here was to get the engine fixed, and to this end Cliff soon located a Portuguese mechanic in perpetually greasy overalls who smiled a lot and called himself Max. He was accompanied by a teenage son, who was shy and never spoke. Together they quickly disassembled the engine and spread its parts all over the galley and saloon in no discernible order. The engine remained in this state for several days, during which time we saw little of Max and his son.

This made Cliff nervous, as he couldn't speak Portuguese and Max spoke little English. We suspected he had no idea what Max was doing. To allay his fear Cliff took to drinking whiskey in the evenings and unfortunately was very much in his cups when we at last held our big crew meeting. Tom for several weeks had been suggesting we do this and now had insisted on a meeting as a precondition to his returning to the boat.

Bud spoke first and wanted only to discuss our itinerary, which he complained was too subject to change. Ron and Tom, meanwhile, were eager to complain about Cliff and how he was always yelling at people. Which prompted Cliff to start yelling about how some crew members seemed to have a problem handling lines and fenders. This culminated in Cliff blaming both Ron and Bud most bitterly for the damage the boat suffered back on the seawall at São Roque. As a result of which Ron, who was normally very calm and polite, completely lost his temper and started yelling at Cliff.

The meeting ended on this sorry note, and the next morning Ron announced he was leaving the boat. He packed his bag that same afternoon and checked into a hotel on shore. With him went Dave, not because Dave was particularly anxious to leave the boat himself, but because he was low on funds and couldn't afford to pay for his berth on the next leg of the voyage. Tom meanwhile had somehow decided the meeting had gone well, so he checked out of his hotel and moved back aboard.

Cliff that night again hit the whiskey a bit too hard and confided to Tim and Tom that he might be willing to let Dave stay aboard for free, as he was so helpful on deck. Tom drank a good bit, too, and he and Cliff fell into a soggy reconciliation, during which they agreed to stand watch together on the next leg of the voyage.

"Jesus Christ!" exclaimed Tom the next morning when he was sober again. "What the hell was I thinking?"

After confirming with Cliff that Dave could come back and ride for free, and that Cliff might actually prefer to stand watch with Dave, Tom grabbed me and said we had to track down Dave before he left the island. We at once rushed ashore and literally ran through town to the hotel where Ron and Dave had spent the night. Unfortunately, they had already checked out, so we immediately hailed a cab and rode out to the airport.

We found them lounging on the lawn outside the tiny terminal, where they were waiting for their flights to be called. We explained all that had happened, and Tom begged Dave to return to the boat.

Dave was ecstatic, laughing out loud, and at once bustled into the terminal to cash in his ticket. Ron was also pleased and I think felt vicariously vindicated that his son had been recalled to service on favorable terms.

We returned together to *Constellation* and found Max and son hard at work muttering incantations in Portuguese as they prodded our debris field of engine parts with their tools. Cliff silently hovered over them, chain-smoking cigarettes. By late afternoon, incredibly, all the parts had disappeared. Max grinned broadly, waved his arm like a stage magician, and pressed the engine's starter button. The engine rumbled to life and Cliff at once ordered that we drop our mooring pennant.

We powered out of the harbor and were immediately caught in the scend of a long sea from the west. Cliff ordered Tim on the wheel to turn into it, and both Max and his son clutched nervously at the back end of the doghouse as the boat started pitching into the waves.

Cliff stood at the engine controls, hand on the red-knobbed throttle, and called out the numbers as he steadily increased RPMs. Oil pressure was normal. Water temperature was normal. Soon we were at full throttle, and the boat shouldered its way confidently through the sea, its motion deliberate and powerful.

"The whole time I've owned this boat I've never heard the engine sound this good," beamed Cliff.

Max and son stood transfixed in a lubber's epiphany, absorbing each passing wave with their legs, faces to the wind, nostrils flaring, eyes and smiles wide with pleasure.

On returning to the harbor we did not pick up our mooring again, but tied up on the seawall and immediately started preparing to leave. While Tim, Dave, and I rushed about doing all the work—tearing down the dinghy, bending on sails, stowing tools and loose gear—Curly roamed the wall with a pair of six-packs under his arm, offering beer to passers-by. Soon he was in the middle of a small group of men, who together stood peering down on us from atop the wall while delivering a running commentary on everything we were doing.

Finally, after Ruth Ann served a late dinner and everyone else had gone to sleep, Tim, Dave, Cliff, and I set sail in the small dark hours of the early morning. We raised the mainsail right there at the wall, tucked in one reef, and cast off our lines with the help of the last two members of Curly's dock committee. They stood watching enviously, with looks of intense longing on their faces, and waved farewell as *Constellation* eased out into the darkness.

THE SWELL FROM THE WEST kept building through the morning sunrise as our view of the mountainous east end of São Miguel steadily diminished. It continued building on through the clear-skied afternoon, and by the end of our first day at sea, as the sun slipped into the horizon behind us, the wind that made the swell finally arrived. By sunrise the following morning, as we settled into the now familiar routine of being on passage, it was blowing a firm 25 knots from west-southwest.

For any well-found sailing vessel, particularly one as large as *Constellation*, these are ideal conditions. As the true wind speed continued climbing to 30 knots we steadily stripped canvas off the front of the boat, then took another reef in the mainsail, and were still making better than 10 knots on a deep broad reach with all sheets well eased. The price we had to pay for this progress, most of it aimed straight down our rhumbline toward Spain, was measured in terms of the motion we endured.

We had sailed off the wind before, but never in my time aboard *Constel-*

lation had we sailed off the wind in such a strong, steady breeze. The seas piling in behind us soon were steeply corrugated, with whitecaps at the top of almost every wave. Each burst of spray torn off a wave by the wind in a line between us and the sun was captured for an instant in the bright light and was resolved ever so briefly into a prism of color. *Constellation*, meanwhile, with her narrow hull, was rolling heavily and corkscrewing as her bow fell and stern rose to greet the walls of water coming up to us.

It was a dramatic motion, but rhythmic and regular, so that it wasn't too hard to adapt to. We quickly learned the sailorly bow-legged gait that best accommodates a lively deck. Most of us, too, had perfected some scheme for wedging ourselves into our berths and felt the boat's gyrations not as an impediment to sleep, but as a narcotic.

The boat, however, was taxed by all this. Often when she rolled some part of her shrieked in protest and after two full days of this we noticed that some of the fasteners securing her interior joinery were coming loose. What was perhaps my scariest moment aboard *Constellation* came on our third afternoon out, when I found Cliff slouched in his easy chair in the saloon pondering a broken screw he had just scooped up off the cabin sole.

"It's this damned cheap Taiwan steel," he muttered and held out the jagged bit of metal for me to see.

It looked familiar to me, and I recalled suddenly, and very vividly, my brief apprenticeship in Key West.

"Cliff, is that a sheetrock screw?"

"I guess it is. It came out of that beam up there."

He pointed up at the top of the forward saloon bulkhead where it had sprung free of the deck beam. The bulkhead I saw was shifting noticeably each time a strong wave swept through.

"I had to be careful not to torque them down too tight. Otherwise the heads just kept shearing off."

It seemed obvious this bulkhead must be a major structural component. I looked at Cliff and wondered: if he could break the heads off screws turning them manually with a screwdriver, how could he not have realized that they couldn't possibly be strong enough to hold the boat together?

"Did you know about this?" I asked Tim later and held up one of the broken-off screw heads.

Tim rolled his eyes. "I warned him."

"Shouldn't we get some sail off? Slow the boat down?"

But Tim said no, he'd been steadily replacing Cliff's cheap screws with good bronze ones whenever he had a chance, and he thought there were enough to hold. And slowing the boat down, he added, wouldn't do much to stop the rolling anyway.

Now for the first time I became interested in our safety equipment. I checked on our life-jackets. I checked to see if there was an EPIRB aboard, though in those days they were much less effective than they are now, and I studied our two life-raft canisters, strapped in cradles on deck.

Tom caught me at this and treated me to a biographical soliloquy.

"Three different times I've had to climb into a raft," he told me. "And every single time the first thing I thought was I didn't spend enough money on this raft."

His first experience was the most dramatic. He'd been aboard a German-built powerboat, a large steel yacht of which he was very proud, the first vessel of any size he'd owned himself. He used it in what he called the export-import trade, smuggling pot north through the Caribbean.

Friends had warned him about metal boats. "But I was young then," he explained. "You couldn't tell me anything."

And so Tom's boat had no zincs, and Tom never worried about isolating metals from each other.

On his last trip he decided to carry a maximum load. He and two crew stuffed every square inch of the boat's interior full of pot bales, leaving open only the engine room and two little tunnels running to the galley and head. Halfway through the run the hull started breaking up around them, chewed to pieces by electrolysis.

They ended up in the life-raft, wishing Tom had spent more on it, and two days later, still surrounded by floating pot bales, were picked up by a Russian spy ship. The Russians kept them locked up in a small cabin, then released them on the nearest island, where the authorities were curious about the pot bales. Tom had to grease many people to get everyone off the island ASAP, before his stressed-out crew starting saying things they shouldn't. And afterwards, after he finally got back to the States, he had an unpleasant interview with the Italian family he'd been working with.

"What about these rafts?" I asked, pointing at the canisters on *Constellation*'s deck. "Are these any good?"

Tom just laughed. "They're probably not the worst I've seen."

We were four days out when we fell into the Portuguese trades, the strong northerly wind that routinely blows down the west coast of the Iberian peninsula. And now, with the wind on her beam again, *Constellation* was still fast, but her motion was less exaggerated.

Soon enough we were in the lee of Cabo de São Vincente, the southwestern tip of Portugal, and the breeze tamped down to less than 15 knots. The sea went flat, and the hazy air again seemed fat with the ripe odor of land. We saw dozens of ships streaming away from and toward Gibraltar. It took some care to avoid them, and any danger posed by the sea or wind now seemed slight by comparison.

Finally, some five-and-a-half days after leaving São Miguel, we arrived on a hot Friday afternoon at Cadiz. As usual we had no chart to guide us, so were momentarily confused by the buoy system, which was the opposite of the system used in North America, with green right returning instead of red.

We were intimidated, too, by the harbor itself, an immense commercial port with no accommodation we could see for yachts or any smaller craft.

Unsure of what to do, we landed at last on a large empty wall in a part of the harbor that seemed inactive. And as soon as the lines were secure, Cliff produced a large magnum of champagne and jumped ashore.

"Guess we have to send a postcard to those Dons," he crowed and started pouring out the bottle's contents into tiny paper cups.

We scrambled up the wall and stood laughing beside him. We raised our paper cups, toasted our skipper and our vessel and ourselves, and kept on pouring champagne in the hot Andalusian sun until the bottle was empty.

SOON THE HARBOR POLICE CAME and chased us away, urging us on to a large marina on the opposite side of the bay. This was Puerto Sherry, a new development with a large luxury hotel overlooking a conglomeration of yacht pontoons and a village of half-finished condominiums. The crews of many other boats who, like us, had signed on to join Jimmy Cornell's America 500 rally were already gathered here, and we received a warm welcome as we pulled into the reception dock.

The crew of *Constellation*, trapped for so long in its own society, was now introduced to the larger society of the cruising rally. Curly, who seemed to become inebriated by simply setting foot on shore, led the way and soon had insulted Wendy, who had sailed to Spain from Miami with her husband and two children, by trying to hit on her. Tom stepped in and tried to soothe her, but only made matters worse when he gave her a patronizing pat on her behind.

"My God!" shrieked Wendy as she ran down the dock away from them. "It's the boat from hell!"

The rest of us, however, quickly made friends, most particularly with the crew of *Compeller*, with whom we seemed to have much in common. Their boat, like ours, was a staysail schooner, and their skipper, like ours, was named Cliff and tended to yell a lot. We also rediscovered other boats and crews we had previously met in St. Augustine, in Bermuda, and in the Azores, so that our arrival at Puerto Sherry, a place we had never been before, a place none of us imagined existed before, in many ways seemed like a homecoming.

From the Puerto Sherry complex it took only a short walk down a beach-front esplanade to reach the old town of Puerto de Santa Maria. Certain members of our crew found whorehouses here and tempted other members into patronizing them, but Tim and I were more interested in seeing a bull-fight. The bullring in town, the Real Plaza de Toros, was one of the oldest in Spain, a small coliseum of stone and brick with rows of arches running around the top.

Neither of us had ever witnessed a fight before, and at first we had trouble understanding what was happening. It seemed unfair that one bull should have to fight all those men—the picadors, the banderilleros, the haughty matador—and as each animal slumped to the sand slathered in blood, it seemed their deaths were cruel and meaningless.

Slowly, however, as the hot afternoon wore on, we noted some of the finer points of the pageantry of the fight, or *corrida*, and of the bullfighters' performances. And when the last bull came out we learned the corrida is not always so one-sided.

This bull was very unpredictable and had great spirit. Early on, as the banderilleros engaged it with their big pink capes, it three times ripped capes from their hands and twice sent them all leaping over the wall around the ring. And when the picadors came out on their horses with their long lances, the bull charged so hard it almost knocked one horse down. And when the banderilleros came back out to plant their colorful banderillas in the bull's back, they were unable to drive home most of their weapons and one man was caught and thrown high in the air over the bull's back.

Finally there came the matador with his sword and a smaller red cape, called a *muleta*. He was clearly nervous as he worked the bull with his cape and miscalculated as he delivered his *estocada*, or sword attack. Here the matador stands directly in front of the bull, one hand with sword held high, the other with the muleta held low to keep the animal's head down. Then he drives in right over the horns and plunges the sword deep between the bull's shoulder blades. If done properly the bull is killed instantly. But our matador leaned to one side going in, anticipating his next move, where he rolls away from the bull after placing the sword. The bull suddenly lurched its head, caught the man on one horn, and gored him badly.

My heart leapt as the banderilleros rushed out to distract the animal with their capes while another team ran out to carry the matador to safety. Here at last the bull was victorious! Surely they would let this one live, bandage its wounds, and put it out to pasture with a harem of admiring cows.

But no. Instead they sent out a relief matador to finish the job. The proud bull, however, survived three more estocadas. Bleeding now from its back, hemorrhaging through its mouth, it was still standing, and only after the matador lunged in with his sword a fourth time did it slump to the ground.

A man in a plain white shirt came forward with a dagger and stabbed the animal directly in the head, right between its ears, to make sure it was dead. The bull, amazingly, leapt to its feet, as though energized by this blow, and staggered around for a few minutes before finally succumbing to a fifth estocada.

In the end, like all its predecessors, it was dragged from the ring by a team of mules. Except this time the crowd rose to its feet to deliver a long standing ovation, and we immediately understood they were cheering not for the bull-fighters, but for the bravery of the bull.

Afterwards we wandered through the milling crowd and at the back of the stadium found a small abattoir. Here the bulls that had died that day had already been butchered and were being loaded on to a waiting truck. We strolled on through the town back toward the shore and by coincidence found a restaurant that served only meat from bulls that had died in the ring.

Obviously, we had to eat here. So we sat down, ordered a bottle of wine, and had a fine feast of calamari and bull's loin. The cycle was complete.

"They all would have been killed anyway," I exclaimed and passed a hand over the table.

"Yes," answered Tim. "They're just cattle. But at least this way they get to go out like bulls, doing what they were born to do."

ESTOCADA ON THE RIO ODIEL

Southwest Coast of Spain
August 1992

HAVING SPENT SO MUCH TIME sailing all the way across the Atlantic Ocean from Florida to Spain, we were now confronted with the question of whether we should immediately leave again. For Jimmy Cornell, in organizing his rally to commemorate Christopher Columbus's voyage to America, had been tortured by the problem of scheduling.

Columbus had guessed correctly that if he followed a southerly route across what was then known as the Western Ocean he would find favorable wind all the way to Japan, or the Bahamas, as the case may be. But he knew nothing about hurricane season and so set out on his voyage at the worst possible time. He departed from Spain, from the town of Palos, about 60 miles north of Cadiz, in early August, bound for the Canary Islands, and then struck out west from the Canaries across the Atlantic in early September, pretty much exactly when he was most likely to get run down by a storm.

It is a minor miracle of history that Columbus was ever heard from again. And, of course, to send a fleet of more than 130 yachts sailing across the Atlantic following in his wake at the same time of year would have been grossly irresponsible. Jimmy Cornell, however, was a man with a deep respect for history. He felt bound to somehow honor Columbus's dates and to do this had decided to split his rally in two. One squadron would leave Spain on August 3, the same day Columbus left, and sail to the Canaries to wait for the second squadron, which would depart from Spain on October 12, the day

Columbus arrived in America. United then, both squadrons would sail out together from the Canaries for the Bahamas along Columbus's original route in the more seasonally correct month of November.

Cliff it turned out was inclined to keep the decision of which squadron to join to himself, so everything we knew of the debate over our immediate fate came to us through the filter of Tim. First he told us Cliff wanted to sail to the Canaries with the first fleet, sail all the way back to Spain, then depart again with the second fleet. Having paid good money to join this rally, it seemed Cliff wanted to participate in as much of it as possible. Next the plan was to just sail with the first squadron and spend the rest of the summer in the Canaries, which at least seemed an improvement over the first plan. Then it was back to Plan A, and finally there came a command decision in favor of Plan B.

It was discouraging to the crew, of course, that Cliff hadn't even considered the most obvious plan, the one we all favored, which was to stay in Spain and leave with the second squadron. But Cliff, I guessed, understood his situation well enough. He must have known that if the boat stayed in one place for very long his crew would bleed away from him, and it would be best for him if this happened in the Canaries. There, where throngs of wanna-be ocean sailors without yachts gather each fall to hitch rides to the West Indies with ocean sailors who actually own yachts, he would be sure to find more crew, and at least some of those might be willing to pay for their berths.

So it was that we set out from Puerto Sherry bound up the coast with some 30 other boats just six days after our arrival in Cadiz. Of the crew who had landed there to drink champagne we had so far lost only one, Bud, who had always planned to leave as soon as we finished our crossing. But Tom now was talking openly of an invitation he'd received to join another boat in the rally, *Tiger Lily*, a modern Swan manned by a gregarious family of Finns. And in private conversations, both Tim and Dave told me they were thinking seriously of leaving the boat. And I, of course, told them exactly the same thing. Only Curly, who suddenly had moderated his drinking, as if crossing the Atlantic had now given him the strength to finally keep his pledge, was evidently content to stay aboard come what may and had said nothing to anyone of wanting to leave.

It was not possible for the rally boats to go to Palos, which was located on the Rio Tinto, because the rio had silted up and was no longer navigable. It was here in Palos that Columbus had formed his own small squadron 500 years earlier and outfitted it for his voyage. One vessel he had chartered, his flagship *Santa Maria*, and the other two, *Nina* and *Pinta*, were donated by the town as compensation for some municipal debt owed to the Spanish crown. By order of the crown, all equipment and provisions were provided by the town, tax free, at reasonable prices. Here, too, Columbus had hired most of his crew, men from all over the western coast of Andalucía, from towns like Palos, Sevilla, Cadiz, and Puerto de Santa Maria.

Though we could not sail to Palos, Jimmy Cornell, in his zeal to adhere to history, directed us instead to the much larger town of Huelva. This was a small industrial port on the Rio Odiel, situated just north of where the Odiel joins the dregs of the Tinto. From here, at least, before we set out for the Canaries, Cornell could lead rally-goers on busses to the chapel in Palos where Columbus and his crews had received communion before their departure.

We arrived in the darkness, almost two hours after sunset. With the rest of the boats we had filed up the black river, past the blazing lights of oil refineries on shore, and gathered together in a strong ebb tide off the Huelva waterfront. Here we attempted to moor in formation, with each boat anchored by both its bow and stern in two parallel lines along the riverbank opposite the town. All this per the instructions of the minions of Cornell, whose voices came crackling at us over the VHF radio.

It quickly became apparent why Columbus had not gathered his fleet here. First one boat that had moored in line dragged its anchors in the hard four-knot current and slid down into another boat, causing it in turn to drag its anchors down into the next boat, and so on, like so many toppling dominoes. Soon great clumps of boats were careening down the river at odd angles with their anchor rodes all tangled up together.

Constellation's anchors were among the first to let go. Tim, Dave, and I, who had now been working the deck together since Bermuda, succeeded in getting them back aboard simultaneously. As we worked we could see the bright lights on other boats twisting by through the black void that surrounded us. And over the radio we could hear the disembodied voices of the strident minions ordering everyone back in line.

Cliff had the engine started before either rode came taut and popped it in gear as soon as he sensed the first anchor was clear of the bottom. Throwing the wheel hard over first one way then the other, with a fierce blast of throttle somewhere in between, he somehow extracted us from the line without hitting or getting entangled with any of the spinning lights around us.

We reset just our bow anchor a short distance downriver and immediately were wondering how well it would hold.

Should we try again to set a second anchor?

Cliff and Tim started discussing the esoteric technicalities of the Bahamian moor, wherein two anchors are set from the bow in opposite directions. Tom meanwhile noticed there was an empty mooring buoy just a short distance behind us off our port quarter.

"Why don't we just take a stern line over there?" he suggested. "That way we don't have to stay up all night mucking around with anchors."

Both Cliff and Tim liked this idea, so we immediately launched the dinghy and set up the line. Once we were secure, however, I saw the boat was lying at an angle to the current. All of my young days on the Kennebec in

Maine, a fast tidal river just like this one, had taught me exactly what would happen when the tide turned. Current flowing the other way from behind us would grow stronger and stronger, and our stern would be pulled inexorably to port as it tried to line up with it.

I mentioned this to Tim, but he just glared at me, as though I were an idiot.

"Don't worry about it. Everything's under control. Just go to sleep why don't you?"

I couldn't believe it. After all we had been through together. And now this: the same old hard-ass bullshit.

"OK then," I answered in an even voice. "I'll do that."

And I went below and lay down in my berth.

Early the next morning I was still lying there half asleep, enjoying the sound of Bud not snoring beneath me, when suddenly I heard two loud cracking noises from on deck—one right after the other, as if a pair of cannons had been fired off in succession. I guessed immediately what had happened and a wave of vindictive joy swept over me. I slipped out of my berth, ambled up the companionway, and found Dave in the cockpit with an unhappy look on his face.

Sure enough, the flood tide had swept our stern hard to port, and Dave had seen that our stern line could not possibly hold us. He had hopped in the dinghy and rigged a second line to back up the first, but as the tide grew stronger both had snapped like over-tightened guitar strings. Dave showed me where the tremendous force of their recoil had torn out a stern chock, a stanchion post, and a good piece of the caprail on our starboard side.

"Almost took my fucking head off too," he muttered.

Having relished the advent of this mishap, I now felt responsible for our situation, so stayed on deck to see if our anchor would reset or would drag up the river on the flood tide. Seen in the light of day, I noticed our environs were less than inspiring. The riverfront was studded with shipping terminals. The water was oily gray with clumps of sewage and feces floating past. The town as a whole, viewed from the river, had a pallid industrial complexion and was surrounded by a low marsh overhung with powerlines and bridges.

Cliff and Ruth Ann had gone ashore at dawn to attend the commemorative ceremony at the chapel in Palos. When they came back aboard, about an hour after the stern lines snapped, Cliff woke up Tim and we decided the best way to stay put was to chain ourselves to a nearby freighter mooring. I asked for and was given the job of leaping down from our bow on to the mooring barrel with a length of anchor chain in hand. I shackled the chain to the mooring ring and just as I was climbing back aboard, a fight almost broke out on deck.

Tim, whenever there was work to be done on deck, had always been most contemptuous of those who helped the least. So when Tom, uncharacteristically, stepped up to the bow while I was down on the barrel and asked what he could do, Tim had simply pushed him aside.

"You motherfucker!" shouted Tom and at once took a swing at Tim.

Tim stepped back to dodge the blow and was about to respond in kind, but then caught himself.

"No! Not on the boat!" And he held up his hands, palms open.

Then Curly stepped forward, grabbed Tom, and pulled him aft toward the transom where the dinghy was tied off.

"Come on, man," he muttered. "We gotta go ashore for a while."

"You better watch out!" shouted Tim as he stood on deck watching the dinghy crawl across the greasy river. "This isn't over yet!"

BUT FOR TOM, AT LEAST, it was over, and no one was surprised the next day when he announced he was leaving *Constellation* to join *Tiger Lily.*

I assumed I wasn't the only one aboard who wondered if he hadn't intentionally escalated the confrontation with Tim to make this decision seem necessary and justifiable. I assumed, too, that both Dave and Tim were also thinking hard about whether they should leave the boat before we sailed for the Canaries.

I was certainly thinking about it. And now, for the first time, there was no innate affection for the boat to hold me back. I understood now what should have been perfectly obvious all along, that *Constellation* simply was not seaworthy, and that all she was really was an overaged boat that had never been properly upgraded.

What was left was the question of obligation. Should I be loyal not to the boat, but to the crew? It was a close call. Tim was an asshole, Cliff was an asshole, but I actually liked Ruth Ann and Dave and was even growing a little fond of Curly, when he was sober.

I asked Dave what he thought, and his view was very straightforward: we should help get the boat to the Canaries, where it would be easy for us to find new boats and easy for Cliff to find new crew.

Meanwhile, as if to taunt us, another technical problem presented itself. Our auxiliary generator, which supplied the boat with electricity when the main engine wasn't running, had been running poorly for days, but Cliff had managed to somehow keep it going in spite of itself. Now, less than 24 hours before our scheduled departure, it gave up the ghost entirely.

At a rally lunch party on shore that afternoon, the other Captain Cliff from the other schooner, *Compeller*, urged our Captain Cliff not to worry about this.

"You don't really need it," he argued. "Our generator broke down weeks ago, and we've been doing just fine without it. All you have to do is keep yelling at your crew not to leave lights on."

Probably it was the old airplane pilot in him that kept our Cliff from subscribing to this view. He had always seemed willing to take chances with our rig, our navigation, and even the integrity of *Constellation*'s hull, but evidently felt too invested in the well-being of our internal combustion engines to let a busted one go unrepaired.

The following morning, while all the other crews around us were bustling around their decks getting ready to leave, we unmoored *Constellation* and took her to the main dock in town. Here we were met by two Spanish mechanics who plucked our generator out the companionway with a small crane, dropped it into the back of a truck, and drove off with it.

We then remoored the boat to our freighter buoy and spent the afternoon on deck watching the elaborate ceremony that Jimmy Cornell had organized. First came a vast fleet of spectator boats, each crammed to its gunwales with ecstatic Spaniards. Then came the king and queen of Spain, Juan Carlos and Sofia, waving at the crowd from the upper deck of a Spanish warship. The ship fired off some guns and slowly cruised past the anchorage as their Majesties reviewed the rally fleet. Then the yachts all hoisted their anchors and slipped downriver in single-file formation.

We sat demoralized and waved halfheartedly at each boat as it passed us. And there, one of the very last to go by, was Tom on *Tiger Lily*, who waved back at us, grinning like a fool.

Later, after dark, there were fireworks, launched from the marsh on the riverbank opposite town. A seemingly endless display, with great bolts of color blossoming in the black sky over our heads. Some of the embers were still burning as they fell and ignited a portion of the marsh just across from where *Constellation* lay moored. Both the fire and fireworks were perfectly reflected in the oily black mirror of the river. And next morning when I came on deck to drink my coffee not long after sunrise, the fire was still going, smoldering away under a vast smudge of heavy gray smoke.

TWO DAYS LATER WE LANDED the boat again at the quay in town and our rebuilt generator was hoisted back aboard. It took most of the afternoon for Cliff and the two mechanics to get it properly reinstalled, and afterward Cliff called a crew meeting.

It was up to us, he announced, to decide where we would go next. And so we resolved we would first return to Puerto Sherry and would then embark on a leisurely summer cruise of the southern Spanish coast. Then later, in October, we would rejoin the America 500 rally and set out with the second squadron for the Canary Islands.

That evening, about an hour after sunset, just as the flood tide went slack and started flowing out the river again, we cast off our lines and left the quay at Huelva under power. We soon reached the junction where the Rio Tinto joins the Odiel. On the eastern bank of the Odiel, right where the two rivers came together, there was a large white statue of Columbus facing west. In the surrounding gloom of the night its pale luminous form stood out like an immense tombstone.

Cliff handed off the helm to Ruth Ann, who had just come on deck after preparing dinner, and one voice, I forget whose, intoned the reading from the depthsounder: 20 feet. No one—not Cliff, nor Ruth Ann, nor any member of the crew passing from the deck to the galley and back again to fetch their meal—had noticed that the flashing red light on the next buoy marking the right side of the navigable channel was in fact well off our port bow, lost in the blaze of refinery lights downriver.

As we went aground, bumping gently at first, Tim, who was standing aft near the taffrail, immediately stepped forward and took the helm from Ruth Ann. Instinctively he knew where the deeper water must be and cranked the wheel hard to port.

The rest of us called out for Cliff, who was down in the galley eating, and in an instant he leapt up the companionway and took the wheel from

Tim. He threw the engine in reverse and goosed the throttle hard, trying to back us off the shoal we had hit. Then he throttled down, shifted into forward gear again, and gunned the engine with the helm still hard over to port, all to no avail.

By now Dave had spotted the buoy we'd missed and stood pointing at it calmly, but intently, as though he were trying by force of mind to move the boat in that direction.

Cliff was wriggling his shoulders now, and his voice was steady and even.

"Let's get the dinghy overboard. We need to set an anchor."

The dinghy was already inflated, lashed down on the foredeck, and it took only a few minutes to launch it and mount its engine on its transom. But the ebb tide was gathering force. Already, in the extra distance I felt in making that familiar leap from caprail to tender, it seemed there was much less water under our hull.

Dave joined me in the dinghy and together we took the main anchor out and set it about 150 feet off *Constellation*'s port bow. Then we stood by watching as Tim wound in the rode on the ship's windlass. The rode went taut and the windlass whined in protest as Cliff gunned the engine again, but the boat did not budge.

"The foremast!" called Cliff. "Take a masthead halyard to the rode!"

Tim eased the anchor rode and grabbed a halyard. He then bent the halyard on to the rode, and he and Curly stood together at the foremast grinding it taut again on a winch. Once again Cliff gunned the engine. The boat's hull twisted a bit and slowly heeled to port, but still it did not come free.

Cliff now called out to Dave and me in the dinghy.

"Get back up to Huelva. Find a boat to tow us out!"

I twisted open the throttle and the outboard screamed as we shot forward into the black night. In just a moment we were caught like thieves in the spotlight of a small police boat. It was a cuddy-cabin skiff, about 20 feet long, with a 45-horsepower outboard engine on the back. Clearly it wasn't big enough to pull out a boat the size of *Constellation*, but Dave and I in broken Spanish urged the two men aboard to head downriver to the scene of the grounding.

"Grande barco, atascado! Vaya rapido!"

And off we sped into the night again, hugging the east bank of the river to stay out the strong ebb-tide current.

At last we reached Huelva, where there was a large coast guard cutter tied up at the quay. We called out for help, but there was just one man aboard standing watch. He got on the radio and called a local tugboat captain, a very jovial man named Luis, who immediately met us on shore.

Luis recalled *Constellation* from our description—grande barco, blanco, Americano—and somehow comprehended our predicament. He explained in his own broken English that his tugboat was too large to help us and quickly led us instead to Pepe, master of a smaller tug that looked just the right size to pull *Constellation* out of the mud.

Pepe gladly agreed to help us and quickly cast off his lines and soon was following us back downriver.

On returning to the scene, however, we found the tide had dropped dramatically. *Constellation*'s masts were canted to port at a severe angle, and it was obvious she could not now be towed out in so little water. Pepe promised he would return in the morning when the tide was high again, and Dave and I tied off the dinghy and came back aboard.

"You did a good job," said Cliff. Which was, ironically, the first and only time I was ever complimented on my performance as crew aboard *Constellation*.

The men in the police boat, Cliff went on to explain, had offered no assistance beyond their repeated advice of the obvious: that we were outside the main channel and had run hard aground.

NOW CAME THE LONG waking nightmare, waiting for daylight and the next high tide. Half of us tried to sleep—Dave, Ruth Ann, and myself—hunkered down amid sail bags and other gear we had hauled to the high side of the deck. Cliff, Tim, and Curly meanwhile sat speechless, crouching on the low side of the deck as they monitored the inexorable progress of the tide.

Wrapped in my own cocoon of distress, wedged against the side of the cabinhouse with a blanket pulled over my head against the persistent buzz of hovering mosquitoes, I persuaded myself this must be only an interval, not an ending. I remembered my old friend *Antje* and how easily she had pulled through her long night on the beach at Block Island. I thought, too, of the bulls we had seen in Puerto de Santa Maria, of how the last one had leapt back to its feet after being stabbed in the head.

If only I could sleep and gain the safety of unconsciousness. Then just as surely as the sun would rise, *Constellation* would likewise rise to her feet again, and when I awoke I should find myself on a level deck, aboard a floating boat.

But none of us could sleep. The last of the tide slipped away from beneath us, leaving *Constellation* lying full on her side, and her hull started making sharp cracking noises at irregular intervals. They sounded like gunshots muffled in the still dark of the night.

"Must be the masts," said Cliff. "Settling against their wedges."

The rest of us knew he was deluding himself, that these noises must be coming from deep down in the frame of the hull, but none had the heart to contradict him.

Eventually the tide turned, rising again, but the port rail did not rise with it. The sharp angle of the deck did not decline, and slowly the interior of the boat began to fill with water.

"Hey, Captain," said Curly. "We might want to get those electronics out of there. You know, just in case."

"Yes," answered Cliff in a firm voice. "We should do that."

And in that small acknowledgment there was implicit, at last, an acceptance of this awful reality: that what we needed to do next was abandon the boat.

We all went below and packed our bags and dragged them up on deck. Then we searched for valuable gear and brought all of that on deck, too. Meanwhile, Tim broke out the big trash pump, our trusted ally that had saved us from sinking on the way to Bermuda, dropped its fat intake hose down the forward hatch, and started it up. None of us were surprised, however, when we saw it could not staunch the flow of water into the boat.

All through the small hours of the morning, while Tim stood silently by the clattering pump, I ran the dinghy and shuttled luggage, gear, and people to a boat-club dock on the far side of the river, not far from where the statue of Columbus stood. Luis, the tugboat captain from Huelva, appeared in a car, and he and Dave went off to search for more pumps. Twice they stopped by the dock to give me progress reports: the coast guard had nothing; the local fire department meanwhile had had one big pump, but it had been sent to Barcelona, where the Olympic games were being held.

I relayed this news to Cliff back aboard the boat, and he grew increasingly sullen. One by one the various props of hope his imagination might feed on were being knocked out from under him. It was impossible not to feel sorry for him. Here was years of restoration work, much of it by his own hand, years of relentless repair and maintenance, years of dreams, all lost in the mud in this ugly river.

At daybreak as the first weak-willed streaks of sunlight stretched out across the water, the trash pump finally ran out of gas and stopped running. The river by now had crept up the deck well past the port rail and was still rising. Down below the interior was more than half full of water. Stray pieces of flotsam—books and loose paper, articles of clothing, settee cushions, a pair of plastic parallel rules—were drifting around the main saloon.

Tim and I sat patiently together for several minutes in the dinghy alongside the boat, watching Cliff as he roamed the dry side of the deck. He was putting things away. He stowed a pair of winch handles in their pockets on the mainmast, replaced the boathook to its proper place under the starboard caprail, coiled a few loose lengths of line and hung them on belaying pins.

Finally, without a word, he joined us in the dinghy and we pushed off from the boat. We cut across the river toward the monument, and when we reached the boat-club dock Cliff at once trudged wearily up the ramp to where the others stood by our pile of gear and luggage. Tim and I, meanwhile, stood for a moment gazing back at the hulk we had left behind.

"Cliff and I worked real hard on that boat," said Tim, frowning.

"Well, at least she went out like a boat," I replied.

And then Tim, too, remembered the bulls, and smiled.

MONTHS LATER WHEN I RAN into Dave again in the Canary Islands—each of us having signed on as crew aboard other boats in the America 500 rally—he showed me photos he had taken of the remains of *Constellation* when he visited Huelva again that fall. We were both well aware of what had happened after we abandoned the boat. That very day Cliff and his insurance company had cut a deal with a salvage crew, and in the week that followed they had swarmed over the wreck trying to float it again. But it proved impossible, as the hull couldn't be moved without it breaking apart. In the end, as compensation for the work they had performed, the salvage crew picked the boat clean of anything of value, including much of its rig, and left its remains in the river to rot.

And though I knew this, the photos were still a shock to me. Though taken less than a dozen weeks after we'd left the boat, the hulk in the pictures, with its masts gone and a few gaps showing already in its deck and topsides, looked as though it had been lying there for years. In less time than it had taken to build the boat, and in much less time than the boat had spent floating about the watery part of our world, the water that had been her element had broken her down into a derelict remnant of what she once had been.

We work so hard to anthropomorphize boats we often forget they are merely objects. We forget that all the life in them comes from us. In remembering *Constellation* now, I think of her very much as an object of my desire. I know she was that. And I remember very specific details: the way her caprail, that immense length of teak I sanded and oiled so laboriously at the yard in Palm Beach, felt beneath my hand; the heft of her helm when steering her; the arrangement of lines on the pinrail at the foot of her mast; the way her gollywobbler filtered all the light that fell on her deck amidships when it was flying; the subtle curve of her deck beams arching over me as I lay in my berth at night.

But it also seems to me that *Constellation* was something my desire created for me, an apparition born of my need to go to sea. An apparition we who sailed on her shared together, born of all our needs, that we believed in together and held afloat with our belief. And as soon as we stopped believing in her, it seemed her demise was inevitable.

I sometimes wonder if she's still there. Just as the pale statue that stood watch over us during all of that long night is a monument to a great dream of the sea that was realized, the wreck of *Constellation* might to an objective observer seem a monument to a dream that failed. But really it is much more than that. In my own mind it testifies to a dream I actually realized: I sailed across an ocean on this boat and in doing so changed the course of my life.

I discovered at last a passion that truly absorbed me and also a sense of pride I had not known before. *Constellation*, while I was aboard her, may never have been truly seaworthy, but in helping nurse her through one last voyage I felt, and still feel, that I accomplished something important.

Just like that bull in the ring in Puerto de Santa Maria, *Constellation*, thanks to our efforts, ended her life doing what she was born to do. With Cliff as our undaunted matador and all the rest of us serving as a hapless band of picadors and banderilleros, we saved her from her most likely fate, the long slow ordeal of withering from neglect on some dock or mooring somewhere. Instead we sailed her across one more ocean, filled her with our own dreams, and in so doing enshrined her in all our memories.

Scott Kennedy

PART II

PRACTICAL MATTERS

JUST ADD WATER
Human Evolution and the Sea

But look! here come more crowds, pacing straight for the water, and seemingly bound for a dive. Strange! Nothing will content them but the extremest limit of the land.... They must get just as nigh the water as they possibly can without falling in.

—Herman Melville, *Moby Dick*

THOUGH MY MOTHER WAS QUICK to blame my wanting to run away to sea on all the sailing magazines I studied as a boy, she might just as easily have blamed herself. She had been born during the Great Depression on an island on the coast of Maine. Her parents were "rusticators," prosperous city folk who wandered around for a while on an old schooner after first getting married and then settled in Maine in a grand ruined house on a headland overlooking the mouth of the Kennebec River. They fixed up the house, filled it with an eclectic mix of then-contemporary Park Avenue furnishings and 19th-century domestic technology, and reared two daughters there before divorcing after the Second World War.

My mother never got along with her mother and had many complaints about her upbringing, but for some reason felt compelled to inflict her island on my two brothers and me. We moved around a lot as we were growing up, in places as varied as southern New England, the Midwest, Texas, the Indian subcontinent, and Southeast Asia, but always we spent summers in Maine, in a tiny cottage half a mile down a narrow trail through the woods from where my mother had been raised.

This was a true island, with no bridge or land leading out to it, and in order to get there we had to handle boats and pilot them across the river. Study a chart of the coast of Maine and you will see it is severely serrated, raked by the claws of ancient glaciers, with knife-sharp peninsulas separated by pencil-narrow sounds and rivers. The fastest and most turbulent river, with the wiliest, most cross-grained waters, is the Kennebec, which reaches all the way to Moosehead Lake in the north and must drain and refill a very large inland body of water, Merrymeeting Bay, with each and every turn of the tide.

My mother had great respect for the river and was constantly warning us about it. "Be careful, or you'll be swept out to sea!" was a favorite admonition. But we were never prevented from exploring both the river and the surrounding coastline in whatever boats were available to us, and in fact this was encouraged.

From an early age this scenery was imprinted upon my mind. The dramatic defile of the river, rimmed with hard rock, studded with dark pine trees, tidal eddies twisting this way and that like loose firehoses, flushing through the narrow mouth, past my grandmother's house on one side, an old Civil War fort on the other, past a broad white sand beach, thence through a small maze of minor islands and shoals, and so out to the Gulf of Maine. Like a sentinel on the horizon stood one especially tall and lonely island, Seguin, crowned with its great lighthouse, and beyond that nothing but open water. The seductive void of liquid and vapor that might lead anywhere on earth.

When I was a bit older my mother explained to me I had a choice to make.

"You can be a mountain person," she declared. "Or you can be an ocean person."

At the time it actually seemed as if she had made this choice for me, raising us as she had, but later I realized this wasn't true. There was never any choice to make, for however much one may admire and pine for alpine scenery, there is no way you cannot be attracted to the ocean. It is ubiquitous, surrounds us, and is always calling no matter how far we are from its shores.

ON A FUNDMENTAL LEVEL our affinity for the sea seems perfectly natural. Biologically we are composed mostly of water, that wonderfully powerful solvent that flushes over the surface of our planet, courses through its atmosphere, and carries dissolved nutrients to all parts of a living organism. Our tears, our sweat, our blood, and our seed all taste of the sea. In embryonic form we look very much like fish. And in certain ways our human physiology, compared to other land-dwelling creatures, seems peculiarly adapted to immersion in water. Like whales, dolphins, and seals, we are hairless with a subcutaneous layer of fat that helps to keep us warm when we're wet. Unlike most other terrestrial mammals, and very much like aquatic ones, we can consciously control our breathing, a useful trick that allows us to inhale big gulps of air and hold them in our lungs when diving under the water.

Some people have argued that these unique features are proof that our distant ancestors must actually have evolved in the water. Even our walking upright on two legs, the defining characteristic that distinguishes us from other primates, has been painted as an adaptation that might originally have been inspired by a need to routinely wade through water.

This concept of "aquatile man" was first posited in the 1930s and '40s by Max Westenhöfer, a Nazi pathologist who was intent on severing the seemingly degrading link between humans and apes that had first been forged by Charles Darwin. Coincidentally, or not, Westenhöfer abandoned his hypothesis soon after the Nazi regime was vanquished in 1945.

In 1960, however, the theory was reiterated by Alister Hardy, a British marine biologist who had no quarrel with Darwin. As early as 1930, Hardy had concluded independently that there must have been some aquatic factor that influenced our early evolution, but he was—supposedly—afraid of ruining his reputation and it took him 30 years to work up the nerve to say so. His "coming out" speech, tellingly, was delivered not to a group of his scientific peers, but to the members of a recreational scuba-diving club.

The very apt Darwin-friendly term "aquatic ape" was first coined by Desmond Morris, a zoologist, in his 1967 popular bestseller *The Naked Ape*. This titillating treatment of human evolution, which proposed, among other things, that we might have lost our body hair to promote pair-bonding through enhanced sexual pleasure, discussed possible aquatic factors in our development only briefly. The idea was taken up, however, by a feminist television writer, Elaine Morgan, who proselytized relentlessly on the subject for nearly 40 years.

Precisely because we have such an affinity for water, the "aquatic ape hypothesis," as it is now known, does seem seductive. Morgan's arguments, which involve various aspects of our anatomy and behavior and are set forth in several books she wrote, are certainly passionate and have garnered support among lay people and certain more adventurous scientists. The theory's most creative proponents, nurtured on a diet of tabloid science, have even urged it helps to prove that mermaids really do exist.

On the whole, however, reputable scientists have treated this all as another fabulist "just-so" story. Paleoanthropologists in particular, in their more mainstream theories of our development, have ignored the aquatic ape hypothesis.

Currently the most widely accepted theory has it that pre-human primates first became bipedal nearly six million years ago, not so they could go wading, but primarily because running upright on two legs rather than four is much more energy-efficient over long distances. Four-legged creatures can certainly run faster over short distances, but two-legged hominids with hairless bodies and sweat glands are capable of running for much longer periods of time.

This unique talent for endurance running allowed our ancestors to engage in persistence hunting, wherein hairy quadrupeds that had to stop and pant to dissipate body heat could be tracked and chased until exhausted.

As for our ability to consciously regulate our breathing, and our descended larynx, another feature that aquatic-ape proponents insist is evidence of a watery past, most serious scientists now agree that their primary purpose is to enable the sophisticated vocalizations that allow us to talk to each other.

But physiology isn't everything. Even if our bodies were not explicitly adapted to an aquatic environment, there is no doubt that we modern humans—*Homo sapiens*, the so-called "wise people"—took to the sea very early in our history.

We often argue over the question of what distinguishes us from all the other creatures on this not-so-green earth. Some say it's our ability to create and use tools, but in fact there are other animals that do this. Chimpanzees modify sticks, stripping them of foliage and sharpening the ends, to fish for termites in termite mounds or to hunt small mammals. Sea otters use rocks to break open shellfish. Dolphins have been known to trap small fish with conch shells and also use sponges to protect their beaks when probing the sea floor for food.

Others urge that our use of language makes us special, but again we share this ability with other species. Chimps and at least one parrot have been taught to express themselves in languages we have created, and several species have reasonably sophisticated languages of their own. Dolphins and whales, we have only recently learned, even assign unique names to each other and most likely communicate over long distances on a fairly abstract level.

But one thing we do, and have always done, that is truly exceptional is travel upon the ocean. Our ability, our apparent need, as terrestrial animals, to leave and transcend the land, to hurl ourselves into a hostile environment where we cannot survive without some machine to sustain us, is extraordinary. From early in our history it has defined us a species. It has formed the sinews of our commerce and civilization. It has even carried us straight out of our atmosphere into space, beyond the thin envelope of air that we breathe.

Ultimately, the earliest maritime adventures of the human species took different groups of us on opposite trajectories that finally intersected in the middle of the Pacific Ocean, halfway around the world from where we first appeared in Africa.

European explorers, who sailed from the east in what were then the most sophisticated machines on the planet, first encountered other humans, Polynesians, on the far-flung islands of the Pacific in the 16th century. They didn't make much of this at the time, as what they were looking for was material wealth, not anthropological puzzles to solve. It wasn't until over two centuries later, when the British explorer James Cook arrived on the scene, seeking not wealth but knowledge, that anyone stopped to reflect on how remarkable this was.

"How shall we account for this Nation spreading itself so far over this Vast ocean?" asked Cook in an entry he wrote in his journal in 1778 after he reached Hawaii during his third voyage into the Pacific.

Cook had previously visited Tahiti, New Zealand, and Easter Island, among others, and already had realized that the people inhabiting all these islands shared a common culture and language. Now he was astounded to find still more Polynesians in Hawaii, more than 2,000 miles northeast of Tahiti. Ironically, he lost his life there, on a beach at Kealakekua Bay, in a dispute with the locals over a stolen boat.

In reaching Hawaii, Cook had barely succeeded in discerning the outer limits of Polynesian migration. This was a vast swath of the planet's surface—from Hawaii in the north, to New Zealand in the southwest, to Easter Island in the southeast—stretching across many thousands of miles of open ocean, from 25 degrees north latitude to 45 degrees south latitude and across more than 90 degrees of longitude, a quarter of the planet's circumference. Somehow, despite having vessels that seemed very crude, in spite of having no compasses or navigational instruments and no written language or maps, these people had already voyaged across all of the Pacific and had settled it long before Europeans, with all their fancy technology, had ever arrived there.

Cook, to his credit, fully appreciated this achievement. He made an effort to learn the Polynesian language and to learn how Polynesians navigated. He concluded that Polynesian canoes, which unlike European vessels of the time were capable of sailing efficiently to windward, were in fact seaworthy and could travel distances of at least 900 miles over the open ocean. He also concluded that the Polynesian people had most likely migrated into the Pacific from the East Indies, from west to east, against the prevailing easterly tradewinds.

For many years Westerners resisted this notion that the seemingly primitive Polynesians were capable of sophisticated navigation and of voyaging long distances to windward. The Dutch navigator Jacob Roggeveen, who on Easter Sunday in 1722 became the first European to visit Easter Island (known as Rapa Nui to the Polynesians), thought perhaps the people of the Pacific had simply been deposited there by God. The French explorer Julien-Marie Crozet, who visited New Zealand and Tahiti after Cook, speculated that the Polynesians had once shared a continent that sank in a volcanic cataclysm that "left us only the mountains and their savage inhabitants."

The more reasonable theory was that the Polynesians had accidentally drifted into the Pacific, from an as yet undiscovered continent, or perhaps from the Americas. As late as 1947, when Thor Heyerdahl set out on his famous raft *Kon-Tiki* to prove that a primitive downwind drift voyage from South America into Polynesia was feasible, certain members of the scientific community refused to accept what the archaeological, linguistic, ethnographic, and ethnobotanical evidence has since established as incontrovertible fact. That the Polynesians did indeed come from the west, and that they did so in a series of deliberate voyages.

Any modern sailor considering the problem can reach only one conclusion. When you are a novice, just learning to sail, you always sail first upwind so that you can easily get back to where you started by sailing downwind. Likewise, if you are an experienced sailor setting out into unknown waters, it is best to explore to windward so you can be certain of getting home again if you find nowhere to land. It is the most sensible seamanlike thing to do.

SCHOLARS ARE STILL QUIBBLING over details and dates, but the general outline of the great aquatic migration that took primitive humans out into the farthest reaches of the planet's greatest ocean is agreed upon and leads all the way back to the origin of our species in Africa. The final phase of this long process began a little over 1,000 years ago, when the immediate ancestors of the Polynesians first struck out exploring from the islands around Samoa and Tonga, their original homeland, which the Polynesians later called Hawaiki.

The speed of their progress was remarkable. They reached what are now known as the Society Islands sometime between 1025 and 1121 AD; by sometime between 1200 and 1400 they had discovered and colonized the Marquesas; New Zealand was inhabited between 1230 and 1280; Easter Island between 1200 and 1263; and finally Hawaii sometime between 1219 and 1269.

In less than 300 years these people explored and populated a vast expanse of ocean of nearly a million square miles and perhaps sailed all the way to the Americas. By the time the first Europeans sailed in from the opposite direction hundreds of years later, Polynesian culture was well advanced, the islands had been transformed environmentally, and people on some of the islands had forgotten about the existence of other islands.

During the previous phase of this diaspora, the predecessors of the Polynesians, a people now known as the Lapita, who came originally from southern China via Taiwan and the Philippines, set out voyaging east from the Bismarck Archipelago and the Solomon Islands sometime after 1500 BC. By sometime around 800 BC they had reached Fiji and had sailed on to Samoa and Tonga. In doing so they shattered a psychological barrier, as these were the first true ocean voyages in all of human history, covering distances of several hundred miles, with no land in sight for long periods of time. We know relatively little about the Lapita and have no clear idea of why they went to sea, but there is little doubt they were the most sophisticated navigators of their time.

Prior to the Lapita, the drift of humanity eastward was less venturesome, but still generally aquatic. The first *Homo sapiens* had reached the Solomons by 25,000 years ago, in the latest ice age, and prior to that prehistoric humans had migrated from mainland Asia across to what are now Australia and New Guinea by about 50,000 years ago. With vast amounts of water trapped in ice-age glaciers at the poles, sea levels then were 150 to 300 feet lower than they are now, and the distances between the relevant land masses were much shorter. Voyages then consisted of trips between inter-visible bodies of land, but this was still seafaring in that people were deliberately transiting bodies of water in vessels they had created.

To put this into perspective, bear in mind this was 40,000 years before humans invented agriculture and launched what we now call "civilization." It was also at least 10,000 years before any members of the species *Homo sapiens* managed to reach what we now call Europe.

Just how did these ancient seafarers get themselves to Southeast Asia and the western shores of the Pacific Ocean in the first place? This far back in time everything is necessarily nebulous, but the current thinking has it that the first humans migrating out of Africa did so via a "Beachcomber Express." The genetic and archaeological evidence suggests the fastest route out of Africa for our ancestors wasn't through the Sinai peninsula into the heart of Europe and Asia, as was once believed, but along the northern shore of the Indian Ocean.

It is not entirely clear when the "express" started running in earnest. The best genetic evidence tells us all humans now living outside of Africa are descended from people who left the continent between 60,000 and 70,000 years ago. The first part of the shoreline route leading east away from Africa was then much easier to negotiate, as the southern end of Red Sea was a narrow strait probably just a couple of miles wide and the Persian Gulf was all dry land, thanks again to those ice-age glaciers. The timing jibes with all sorts of other evidence and leaves 10,000 to 20,000 years for people to migrate to New Guinea and Australia before ultimately striking out into the Pacific.

The most recent archaeological evidence, however, points to an even earlier exodus, as stone tools dated to 125,000 years ago, similar to tools used by *Homo sapiens* in East Africa at around the same time, have been found in eastern Arabia. This suggests that an older group of migrants who settled in Arabia were overrun by a later group, or that the first group had already died out before the second arrived.

Either way, the advantage of migrating along a coastline is fairly obvious. The sea and the shore, in an age predating agriculture and animal husbandry, must have been a far richer source of calories and protein than the continental interior.

Indeed, we now know that a taste for seafood may have saved the human species from extinction long before we ever left Africa. Beginning about 195,000 years ago, as the planet entered a strong glacial phase, the African climate became much cooler and drier with fewer food resources and consequently was much harder to survive in. According to the genetic evidence, the human population decreased dramatically, perhaps to as few as 600 individuals. Recent archaeological finds dated to about 164,000 years ago also tell us that some or all of these people lived in caves on the coast of what is now South Africa and subsisted on a diet of shellfish.

These same caves also contain the earliest known examples of heat-treated tools made by *Homo sapiens* and ground-up red ochre that may have been used to create pigment for painting. Some anthropologists theorize that the Omega-3 fatty acids in the seafood consumed by these early humans may have led to a dramatic increase in cognitive ability that made possible the development of both symbolic representation and sophisticated tool-making.

DOES ALL THIS MEAN that our affinity for the sea is part of our evolutionary hard-wiring? Not necessarily. After all, things we learned after becoming fully human aren't necessarily the things that made us human in the first place.

There is a growing body of evidence, however, that hominid species predating *Homo sapiens* were also capable of going to sea. Primitive tools discovered on the island of Crete suggest that Neanderthals or perhaps even *Homo erectus* were making voyages on the Mediterranean Sea about 130,000 years ago. Going back even further, tools found on the island of Socrata, 240 miles off the coast of Yemen, suggest that *Homo erectus* was putting to sea in the Indian Ocean over 500,000 years ago. There is also evidence that *Homo erectus* did some voyaging in Asian waters long before *Homo sapiens* ever got there.

More importantly, the current thinking among many paleoanthropologists is that contact with unruly bodies of water may be what prompted the development of the single most important piece of hominid physiology. As mentioned, bipedal primates are believed to have first evolved about six million years ago. These early bipeds, however, like the species *Australo-*

pithecus afarensis, were small-brained creatures with no more cranial capacity than a modern chimpanzee. It wasn't until about two million years ago that large-brained bipedal hominids like *Homo habilis* appeared on the scene.

What prompted the quantum leap in cranial capacity? Geological evidence now indicates that the Rift Valley in East Africa, where hominid species and their ancestors first evolved, was at that time extremely unstable. Vast portions of the region were frequently inundated in catastrophic floods, with very large lakes or inland seas, equal in size to the American Great Lakes, suddenly appearing and disappearing over relatively short periods of time. Some floods may have been Niagara-like onslaughts, with immense walls of water instantly inundating previously habitable terrain.

Is it just a coincidence that some of our oldest legends and myths are ripe with accounts of all-encompassing floods? We have Noah and his ark, of course, in our Judaic tales of prehistory. Even further back we have the Mesopotamian story of Utnapishtim, who, like Noah, was warned by a vengeful deity to build a ship to survive a coming cataclysm.

Certainly there can be no direct correlation to Rift Valley floods two million years ago, but the presumptive paleoanthropological narrative does offer an intriguing parallel. Small-brained primates were destroyed in the great aquatic purges, while hominids who were smarter and more adaptive managed to survive all the chaos and turbulence. Surely it isn't too far of a stretch to think that discovered or improvised vessels of some sort were one of the tools that helped them do so.

In the end, we may not be "aquatic apes" in quite the way that Elaine Morgan imagined. But she would likely be gratified to know that her basic premise has bit by bit crept into anthropological orthodoxy. Today we do know that we are descended from apes, but we also know that our interaction with aquatic environments has played a large part in our becoming what we are today.

FIRST BOATS
Learning to Be a Sensuous Sailor

Often as a boy I had thought of the pleasure of being one's own master in one's own boat; but the reality far exceeded the imagination of it, and it was not a transient pleasure.

—John MacGregor, *The Voyage Alone in the Yawl Rob Roy*

YOU HEAR LOTS OF COMPLAINTS these days about how there aren't enough young people coming into the sport of sailing. Modern sailors, with much gnashing of teeth and rending of garments, love to debate the reasons for this. Many heap blame upon the venerable Optimist, the default training dinghy for the last half-century or more, and deride it as being too slow and boring to interest today's media-addled youth. Racing sailors in particular seem to believe we must somehow make our sport more exciting and more telegenic if it is to survive.

Speaking from my own experience, I'd say a keen interest in sailing depends on something other than raw speed and action. For children, or anyone, to learn to love sailing, and to get good at it, I think they must experience it as a magical process. They must be captivated by the mystery of how the sky can make their boats go. Given this, there are two other important ingredients: access to the water and a boat they can think of as their own. It need not be a fast boat, or a fancy one, or even a pretty one. But they need to feel it belongs to them, figuratively or actually.

In one sense I was very lucky. Thanks to the island my mother dragged us to each summer, my two brothers and I were exposed to rowboats and outboard-powered skiffs at an early age and were taught how to handle them. We were also given a boat—a small wooden duck boat that had been exhumed, I believe, from my grandmother's coal cellar. It was a simple craft, drew only a few inches of water, and was easily controlled with a kayak paddle. Unlike a kayak, however, it had great form stability, as its hull was wide and flat, with a fine entry forward and very broad hindquarters, so that it did not mind being overloaded with children and dogs and mindlessly romped upon.

We had that duck boat only one summer, but for me it was an important one in that it was the first summer I was allowed to use a boat alone and unsupervised. I paddled about the narrow channel that bounded our island to the east, much of which was mudflat and sandbar at dead low tide, and explored the shore on both sides in detail. I felt intently free and independent, and this sharpened my appreciation of my surroundings. Hacking about on foot through the woods on our island, the dense pine thickets and dramatic rock ledges were annoying obstacles. Seen from the water, from a boat I commanded, they seemed mysterious and beautiful.

At the end of that summer we stored our duck boat upside down in the open pasture behind the little beach from which we routinely launched it and covered it with a tarp to protect it from the winter weather. That fall, however, Henry Blake, one of the lobstermen who lived across the narrows, discovered it and decided to conduct experiments.

What I was told was that Henry mounted a 35-horsepower outboard on the back of the boat, to see how fast it could go, and took off down the narrows at full throttle. The little boat went airborne, then shattered into pieces when it hit the water again. Henry and the engine barely survived. Of course I should have been upset that he had so thoughtlessly destroyed a boat I thought belonged to me, but really I was awed by Henry's audacity.

In terms of learning to sail, I was less fortunate. There was no yacht club for us to belong to. There was no "youth program" for me to enroll in, and none of the adults in my life were inclined to teach me, even though my mother's parents had cruised and lived aboard a large schooner before settling on the island and my father, who was raised in the Midwest, had raced on scows as a boy.

I do have some vague memories of excursions made on a small cruising sailboat my grandmother kept when I was very young. I remember a rainy afternoon spent in a cold cabin trying to heat food over a can of Sterno, and I remember motoring through some scary-looking whirlpools in a place upriver appropriately called Hell's Gate, but I have no memory of ever sailing on that boat.

In this respect, too, our island was not well situated. In the narrows on the east side we could at high tide paddle about safely in the duck boat, or in a cheap inflatable kayak we owned for a while, but it was too sheltered from the wind for sailing. In the open river on the west side there was wind, particularly in the afternoons after the sea breeze filled in, but the current was very strong. Especially on an outgoing tide there was a real danger that an inexperienced child in a sailing dinghy might get into trouble.

My desire to sail was at first abstract. Sailing vessels were prominently featured in certain books I enjoyed, most particularly *Song of the Sirens*, by Ernest K. Gann, which starred a large schooner on which the author voyaged from Holland to the South Pacific. I was also keenly inspired by the movie *Captain Horatio Hornblower*, starring Gregory Peck, which I first saw on television one Saturday afternoon.

After watching this film, I read all the Hornblower books and taught myself how to draw square-rigged vessels in detail. I also started building crude model boats that I sailed across our swimming pool.

Eventually I found the book *Dove*, by Robin Lee Graham, and was transfixed. Here was a boy just a few years older than me, equipped with a sailboat just a few feet longer than the outboard skiffs I was by now allowed to handle on my own, who had sailed by himself all the way around the world. That could be me, I realized, if only I learned how to sail.

I developed a plan to convert a small pram we kept on the island into a sailboat. At school, on scraps of looseleaf paper, I sketched out the details: an oar for a rudder, some plywood scraps for leeboards, a slender sapling for a mast, an old bedsheet for a sail, and I thought I'd be all set. But when I showed my drawings to a friend who knew something about sailing, he laughed and assured me this crude concoction would sail very poorly.

Then I spotted an ad for Kool cigarettes in a magazine. Send us $88 and a Kool carton top, proclaimed the ad copy, and we'll send you a real sailboat—a Sea Snark. I immediately tore out the ad, convinced my parents to switch to smoking Kools for a while, and started saving my allowance. Eventually, with the help of a parental subsidy, I had enough money to send away for the boat.

The Sea Snark arrived in a large cardboard box. Inside the box I found an 11-foot slab of unfinished styrofoam shaped like a hull, a small lateen sail, a daggerboard, a small rudder, and two lengths of light polyester line. There were also two pamphlets: one explained how to assemble the boat, the other how to sail it.

I in fact had little trouble putting the boat together, which says something, as I had (and still have) no inherent mechanical ability. Learning to sail it was something else. I read the instructions carefully, but was confused by the section (really it was just a paragraph) on sailing to windward. I could easily understand how a boat could be propelled sailing with the wind behind it. But I had to wonder: how could a boat possibly use the wind to sail against the wind? The pamphlet offered no explanation of the principle involved, just a crude diagram that showed a Sea Snark magically zigzagging upwind.

Oh, well, I thought, all things will become apparent on the water. And I tossed aside the pamphlet and launched my new boat.

TEACHING MYSELF TO SAIL turned out to be surprisingly easy. I can tell you most everything you really need to know in just one sentence: as you point your boat closer and closer to the wind, pull the sails in tighter and tighter; as you point it further and further away from the wind, let the sails out more and more.

This is oversimplified, of course, and you can if you like spend a lifetime absorbing the technical minutiae of sailing, which is one of its many attractions. But really the most important thing is just figuring out where the wind is coming from. Anyone who can sense this instinctively can quickly learn how to sail a boat reasonably well on their own; people who cannot (there are more of them than you would think) may well never learn.

For this really is what is most unique about sailing: it is the only mode of vehicular transportation in which the vehicle derives non-gravitational motive energy from its surrounding environment. And to make this happen, to make their boats go, sailors must perceive and interpret their environment in a sensual manner.

A sailboat quite simply is a machine with foils deployed simultaneously in both the air and water. A sail acts as a drag device when the boat beneath it is going downwind, but also acts like an airplane wing, creating lift through the fluid pressure differentials on either side of it, while going upwind. A keel, meanwhile, may just as well not be there when a boat is going downwind, but also acts like a hydrodynamic wing, creating lift underwater, when a boat sails to windward. The process of sailing consists of balancing the two foils, the air wing and water wing, against each other, and to do this well you must perceive the wind and water as acutely as possible. Ideally, your body and mind should become a pure sensory interface between your boat and its surroundings.

We are primarily visual creatures, and so our eyes are the sensory organs we use most when sailing. Even if you are so insensitive you can't deduce the direction of the wind from its caress on your cheek, you can easily detect it visually. As a novice you may need to turn your boat to windward and actually see your sails luffing before you grasp exactly where the wind is coming from, but as you gain experience, you will pick up on subtler clues. You will notice a faint shiver in the leech of a sail or a small change of angle in a flying telltale. Your eyes will assess the shape of your sails in detail so you can fine-tune their effectiveness as aerodynamic foils. You will also see direct evidence of the wind's doings in the direction and the height of the waves or ripples around you. And when you are very experienced you will be able to see into the future and predict even small changes in wind speed and direction by studying the water's surface well away the boat.

Your ears are also important. You will soon learn that the dramatic machine-gun chatter of a flogging sail is not as calamitous as it seems, and will develop an ability to distinguish and identify much subtler sounds. You will gauge the speed of the wind from the noise of it and also the speed of your boat from the burble of its wake. Almost all of a boat is under tension when sailing, and variations in tension often make noise, so you will also use your ears to assess your vessel's physical status. You will listen for creaks and groans and screams in its hull and all its standing and running rigging, and will assess loads carried accordingly. And when the fog rolls in, your hearing will become even more sensitive as you listen for faint bells and whistles and running engines and breaking waves in the invisible world around you.

Most importantly, to become a very good sailor you must become attuned to seat-of-the-pants kinesthetic sensation. Not just the simple touch of the wind on your skin, but the feel of everything, most particularly the motion of your boat in relation to the water around it, in your body and in your gut. And you finally must integrate this with all the rest of your sensory input.

The primary business of steering a sailboat offers the best example of how this works. You of course will use your eyesight while steering—noting points on your compass card, or landmarks in the distance, and the trim of your sails, and the action of the wind on the water—while feeling the pressure on the helm, be it a tiller or wheel, with your hand. The sound of the pattern of waves slapping the hull will help you maintain course.

But you will also feel the boat's motion, and this is what ties the whole package together. As the boat rounds up, you will see your course change with respect to the compass and horizon, you will feel an increase of pressure on the helm, you will hear the pattern of waves slapping the hull change. But you will feel it also in your gut, and most importantly, once you are practiced you will feel it here first. You will feel the boat beginning to round up before it actually rounds up, and it is precisely this element of anticipation, the ability to correct before a correction is explicitly required, that allows a good helmsperson to steer a true course under sail.

THE SEA SNARK, IT TURNED OUT, was well suited to my cavalier trial-by-error approach to sailing. It was, above all, a very forgiving boat. Though it weighed just 30 pounds, it did not carry enough sail to make it especially tender and could be handled by a novice like myself in pretty stiff air. I soon discovered, however, that it was possible to capsize the thing, particularly when jibing in a breeze. But I also found it was easy to right again, and indeed enjoyed this, and sometimes capsized the boat just for the fun of it.

The Snark was not a fast boat by any means, but it sailed well enough to keep me interested. Because it was so light it needed very little air to get moving; in a strong wind on a broad reach it would actually plane a bit. It did have some quirks. Upwind, sailing alone, I found it was best to have a 15-pound rock up forward to keep the bow down, though downwind the boat was faster without the rock. In any sort of decent breeze the Snark had a heavy weather helm, and in a really strong breeze sailing to weather the entire hull would twist in a rather alarming way. Also, since there was no way to fasten a cleat onto the styrofoam, I had to constantly hold the sheet in my hand, which became painful when the wind was strong.

After they saw me sailing in the Sea Snark, my brothers wanted to try, too, and learned to handle it as easily as I had. Soon we were lobbying my parents for a bigger boat, so we could all go sailing at the same time, but they suggested instead we just get more Snarks. This perhaps was the boat's most significant virtue: it was cheap enough that a family of modest means could acquire an entire fleet of them.

One boat was purchased brand new from a dealer. Another one (another Kool boat, in fact) we purchased secondhand from a private owner, and two more were acquired in a manner similar to the first, through an offer made by a beer company. In all I believe we spent less than $500 on our five boats, which, even in those days, was a great bargain.

Inevitably, my brothers and I and the many friends who visited us on the island wanted to do something organized with the boats, so we formed a club, which we pompously named the Long Island Corinthian Yachting Association. We especially liked to pronounce the acronym of the club's name out loud.

LICYA's very first event was an around-the-island race, in which three boats participated, each with two crew aboard. The Race Committee (our parents) decreed this must be held on an incoming tide, as they were worried, as always, about our being swept out to sea. Because of the tide, however, some legs were very slow, and eventually the Race Committee became bored, towed one boat across the finish line, and declared it the winner. Several protests were filed—two against the winning boat concerning the propriety of the finish; two against the losing boats, which had tied up to trees onshore to await the turn of the tide; and one more against the winning boat, which allegedly at one point had been dragged several hundred feet across a sandbar.

To promote less controversial competitions, LICYA then established a short round-the-buoys course on which to hold races. It was a challenging circuit, designed so that the tide remained a factor, but not prohibitively so, and included such interesting features as a barge wreck and a large rock on which seals liked to sunbathe. These races were very successful, and we all learned a bit about the finer points of sailing while trying to beat each other. For the better part of two summers we raced the boats almost every day.

I enjoyed racing Sea Snarks, but really was more interested in voyaging. In considering what voyages I might undertake in an 11-foot styrofoam boat, I hit first on the idea of sailing out to Seguin Island, which lay three miles offshore. The Race Committee immediately vetoed this proposal, but said I was welcome to go exploring in the other direction, up the river, as far as I liked.

A friend and I then developed a bold plan to sail up the river to the city of Bath, a distance of about 15 miles, in two separate boats. Our passage was, at first, very pleasant. People in other boats paused to talk with us, and we had fun pulling their legs, telling them we were going all the way to Augusta, about 40 miles upriver. To see their eyes widen at the thought of this was most gratifying. By the time we reached Bath, however, the wind was blowing hard and our hands were bleeding from clutching the sheets for so long. We went ashore, had a meal, considered the prospect of beating against the wind all the way back downriver, and then called the Race Committee for a lift home.

This taught me that Snark voyaging definitely had limits, but it did not dampen my enthusiasm. On days when the others did not want to race, I took my boat and went off on my own to explore the river immediately north of our island. There were five uninhabited islands within two miles of us, four of which had abandoned houses on them. As I had on the duck boat earlier, I savored each shoreline in detail as I sailed along. Often, too, I went ashore on one island or another, secured my boat, and threaded my way inland to creep around the lonely houses, most of which had been vacant since the 1920s and were filled with artifacts. The sense of discovery this provoked was intoxicating.

What I valued most during these tiny voyages was my autonomy. For me it was a point of pride to be able to set out and return from these ventures entirely under sail and without assistance. Often, after I'd been gone for two hours or more, the Race Committee would send someone in a skiff to check on me. The search party would find me creeping along some back channel in a mere whisper of wind, working my way home inch by painful inch, and would ask if I'd like a tow. No thanks, I'd say cheerfully, I can do this, and I waved them away.

Usually I did make it back on my own, but sometimes I miscalculated and would still be laboring against some contrary current or breeze when it came time for dinner. Out would come the skiff again, but this time with an explicit order from the Race Committee: you must accept a tow. I surrendered my painter reluctantly and sat silently in my Snark as it rumbled along in the wake of the skiff, thinking glumly to myself that my adventure had been ruined.

IT WASN'T UNTIL AFTER we got tired of conventional racing that we learned just how mortal our Sea Snarks really were. One year, to spice things up a little, LICYA abolished the rules pertaining to right-of-way and decreed that boats could hit each other while racing. We called this "bumper-boating" and enjoyed it immensely. Soon we forgot all about the pedestrian business of trying to be first around the course, and our races deteriorated into wild melees in which we concentrated solely on trying to capsize, dismast, or otherwise disable one another.

Bumper-boating was much more visceral than regular racing and demanded more skill, as skippers who were best at maneuvering their boats quickly in a tight spot under combat conditions always had an advantage over their opponents. The climatic moment came one windy day when one skipper found some running room, quickly built up a great head of speed, and T-boned another boat full out directly amidships, causing it to break into two pieces. This drew wild applause from those watching on shore, but also marked the beginning of the end of our fleet of Snarks. A few days later, when another boat broke apart in a similar incident, the Race Committee immediately banned all bumper-boat competitions.

I remembered Henry Blake and our duck boat and thought the Race Committee was overreacting. There is honor, I argued, in pushing your ship beyond its limits. But the problem was our ships were essentially disposable. As the Snark hulls got older, the styrofoam, after much exposure to the sun, became brittle and less resilient and much more likely to crumble and crack. We tried fiberglassing one hull, but this was an abysmal failure. The glass added much weight and did not take well to the old foam, and we ended up with a bubbly, blistered, heavy boat that sailed poorly. And even without the stress of bumper-boating, we soon learned our surviving hulls were none too sound when one day the mast on one boat, my old Kool boat, suddenly dropped right through the bottom of the hull while I was sailing it.

For most LICYA members the demise of our Snark fleet spelled the end of their interest in sailing. Of the several kids who played on those boats, I was the only one who stayed involved in the sport. Even before the Snarks started dying, I had acquired a more sophisticated boat, a Hobie 10, that had all sorts of fancy controls—a boom vang, an outhaul, and a cunningham—that I had never used before. It was also light-years faster than the Snarks and much more fun to sail, at least as far as its performance was concerned.

My brothers had access to the Hobie, for I wasn't proprietary about it, but they were never too interested in it. One became obsessed with cars and eventually with racing them; the other one went all nutty about baseball and computers. Where I thought of the Sea Snark as my "first sailboat" and looked forward to learning to sail on other sorts of boats, my brothers thought of it merely as a toy they once had some fun messing around with.

I do not believe you can ever permanently capture the interest of people who are not inherently fascinated by sailing by tantalizing them with speed. Yes, the fastest sailboats today can run at 40 knots or better, and to a sailor that is like breaking the sound barrier, but to everyone else it is barely highway speed.

My perspective on this is skewed, because I am much more a cruiser than a racer, but I do think cruisers and racers have certain things in common. We love sailboats because they demand that we be self-reliant and because we enjoy being on the water, but mostly because we are captivated by the idea of harnessing a natural element, the wind, to move us from place to place. If that in itself does not seem exciting to you, I doubt you will ever be excited by sailing, no matter how fast you are going.

WEATHER RULES

A Theology of Ocean Sailing

The spiral is a spiritualized circle.

—Vladimir Nabokov, *Speak Memory*

FROM THE TENUOUS SECURITY of a sailing vessel at sea, where wind and wave are the ultimate arbiters, where there can be no immediate aid and no witness to any crisis they might create, it is easy enough to think like a primitive. It is an inherently existential predicament. Look as far as you can in all directions and you see nothing solid save the deck you stand upon. Everything else is insubstantial, consisting only of liquid and vapor.

Even the horizon, though often visually distinct, is amorphous. Liquid water heated by the sun constantly evaporates from beneath you into great clouds of flying water overhead. And eventually it pours back down, sometimes so hard the horizon becomes invisible. And the wind, too, when blowing its hardest, with or without rain, can sometimes push the ocean so hard the horizon is obscured in a blur of driven water molecules. Or clouds may form through condensation without convection right over the water's surface as fog, and then everything is invisible.

You meanwhile are an acute singularity, a land animal that presumes to exist here but cannot survive without a vessel to ride upon.

Historically then, sailors have had strong superstitious tendencies. Adrift in an alien environment they cannot pretend to control, they must hope instead to somehow propitiate whoever or whatever might be in charge of it.

The list of proscriptions and recommended procedures is seemingly endless. Sailors we are told must throw prophets and priests overboard, must never leave port on a Friday, must insert coins beneath their masts, must be careful when whistling, must banish bananas from their larders, must never kill an albatross or a dolphin, and must grease the ways (at least if they were Vikings of old) with the blood of virgins when launching their vessels for the very first time.

Even modern sailors are apt to read omens into the circumstances of their existence. And in very ancient times, when all of humanity was primitive and vulnerable in this way, this presumably is how the first deities were born. For the simplest way to comprehend elemental forces is to somehow personify them.

THE SEA HAS ALWAYS SEEMED PRIMAL to humanity and is prominently featured in many creation myths. The very word "ocean" derives from one of these. In Greek mythology the sea that bounded all of the world as the Greeks knew it was personified by Oceanus, one of the Titans, the proto-gods who spawned the upstarts who came to inhabit Olympus. Poseidon, though better remembered now, had a much smaller jurisdiction and ruled only over the Middle Sea that was surrounded by all the land that Oceanus himself embraced. And Hera herself, queen of Olympus, acknowledged (per Homer in Book XIV of *The Iliad*) that she and the others must return "to the ends of the generous earth on a visit to Oceanus, whence the gods have risen."

In the cosmogony of ancient Egypt the world was born of an oceanic abyss inhabited by four pairs of frogs and snakes. The most important pair were Nun (a male frog) and Naunet (a female snake), who personified water itself and gave birth to Ra, the sun god, who rose from the first land to emerge from the water and was himself father of all subsequent gods. Nun the frog had no priesthood, but was represented in sacred lakes installed around the temples of other gods and was present, it was believed, in every molecule of water and encompassed all aspects of existence.

In Mesopotamia there was Tiamat, an aquatic "chaos monster" who mated with Abzu, the god of fresh water, to produce a pantheon of younger gods. She was also known as Ummu-Hubur, or the one who formed all things.

In India we find Varuna, the elder Hindu god, sovereign of water, who was believed to have created the world. The Polynesians, not surprisingly, also believed that the world was formed out of a watery chaos, from which the great god Ku extracted the male and female forces of Ao and Po, who made all things possible. And even in our own Judeo-Christian tradition, the Book of Genesis tells us "in the beginning... the earth was without form, and void; and darkness was upon the face of the deep. And the Spirit of God moved upon the face of the waters."

All of these belief systems presuppose the existence of water, and of a primordial ocean, but do not presume to tell us where they came from. Fortunately, we now have a little science to help fill in the blanks.

Imagine this: a whirling vortex of interstellar gas and plasma, spirals within spirals, and eventually some choice bits of matter within each spiral are violently compressed by gravity into spheres. When pressed hard enough some of these ignite into gaseous nuclear bonfires. These blow off explosive waves of matter as they are formed, and this matter in turn swirls about in still more spirals and is compressed to form smaller spheres. Some are still too large and too gaseous to be truly solid, but some are smaller still, with hot molten cores surrounded by hard solid crusts.

It takes an awfully long time for all this turbulence to settle down. Even after the solid and semi-solid spheres have started spinning in a somewhat organized fashion around their central star, they are bombarded by great fusillades of smaller, more disorderly objects, which they must ultimately absorb. And many of these projectiles are coated in water, or are entirely composed of water, dihydrogen monoxide, an important byproduct of stellar birthing explosions and a ubiquitous compound molecule.

Space is normally very cold, so the water in and on these projectiles is frozen hard. But when the projectiles collide with solid planets that hard ice melts and becomes liquid water. This water joins whatever water has been pressed out of the planet itself, and if the planet is fortunate enough to have the right elemental chemicals onboard, and enjoys the right mix of heat and moisture, and is large enough to have a decent gravitational field, it might form enough of an atmosphere to keep much of that water from boiling off into space.

How much water must be trapped on a planet's surface to create a primordial ocean? From a small sailboat the ocean seems infinite, but thinking objectively we know our planet is finite and that the quantity of water circulating in, on, and around it must therefore also be finite. Over 70 percent of our planet's surface may be covered with water, but it is in fact thinly distributed. If you were to gather it all together—all the liquid water in our oceans, rivers, lakes, ponds, and puddles; all of the liquid groundwater trapped beneath the land; all of the frozen water trapped in ice caps and glaciers; all of the water vapor circulating in our veil of an atmosphere—and collect it in a single liquid drop, you'd have a sphere measuring just 860 miles in diameter—the distance, say, from New York City to St. Louis. Compare this to the planet's diameter, which is about 7,900 miles. To get an accurate differential, consider the respective volumes of the two spheres. The planetary orb comes in at about 260 billion cubic miles; its droplet of water has a volume of 332.5 million cubic miles, a little less than 0.13 percent of the whole.

Yet because water is so unique, it has had an inordinate influence on the planet's destiny. First and foremost, it has an unusually high boiling point compared to other common substances, which is precisely why so much of the water on Earth can exist as a liquid. And liquid water itself has some unusual qualities. It is the most powerful solvent we know of, dissolving more substances in greater quantities than other liquids, and is an excellent suspension medium. It is highly transparent. It also has tremendous surface tension, higher than any other common liquid.

All these qualities are critical to the sustenance of biological life. All components in living cells are dissolved in water, and the structure and actions of all cells are determined by how they interact with water. Water carries dissolved oxygen and nutrients to all parts of organisms. Its high surface tension gives rise to the capillary action that allows it to defy gravity and creep up narrow tubes, an important process exploited by all vascular plants. Water's transparency is what permits the miracle of photosynthesis, wherein plants utilize sunlight to produce glucose, and water is also critical to respiration, wherein animals absorb the oxygen given off by plants and in turn give off the carbon dioxide that is absorbed by plants.

Life first evolved in water, and life as we know it cannot exist without it. Some 90 percent of the planet's biomass is in its oceans. We ourselves are fully saturated in water. Between 50 to 70 percent of the human body consists of water by weight; or, if you prefer to simply count the molecules in your body, 99 percent of those are water. Water, ultimately, is the glue that binds us together. It has no form or individuality, yet it connects everything to everything else.

AS FAR AS SAILORS are concerned, what is most important about water, aside from the fact that our boats can float in it, is how it creates weather. For one of the most remarkable things about water is its ability to absorb and transfer heat. Its heat capacity—the amount of heat it can absorb before its temperature rises—is higher than all other common liquids and solids, as is its latent heat, which is the amount of heat it absorbs and releases during phase changes between its solid, liquid, and gaseous forms.

As the only substance that can exist in all three phases on our planet's surface, water is the medium through which most of the heat we receive from the sun is regulated. It greatly moderates the planet's overall temperature by absorbing and storing heat and by circulating it both vertically and horizontally through the atmosphere and oceans. Horizontal heat circulation through water helps to create the planet's great ocean currents, which obviously are significant to any mariner, but it is the vertical atmospheric circulation that makes sailing possible.

Look at any weather map and you will see its primary features are vast cells of low and high pressure. Quite simply, low-pressure cells form where areas of concentrated heat have caused warm moisture-laden air to rise up into the atmosphere, and the air that rushes into the void to replace the rising air is the wind that fills our sails.

The high-pressure cells are where the once risen air, now stripped of warmth and moisture, falls to Earth again. Because of the planet's rotation, the air around both sorts of cells is itself rotating—in opposite directions, away from high-pressure cells and toward low-pressure cells—in vast spirals that mimic the great spirals of matter that formed our star and planet in the first place. These rotations, which can be temporarily bent and corrupted into fronts, ridges, and troughs, determine the direction of the wind, which in turn determines the direction in which any given sailing vessel can most easily travel at any given point on an ocean's surface.

What this is, of course, is simply turbulence, a slow-boiling mix of liquid and vapor that absorbs and disseminates heat from the sun throughout the planet's aqueous skin. And though the turbulence of weather may seem random and chaotic, it is certainly not anarchic. Indeed, what we now call the science of chaos was born of our efforts to comprehend the weather. The earliest glimmerings of "chaos theory" may have been manifest in an odd puzzle worked out by French mathematician Henri Poincaré during the

1880s, an irrational-seeming monster he was then unwilling to confront. But it wasn't until Edward Lorenz, an American meteorologist, tried for the first time to model weather on a computer in the early 1960s that the overarching dimensions of this new science first became apparent.

To create his model Lorenz greatly oversimplified meteorology and distilled the behavior of Earth's weather into as few mathematical equations as possible. Then when running his computer model he made a remarkable discovery: he could not rewind and replay it. He tried to scroll his toy weather machine back in time, queuing it to a prior set of conditions, but when he hit the play button again a very different scenario unfolded. Though initially similar to the first scenario that played out from the same starting point, the new scenario quickly diverged into something entirely dissimilar. Though governed by the same set of relatively simple equations, each extrapolation seemed random and unpredictable.

Anyone who has ever coped with real weather in real time won't be surprised by this. Though created through physical processes we can describe and understand, and constrained by deterministic rules that cannot be violated, the behavior of weather always is ultimately unpredictable. No one knows this better than a sailor.

It is seemingly oxymoronic, this deterministic unpredictability, but we find examples of these systems all around us. The seemingly random gyrations of financial markets, fluctuations in automobile traffic, Internet traffic, the frequency of earthquakes, variations in animal populations, the evolution of biological systems, the patterns in which snowflakes and ice crystals form, and yes, even the unfolding creation of galaxies, stars, and individual planets—all these things and many more are both deterministic and unpredictable.

What is surprising, and seemingly magical and divine, is that the unpredictable turbulent behavior exhibited in all these systems falls into patterns

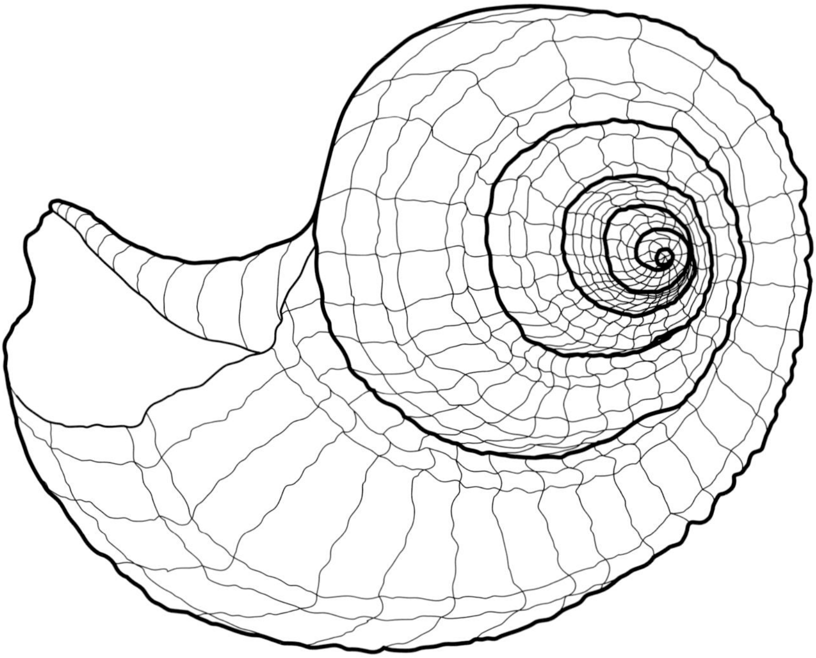

The spiral patterns that define the structure of galaxies on a cosmic scale and weather systems on a global scale are replicated on a microcosmic scale in the shape of many seashells and other natural structures.

that are universal. Across all sciences, across all disciplines, at all scales from macro to micro, these patterns are self-similar and govern the way in which things change.

Will our growing ability to see the patterns in chaos someday make it possible for us to predict the unpredictable? Will our marine weather forecasts someday come with guarantees? That would be convenient, but it misses the point. Our understanding of unpredictability may mitigate it to some extent and may ultimately improve our forecasts, but it can never negate it.

What our comprehension can do, however, is help us accept and commune with uncertainty.

For what we are doing when we are sailing, most particularly when we are sailing across an ocean, is surrendering ourselves to chaos. We submit our bodies and minds to the turbulent interplay of ocean and atmosphere, commend ourselves to the liquid and the vapor, and in so doing become the siblings of universal things.

THIS BLENDING OF OURSELVES into the greater whole is, I believe, a fundamental attraction of ocean sailing. At sea, in the light and space of a long voyage, you may sometimes become acutely aware of your own mortality, but you will also sometimes feel it expanded into something seemingly infinite.

It is interesting that our three major monotheistic "revealed" religions—Judaism, Christianity, and Islam—are all the fruit of mystic transmissions received by prophets who isolated themselves in the desert. And in Buddhism, of course, though it is not really theistic, we have a belief system based on the enlightenment of a man who isolated himself under a tree. But curiously, though humans from the very beginning of our existence have wandered across the watery part of our world, an inherently isolating experience, we have in our history no real prophet of the sea.

Many modern sailors will readily agree that the man who most closely fits the description is Bernard Moitessier, the iconoclastic French singlehander who became notorious in 1969 when he abandoned the first nonstop solo round-the-world race so as to "save his soul." Most will also agree that the book Moitessier wrote about his experience, *The Long Way* (*La longue route* in the original French, 1971), though it never spawned any sort of religion, is the closest thing we have to a spiritual text.

Moitessier did not originally go to sea seeking enlightenment. Instead his goal was simply to emigrate from war-torn French Indochina, where he was born and raised. His first boat, a decrepit Malaysian proa called *Snark*, in which he hoped to reach Australia, was turned back to Saigon by Indonesian authorities, but on his second boat, a gaff-rigged Siamese junk called *Marie Thérèse*, he achieved exit velocity into the eastern Indian Ocean and beyond.

Though Moitessier ultimately lost *Marie Thérèse* on an Indian Ocean reef, he built himself a new *Marie Thérèse* from scratch in Mauritius. He later lost this boat on a reef in the West Indies. The book he wrote about these adventures, *Sailing to the Reefs* (*Un vagabond des mers du sud* in French, 1960), made him famous in France and provided him with the funds needed to build *Joshua*, a crude 40-foot full-keeled steel ketch with solid-wood masts and a remarkably large sail plan. As part of a honeymoon cruise from Europe to the South Pacific and back, he sailed this boat doublehanded with his new wife nonstop halfway around the world from Tahiti to Alicante, Spain, by way of Cape Horn.

This very impressive accomplishment—the voyage in fact set a new nonstop long-distance sailing record—and the book he wrote describing it, *The Logical Route* (*Cap Horn á la voile* in French, 1967), heightened his fame in France, but was not universally recognized by the international yachting community at the time. At least Sir Francis Chichester knew nothing of it before setting out on his famous one-stop circumnavigation to and from Great Britain via Sydney, Australia.

The immense public acclaim Chichester received (he was knighted by Queen Elizabeth on stepping ashore in May 1967 and was featured on the cover of *Life* magazine) immediately inspired other sailors, including Moitessier, to start preparing for the ultimate voyage—a solo nonstop circumnavigation. Seeking to organize these disparate efforts into a coherent whole it could more easily exploit, the British weekly *Sunday Times* announced it would award a Golden Globe trophy to the first person to complete the trip and a separate £5,000 prize (equivalent to almost $100,000 in current U.S.

dollars) to the one who did it fastest.

Moitessier up to this point had never publicly revealed any spiritual inclinations, but it was clear even before the great race started that he viewed it in a very different light than his competitors. Intently self-obsessed, he had berated himself for writing a book he felt betrayed the spirit of his long Alicante voyage, became depressed as a result, and decided the only way to redeem himself was to write his next book while sailing on this much longer voyage.

As he later wrote, being propositioned by the *Sunday Times*, who sent a man to France to urge him to join the race by starting his voyage from Britain, "made me want to vomit." And he expounded on this sentiment in an article he wrote for the French magazine *Bateaux*: "In a passage like this, a man must look into himself without facing a competitor. I disapprove of a race; it makes you lose sight of the essential: a voyage to your own utter limits, this search for a profound truth with as sole witness the sea, the wind, the boat, the infinitely big, the infinitely small."

In the end he yielded, however, moved his starting port to Plymouth, England, and explained to the *Sunday Times* that if he won the race—which was a distinct possibility, as he was the only competitor who had already rounded the Horn and had sailed halfway round the world nonstop—he would "snatch the check without saying thank you, coolly auction off the Golden Globe, and leave without a word."

And though ultimately Moitessier did not write his book while sailing (this in fact took him two torturous years of effort after the fact), he did write it all in the present tense, which serves to heighten a reader's sense of the voyage as an unfolding 10-month-long epiphany.

To some extent what clearly became a spiritual adventure can be seen as a product of certain happenstances. Moitessier, unlike most other European sailors, had been raised in the East, had been steeped in local lore and wisdom by Asian nannies, so was predisposed toward an eastern view of the mystic. Also, a friend had casually left onboard a copy of a then seminal how-to text, *Yoga for Everyone*, by one Desmond Dunne.

Finally, and not insignificantly, *Joshua* had been vastly improved since her Alicante voyage. She now had modern polyester sails and lines and a full complement of winches (where previously she had only blocks and tackle), so it was much easier for Moitessier to keep her sails properly trimmed. He'd also removed thousands of pounds of miscellaneous cruising gear and concentrated most of what stayed aboard in the middle of the boat. The result overall was a vessel that was much more responsive, faster and more easily handled, and much more exactly an extension of her master's identity and will.

All this is manifest in Moitessier's book, which starts with a fairly prosaic, if expressive account of the voyage's early stages. The key event being a collision with a freighter off South Africa that damaged *Joshua*'s rig and bent her bowsprit. Moitessier dealt with the crisis like a Zen master. He spent a full day hove-to pondering the problem, then engineered a brilliant, yet simple solution. Taking a tackle to a gin-pole and line leading to the end of the bowsprit, he led the fall of the tackle aft to a sheet winch. With all this leverage and mechanical advantage, he then was able to straighten the sprit by grinding on the winch and soon had restored his rig.

"Incredible, the power of a tackle on a winch," he wrote. "I feel I am going to start crying, it's so beautiful... the bowsprit begins to straighten out, very, very slowly. I am wild with joy!"

From there his tale devolves into an ongoing exaltation. Moitessier (in time-honored solo-sailing fashion) happily hallucinates an extra passenger to keep him company and succeeds (to some extent) in taming a group of seabirds that follow his boat. He is ecstatic when he figures out that a pod of dolphins he encounters off New Zealand are dancing at his bow in such a way as to warn him of danger ahead. He starts practicing yoga, sometimes in the nude, and stops bathing. Soon he even looks like a filthy mystic.

"My hair has grown a lot; it is almost down to my shoulders," he wrote. "My beard is so long I have to trim it around my lips every week, so as to eat my morning porridge without smearing it all over. My last complete soaping dates back to a rain squall in the doldrums, months ago… yet I do not have a single pimple on my skin."

One coincidence that aided Moitessier in his enlightenment was the unusually calm weather he encountered as he plunged into the famously turbulent waters of the Southern Ocean. It gave him a happy breathing space after his tumultuous departure and his unlucky freighter collision, and created a peaceful environment in which his view of things dramatically expanded.

"This is the first time that I feel such peace," he wrote of this interlude, "a peace that has become a certainty, something that cannot be explained, like faith. I know I will succeed, and it strikes me as perfectly normal; that is the marvelous thing, that absolute certainty where there is neither pride nor fear nor surprise. The entire sea is simply singing in a way I had never known before."

And when the foul weather inevitably did come, most particularly as he approached Cape Horn, in fantastic scenes of angry phosphorescent water and glorious displays of seemingly supernatural *aurora australis*, his incipient state of grace was tempered like hot steel plunged into cold water. From inside his boat, he wrote, "the rumble of the sea sounds muted, as it tells me lots of things. Present things, past things, future things. It is all there, in the sea." And the turmoil helped him to "[l]ive only with the sea and my boat, for the sea and for my boat."

What was not coincidental was that Moitessier's experience was explicitly tied to his environment. Unlike those famous prophets of the desert, his revelations were inextricably bound up with the place that produced them.

"Sailing in these waters," he wrote, "if man is crushed by his feeling of insignificance, he is borne up and protected by that of his greatness. It is here, in the immense desert of the Southern Ocean, that I feel most strongly how much man is both atom and god.

"And when I go on deck at dawn, I sometimes shout my joy at being alive, watching the sky turning white above the long streaks of foam on this colossally powerful, beautiful sea, that tries to kill at times. I am alive, with all my being. Truly alive."

And though he never articulated any specific tenets of his faith (again, unlike those prophets of the desert), his tendency, like some sort of ocean druid, was to both worship and anthropomorphize the nature that surrounded him. Anticipating James Lovelock's Gaia hypothesis, he conceived of the entire planet as a single living entity, and his ultimate metaphor for divinity was a friendly bird that came to visit him: "She is the Fairy Tern, who lives on all islands where the sun is the god of men. She flies out to sea in the morning and always returns to her island by dusk. So all you have to do is follow."

Many ocean sailors, though unable to describe them at such length, have had similar revelations while sailing offshore. For even more than the desert, the ocean is inherently a place that encourages spiritual thought.

In scientific literature, there is a term for this. "Oceanic feeling" is an explicit psychological expression first coined by Romain Rolland in 1927 and later popularized by Sigmund Freud. Rolland, in correspondence with Freud, described it as a "spontaneous religious sentiment" born of a sensation experienced by those who have formed an insoluble bond with the external world.

Freud acknowledged the phenomenon, but dismissed it as a "primitive ego-feeling" related to breast-feeding. Years later it was redescribed as the "overview effect" after astronauts reported experiencing spiritual revelations while observing our planet from space. Most recently it has been scrutinized by certain academics seeking to establish a neurological and evolutionary basis for spiritual and religious experiences as part of a nascent science known as neurotheology.

Neurotheology still stands well outside the mainstream of science. Theorists in the field have focused on repetitive rhythmic stimulation as a common characteristic of human religious rituals, and they believe such stimulation may provoke transcendental feelings of universal connectedness, or "a unitary state," in the human mind.

According to one group of authors (Andrew Newberg, Eugene D'Aquili, and Vince Rause), rhythmic experiences "can lead to unitary states by causing the orientation area [of the brain] to be blocked from neural flow. The intensity of those unitary states depends on the degree of neural blockage. Since the degree of that blockage can increase by any increment, and theoretically until there is a total blocking, a large spectrum of increasingly unitary states is possible. We call this span the unitary continuum. The arc of this continuum links the most profound experiences of the mystics with the smaller transcendent moments most of us experience every day, and shows that, in neurological terms, the two are different essentially by degree."

Repetitive rhythmic stimulation obviously is inherent to any ocean sailing experience and, from a human perspective, is perhaps the most unique aspect of the ocean environment. You cannot adapt to a life at sea without adapting to the motion of the ocean. You must learn the rhythm and must learn to focus solely on whatever it is you are doing as you are doing it, lest some impertinent wave disrupt your immediate project—be it a repair job, the keeping of a log, the donning or removal of clothing, the brushing of teeth, or the boiling of water for coffee. Achieving this focus is fundamentally an act of meditation. To live well at sea you must live as much as possible in the present moment while simultaneously maintaining maximum awareness of your surroundings.

Add to this the inherent isolation of being at sea, your singularity in a hostile environment composed of a universal life-giving element, and you have everything you need, as Moitessier did, to climb as high as possible on the unitary continuum and devise a religion of your own.

The culmination of Moitessier's own transcendental experience was his decision not to finish the race. He announced this by hurling a film canister with a note in it on to a freighter, then sailed on to Tahiti, where he finally landed and ended a nonstop passage that had taken him one-and-a-half times around the world. It was an act that suddenly made him famous, and he worked to capitalize on this by writing about his voyage, but his fame did not last long outside the sailing community.

To prove the purity of his experience Moitessier tried to give the royalties from his book, this bible of ocean sailing, to the Pope, but the Pope ignored the offer. Moitessier stayed on in the Pacific for several years, fathered a son there, and lost a battle with marauding rats on a lonely atoll in the Tuamotus where he tried to settle with his family. He finally lost *Joshua*, as he had his previous boats, when she was wrecked on a beach in Mexico. He ended up in France and tried to stay true to his vision of the Long Way by working to plant trees throughout the country in the years before his death.

It is amusing to think there might someday be a sailor who does Moitessier one better. Someone who writes a real bible and somehow makes it stick, and so becomes a real prophet espousing a real religion. Like robe-clad Hari Krishna monks wandering through an airport terminal, the prophet's acolytes might wander the globe under sail in a great fleet of boats, proselytizing and spreading the word, drawing more and more sailors out on to the ocean with them.

But this is a blatantly idle vision. The ocean might carry us to the very top of the unitary continuum, but it cannot spawn a religion. The truth it offers is unique to every individual who finds it and cannot be shared. In the end it is a truth we must each follow on our own.

KISS ME (YOU FOOL)

Selecting and Preparing a Boat for Bluewater Cruising

Most of the luxuries, and many of the so-called comforts of life, are not only not indispensable, but positive hindrances to the elevation of mankind. With respect to luxuries and comforts, the wisest have ever lived a more simple and meager life than the poor.

—Henry David Thoreau, *Walden*

RECREATIONAL MARINE SYSTEMS TECHNOLOGY has advanced mightily in the past 50 years, and it is now possible to live just as profligately afloat as you do ashore. If you have the money and are willing to spend it, you can cruise aboard a palace of a craft while manufacturing as much fresh water and electricity as you like. You can enjoy fridges and freezers, central heat and air conditioning, showers whenever you want, dishwashers and washing machines, even full phone and Internet service. And as technology has marched ever forward, those giving advice to aspiring bluewater cruisers have increasingly urged that when selecting and equipping a bluewater boat you should always adhere to the overarching principle of KISS, or Keep It Simple Stupid. And amazingly, no matter how complicated their boats are, almost all bluewater cruisers swear that they do this.

The advantages of KISS are usually described in terms of the time and money saved in not having so much broken equipment to fix. It is true all technology at sea must eventually fail, but really the more important point is this: none of the peak experiences of bluewater sailing are augmented or improved by luxury and convenience. They can save you from some of the discomfort of sailing offshore, but not the ultimate discomfort, and never from the fear, and in deadening the low points of the experience they only dilute the high spots. Ultimately they can only inhibit your ability to become one with the ocean.

It certainly helps to be younger when you start. Young people, having less money and more endurance, can more easily appreciate discomfort and inconvenience. Most older people, meanwhile, will buy their way out of all that virtue if they can. In my case, I emerged from my baptism aboard *Constellation* while still in my early 30s and was determined to sail around the North Atlantic again. Except this time I wanted to go further south to West Africa and the Cape Verdes before coming back, and I also wanted to go on a boat of my own. To acquire and equip it I had about $50,000 to spend.

The good thing about a constrained boat-buying budget is that it limits your options. It is not hard to get lost and confused in the modern market, and staying focused is easier if you are restricted to the bargain basement of brokerage listings. In selecting my own boat all I really wanted was something strong and cheap, and because they were familiar to me I was naturally attracted to older designs built to the long defunct Cruising Club of America (CCA) rating rule.

The CCA rule dominated American boat design through all the middle part of the last century, including during the period when boatbuilding shifted from wood to fiberglass. The club that created the rule sponsored and promoted offshore ocean races precisely because it believed such events stimulated the development of proper cruising boats. In furtherance of that goal the rule was kept intentionally conservative and imposed boundaries on designers that prevented dramatic exaggerations of hull forms. The ideal CCA form—which seems natural and organic to many sailors—features a graceful cutaway full keel with an attached rudder under the water, a relatively narrow beam, and long overhangs at both the bow and stern.

This is a very seakindly shape, with lots of reserve buoyancy in its ends, but it does have two obvious drawbacks: there isn't much room inside for living, and the deck, being low to the water, is wet when conditions are strong. The next generation of more dedicated cruisers, fat double-ended boats like the iconic Westsail 32, which were built in the 1970s, were roomier and somewhat drier, but they were also slower and more expensive to buy.

Another advantage of this first generation of fiberglass boats is that they really were quite rugged. Owners of early fiberglass boats like to boast that their solid laminate hulls are just as thick as wood hulls because builders back then didn't know any better. This is an exaggeration, but these boats are generally stronger than more modern boats constructed by those who have learned the tolerances of the materials and economics of their trade.

I looked at several old CCA boats over the course of one fall and winter, and finally purchased a Pearson Alberg 35 yawl that was stored in the back of a crowded open-air shed in a boatyard in Connecticut. It had been built in Bristol, Rhode Island, precisely three decades earlier and cost me $28,500.

Wanderlust, as she was then called, had been in the same family for 18 years and had been well cared for. She was a seasonal boat, was always stored under cover during winters, and had been continually upgraded. Her original Atomic Four gasoline engine (known as the Atomic Bomb to those with experience of them) had been replaced with a 27-horsepower Volvo diesel engine, and she had a good sail inventory, new spars, a pedestal-mounted autopilot, two refrigeration systems, and a pressure-water system. Still, she was equipped only for coastal cruising, and there was much work to be done.

I feel embarrassed now remembering how hastily I prepared to go offshore. My new boat was out of the water when I purchased her, and because she was far from home, deep in the back of that crowded shed, it wasn't possible to do much work prior to launching her. With the help of a good friend, Nim

The Pearson Alberg 35, a typical CCA design, was drawn by Carl Alberg and could be ordered as a sloop or yawl. First introduced in 1961, over 250 hulls were built over a six-year period.

Marsh, I finally launched her in early June 1995, renamed her *Crazy Horse*, and after about six weeks of frenetic activity we set off for Bermuda.

The boat wasn't really ready when we left, but we were passionately committed to somehow getting to sea that summer. I cannot recommend this as a *modus operandi*, but at the opposite extreme there are those who are so obsessed with getting everything just right they never actually go anywhere. Different people must draw the line in different places, but if you are a novice boat-owner and want to sail sooner rather than later, you should resign yourself, on some level, to preparing the boat as you go along.

BELOW THE WATERLINE

One reason I bought *Crazy Horse* was because she had a very clean bottom with no osmotic blisters. This is not uncommon in New England, where the water is cold and boats spend a lot of time stored on shore. Further south the warmer water not only migrates into a glass laminate more easily, but also has much more time to do so if a boat is constantly afloat. On *Crazy Horse*, the surveyor's moisture meter turned up some damp spots, but nothing dramatic. The previous owner, in spite of the lack of blisters, had also recently treated the hull to an epoxy barrier job, so I felt I had an excellent foundation on which to build.

The rudder was a different story. Pearson built its Alberg 35s with wooden rudders—mahogany planks mounted vertically on horizontal drift pins—and *Crazy Horse* still boasted an original example. It seemed wobbly, but several people assured me it would swell up tight once it was immersed in water for a while, so I left it alone. One nice feature of full-keel sailboats is that they are not absolutely dependent on their rudders for directional stability. In an emergency they require a less substantial jury-rudder, or, if you are good at trimming sails (and particularly if you have a yawl), can sometimes be sailed without any rudder at all.

The rudder did cause concern during my voyage. When I hauled the boat more than a year later in Gibraltar, there was some play in it, and just to be safe I screwed horizontal support beams on either side of it. This made for a strong, but not very hydrodynamic foil that remained intact for the rest of the trip.

The other issue was the bronze rudder heel. It was corroded along its leading edge, and as a purchase condition I insisted the previous owner replace it. This proved a mistake, not because he did a poor job, but because he was so slow about it and I ended up launching the boat a month late. I would have been better off demanding a price reduction and taking care of it myself.

TOPSIDES AND DECK

The boat still had her original gray gelcoat, which was thoroughly crazed. My research told me this was likely because it had been laid on too thick when the hull was built. After a good waxing, however, the gelcoat shined up nicely and the crazing was barely noticeable. I thought about painting the boat, but it seemed silly to go to much trouble over a cosmetic issue prior to an extended cruise. Instead, I just waxed her every few months. In a few places, tiny chips of gelcoat started falling out, but I just puttied over these spots and kept on cruising.

On deck there were several things to attend to. The boat had only a small pramhood over her companionway, and since we expected she would be wet in a seaway, we removed this and installed a full cockpit dodger. As soon as we got to Bermuda, after a brush with a storm, we also added some cockpit weather-cloths. Up forward we added a strong bow-roller to carry an anchor, and on the cabintop amidships we mounted a four-man life-raft in a canister. I also had a seahood for the sliding companionway hatch fabricated in fiberglass.

During the survey, the balsa-cored decks had, with a few minor exceptions, read dry on the moisture meter, so I did not waste any time rebedding deck hardware. I did this instead bit by bit after we reached the Azores. As it was, I should have paid more attention to the hardware before leaving, as one cleat without a backing plate pulled right out of the deck when we were tied to a wall in Bermuda.

The boat came equipped with just one lifeline running along the tops of her stanchion posts, and though conventional wisdom dictated there should be a second line running through the middle of the posts, I never bothered about it. The stanchion posts were rather low, and to me it seemed anyone going overboard was going over the lifeline and not under it. In the Azores I did add netting under the lifeline up forward, as this made it much easier to keep everything on deck when changing roller-furling headsails at sea.

I also never installed any special hardware for jacklines. Instead, we just set up lines running from the bow cleats to the stern cleats on either side of the boat and clipped on to these. Nor did I install any dedicated D-rings for lashing down gear on deck, and this was probably a mistake. Most of the time we had a rolled-up dinghy and a few sail bags lashed to the teak handrails on the coachroof, and we were lucky they held up as well as they did.

We did go to the trouble to make up emergency storm shutters for the four large cabin portlights in the event they were punched out by waves. We pre-assembled kits of the gear and fasteners needed to install these, and stored them below with the shutters.

SAILS AND RIG

My biggest mistake was not paying more attention to the standing rigging. Though the rig looked good before we left, by the time I finished my two-year circuit of the Atlantic I had replaced every shroud on the mainmast, plus the backstay, piece by piece. Most of the shrouds I replaced in Gambia, which was difficult, as it was hard to source parts there. Fortunately, I was religious about polishing and inspecting the swage terminals, and found each cracked terminal before any had a chance to fail.

We did take apart the roller-furler, an old Harken unit, for an inspection before casting off. Unfortunately, I did not learn until after the rig was up that the big problem with these units is that the roll pins that hold the foil extrusions together like to fall out. The best way to prevent this is to peen the ends of the pins, but it is impossible to do this unless the rig is down. As it was, I laid in a supply of spare pins and inspected the foil regularly. Fortunately, it never caused me any trouble.

The running rigging was in good shape and presented no problems. We did reeve a heavier topping lift, so it could serve as a backup main halyard if necessary. Both the jib halyards were wire spliced to rope, and eventually I replaced one of these with an all-rope line, as I felt more comfortable going aloft on this.

As for the sails, these also were in good shape. The inventory consisted of a mainsail, mizzen, mizzen staysail, a drifter, a 150 percent genoa, a 130 percent genoa, and a working jib. The only new sail I added was a storm jib. Instead of a trysail, I had a deep third reef put in the main and also had a reef added to the mizzen. At the sailmaker's suggestion, I also had a full batten installed at the top of the mainsail, and this, I found, worked well. It is a good compromise for those unwilling to commit to the extra expense and hassle of a completely full-battened main.

One feature I never addressed was the lightly stayed mizzenmast. It would have been more useful in stronger wind if its midsection was better supported, and I soon concluded it wanted spreaders. I also thought many times about removing the mizzenmast altogether, but in light air, particularly with both the mizzen and mizzen staysail up, it often gave me an extra knot or so of speed, and thus I grew fond of it.

ACCOMMODATIONS

Crazy Horse had a simple seagoing interior that needed few changes prior to our heading offshore. The two settees in the main cabin made very good sea-berths, and the big V-berth up forward was used for storage while underway. We did add canvas lee-cloths to all the berths and learned that canvas is a poor material for this, as mildew grows on it quickly when the lee-cloths are stowed under their berths.

The biggest change we made was rebuilding the engine box. When repowering the boat the previous owner had installed a steel ladder over the box, and this made a huge part of the galley counter inaccessible. We chucked the ladder, and a talented friend devised a clever new box with integral companionway steps, a little galley seat, and some extra storage cubbies. This was a huge success, as it opened up scads of counter space and made it possible to cook, navigate, and con the boat from the same spot.

Up in the head, which was between the saloon and forepeak, I removed the shower curtain and the sump pump under the drain pan and decreed that all bathing would henceforth take place on deck. This made the head much more functional and opened up a lot of deep storage space for canned goods under the drain pan.

ENGINE AND SYSTEMS

Both *Crazy Horse*'s exhaust line and fuel vent exited the boat through the transom, which was quite low, and I was worried big following seas might overwhelm and flood them. To prevent this, we installed shut-off valves at the end of both lines. After we left, I also learned (the hard way) that with the boat fully loaded the top of the engine was below the waterline, so in Gibraltar I installed a siphon break on the cooling circuit.

Otherwise, the biggest issue was the electrical system. I did nothing with it prior to leaving and ended up constantly fretting over it during the cruise.

The boat came with just two 85-amp wet-cell batteries charged by a small 50-amp alternator, and we soon had problems keeping the system topped up. In the Azores I added a flexible 22-watt solar panel and also adopted the practice of running dark at night while on passage, except when other vessels were in sight. I often joked that the only thing I had to worry about were other dopes like me.

Ultimately, I became hyper-conscious of every little bit of power we used, monitored the batteries closely, and we managed to squeak by. We never used the electric pump to draw water from our tanks, always used a kerosene anchor light instead of the electric one, carried a few kerosene lamps to light the cabin when power was low, and in the end, believe it or not, rarely had to run the engine just to charge the batteries. This is a fundamental rule of electrical systems on boats: using less electricity in the first place is always the most effective (and least expensive) way to increase a system's efficiency. Life aboard *Crazy Horse* did sometimes seem spartan, but I didn't mind this at the time and looking back now remember our lack of power as anything but a hardship.

Likewise I kept all other systems as primitive as possible. We immediately removed the 12-volt refrigeration, for example, and I swore the engine-driven Sea Frost system would follow as soon as it broke down. It worked fine the entire trip, but we only used it occasionally, as I was unwilling (and unable, due to our small fuel tank) to run the engine just to keep things cold. Most of the food we carried did not need refrigerating, yet still we ate well. There are many fresh foods that keep for long periods at room temperature (including cabbage, onions, garlic, carrots, potatoes, cured meat, and most types of nuts), and by mixing these judiciously with canned food and dry staples like rice and pasta we always managed to make our meals palatable.

Initially there was much debate about the pressurized alcohol stove in the galley. I agonized over whether to replace it with a propane system, and in the end did nothing. I never regretted this and grew fond of the alcohol stove. It was easy to strip and maintain, far simpler than a propane system, and we never had any trouble finding good alcohol to burn. In most places we visited it was cheaper than in the U.S., as we could buy it in bulk.

There was also a great debate concerning the boat's through-hull fittings, as the cockpit drains and both sink drains had no seacocks on them. Instead the drain hoses were clamped to tall fiberglass standpipes that reached above the waterline and ran straight out the bottom of the boat. None of these pipes were very accessible, and cutting them down and replacing them with seacocks would have been a difficult job. The end result would have been four more seacocks to service, and as I couldn't think of any way the standpipes could possibly break, I elected to leave them alone. In a worst-case scenario, if the hose on a pipe failed, I figured it would be easy enough to plug the pipe with a simple wood bung. I screwed bags of these to the bulkheads near every standpipe on the boat.

WATER AND FUEL

Crazy Horse carried 50 gallons of water in two separate tanks under the cabin sole and about 30 gallons of diesel in one tank under the cockpit sole. All these tanks were made of Monel, an excellent marine metal, and were clean and in good condition when I purchased the boat. We did have to replumb the water tanks so we could isolate them from one another.

To augment capacity we carried jerry jugs on deck. I lashed heavy strips of wood to the shroud turnbuckles on either side of the boat and lashed the jerry jugs in turn to these. This worked well enough and I never had a problem with jugs working loose. Unlike some contemporary cruisers, who carry vast quantities of jugs on deck, we carried just four 6-gallon jugs in total—one each of water, diesel, alcohol, plus gasoline for the dinghy's outboard engine. I also had one collapsible 5-gallon water jug, which made it possible, when necessary, to completely refuel and water the boat with just five trips to shore in the dinghy.

Because I was worried about our water capacity, I also purchased a hand-powered watermaker, a rather expensive item, but we never had to use it. At sea, and often also at anchor, we used sea water to wash dishes and ourselves, using just a bit of fresh water afterward to rinse with. Consequently, we never came close to running out. On our longest passage, 19 days sailing from Bermuda to the Azores with three people aboard, we used only half our supply.

Nor was our low fuel capacity ever a problem. We often motored the first and last few miles of a passage, but once offshore *Crazy Horse* was a sailing vessel pure and simple. If there was no wind, we furled our wings, rolled our brains out, and waited for a breeze. Only in Africa, while motoring 400 miles up and down the Gambia River, was it necessary to carry extra jugs of diesel.

NAVIGATION AND COMMUNICATIONS

The boat came equipped with a VHF radio, and all I added was a portable shortwave receiver with a SSB switch. With this I could pick up NOAA voice broadcasts, the popular volunteer weather-router Herb Hilgenberg, and the French Meteo Marine broadcasts, which between them provided more than enough weather information.

As for navigation equipment, I purchased a small handheld GPS receiver and installed an external antenna, and this worked perfectly the whole trip. I already owned a sextant and sight-reduction tables, but also purchased a Celesticomp calculator, which turned out to be great fun. Because it made it so easy to reduce sights and could even identify stars for me, I practiced with the sextant a lot and would have been in good shape had the GPS failed.

For an EPIRB (Emergency Position Indicating Radio Beacon), I bought one of the older 121.5-MHz models, which are now no longer available. I figured in the relatively crowded North Atlantic there would be enough airplanes passing overhead to catch any distress signal we might send. I also bought a handheld VHF radio, which I stowed in the ship's ditch bag on passages.

SELF-STEERING

I had no confidence in *Crazy Horse*'s autopilot, a small pedestal-mounted unit, so I removed it and never missed it, except on the rare occasions when we motored more than a few miles. Having to hand-steer while motoring encouraged us to sail whenever possible and so saved a lot of fuel.

In place of the autopilot I installed a Monitor servo-pendulum windvane, and this performed flawlessly. These machines are as simple as bicycles and there is very little that can go wrong with them. Over two years of constant use, I never even had to replace the control lines. If you are already attuned to the subtleties of sail trim, learning to use a vane is easy. If you are not, the vane will soon educate you if you are persistent and patient.

As to its installation, the only issue was the vane quarreling with the boom of the mizzen sail, which extended out past the transom. Rather than remove the mizzen or extend the Monitor's mounting tubes so as to clear the end of the boom, I played referee. I always kept a preventer on the mizzen boom and when tacking or jibing first lowered the mizzen, hoisted the boom over the vane with the topping lift, then reset the mizzen. It was a small sail, so this wasn't too much of a hassle. When short-tacking to windward, I simply left the mizzen down.

GROUND TACKLE

Crazy Horse came equipped with a 25-pound CQR anchor and a 12-pound Danforth anchor. I added a big aluminum Fortress anchor and a 35-pound CQR and used the latter as our main anchor. Though conventional wisdom dictates you should have all-chain rode and a windlass, I went with heavy rope and just 30 feet of chain and hauled it all by hand. One nice thing about being young and cruising in a small boat is that you can get away with this.

We carried two extra rodes with chain leaders in buckets, and this made it easy to deploy extra anchors, which I did fairly often. Anchoring on rope tends to inspire caution, and when it comes to anchoring, this is always a good thing. I inspected my rodes often, took great care in picking my spots, and dove on my anchor whenever possible. I never dragged the whole two years I was cruising on *Crazy Horse*, nor did I ever see anyone else on a rope rode get into serious trouble. The ones with problems always seemed to be people with chain rodes who had grown lazy and complacent.

THE HARD NUMBERS

This was the first time I was solely responsible for preparing a boat for sea and I found it overwhelming. Even when prepping a modest boat like *Crazy Horse* it feels like you are hemorrhaging money, and every decision seems fraught with horrible consequences. I had some offshore experience and some idea of what to expect, but for those without any experience it must be harrowing. As it was, what with our hasty departure, I was cranky and irritable during the first part of the cruise, as Nim will attest.

As for what this cost me, the list opposite shows what I spent before we left the U.S. in 1995 dollars. During the cruise my expenses were only about $10,000 a year, much of which was spent on boat gear and maintenance.

Storm jib	$397.00
Sail modifications	$281.76
Seahood for companionway hatch	$1,500.00
Monitor windvane w/spares	$3,285.00
Cockpit dodger	$1,025.00
Bow roller	$208.65
Life-raft w/mounting bracket	$2,750.00
Manual watermaker w/spares	$1,490.00
Used 35-pound CQR anchor	$250.00
Engine exhaust valve	$62.75
Portable shortwave receiver	$216.25
Spare rope	$346.88
Extra snatch blocks	$164.25
Handheld VHF radio	$179.95
121.5-MHz EPIRB	$234.95
GPS receiver w/external antenna	$449.00
Binoculars	$198.00
Celestial nav calculator	$265.00
Small inverter	$69.00
Lifesling MOB recovery kit	$99.00
Boarding ladder	$22.95
Radar reflector	$32.95
New companionway boards	$45.00
Safety harnesses	$120.00
Preventer tackle	$68.50
Bosun's chair	$71.95
Lee-cloths	$43.80
Miscellaneous	$1,638.88
Total:	$15,516.47
Including the boat's purchase price:	$44,016.47 (or about $68,000 in 2015 U.S. dollars)

WHAT I'D ADD NOW

The march of marine technology has brought not only frivolous comfort and convenience to the realm of bluewater sailing, but also improved safety. Certain devices are too important to ignore and should be carried by even the most economical cruisers. Number one is the modern 406-MHz satellite EPIRB, which immediately broadcasts your plea for help and your GPS position around the world via satellite. These have completely replaced the old 121.5-MHz models, which only broadcast locally and relied solely on radio direction-finding for position data. Number two is an invaluable collision-avoidance tool, the modern AIS (Automatic Identification System) transceiver, which constantly broadcasts your GPS position while also receiving positions from similarly equipped vessels within a range of about 50 miles.

I am on the fence regarding modern weather communications. You can still get lots of simple voice forecasts via a portable radio, just as I did on *Crazy Horse*, and I suppose I would still consider this the minimum requirement. But thanks to improvements in both communications and weather forecasting, it is now possible to receive much more detailed information, and this is so useful it seems almost negligent not to take advantage of it.

On my current boat, *Lunacy*, a 39-foot aluminum cutter I have sailed several times between the West Indies and New England, I have punted a bit. I have invested in a handheld Iridium satellite phone ($1,000 for the phone, plus approximately $600 a year for service), which I can carry on any boat I am sailing aboard. On my West Indies passages I use this to call a professional weather-router, particularly on the dodgy leg between New England and Bermuda in the fall, and pay him about $200 per passage. If I were to do another transatlantic run I would probably also invest in the technology needed (there are various options) to receive long-range computer-modeled graphic forecasts (commonly called GRIB files) via satellite. These are less accurate than the short-term synoptic maps generated by human meteorologists, but they are easier for lay people to interpret and give a more granular picture of how the weather is unfolding.

Lunacy otherwise is not much more complex than *Crazy Horse*, though she is significantly bigger inside, being both four feet longer and four feet wider. The most notable improvements are the addition of a small electronic autopilot, a tiller-pilot I can use to drive the head of my Aries servo-pendulum windvane (allowing the vane to steer to a compass course and without any wind); a radar set (it came with the boat, and I'm still not sure I consider it essential); a windlass (I now wouldn't think of doing without one, given my advancing years); a GPS chartplotter (but I still carry and often refer to paper charts); and most importantly a much larger and more sophisticated electrical system with a 400 amp-hour house battery bank fed by a wind generator, two 70-watt solar panels, and a 125-amp alternator.

The larger electrical system helps service new loads from equipment like AIS transceivers and chartplotters and also allows my family to recharge their ever-burgeoning array of personal electronic devices. But still I am frugal with power. Because I do not rely on a large electronic autopilot, I can keep consumption low enough while sailing that I almost never need to run the engine just to charge the batteries. Likewise, when at anchor or in a marina, I can rely solely on the wind generator and solar panels to keep everything running.

In terms of the rig, the most significant improvement on *Lunacy* has been the addition of a large lightweight "gennaker" or "screecher" headsail that furls on its own luff courtesy of a removable continuous-line furler. Such sails are now commonly called "Code Zero" sails, but this is a gross misnomer. Really they are just overlapping genoas built light enough to fly and furl without a solid luff foil. They are set and struck as long rolled-up sausages that are much easier to handle than loose sails.

Having the screecher aboard allows me to shift quickly and easily between a working jib and a genoa-sized headsail, which is very useful if you want to sail much more than you motor. When sailing aboard *Crazy Horse* I used to change regular roller-furling headsails underway, but this is enormously difficult and even then seemed the height of zealotry.

The bottom line is you can almost always make your boat simpler if you really want to. I could have made *Crazy Horse* simpler by removing her toilet and using a bucket instead and by using only kerosene lights instead of electric ones. There are any number of ways I could make *Lunacy* simpler, and I am sure there are as many or more ways most other ocean sailors could simplify their boats. Anyone who tells you differently probably does not have a very simple boat. More likely they have a very complicated boat and are more addicted to luxury and convenience than they are willing to admit.

CELESTIAL REASONING

The Art of Where We Are Now

Measured in terms of enchantment, is there anything can compare with a chartroom?

—Sterling Hayden, *Wanderer*

QUIZ ANY CURMUDGEON THESE DAYS on the subject of proper wayfinding and you'll soon find yourself reefed down in a gale of conventional wisdom about the importance of paper charts, compass bearings, dead reckoning, sextants, and the like. But what even curmudgeons tend to forget as they rail on about how modern navigational tools are corrupting us, is that many of their sacred cows are also just tools. They are more primitive, simpler, and more reliable in one sense, because they don't require electricity, but they are not the organic root of navigation.

Reduced to its purest form, human navigation (as opposed to more advanced forms practiced by certain migratory animals) is simply a matter of being able to look at something from a distance and say what it is. In a state of nature, using no tools whatsoever, we can travel knowingly only as far as we can see.

I am now almost old enough to qualify as a curmudgeon myself, and this is what I wonder about modern satellite navigation: will it ultimately destroy our ability to just eyeball our way around a body of water? Will it cut us off from the root of navigation?

What satellites do is turn navigation into a video game. You are a throbbing dot on a glowing screen, and the object of the game is to maneuver your dot through the various hazards on the screen using the controls on your boat. All you have to see to do this (unless you're trying to do something very precise, like bringing a boat to a dock or a mooring) is the screen itself. Everything else you see around you—the buoys, the landmarks, the textures and contours of the shore, those ripples in the water that might be hiding rocks beneath them—precisely because you are not trying to extract any information from it, is little more than scenery.

Shut the game down and the scenery is immediately more meaningful, and much more vivid, because it now poses a threat. If you are in a place you've never been before or have no memory of, you cannot tell what land is what, what buoy is ahead, what tower is on the horizon, or where the rocks and shoals are hidden. All you can do is pray you'll be able to get yourself out of all the trouble you will likely fall into.

The ultimate navigation tool before the advent of the video game was the humble paper chart, a printed pictorial database representing the recollections of those who have gone before us, often creased and printed over with coffee-cup stains. It is a valuable reference, but unlike an electronic chart can give no hint of a user's current location. To figure that out, you have to figure out what you're looking at and relate it to the chart on an ongoing basis.

This can be an intense process. I will always remember the first time I sailed south down Buzzards Bay into the teeth of a summer sea-breeze, because my two buddies and I, as we slashed to windward through the vicious chop in our 28-foot ketch, spent the entire afternoon quarreling over the identity of the distant humps we spied on the horizon. We agreed the humps must be the Elizabeth Islands, but had very different opinions on which hump might be which island, a debate aggravated by the fact that the most prominent landmark in view, a tall windmill on what turned out to be Cuttyhunk, was not marked down on our chart.

One thing I realized that day is that uncertainty is a powerful stimulant. It heightens the senses and sharpens the intellect (and an appetite for argument) in a most wonderful way. As a result, I really learned the layout of Buzzards Bay that afternoon in a way I never would have had we simply been following our progress on a plotter screen.

What I also learned is that navigation must always be a debate. Even when you're alone, sailing without debating partners, you must question every conclusion you reach and be willing to change it as soon as any doubt is cast upon it. You must revel in the uncertainty, and your mind and eye must always be probing, asking questions, testing assumptions. What if the chart is wrong? What if this buoy is missing? What if this tower is not visible at this angle? Have atmospheric conditions obscured or enhanced my visual range? And so on.

In the end, when you have solved the puzzle and have confirmed the identity of everything you see, with the relationships between the puzzle pieces you see matching all those you see on the chart, you will most likely know where you are.

THE GREAT PROBLEM OF OFFSHORE NAVIGATION is that when transiting a seemingly featureless void there is ostensibly nothing to identify. Voids like this, which also occur when visibility is badly reduced, are always the greatest challenge in navigation. In my own case my earliest experience involved crossing our river in Maine in a thick of fog, with a bit of gunfire thrown in, hence was fraught with peril.

We had to cross that morning, fog or no fog, to visit my grandfather on shore and could barely see the bow of our old West Point skiff. My dad had a plotted a compass course straight to the old Civil War fort on the other side and was cautiously motoring toward it with one eye glued to the old box compass he'd set on the floor of the skiff just before him.

About halfway across my mom started pointing off to the left, insisting we must be off course, and my dad pointed at the compass muttering no the hell we weren't. He seemed alarmed when he picked it up to show her and it dramatically changed its opinion of where we were heading. My mom became irate, going on, as ever, about the danger of being swept out to sea. My dad in response shouted something unprintable and threw the compass overboard.

Soon afterward we ran aground on a mudflat. This gave us no clear idea of where we were, because the mouth of the river at low tide is studded with mudflats, and because mud, like water, is mostly featureless. My dad set an anchor, and we left the boat and started walking across the mudflat toward where we thought the shore must be.

Eventually we found some big rocks and behind those an empty summer cottage we did not recognize. My dad started walking inshore to the road to find out where we were, while my mom stayed with my brothers and me on the porch of the cottage staring out into the fog. After a little while we heard guns being shot off out on the mudflat where we had come from.

"Must be clam-diggers," explained my mom. "They shoot at the gulls to keep them from stealing their clams."

She made my brothers and me lie down behind the cottage while she stood out on the porch shouting.

"There are children up here!" she shrieked, her voice as shrill as a gull's.

Which seemed only to provoke more shooting. But my mom kept on shouting, until the clam-diggers realized she was human and ceased fire.

Later my dad showed up with a borrowed car and rescued us. But we also had to find a boat to borrow to get our boat back after the tide came in and the fog lifted, so we ended up not having time that day to go see my grandfather.

As I grew older I learned how to navigate the river in the fog on my own and could get all the way up to Bath and back, a distance of some 30 miles, without losing my way no matter how thick it was. My trick was to stay within sight of one shore or the other and always cross between the two on a reliable compass heading, preferably where the river was narrow, going as fast as possible to minimize the offset from the always-strong tidal current.

I also learned, as I started wandering up and down the coast in small boats, studying charts more closely and going to places I'd never been before, that the next most important trick in navigation, after being able to identify what you're looking at (assuming you can see it), is being able to take two or more bearings on known objects and cross them on top of each other.

This is something we do instinctively in coastal navigation when we have landmarks in sight, regardless of whether we have been trained to do it and have a chart as a reference. Comparing line-of-sight angles on things we see is the most fundamental wayfinding technique there is, and we use it even when just walking across a room. It allows us on an instantaneous real-time basis to judge not only our position relative to objects around us, whether we know what they are or not, but also our speed as we move among them.

Crossing bearings is also the fundamental basis of any accurate offshore navigation system. This is especially true of electronic satellite navigation, where extremely precise real-time positions can be plotted by comparing angles of radio signals received from a constellation of flying transmitters. It is also true of its immediate predecessor, celestial navigation. It remains true all the way back to the earliest accurate offshore navigation performed by Polynesians in their voyages across the Pacific.

Instead of taking bearings on satellites or solely on celestial objects, Polynesians used all sorts of angles to help them find their way. When navigating they were totally plugged into their environment. Their system was celestial in that they had memorized, and had transmitted their memories orally through multiple generations, which stars rose and set over specific islands as viewed from other specific islands. Combining intricate knowledge of this web of angles with observed angles of prevailing wave trains, bird tracks, and cloud formations allowed them to orient themselves at sea, in a void with no obvious landmarks, in a way that modern mariners can scarcely conceive.

Simple celestial navigation seems boringly reductive by comparison, but it is the most environment-oriented offshore navigation system that Western technology has on offer. Become proficient in celestial and you not only have an excellent backup offshore navigation system to rely on should your electronics fail, you also have a medium through which you can bond more closely with both the sea beneath you and the sky above you as you voyage between them.

THOSE WHO ARE TRULY EXPERT at celestial navigation do seem to enjoy making it mysterious and incomprehensible to the rest of us. Joshua Slocum, for example, was extremely coy on the subject. Early on in his seminal *Sailing Alone Around the World*, the book that effectively launched the modern sport of bluewater cruising, he boasts of his five-and-dime alarm-clock chronometer and lets us believe he was quite casual about his navigation. Only much later, in an arch aside, does he note he was in fact a "lunarian," meaning he solved for longitude using the impossibly arcane lunar-distance method, and so did not need an accurate chronometer to fix his position.

In reality locating yourself at sea with a sextant can be pretty simple. You need not learn spherical trigonometry and differential calculus; you don't even need to learn how to use those gruesome-looking sight-reduction tables. All you really need is a sextant, an accurate quartz watch, and a current copy of the Nautical Almanac. With these you can always shoot the sun at noon and get a very good idea of your latitude and a rough idea of your longitude without having to do anything terribly complicated.

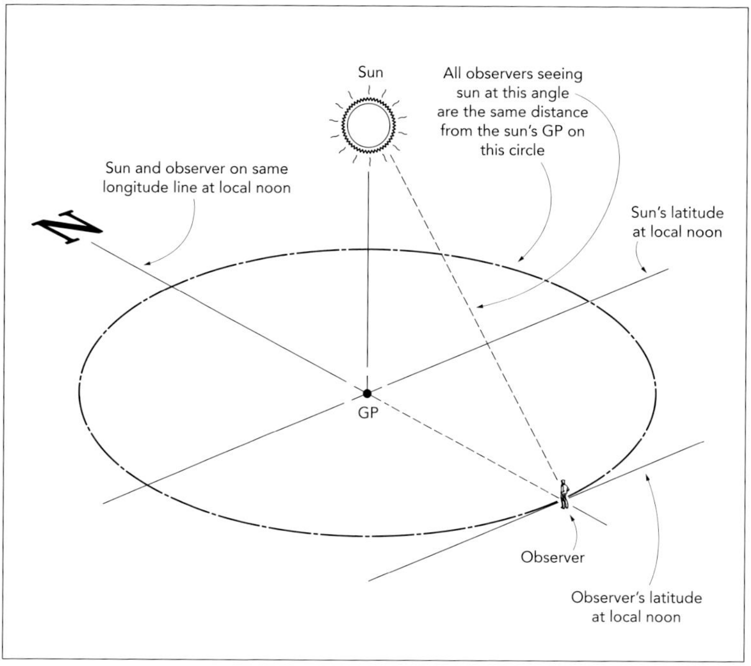

The angle defined by the observed altitude of the sun from an observer's location tells you how far the observer is from the sun's geographic position (GP). At local noon the observer's location and the sun's geographic position are on the same longitude line, and it is also very easy to calculate your latitude.

SOLVING FOR LATITUDE

Imagine the sun is aloft at the top a giant pole. You know the height of the pole and the location of the base of the pole, for these values can be accurately predicted by astronomers and are revealed in your Nautical Almanac. If you measure the angle between the ground and your line of sight to the sun (or, same difference, the altitude of the sun as it appears over the horizon from your location), you can figure out how far you are from the base of the pole.

All persons the same distance from the base of the pole as you are will see the sun at the same angle or altitude and can be ranged around the pole in a perfect circle of 360 degrees. This circle is one of your bearings, or one line of position (LOP). You can theoretically get a second LOP simply by taking a straight compass bearing on the sun. It will intersect the first LOP at your location.

In reality, however, compasses are not sensitive enough to take an accurate bearing on the sun or any other celestial body and can only provide a vague idea of where you are among the vast circle of observers surrounding the base of the sun's pole at any given time. The one time during the day when you can obtain a precise bearing on the sun is at local noon, when the sun as you see it is as high in the sky as it will get that day.

At the moment of local noon the sun is either directly north or south of you and any LOP obtained from it by measuring its altitude will coincide exactly with your latitude. Finding latitude from a noon sight is the simplest celestial nav calculation there is and yields very accurate results. It runs as follows:

1. Subtract the sun's precise observed altitude (in degrees, minutes, and seconds) at local noon from 90 degrees (the total number of degrees of latitude within your hemisphere). The result is called your Zenith Distance (ZD).

2. Look in your Nautical Almanac to see what the declination of the sun was to the nearest hour of when noon occurred at your location. (Note that the sun's declination is the same as the latitude of the base of the pole we imagine it is sitting upon.)

3. Add the sun's declination to ZD if you and the sun are in the same hemisphere; subtract it from ZD if you are not. This result is your latitude.

If you're so clueless you're not sure which hemisphere the sun is in, don't worry. The almanac has the answer. If you're not sure which hemisphere you are in, which normally only happens when you are very close to the equator and could be on either side, just run the equation both ways. One answer will make perfect sense; the other will be nonsense.

Even without a sextant or a Nautical Almanac, you can with experience roughly estimate your latitude by simply eyeballing the height of the sun at noon or, if you are in the northern hemisphere, the height of Polaris, the North Star, at any time it is visible. In ancient times this is how many mariners navigated, including the Vikings, who purportedly used hands and fingers held out at arm's length to measure the sun's altitude. They also, according to a legend that has recently been substantiated, used a crystal known as a "sunstone" to help them see exactly where the sun was on overcast days.

The ancient Arabs, as they navigated back and forth across the Indian Ocean, used a rather ingenious tool known as a kamal to help them gauge the North Star's altitude and thus their latitude. This was a simple wooden card of fixed dimensions with a small hole in the middle through which a string was run. Holding the card before them, Arab navigators would line up its bottom edge with the horizon and its top edge with the North Star and correlate its altitude to the distance between the card and the end of the string, which they held in their teeth. Knots were tied in the string to mark these distances and could be used to record either fixed units of angle measurement or the fixed angle at which the North Star should be kept when voyaging from one specific port to another.

For many centuries this sort of simple latitude navigation was state of the art. Its efficacy is obviously limited, as it yields just one LOP. But still, if you know the latitude of your destination and whether you are east or west of it, all you have to do to get there is sail first to that latitude line and then sail along it until you get to where you're going.

FINDING LONGITUDE

Since the sun is directly north or south of you at local noon, you and the sun must obviously be on the same longitude line at that time. If you know precisely what time noon occurred at your location, you can simply look in the Nautical Almanac to find your longitude. This will be same as the sun's Greenwich Hour Angle (GHA), which is equivalent to the longitude of the base of the pole upon which we have imagined the sun is suspended.

The tricky part is getting the exact time of the event. The sun moves quickly across the sky (or rather the Earth turns quickly), and even a couple of seconds of timing error will throw your position fix off by several miles. Even if you have a perfectly accurate watch, getting an exact time for noon is problematic. The sun always seems to hang at its highest (or meridian) altitude each day for a couple of minutes, and to time noon precisely you need to figure out exactly when the middle of that "hang time" is.

The technique I figured out for doing this is fairly straightforward. I get out my sextant 15 to 20 minutes before I expect noon to take place (you can easily get a rough estimate from the almanac) and take a leisurely series of sights as the sun climbs ever higher in the sky. The sights I feel good about I mark in my notebook with an asterisk.

After the sun reaches its meridian altitude, I preset the sextant to the altitudes for the three or four sights I felt were my best when the sun was going up and carefully record the time when the sun again hits those altitudes going back down. I then calculate the time spreads between each set of matched sights and figure out the midpoint of each spread. These times I then average together to arrive at a best estimate of when precisely noon took place.

CORRECTING SEXTANT SIGHTS

There are various fiddly corrections you need to make to any raw sextant sight, and this does complicate the business of taking noon sights. Before writing this I took some sights during a singlehanded passage between the West Indies and Bermuda—the first sextant sights I'd taken in many years—and remembering what corrections to make was what slowed me down the most.

Really, though, it's not a big deal. You may first need to make corrections for watch error, which means adding or subtracting a few seconds from your observation times if your watch tends to run a little fast or slow. To do this, you must know the rate at which your watch loses or gains time and will need to have figured this out in advance. These days you can most easily check your watch against perfectly accurate master clocks online (www.time.gov, for example, takes you to a clock maintained by the U.S. Naval Observatory), or you can still get time-check signals over a high-frequency radio from, among others, the U.S. government's WWV station, which broadcasts continuously on frequencies of 2.5, 5, 10, 15, and 20 MHz.

You may also need to correct for what is called "index error," which relates to small flaws in sextants, usually having to do with the mirrors, that cause altitude readings to be off slightly. This error is often variable (especially with plastic sextants), so you need to check it each time you use a sextant, which is easy to do. Just set your sextant angle at zero degrees, then peer through the sextant at the horizon. If the horizon is split you have some index error. Turn the sextant's micrometer dial, which controls the sextant angle, until the horizon is level, and then you can read off the amount of error and whether it is positive or negative.

There are also two other sight corrections you always have to make, even if your watch and sextant are perfect. The first is for dip, which relates to the height of your eye above the water when you take a sight. The second is called an altitude or diameter correction. This compensates for the fact that you are measuring the distance between the horizon and the bottom of the sun (or "lower limb," as it is called), rather than the center of the sun. The correction varies depending on the sun's altitude, as the apparent diameter of the sun varies depending on how much atmosphere you are seeing it through. (The closer to the horizon, the more atmospheric refraction there is, and hence the sun looks fatter.) Tables for both dip and altitude corrections appear in the Nautical Almanac.

QUICK-AND-DIRTY NOON SIGHTS IN PRACTICE

Classically trained celestial navigators usually take a series of three sun sights over the course of a day. The morning and noon sights are advanced according to the estimated course and distance traversed in the interim and are merged with an afternoon sight to create three different LOPs that criss-cross to produce what should be a very accurate fix as of the time of the last sun sight. The navigator also takes sights of various stars and planets at sunrise and sunset, during the brief intervals when both bright celestial bodies and the horizon are simultaneously visible, and consequently is busy for much of the day. This is why navigators on sailing vessels of old were treated as minor deities and never had to stand any watches.

A regimen like this obviously makes no sense for a modern navigator who merely wants to use celestial as a backup to electronic navigation. After I first took a formal celestial nav course in the early 1990s, I quickly deduced for myself the longitude-finding method described above and resolved only to take noon sights on a regular basis. A couple of hoary old salts I knew assured me that my quick-and-dirty longitude method was an insult to the art of celestial navigation, but I was very gratified when I later learned Bernard Moitessier used the same method on his voyages.

I was also gratified when I found it in fact works pretty well. While crossing the Atlantic for the first time on *Constellation* I took quick-and-dirty noon sights every day. Once I really got the hang of swinging a sextant and parking the sun's butt on the horizon, my noon fixes were routinely accurate within less than one mile on latitude and within five miles on longitude. In the age of GPS this seems grossly inaccurate, but if you're making a landfall after many days at sea, it should be good enough to get you where you want to be.

My most recent foray into the sky with my sextant was sobering. In a sense it accurately simulated the predicament I might find myself in if, after many years of not practicing, I had to break out a sextant after losing GPS service while at sea. My results were very good as to latitude (again, within one nautical mile), but very poor as to longitude (within 16 to 25 miles, over three days of sights). I am confident, however, given several days of practice, I could achieve my old level of accuracy. By far the hardest part of celestial navigation is handling a sextant and taking good sights on a moving boat with waves obstructing the horizon. The only way to get proficient is to do it repeatedly, which is why it isn't a bad idea to break out the sextant for some practice on every passage you take.

Still, even without practice, the sloppy sights I was taking as I approached Bermuda were not without value. With accurate latitude lines and fuzzy longitude lines you can still make safe landfalls by simply "running down your latitude" just like old-time navigators used to do. In this case, for example, coming at Bermuda from the south, if I had lost GPS service all I had do to was sail well east of Bermuda (the only port of entry, St. Georges, is on the east end of the island) and then approach it on the appropriate latitude line.

One valuable thing I learned by taking noon sights for the first time in so many years was just how broad my unpracticed margin of error could be. Now if I ever do need to sail down my latitude to make a landfall, I know I need to make sure I am at least 25 miles east or west of my destination before turning toward it.

SELECTING AND LEARNING TO USE A SEXTANT

No matter how many GPS receivers you have on board, it is a good idea to carry a sextant as a backup if you plan on doing much offshore sailing. You should also obviously learn how to use it. If you're truly dedicated you can learn from a book (I'd recommend trying *Celestial Navigation Step by Step*, by Warren Norville, or the classic *Celestial Navigation for Yachtsmen*, by Mary Blewitt), but it's much easier to have someone else show you. You can have a friend who already knows celestial teach you how to do it, or you can take a class. It's also a good idea to start out by taking sights on shore before trying it at sea.

If you really want to learn sextants, I think it's best to start out with a plastic one. The mirrors on these need a bit of tuning each time you use them, and this forces you to get good at it. They're also cheap and reasonably accurate. I used a plastic Davis Mark 15 sextant (new ones currently sell for around $180) during my voyage on *Constellation* and had good results, as described above. One big advantage to using a plastic sextant is that they are very light and easy to handle. They do not last forever, however, as eventually the plastic threads for the metal tuning screws on the mirrors wear away and it becomes impossible to tune the mirrors properly. Plastic sextants also tend to vibrate in high winds, so are not reliable when used in strong conditions.

When you're ready to move to a more durable metal sextant, you'll find there are still three or four manufacturers to choose from. The most popular is the Astra IIIB from China, which costs about $800 new. These are a great value and definitely give you the most bang for your buck. A very fine sextant, such as a top-of-the-line Cassens & Plath model, can cost over $2,000. Quality used sextants in good condition, meanwhile, normally sell for much less. These can be found online at eBay or at specialist websites like Landfall Navigation (landfallnavigation.com) and Celestaire (celestaire.com). If you find a used sextant you like that needs work, you can send it to Robert

White Instruments (robertwhite.com) and they will be happy to repair and refurbish it for you.

When selecting a sextant, you should be most interested in its mirrors. Large mirrors are easier to work with than small ones, as they capture more light and it is easier to keep errant celestial bodies within their boundaries. Full-horizon coated mirrors are easiest to use when shooting the sun, but the coating absorbs a fair amount of light and can make it difficult to shoot planets and stars. If you plan to take more than just noon sights you should opt for traditional split-horizon mirrors (or look for a sextant that allows you to change mirrors).

If you want to shoot stars and planets (including the moon), you should also invest in a celestial nav calculator, as this will save you from tearing your hair out over sight-reduction tables. A good nav calculator will have an almanac programmed into it, plus can identify stars for you, so you can shoot shiny objects first and ask questions later. With a tool like this you can easily forge all sorts of relationships with objects in the sky overhead.

I have often imagined an ideal instrument—a sextant with both a satellite-corrected quartz clock and a sophisticated nav calculator built into its handle. You could take a series of shots, pulling a trigger on the handle each time you bring a body, whatever it might be, down to the horizon, and then finally press a button to get a final result. The sextant would record the times and altitudes of each shot, identifying the bodies involved, run the numbers, and display your lat/long coordinates on a small LED screen.

Technologically this is perfectly feasible, but I doubt anyone will ever build such a device. There simply is no market for it, so instead celestial navigation must remain an archaic art, which may be for the best. This way those who take the trouble to join the ancient priesthood and learn the art can still feel a little superior to everyone else.

HEAVY-WEATHER SAILING

Too Much Wind and What to Do With It

The sky, it seems, would pour down stinking pitch
But that the sea, mounting to th' welkin's cheek,
Dashes the fire out.

—William Shakespeare, *The Tempest*

OCEAN-SAILING EPIPHANIES MAY COME in all shapes and sizes, but there is little doubt the most intense ones involve heavy weather. One tends to pay much closer attention to the sea when it is angry, and it is an awful truth of ocean sailing that there are just two sorts of sailors. There are those who, in spite of feeling afraid, derive an intense and perverse pleasure from the sea's anger, who can cast eyes across a field of breaking waves and perceive a scene of unparalleled beauty and perhaps even feel at one with the soul of the planet for being caught in the middle of it. And there are those who experience nothing but the fear.

It is a good idea to figure out which sort you are while sailing on a boat you are not responsible for. For it is possible to nurture a dream of sailing offshore and then suddenly feel that dream morph into a nightmare once you actually get offshore. I have in a few instances been paid to take groups of the uninitiated out on their first passages and have sometimes witnessed this at first hand.

The most dramatic example was a fellow named Roger, a doctor from Tennessee, who joined a crew of five I once led on a fall delivery from

Newport, Rhode Island, south to St. Martin in the West Indies on a Swan 46. Roger was very full of the dream. He had read all the books and owned a boat he sailed on a lake near his home. When he retired he planned to buy a bigger boat and become a full-time bluewater cruiser.

As so often happens in the fall we rode the coattails of a cold front out of Newport and had strong wind and seas behind us from the very start. Roger's eyes were wide with apprehension when I asked him to take a turn steering that first afternoon, and within minutes of his touching the wheel he was caught by surprise by the power of one wave passing beneath us and was thrown hard across the cockpit. He immediately diagnosed himself as having broken one or more ribs and took himself below. He made himself a nest in the forward V-berth—which was considerate, as it left the better sea berths in the middle of the boat open for working crew—and remained inert there, save for one foray to the galley for food, for the rest of our four-day passage.

During the worst of it we were running off through the Gulf Stream getting chased by squalls with long sustained gusts over 50 knots. We had the mainsail triple-reefed, and just before sunset on our second day out its luff slides started blowing out one by one, moving up the mast track like a giant zipper unzipping. I called out all hands, save for Roger, to help douse the sail. We struggled to scrape the sail inch by inch off the spreaders and then raised a storm jib on a removable inner forestay, under which we sailed the rest of the way to Bermuda.

The moment we tied up at the customs dock in St. Georges Roger was magically revived and popped out the companionway like a jack-in-the-box. He showed no sign of being injured and had already packed his bag. He shook hands with each of us in turn, thanked us fervently for saving his life, and then explained himself: "Now I know for sure. I'm a lake sailor."

This was an expensive lesson, as Roger had paid several thousand dollars in fees and airfare to join us and now was jumping ship just halfway to St.

Martin. But it was also a fantastic bargain, as he would have squandered much more had he pursued his dream and bought his own bluewater boat without first conducting this experiment.

Even if you've passed such a test, there are a series of thresholds you cross as you gain experience sailing in strong conditions. Some have to do with the amount of responsibility you assume on a boat, but most have to do with the amount of wind you are sailing in. The simple physics of the matter are daunting, for increases in the strength of the wind are not simply sequential. A doubling of wind speed does not translate to the wind blowing twice as strong as before. Rather the equation is exponential, and the driving force of the wind increases in proportion to the square of the wind's speed. A 10-knot breeze (10x10=100) generates slightly more than twice the force of a 7-knot breeze (7x7=49), and a 20-knot breeze (20x20=400) is four times as strong as 10-knot breeze. A 40-knot breeze (40x40=1600), officially strong enough to be termed a gale, is four times as strong again, or 16 times more forceful than that 10-knot breeze you'd much rather be sailing in.

MY OWN INITIATION into sailing in heavy wind at sea on a boat I commanded myself came on my very first passage aboard *Crazy Horse*, from Newport to Bermuda in early July 1995. I had two experienced crew with me, and I had some experience myself, but still I was unnerved by the weather we found. Already there had been two named storms in the North Atlantic, so I should have twigged to the fact that the weather gods were warming up their arms early for hurricane season. The first storm, Alison, had been a gutter-ball. She was born south of Cuba, then hooked up through the south-eastern U.S. and degenerated into a warm wet blob off the Carolinas. The second, Barry, was a clean shot straight up the bowling alley all the way to Nova Scotia.

We had some warning of the third shot. We were lying to a fuel dock at

Goat Island in Newport, topping off on water and diesel before heading out, and one of my crew, Tim, who had spent part of his childhood on a bluewater boat, conscientiously volunteered to go check on the weather one more time. He returned a few minutes later with an ambivalent report.

"It looks clear," he said. "Except there is a little tropical wave east of Antigua."

I wish I could tell you that I digested this information and coolly calculated the risk involved. After all, what were the odds that this one kink in the normally smoothed-out barometric isobars of the tropics, more than 1,600 miles away from us, would deform into a closed loop, send a whirlwind of convection rising up through the atmosphere, and then careen in just two or three days on a path that might intersect our own? Surely they must have been small.

What really happened was that I simply dismissed the information, which at that point in my career I didn't fully understand. I had been scrambling madly for six weeks to prepare my boat for sea, and now I was eager to get going. I wasn't about to let this seemingly small anomaly stop me.

We spent three days sailing southeast on a hard close reach, had crossed the Gulf Stream, and were just 100 miles from Bermuda when I switched on my portable shortwave radio receiver shortly after coming on watch at 0600 hours on July 17. The news that emerged from it, courtesy of the National Weather Service's November Mike November station in Norfolk, Virginia, was certainly disquieting. Our tropical wave was now a tropical storm, Chantal, and was headed straight for us. Even worse, she was forecast to achieve hurricane status by mid-afternoon.

Now finally, inspired by the anxiety that gripped my mind, I tried to analyze the situation as closely as I could. Coincidentally, our news had arrived during the first lull in the wind we'd experienced since leaving Newport, so the very first thing we did was start the engine and pile on for Bermuda.

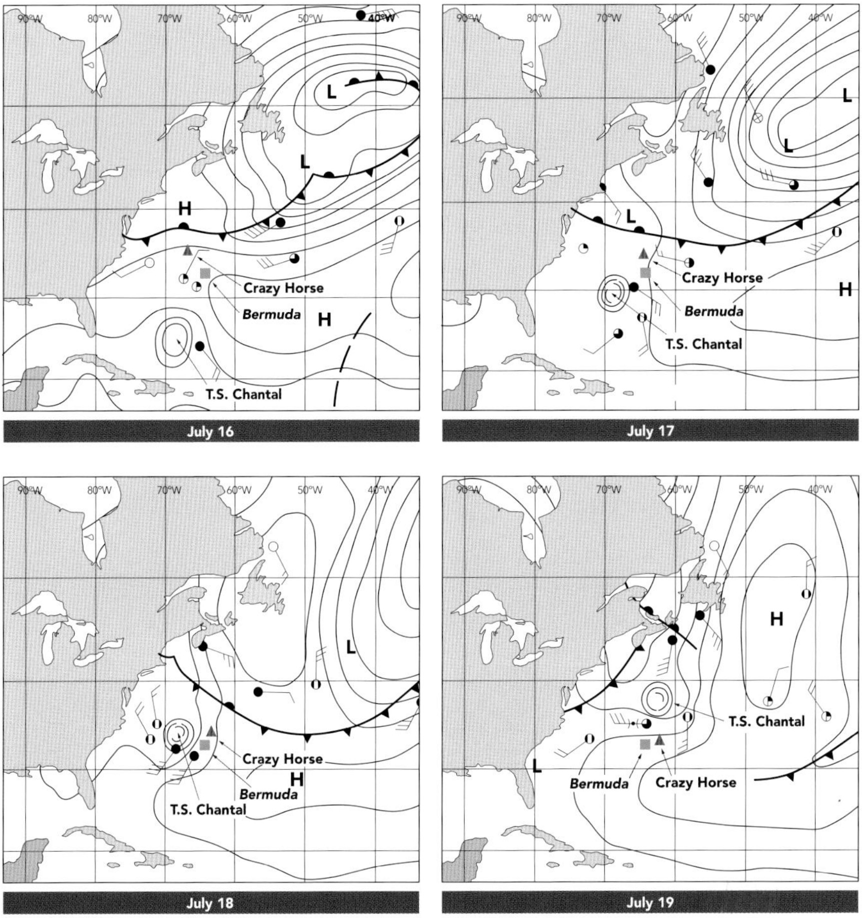

To keep our distance from the center of Chantal
we had to sail past Bermuda and then beat to windward back to it.

Plotting the storm's projected track on our chart, I could see she would pass west of us, so it seemed obvious we should not go in that direction. We had no chance of getting west of the storm before it reached our latitude, and we certainly didn't want to go back into the Gulf Stream and find it there. This meant we were committed to the storm's right side, the so-called dangerous sector, where the speed of its wind would be augmented by the speed of its forward motion.

By 1300 hours that afternoon the wind had returned and was blowing 20 knots straight against us. We carried little fuel, just 35 gallons, and had already burned at least five of those, so we had no hope of motoring very far dead into the wind and building seas. We had to start sailing again, which meant we had to decide: port tack or starboard?

If our goal was simply to get to Bermuda as quickly as possible, port tack was obviously the way to go. As the storm passed by us the wind it generated as we experienced it would veer, shifting from southeast to south to southwest to west. Port tack would be favored slightly in the first part of this progression, then we could tack over toward the end of it and steadily ease sheets while sailing straight toward our destination. But this would also inevitably pull us in ever closer to the heart of the storm.

Starboard tack was the safer option, as it put the most distance between us and the center of the storm. Of course this is what we chose to do, but sailing on starboard tack also put the most distance between us and Bermuda. In the end, thankfully, Chantal never did become a hurricane and the storm center missed us by almost 200 miles. For at least 12 hours, however, it definitely looked like it was homing in on us. I remember Tim wore the same pair of sweatshorts every day, and for a while I was convinced those damn shorts had something to with our predicament. I imagined them getting warmer and moister with each passing hour, and I imagined, too, that the storm, like the Nazgûl seeking the One Ring, had sensed their presence and was drawn to them.

We didn't see the worst of the wind, 35 knots, until after the storm had passed north of our latitude. I had sailed in 35 knots before, so this never seemed cataclysmic, but we were closehauled through all of it and had to sail well east of Bermuda before we could finally beat up to it. Ultimately it took us two full days to sail the last 40 miles to the island. During all that time the seawater mimosas, as I liked to call the flying sheets of spray that constantly passed over us, were served up overhand in 10-gallon buckets. The motion as we slammed into the oncoming seas was quite violent, and *Crazy Horse*'s low-slung deck was continuously drenched. We had water in our faces, down our necks, up our sleeves. It was, to this day, my wettest experience ever on a boat.

As it turned out, the 1995 hurricane season was rather dramatic and marked the beginning of a trend of strong seasons that reached a crescendo 10 years later when Hurricane Katrina destroyed the city of New Orleans. Every single tropical wave in 1995 developed into a tropical depression. Every depression save two became a storm. Eleven of the 19 named storms became full-fledged hurricanes. I had learned my lesson about carefully picking weather windows, one of a skipper's key responsibilities when sailing offshore, and I was if anything gun-shy the rest of that year. I managed to get out of Bermuda just before Felix, a Category 4 hurricane, pasted the island in August, and then weathered two more storms, Noel and Tanya, while tied to a dock in a marina in the Azores. Soon afterward, when I read the season might run on into December and they were dusting off the Greek alphabet so as to have extra storm names just in case, I got spooked and decided to stay put for the winter.

I didn't have to cope with sailing in heavy wind again until the following spring when I started cruising around the Azores. I had by then taken up with an adventurous Dutch woman, Carie, who lived in the Azores and whom I first met while passing through on *Constellation* three years earlier. We had put into the town of Velas on the island of São Jorge, where in those days there was nothing but a short seawall for visiting yachts to land on. We had been there only a day when the harbormaster suddenly asked us to leave. The monthly freighter was coming in ahead of schedule, he explained, and needed to land on the wall immediately.

Peering out the companionway, I could see the ship was just about a mile away. Before I knew what was happening, the very instant I started my engine, the harbormaster and his assistant suddenly cast off our lines. *Crazy Horse*'s starboard aft quarter smashed into the wall as I pulled away from it and her caprail was smashed to splinters. Then, soon after we cleared the harbor and started sailing toward Faial, just 15 miles away, in a seemingly sedate 12-knot breeze, an unforecast gale suddenly blew in. It came from the southwest, which was exactly the direction we wanted to go.

My eyes nearly popped out of my head as I watched the numbers on the wind-speed display pump higher and higher. These were numbers larger than any I'd seen before, and they inspired something like panic in my mind. The laws of nature, I feared, had been cancelled. It seemed the wind might do whatever it wanted—increase to some impossible velocity, obliterate us, and leave no trace of our existence.

Instinctively I turned the boat downwind. This decreased the apparent wind speed and is always much more comfortable than sailing upwind. With the mainsail doused and just a scrap of jib unrolled I found the boat was perfectly under control. It felt as though we were on rails as the Monitor windvane steered us down the ever-growing seas on an unwavering broad reach. Carie lay seasick on the leeward berth in the saloon, and I lay on the cabin sole fully dressed in my foul-weather gear with my heart in my mouth.

Every 15 minutes or so I climbed up to the cockpit. I marveled at how well the boat was behaving in this breeze I had until then thought must be much too strong to sail in. I also fretted over the condition of the backstay. I had just installed a new one, which had come up just an inch or so short, and I'd made up the difference with a stainless-steel shackle I found in my bag of rigging spares. Now the shackle was slowly deforming under the force of the wind, and I worried it might at any moment snap and that we would then be dismasted.

We sailed on in this way, running off in the general direction of Iceland, for most of that day. I kept studying the bent shackle every few minutes, debating whether I should turn the boat upwind to reduce the strain on it, but I couldn't bring myself to face into that awful blast of wind. Finally, however, in the early evening, it subsided just as mysteriously and suddenly as it had come up. We were by then many miles north of Faial, and it took all that night and most of the next day to sail back down to it. Once there, safe and sound in the marina in Horta, I immediately replaced the deformed shackle with a much stronger one. I then spent two more days repairing the damage to my caprail.

I LEARNED A GREAT DEAL from this experience, and I think of it often. The apparent wind speed that day in fact topped out in the mid-50s, which meant the true wind was probably a little over 60, and the fact that it was possible to keep sailing in such a breeze seemed revelatory. This is the unfailing pattern. You sail in more wind than you ever thought possible, are reassured that it is feasible, but believe you may have reached the limits of that feasibility, until you sail in even more wind. I have sailed in winds over 50 knots on a few more occasions since that day in the Azores, most memorably to windward for the better part of two days in a perfectly miserable Sydney–Hobart Race. It was literally painful, as the spray flying down the deck felt like gravel blasted out of a cannon, but it was doable.

I also figured out sometime later that my decision to run off before the wind that day was, in that particular instance, not necessarily the best one. Though at the time I assumed the breeze that assaulted us was meteorological, I eventually realized it was more likely a topographical phenomenon. When the ambient wind shifted southwest that morning and perhaps also increased a few knots in strength, I now believe it must have set up a wind-acceleration zone between the very high island of Pico to the east and the less

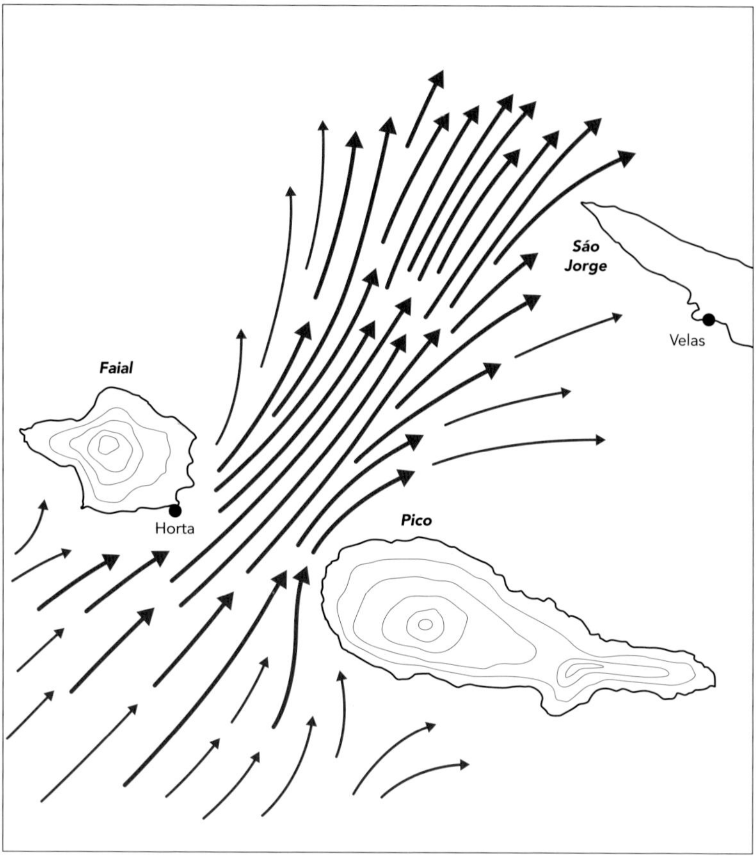

The height of the land around you can have very dramatic effects on wind speed, even if the land doesn't look very high from a distance.

high but still lofty island of Faial to the west. Carie and I aboard *Crazy Horse* were caught in this alley of greatly reinforced wind and ended up running down the length of it by bearing off and putting the breeze on our quarter. If instead we had bitten the bullet and endured the enhanced discomfort of sailing at a much tighter angle to the wind, we might have gotten out of the acceleration zone much sooner.

As a general rule, however, the principle of keeping a heavy breeze on your transom whenever possible is a good one. This is true not only in strategic situations, when you are trying to cope with an intense weather system, but also in tactical ones, where you simply would like to perform a potentially onerous sail-handling chore in a calmer, more deliberate manner.

Take for example the simple business of rolling up your headsail, whether you are furling it altogether or simply making it smaller. If you do this when you are sailing on the wind in a breeze of any strength, it will seem a violent experience. The sail will flog angrily when you release its sheet, and the load on the furling line as you roll the sail up will be quite heavy. In very strong conditions there is some risk of damaging the sail, and the free-flying sheets may tie themselves into what are known as wind-knots as they are whipped about by the sail.

You can avoid all this by turning downwind before you do anything. The boat's motion will be easier, the apparent wind speed will be reduced, and if you turn far enough downwind the headsail will be buried in the lee of the mainsail. It will then be limp, and rolling it up will be easier and much less dramatic.

This tactic can save trouble and anxiety in all sorts of situations. Pretty much anything you might have to do with a headsail—be it a jib, genoa, staysail, spinnaker, or some other modern-named something-or-other—is easier to do if you are sailing off the wind. The same is true of any job you might need to perform forward of the mast, even if it's only to secure a loose piece of gear: it will always be much safer and easier if you do it while sailing downwind.

This may feel counterproductive. Going the wrong way, even for only a few moments, may seem like the wrong thing to do, but the cost of giving up some distance to leeward is outweighed by the benefits. If you need any proof of that, consider that this is the modus operandi of sailors who race boats like IMOCA Open 60s singlehanded around the world in events like the Vendée Globe. The Open 60 sailors I've sailed with, even when tacking a genoa around a staysail stay in very moderate conditions, will bear away downwind to roll up the sail before tacking over and unrolling it again, all just to save stressing the sail. And they will turn downwind as far as they can, as a boat moves more slowly sailing at its deepest apparent wind angle and less distance is lost that way.

HERE'S ANOTHER LITTLE SECRET about sailing off the wind in heavy weather: it is just plain fun. If indeed you are one of those people who enjoys sailing across an angry sea, you will quickly learn that steering a boat downwind through large waves is exhilarating. Done properly it is one of the peak experiences in the sport and is something many experienced sailors look forward to.

The safest way to transit very large seas is by quartering them rather than sailing dead downwind. With the wind right aft a boat is apt to roll badly, and it is then much easier for a following sea to throw the boat's stern far enough out of line to backwind a sail, which in turn can lead to a bad broach and perhaps a knockdown or capsize. If instead you sail on a broad reach with the boat running at an angle to the waves, rolling is reduced, it is much harder to backwind a sail, and it is easier for the helmsperson to maintain control and steer around breaking seas.

When sailing over large waves at an angle, whether you are going upwind or down, the fastest, smoothest course is never a straight line. Instead you want to do what is called sculling the waves, sailing a more scalloped course that matches the vertical shape of the seas. This is particularly important when sailing upwind. Beating to weather in heavy seas, a poor helmsperson who doesn't scull the waves properly will often bring the boat to a near standstill by pinching too close to the wind, or will fall off the wind too far and let

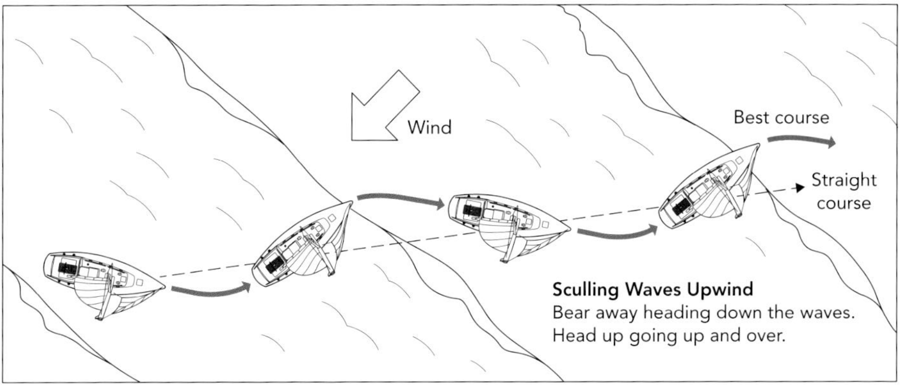

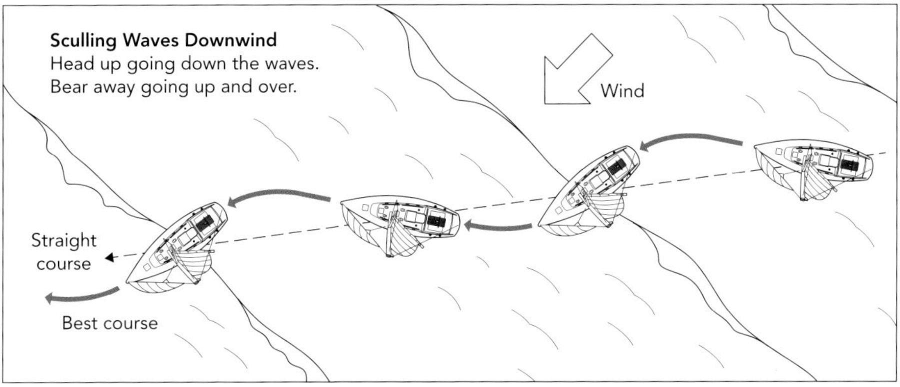

The smoothest route through a field of waves, whether you're going upwind or down, is a scalloped course that itself looks like a series of waves.

the boat get pushed down on to a beam reach. To prevent this you need to fall into a simple pattern, pinching the boat to weather a little as it approaches a wave crest and bearing away again as it sails down the back of the wave into the trough behind it.

Sailing off the wind, to achieve the same result, you need to reverse the pattern. As a wave crest approaches the stern of your boat you should bear away a bit, and once the crest is past you should head up a little.

The end result in both cases is the same: at the wave crest the boat is depowered slightly, with the bow or stern closer to the eye of the wind; heading down into the trough the apparent wind angle is increased and the boat is more powered up. Sailing to windward this allows a boat to get over the top of each wave with less resistance and reduces the chance of it flying off crests and slamming down into troughs. Sailing off the wind it keeps the hull flatter as the wave crests approach, reduces torsional twist on the stern that can lead to a broach, and sets the boat up to perhaps surf down the front of the wave. Powering up the boat as it heads into the troughs in both cases increases control and speed, so you can more easily avoid obstacles and negotiate the next wave crest as it approaches.

The illustrations show a simplified view of wave-sculling courses upwind and downwind with the course adjustments exaggerated a bit for clarity. As a general rule, larger waves require larger corrections. In the real world wave patterns are also normally less organized, with two or more wave trains interacting with each other. Steering over or around offline waves, and of course avoiding breaking waves when possible, will require additional course adjustments.

Another factor not accounted for in the drawings is surfing downwind, which is where the fun and exhilaration comes in. This happens to some extent even in a traditional heavy-displacement boat, but is more common when sailing in more modern light-displacement boats with shallow bilges. Once a hull breaks loose and starts surfing down a wave, you are basically riding the wave crest and you'll feel a very satisfying and thrilling acceleration. This is when a boat most readily exceeds its theoretical hull speed, and the lighter the boat the more excessive its speed will be. On many boats you will simply maintain course while surfing and then head up a bit after the crest passes to set up for the next wave. On faster boats you may want to head up a bit while surfing to make up for the loss of apparent wind speed and to keep the boat surfing longer.

The best helmspeople automatically scull waves as they steer a boat through heavy seas. They feel the boat under them as they steer and instinctively head up and bear away as waves pass beneath them, whether they are conscious of what they are doing or not. Even if you are not a naturally talented helmsperson, however, you can learn to do this if you apply yourself and open your mind to the relationship between your boat and the water around it.

Body position while steering is particularly important. You need to find a posture in which you can comfortably grasp the wheel or tiller and can easily feel how the boat is moving under you. This is largely subjective, and different people steer better in different positions. Some people can feel a boat easily through their butts and can sit while steering; many more feel a boat best while standing with their legs spread wide. Compromise positions, where you sit with one leg braced against a vertical cockpit feature, like a coaming, footwell side, or wheel pedestal, can also be effective.

By steering with your body in its most perceptive position, you'll find it is easier to react to the boat's motion. As a wave crest approaches you will feel your boat's bow or stern rise with it, and once you are experienced the nature of this motion will tell you a great deal. Depending on its speed and torsional twist, you can sense the size and shape of each wave and its direction relative to other waves and should be able to steer the cleanest course over or, in some cases, around it.

Vision, of course, also plays an important role. Steering to windward in daylight you can easily see approaching waves and can make course adjustments accordingly. If you don't scull waves instinctively, this is usually the best way to learn when starting out. When steering downwind with waves behind you, or at night when it is much harder to see them, you can also rely on your hearing a bit. Your ears can easily tell you when a wave is breaking.

Listening to the pattern of noises waves make as they pass in conjunction with their motion can also tell you something about the size and angle of an approaching wave, even if it isn't breaking.

Getting good at all this, even if you do have an instinctive feel for it, does require practice. It is always tempting to let an autopilot or windvane do the steering for you, but the bigger the seas are, the less efficient these devices will be, as they normally cannot scull waves. Unless you have a very advanced autopilot with multi-axis sensors like those now used on singlehanded ocean racers, you need a human on the helm to steer the cleanest course in rough conditions. Which isn't to say you must always steer your boat when the weather is bad, but the more time you spend steering in bad weather, the more confident you will feel sailing in it.

THE GOOD NEWS IF YOU are still nervous about sailing in heavy weather (or the bad news, if you truly do enjoy it) is that usually you don't have to do it too often. In this age of enhanced forecasting and communications it isn't hard to pick comfortable weather windows as long as you are patient, have some time in hand, and are sailing at the proper time of year in appropriate latitudes. All bets are off, however, if you want to sail to more extreme destinations or if you are pushing the edge of a season in a potentially volatile area.

Even if you don't care to gamble like this, it is a good idea to be prepared. First and foremost you should have a stout vessel you have faith in. I have already described at some length what this means in my book *The Modern Cruising Sailboat* (International Marine, 2010), and if you have doubts about your own vessel I urge you to consult it.

Assuming a sound vessel, my primary recommendations are as follows:

Appropriate sails and rig. Traditionally this meant carrying a storm trysail to fly in place of your mainsail and also a storm jib. If you have a heavily constructed mainsail with a deep third reef, most agree now you can leave the trysail behind. It is important, however, to be able to reliably reef your mainsail while sailing downwind. This can be problematic on some boats with in-mast furling mainsails or with very swept-back spreaders on their masts.

Whether you really need a storm jib is more of a question, depending on your rig. If you have a cutter rig with a sturdy roller-furling staysail, you can probably leave off a storm jib, though it isn't a bad idea to carry one anyway, in case you lose the ability to roller-reef your staysail. If your staysail isn't on a furler, you should either have reef-points in the staysail, so you can reduce its size, or you should have a storm jib to fly in its place.

If you are a sailing a sloop, you absolutely need some sort of storm jib. Assuming your regular headsail is on a roller-furler, you might try something like the ATN Gale Sail, which is designed to be hoisted over a rolled-up headsail. Or you could fit a removable inner forestay on which to fly a conventional storm jib.

Precisely because you are much more likely to be sailing in too little wind rather than too much, you should also give thought to the other end of your sail inventory. Some good light-air headsails—an asymmetric spinnaker perhaps, or a light gennaker—will save much fuel and many engine hours.

Self-steering and emergency steering. Though I have just urged you to spend time steering by hand in bad weather so as to get the hang of it, you also should have a self-steering system you can rely on when conditions are gnarly. This is especially true if you are sailing shorthanded. Modern autopilots are much more dependable and energy-efficient than they were when I started sailing offshore, and most sailors rely solely on these now, but I still believe it is a good idea to have a self-steering windvane, at least as a backup. If you follow this advice, you must of course also learn how to use a vane.

Emergency steering is more or less important depending on what sort of steering system you have. If you sail a boat with a long full keel to which a rudder is very firmly attached, and said rudder is turned with a tiller, pretty much all you have to worry about is breaking the tiller. If you sail a boat with a fine high-aspect spade rudder, you need to think about what happens when that rudder is gone.

There are various ways to make up for a missing rudder. If your boat has a yawl rig and a long keel, you may be able to steer just by trimming sails. Some windvane systems incorporate auxiliary rudders that can steer a boat if the main rudder is lost. Servo-pendulum vanes have steering oars that can be turned into rudders with some modifications. A dedicated emergency rudder can also be designed and fit on to most any boat. But the simplest solution is to carry a drogue. When streamed behind a boat on a bridle a drogue can serve as crude, yet effective steering system.

On boats with steering wheels the most common failures involve the steering quadrant (which is mounted on the rudder stock above the boat's waterline) and the apparatus that controls it. Almost all such boats have emergency tillers that can be installed directly on the head of the rudder stock in case of such a failure, but you need to be sure any such tiller is actually functional. An autopilot with a steering ram that has an independent connection to the rudder stock can also save the day in these situations.

Interior security. Advice here usually begins with an admonition: imagine your boat is turned upside down. A traditionalist will tell you that in this situation nothing inside should come loose, except perhaps the pencil you use to mark your position on your chart. And maybe the chart itself. Which is obviously absurd. Realistically there is no way to prevent all hell from breaking loose, but you do need to be sure that important heavy objects such as the engine, the batteries, and the stove are absolutely secure. Potentially troublesome lesser items, such as galley knives and large floorboards, as well as essential tools and other useful items you want to be sure of locating after hell has broken loose, should also be secure.

WHEN IT COMES TO BOAT-HANDLING TACTICS in truly extreme survival situations I have no firsthand knowledge to share with you, which should give you some idea of how unlikely it is you will ever be in such a situation. I have never deployed a sea anchor or drogue in extremis, though I have hove-to in several instances. This is an important trick to learn. It can be used not only to deal with heavy weather, but also in any situation where you want to "park" for a while to get some rest or to perform an important job (like fixing something or cooking and eating a meal) in relative peace and quiet.

My most educational experience came in the fall of 1998, when I sailed as first mate on a Swan 48 in Steve Black's Caribbean 1500 rally, which that year sent two squadrons of boats—one from Newport, Rhode Island, and another from Hampton, Virginia—down to Tortola in the British Virgin Islands. The Hampton boats ended up tangling with the remnants of Hurricane Mitch, and though I sailed from Newport and sat out the storm in Bermuda, Steve ran a fantastic debriefing seminar after everyone reached Tortola. Here crews had a chance to directly compare different tactics they had employed.

The first thing to note is how remarkably unstable the weather can be on this very popular route at this time of year. Mitch had originally formed as Tropical Depression 13 south of Jamaica on October 22 and within just four days became the fourth strongest Atlantic storm of the 20th century, a fearsome Category 5 hurricane with sustained winds of 150 knots and gusts to 170. The storm stalled off the north coast of Honduras before grinding into Central America, where it caused flooding and mudslides that killed nearly 10,000 people, the third highest Atlantic-storm death toll in history. But by October 31, when our squadron of 14 boats left Newport, and November 1, when the other 40 boats left Hampton, almost 2,000 miles away, Mitch had been downgraded to a tropical depression and was dying fast in the mountains of the Pacific coast of Guatemala.

The next day, November 2, as the Hampton squadron pottered on toward the Virgin Islands in light air, Mitch was officially nonexistent. Then, on the afternoon of November 3, the storm suddenly reappeared over the Bay of Campeche on the west side of Mexico's Yucatan peninsula, regained strength, and quickly moved northeast. Over the next 48 hours it covered a distance of about 1,100 miles, crossing the Yucatan, the Gulf of Mexico, and southern Florida. By the afternoon of November 5 Mitch was extratropical, but still packed winds of over 50 knots. It was still moving northeast at about 30 knots and had the bulk of our Hampton squadron dead in its sights.

For those of us who had left from Newport and were by now in Bermuda, Mitch was something of a holiday. We laid out extra anchors and docklines, monitored for chafe and displaced fenders, and watched the harbor at St. Georges get swept by 50-knot winds. The storm center passed 60 miles north of the island that morning, on November 6, and that evening we had a party at the St. Georges Dinghy Club. In the midst of this celebration, rally officials delivered up the first sobering bits of news from the Hampton squadron.

Circe, a Kadey-Krogen 38, had been abandoned, purportedly because her crew was severely seasick. *Kampeska*, a Tayana 42, had been dismasted, and her crew was injured, waiting to be airlifted off the boat. At least one boat had turned back to the U.S.; several others were diverting for Bermuda.

Only later, at the debriefing seminar on Tortola, were we able to piece together a more complete picture of what had happened. Mitch, we learned, caught the Hampton boats starting at about 1800 hours on November 5 and was the dominant factor in their reality into the early hours of the next morning. As the storm approached, boats scattered north and south trying to avoid it, but the bulk of the squadron was caught on the depression's south side in its "dangerous" semicircle, and suffered through 50-knot sustained winds, with gusts over 60, for about six hours. A handful of boats were far enough south that they experienced top wind speeds of less than 30 knots, but the storm's swath was very wide. Boats as far as 180 miles from the storm's center experienced gale-force winds of 35 knots or better.

During the debriefing some skippers complained of "confusing and inconsistent" weather communications, and Steve Black readily acknowledged this had been a problem. Confusing weather information certainly seemed to play a role in the abandoning of *Circe*. Contrary to early reports, only two of the five people aboard were seasick, and an e-mail account I later received from the boat's owner, Chris Stevenson, made clear she was abandoned because weather communications led the crew to believe they had been trapped by the storm.

According to Stevenson, during radio chats on November 3 the fleet was urged to move southeast as quickly as possible. On the morning of November 4, *Circe* and other boats in the northernmost part of the fleet were advised by Steve Black to keep pressing on in that direction. But then that evening, via a secondhand VHF transmission, Stevenson was told he must sail northwest to avoid the storm. *Circe*, at that point, was beset by strong winds and seas from the northwest, the crew was tired from hand-steering, and Stevenson did not believe the boat could make significant progress in that direction.

"I considered continuing southeast," Stevenson wrote to me, "but I assumed the advice not to continue that way was well-founded. I went below and tried without success to raise someone on the SSB radio. I then asked my crew to think over our situation and offer independent judgments about our options. No one offered a solution, so I reluctantly introduced the possibility of seeking rescue."

Stevenson lit off *Circe*'s EPIRB that evening, and by 0200 hours on November 5 he and his crew had abandoned the boat and were aboard a freighter that diverted to meet them. *Circe* had suffered no damage, and her position at the time she was abandoned was more than 120 miles north of the storm's track, in its "safe" semicircle, when it reached the area 16 hours later.

Meanwhile, most boats in the fleet chose the much less drastic alterna-

This is the traditional method of heaving-to, which usually works best with traditional boats that have long full keels. In practice every boat heaves-to differently. On modern boats it may take a lot of experimenting to figure out what works best.

tive of heaving-to during the worst of the weather and survived in good form.

"It was like a parking lot out there," said Bob Brickman, owner of *Peregrine*, a Morris 40. "We all just stopped our boats, lay down to rest for a while, then picked up and started sailing again when the wind went down."

A couple of skippers who had no experience heaving-to elected not to try it and continued sailing, though some found this tiring. Some went ahead and tried it for the first time and were very pleased with the results. The most experienced offshore sailors—including Steve Black himself, who was sailing his Hunter 54 *Caribbean*—preferred to simply run off with the storm and pick up easting, which is always useful when trying to sail from the U.S. to the Caribbean.

Crews on a handful of boats decided to deploy parachute-style sea anchors, which are designed to hold a boat in place with its head to the wind. No one who did this, however, was able to recover their gear again.

"It worked great," said Jim Hagy of the ParaTech chute he used to anchor *Blue Devil*, his Caliber 38. "Only they never told me when I bought the damn thing that it was disposable."

Hagy explained to me that the small dinghy fender he used as a float on the end of his sea anchor's retrieval trip-line did not have enough windage to blow it downwind of the anchor. Hagy could not reach the float from his boat, and in the end had to cut the anchor free to resume sailing. On another boat, *Endymion*, a Freedom 40, efforts to set a sea anchor were abandoned after the trip-line failed to deploy and the anchor's rode wrapped around the boat's propeller.

The crew on *Kampeska*, the only boat in the fleet that suffered serious damage, chose to lie ahull during the storm. This worked through the worst of the weather during the night of November 5, but at some point the next morning *Kampeska* was rolled by a very large wave and dismasted. The skipper, Roy Olson, suffered a severe back injury, and two of the other three

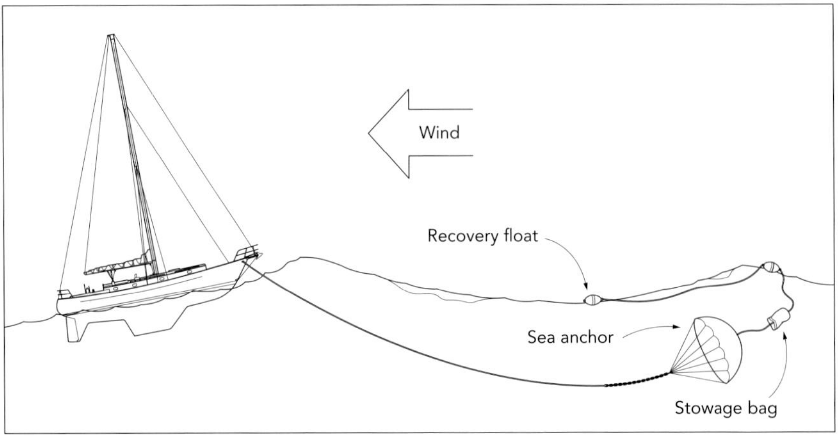

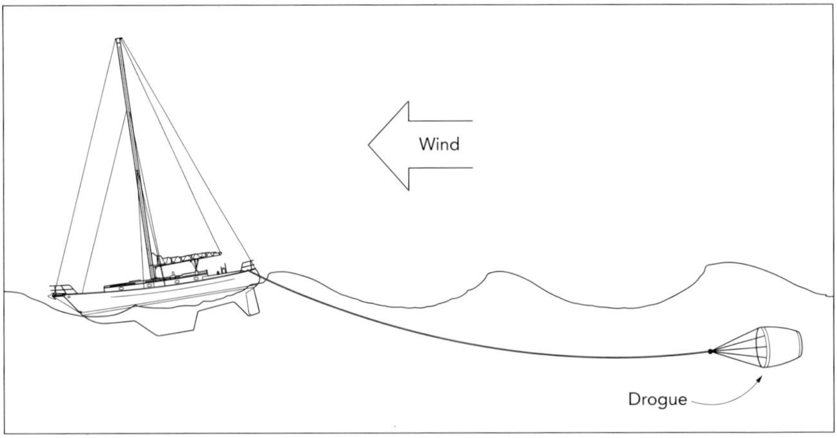

A sea anchor is a very large drag device designed to hold a boat with its head to the wind and seas as it drifts to leeward as little as possible. A drogue is a much smaller drag device that is normally streamed astern so as to slow a boat down as it runs off before very large seas.

crew suffered lacerations and broken ribs. The boat's EPIRB was activated at 0606 hours. A passing tanker and another rally boat, *Elixir*, a Bristol 41, diverted to her position and stood by until the morning of November 7, when a U.S. Coast Guard helicopter finally arrived to evacuate the crew to a hospital on Bermuda.

One other boat that lay ahull during the storm—*Perseverance*, a Tayana 42—fared significantly better. Her owners, Jack and Abbie Fassnacht, decided to adopt the tactic only after they failed to get the boat to heave-to, but reported they were relatively comfortable and suffered no damage. During the worst of it, Abbie even managed to bake a cherry pie from scratch, an accomplishment that drew vigorous applause from the large crowd at the debriefing.

To me the lessons to be learned from all this seemed fairly clear. In conditions like these, strong gale-force winds that do not actually rise to "survival" levels, the most successful tactics were either to heave-to or keep sailing and run off downwind. Significantly, several skippers at the debriefing stated they wished they had practiced heaving-to prior to the storm.

As *Kampeska*'s experience illustrated, lying ahull entails serious risks. *Kampeska*'s position when she was rolled was close to the track of the storm center, where seas were most confused and most likely to generate breaking rogue waves. In situations like this especially, I have always believed more active tactics should be employed if at all possible.

As for those folks who deployed sea anchors, I honestly don't think it was necessary in those circumstances. Not that it did any harm, but if they had first practiced using the gear in calmer conditions I'm sure they would have had better luck getting it back aboard. If you are inclined to try a sea anchor, I suggest you also study a technique employed by Lin and Larry Pardey that is described in their excellent book, *Storm Tactics Handbook* (Pardey Books, 3rd Edition, 2008). They recommend rigging a bridle off one side of the bow or the other so that the anchor holds the boat at an offset angle to oncoming seas.

None of the crews in the '98 rally tried streaming a drogue, which is designed to stabilize the behavior of a boat's stern when it is running off before very large seas. Again, as with the sea anchors, I doubt this was necessary in this situation. What intrigues me about drogues, however, is their versatility. As mentioned earlier, they can be used to help steer a rudderless boat. In his classic book *40,000 Miles In a Canoe*, Captain John Voss also describes how he used one to keep his unique craft *Tilikum* from broaching when entering dangerous inlets. More recently, John Harries, who maintains a very useful website at morganscloud.com, has suggested a drogue can also be used to help a boat heave-to much more effectively.

Of course, the biggest take-away from that ill-fated rally comes from *Circe*'s adventure. To this day I am still astounded by the fact that Stevenson and company decided to abandon their boat seemingly on the basis of nothing more than a depressing weather forecast. I understand they were tired and demoralized, and yes, two crew were seasick, but I am sure they would have been fine if they had hove-to or had simply sailed off downwind under a small headsail.

It is a lesson every modern ocean sailor should keep in mind when caught in heavy weather: even if you're scared, you shouldn't leave the boat unless you really have to.

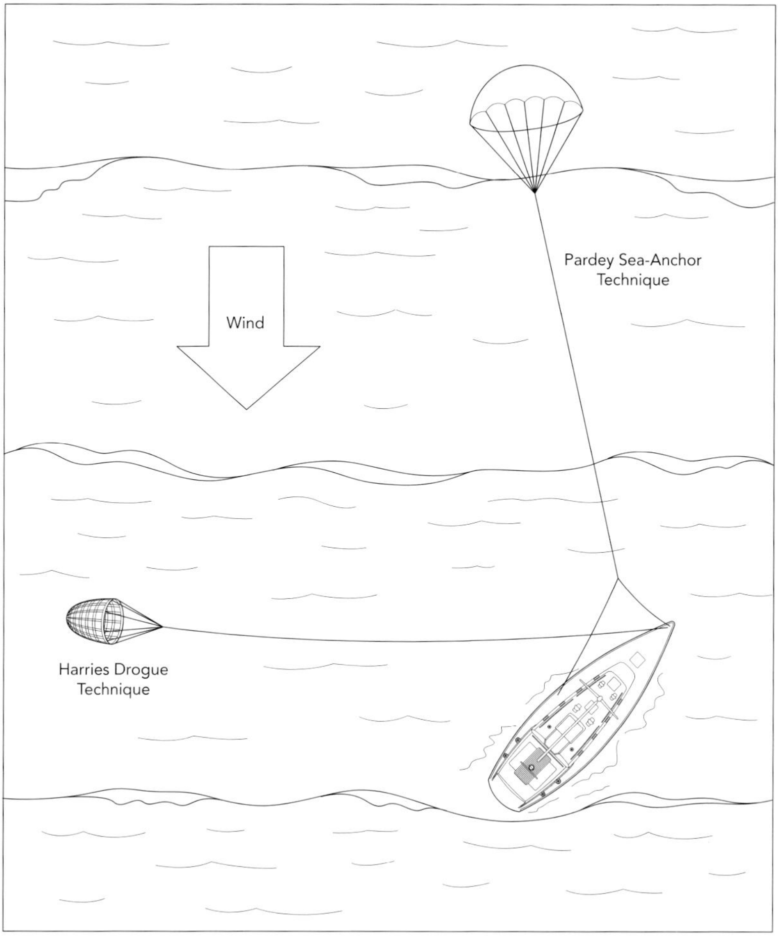

Lin and Larry Pardey always liked to stream a sea-anchor from a bridle so as to hold the boat's bow at an angle to the wind and seas. John Harries has had success streaming a drogue from his bow while hove-to, as this also helps hold the bow up to windward at an angle to oncoming waves.

Hank Schmitt waits patiently for a marina pump-out boat
to break us out of the ice so we can start
our voyage south on the catamaran *Be Good Too*.
(Photo by the author)

The view through *Be Good Too*'s starboard saloon window as the gale gathers strength. (Photo by the author)

After she was released by the U.S. Navy after World War II, *Constellation* was purchased by Stanley Dashew, father of Steve Dashew, who later became a renowned ocean sailor and boatbuilder. The Dashew family cruised on the boat starting in 1948 from Michigan to California via the Panama Canal. Once on the West Coast *Constellation* was rerigged and won her class and came second overall in the 1955 Transpac. She won her class in the Transpac again in 1959, under the command of Sally Blair Ames, a young yachtswoman from Boston. During the 1970s *Constellation* was cruised around the world by Roberta Erb and by the 1980s had landed in Florida. (Photo by Diane Beeston)

Out she comes at last! *Constellation* on the ways
at the Rybovich-Spencer yard in West Palm Beach.
(Photo courtesy of the author)

Captain Cliff stalks the deck of *Constellation*
during our passage from Bermuda to the Azores.
(Photo courtesy of the author)

Carie feeling feisty, standing watch during a passage aboard *Crazy Horse*.
(Photo courtesy of the author)

The author atop Kuntaur Hill, the highest point on the banks of the Gambia River. *Crazy Horse* lies to an anchor below. (Photo by Carie van der Krüys)

Ebrahim with Carie aboard *Crazy Horse* at Bambale.
Elephant Island is in the background.
(Photo by the author)

Don Street steers his famous yawl *Iolaire* down the Solent
shortly after the start of the 2005 Fastnet Race.
(Photo by the author)

Reid Stowe and Soanya Ahmad aboard the schooner *Anne*
shortly before they set off on the Thousand Day Mars Odyssey in April 2007.
(Photo by the author)

The author (on the right) and Reid Stowe prepare
to sail *Anne* up New York Harbor to celebrate Reid's
completing the longest non-stop ocean voyage in history.
(Photo by Tania Aebi)

The Hobie 18 catamaran *United States of the World* at the start of Jimmy Cornell's America 500 transatlantic rally off Las Palmas de Gran Canaria in November 1992. She did not make it very far and was later towed into Gomera by one of the rally boats. Later that same winter, however, Federico di Benedetto and his son Alessandro (seen steering here) did succeed in sailing this craft all the way across the Atlantic. Alessandro later sailed small beach cats singlehanded across both the Atlantic and Pacific, sailed solo around the world nonstop on a 21-foot Mini, and also competed in the 2012-13 Vendée Globe. (Photo courtesy of the author)

Jimmy Cornell (left) aboard *Aventura IV* after hoisting a spinnaker en route from Florida to Panama.
(Photo by the author)

First Mate Dunbar (left) and a local line-handler stand by on the bow of *Aventura IV* as we approach the Gatun Locks leading into the Panama Canal.
(Photo by the author)

The port-side rudder stock and tiller arm on *Be Good Too* after we pinned them back together with an Allen key. The tiller was originally set higher on the stock, at the mark shown, and was secured with a small set-screw that failed. (Photo by the author)

One of the owners of *Be Good Too*, Gunther (without the helmet), is hoisted aboard a U.S. Coast Guard helicopter. (Photo by the author)

Be Good Too, right after we abandoned her in January 2014,
as seen from the helicopter that rescued us.
(Photo by the author)

Almost exactly three years after we left her, *Be Good Too* washed up on a beach on the island of South Uist in the Outer Hebrides off the west coast of Scotland. At some point during her drift across the Atlantic she was capsized and dismasted. Her cabinhouse was torn off on a reef as she came ashore. (Photo by JF Martin)

Scott Kennedy

PART III

WANDERINGS IN WEST AFRICA

The continent is too large to describe. It is a veritable ocean,
a separate planet, a varied, immensely rich cosmos.

—Ryszard Kapuscinski, *The Shadow of the Sun*

SOUTH TO SENEGAL

Gomera to Dakar
November 1996

EVEN MORE THAN THE WEATHER what most gnawed on me as I sailed across the Atlantic on *Crazy Horse* was the simple business of maintaining the boat. Just as there is a dichotomy among sailors between those who enjoy strong weather and those who do not, there is another regarding the maelstrom of maintenance. There are engineers who become poets in spite of themselves, the technically inclined who rather enjoy solving mechanical and electrical problems, but must learn to commune with and appreciate the magical environment of water and air. And then there are poets who become engineers in spite of themselves, those who instinctively revel in the environment, but must agonize over the hard lessons of technical boat lore.

I was most definitely in the latter group. I was lucky during the early part of my voyage, on the leg from Bermuda to the Azores, as I had my old friend Dave, from *Constellation*, aboard as crew (he replaced Tim and joined Nim and me in Bermuda), and he solved the first problems that confronted me—replacing a blown bearing in the boat's steering system and reglassing a portion of the deck that was damaged. But after Dave and Nim left the boat in Horta I had to manage things on my own.

Crazy Horse's engine promptly rebelled against the poet's regime by spontaneously filling the bilge with motor oil. In the reluctant fit of engine-awareness that followed, I inspected the Racor fuel filter and discovered there were also plants growing in my diesel fuel.

I was aghast. I had read of such things in boat magazines, just as I had seen stories about space aliens and Loch Ness monsters in supermarket tabloids, but I never expected to encounter them face to face. Somewhere in this universe, I now realized, there might well be a planet covered with an ocean of diesel oil, and on the shores of that ocean intelligent creatures might be found lounging in beach chairs while sipping on carbonated kerosene cocktails garnished with maraschino cherries and little paper umbrellas. That the seeds of such an evolution could be found in my fuel filter seemed horrible to contemplate.

So began my education. With the help of my neighbors in the marina at Horta I polished my fuel and dosed it with algicide, and then I apprenticed myself to a Portuguese mechanic, Mario, who replaced the failed main seal on the engine's crankshaft. When he was done I immediately prepared to leave Horta for São Miguel and before starting the engine thought to check the oil. I was shocked to find the crankcase was full of water and at once remembered Cliff and his awful ordeal with the engine on *Constellation*.

This was a turning point for me. Instead of calling Mario again, I studied my copy of Nigel Calder's invaluable reference, the *Boatowner's Mechanical and Electrical Manual*, and carefully followed the instructions in the section improbably entitled "Water in Engine." The prescribed cure, in case you're interested, was surprisingly simple. I turned the engine by hand to pump the water out of the cylinders, then alternately changed the oil and ran the engine for very brief periods half a dozen times. When I was done, the engine worked perfectly and seemed to have suffered no ill effects. The feeling of accomplishment I experienced was every bit as profound as the joy I felt when contemplating my relationship to the sea and sky and cosmos that surrounded me.

WITH CARIE NOW as my only crew, after a winter spent at Ponta Delgada attending to various maintenance chores, I sailed east from the Azores in the late spring of 1996 feeling much more confident in my ability to manage the boat. We visited some places I had been before during my previous adventures: the marina at Puerto Sherry, where I dragged Carie off to see more bullfights, and Gibraltar, where we hauled out at Sheppard's yard in the shadow of the almighty Rock for a bottom job and a rudder repair. I also added a siphon loop to the engine's exhaust circuit to (hopefully) permanently cure the water-in-engine problem.

Carie was an excellent companion and also very helpful in certain respects. She was irrepressibly optimistic and spoke several languages—her native Dutch, plus German, English, French, and Portuguese—and strove instinctively to express herself in those she didn't know, as she could never conceive of not talking to people. She thus could be counted upon to interpret my needs and desires to the world, wherever we might land. She also willingly tackled any onerous and filthy boat job I assigned her, and when we sailed together cheerfully stood watch and looked out for ships and squalls while I was sleeping, in spite of often feeling seasick. But she had no interest in learning anything about sailing or handling the boat. Though I did make an effort to teach her, she was very content to leave all this to me.

"You need to know certain things," I urged. "What if I fall overboard when we're in the middle of the ocean?"

"Well then," she answered in a very matter-of-fact tone. "I am sure I will figure it out."

We cruised together that summer to some places in mainland Portugal and Spain I hadn't been to before—the Rio Guadiana and the Costa del Sol—and in the early fall made short passages to places I'd visited on other boats after we lost *Constellation* in 1992—Madeira and the Canary Islands. During all this time, in the several months since we'd left the Azores, I felt competent and in control, but finally in November as we sailed south from the Canaries toward our next destination, I felt a great stone of uncertainty growing within me.

Africa! The very name conjured thoughts of the unknown and the unknowable. Ever since acquiring *Crazy Horse* I'd sailed in familiar waters, voyaging to places I had been before, or places close to places I had been before. Now, at last, I was wandering on to charts that were utterly alien to me, aboard a vessel I owned and commanded, and I felt as though I was stepping off a cliff into a void.

THE SKY TO THE SOUTH as we sailed away from the Canarian island of Gomera looked bruised and hazy, as though the blue had been sucked out of it by some meteorological vampire. It made me very nervous, and I was of half a mind to turn back, though there was no rational reason to do so. The wind was light as we departed the village of San Sebastien that afternoon, and the forecast was for moderate northeasterlies in the days ahead.

Forecasts, however, are never right all the time, and by midnight the wind had increased to over 20 knots and had veered south of east. The cold stone within me grew a bit larger as I struggled to maintain perspective. The breeze will soon back again, I told myself, and to demonstrate that I believed this, I swerved away from our rhumbline route to the south-southeast and set a course a little west of south to keep the wind just behind the beam. By daybreak, unfortunately, it was blowing over 30 straight out of the southeast, what some might call a small gale, and we had little choice but to sail into it.

We slammed to windward all through that second day, drenched in spray as steep waves hopped aboard at irregular intervals. Carie sat stoically through her watches with a bucket at her side. When not on watch she lay unconscious below, as though felled by some magic potion. I felt queasy myself and was very tired, but the stone within me, and the awful motion of the boat, made it hard to sleep.

The sky, meanwhile, maintained its ominous hazy appearance. I thought this might be due to the harmattan, a strong east wind that blows off the hot Sahara desert. The harmattan, it is said, can carry dust from the Sahara out to the Canaries and the Cape Verde Islands, and indeed, according to some, all the way across the Atlantic to the West Indies. But I could not see or feel any dust. There was only the haze and the strange pale sky.

Fortunately, toward the end of that day the miserable wind and sea abated. By sunset the wind was veering east again, the deck was dry, the boat's motion had improved, and Carie finally stopped vomiting. Gratefully, I crept to a berth. At last, I felt some of the familiar contentment of the routine of being on passage creep over me as I quickly drifted off to sleep.

Just an hour later Carie poked me awake again.

"You must come see! It is very strange. A flashing yellow light in the sky."

I jumped from my berth as though I'd been stuck with a cattle prod. I stumbled up to the cockpit, where I stood in my underwear and studied the eerie night sky. Sure enough, there were huge flashes of yellow light off to the east, followed by dull rumbling sounds and a faint acrid burning odor. The quality of the flashes, so sharp and precise, and the strange smell led me to think this might be artillery fire.

Were we sailing into some sort of a naval battle? Should I show more lights, I wondered, so they'll know not to shoot at us? Or could these be pirates? Much better then not to show lights. And I ordered Carie to switch everything off.

But, of course, it was just lightning. A thunder squall viewed through the prism of the hazy night sky, creeping out to us from the desert with probing fingers of hot, unhappy air. The leading edge passed over us, and finally the jagged sheets of lightning were plainly visible, striking down at the sea less than a mile away.

I HAD A BOOK I WAS READING, *Narrative of a Voyage to Senegal*, by Jean-Baptiste Henri Savigny and Alexandre Correard, published in 1818. The authors were both survivors of the wreck of *Medusa*, a French frigate that was sent with a small squadron of vessels full of colonists and soldiers to reclaim Senegal from the British after the end of the Napoleonic wars. *Medusa* lost contact with the rest of the squadron and ran aground on the Arguin Bank, a long reef off the coast of what is now Mauritania. While working to get off again, the crew built a large raft over 60 feet long out of spare spars and timber on to which they planned to offload gear and supplies so as to lighten the ship. Before they could do so, however, a gale blew up. *Medusa* started to break up on the reef, and the captain ordered that the ship be abandoned.

There were 240 people aboard, far too many for the ship's boats to carry, and most of them, 150 in all, were compelled instead to board the raft. In their book Savigny and Correard, who were among those on the raft, continually refer to it as "the machine" or, even better, "the infernal machine." The plan was for the boats to tow the raft, which was continually awash once loaded with its passengers, some 30 miles to shore.

"Vive le Roi!" cried the horde on the raft as those in the boats pulled hard on their oars. But soon another cry was heard: "We forsake them!" And the boats cast off their tow lines and left the raft behind. The only provisions aboard were six large barrels of wine and two small casks of water.

Question: what is most likely to happen when you heap 150 Frenchmen and several barrels of wine on to a makeshift raft and leave them to fend for themselves standing in water up their shins many miles from shore? Do they: (a) sip their wine politely and discuss ways to preserve the purity of the French language while patiently awaiting rescue; or (b) get raving drunk and fight and murder and eat each other?

It truly is an appalling tale. When the raft was found by one of the other ships in the squadron 13 days later, only 15 survivors remained. All the others had been swept away, had killed themselves, or had been consumed.

This tragedy has meant many things to different people over the years. To the young Romantic artist Théodore Géricault it provided the inspiration for his first major painting, *Le Radeau de la Méduse*, an enormous work (over a third the size of the infernal machine itself) that is still prominently displayed in the Louvre. For others it was (and is) a sad commentary on the hapless Bourbon monarchy that was restored to power after the fall of Bonaparte. For many, of course, it is simply a titillating and gruesome survival story.

For me, at this particular point in time, it raised just one question. I studied those alien charts of mine quite closely. I located the Arguin Bank just south of Cap Blanc—some 240 miles north of Port St. Louis in Senegal, *Medusa*'s destination, some 100 miles east of our own position—a threatening lump of shoal water if ever there was one, with nothing to this day but a wilderness of endless desert behind it. I read the sailing directions for ships traversing this area: "The hydrography of this region is incomplete and vessels are advised to keep in depths of at least 30 meters. The tidal currents in the vicinity of the bank attain rates up to 1.5 knots, and eddies render the steering of a vessel difficult."

And I wondered: whatever were they doing sailing so close to this godforsaken coast?

SEVEN DAYS AFTER LEAVING GOMERA we finally closed the coast ourselves. I had no real expectations as to what it would be like, but still I was puzzled by what we found. On our port bow, to the east, we saw the low silhouette of the long isthmus of Cap Vert lying under a pall of thin smoke. As we continued south the faint smell of burning dung wafted out to us on the breeze. This was familiar to me and reassuring, as it recalled parts of my childhood that had been spent in south Asia. What was surprising were the thin columns of heavier smoke we saw rising on our starboard bow, to the west, over what should have been open water.

Soon the skyline of the city of Dakar started jutting up out of the land to the east, but the source of the columns of smoke to the west remained a mystery. I studied them intently through binoculars and eventually saw they were emanating from a group of brightly colored open longboats—I later learned these are called pirogues—that lay offshore, rolling in the ocean swell. Finally, when we were close enough, I could see the men aboard were fishing and tending small cooking fires in the bilges of their boats. We waved eagerly as we passed, but the fishermen only stared in return, as though mystified by our appearance.

Turning east finally toward the city itself, my stone of anxiety started swelling again. Unlike every other place I had visited so far in my travels, I now had no reference book to consult, no "Cruiser's Guide to Senegal" full of friendly advice on where to go and what to do on arrival. All I could think of was to hail "Dakar harbor control" on the VHF radio and ask for instructions. They came back promptly, speaking good English, but they also seemed mystified when I described my vessel to them. After a long delay they at last ordered me to enter the main port and come alongside the south mole "between the Cuban freighter and the Liberian tanker."

This, on its face, sounded like a bad idea. And as we turned north past the old slave fort on Île de Gorée and at last got a good view of the port, it also looked like a bad idea. The wall between the freighter and tanker was very high, obviously meant for large ships rather than small yachts, and was coated in black oily filth. At the top of the wall, as we approached the large gap between the two ships, there quickly gathered a huge crowd of men. As we came alongside they shouted at us in various languages in a very excited state, waving their arms and gesticulating madly.

Never mind the stone metaphor. I was by now flat-out scared. Who the hell were these guys? What in God's name did they want? Just as my imagination had several days earlier converted the thunder squall into an artillery barrage, it now supposed this must be a lynch mob and that I was about to be torn limb from limb in a riot of revenge for all the indignities and oppression that the white race had ever visited upon black Africa.

But no, all these men wanted were jobs. With heart in mouth I tossed my dock lines up to the top of the filthy wall and dozens of hands fought for the right to take hold of them. Once the lines were made off, I scaled the wall, and those same hands all held out scraps of paper, letters of reference urging that the bearer was highly qualified to serve as a harbor guide and watchman. The awful din of all these men shouting and pleading with me grew louder and louder, and I realized there likely would be a riot if I didn't hire one of them.

"Very important paper! Very important paper!" cried one man, who somehow managed to out-shout the others as he pushed his way through the crowd. He thrust his paper into my hand, and I saw it was from an American yacht, *Sea Shantey*, whose owners I had met and befriended back in the Canary Islands just a few weeks earlier.

"I know these people!" I exclaimed and felt immensely relieved. I quickly read through the recommendation and then announced: "You're hired!"

The unruly mob around me immediately wailed in protest and throbbed with angry energy, but now I had a powerful ally. My new employee, Abdul, waved his arms dismissively, barked a few choice words in several dialects, and soon the crowd started to disperse. Abdul then explained to me that he had a highly qualified colleague, Willy, who would stay with Carie and watch the boat while he and I went to visit the police and the port captain.

I reboarded the boat to retrieve my papers, shook hands with Willy, who now stood impassively in the cockpit, and Abdul and I then started the long march down the mole and around the port to the offices in town. One of the men from the disappointed crowd of job applicants—he called himself

Jean—followed us most of the way, bouncing up and down like a puppy. He kept insisting I owed him money because he had handled one of my dock lines. I kept telling him no, I would not pay him anything, as nicely as I could, and then finally I just ignored him.

"You are American, yes?" he demanded.

"Yes, yes. I am American."

"Americans are very bad people!"

He spat the words out with a vicious scowl on his face, as though he might be perfectly willing to murder me. I said nothing in response and kept marching resolutely forward. He stalked beside me for several more yards, then suddenly brightened and grabbed me by the shoulder.

"Hey, man," he proclaimed. "I is only joking. Just joking with you." He shook me by the hand and gave me a big smile and a thumbs-up. "Welcome to Dakar!"

And he then marched off and disappeared into the hive of the city.

IN THE END I WAS GLAD to have hired Abdul, for I soon realized it would have been difficult finding the appropriate offices to report to without him. Neither office was clearly labeled and both were located in odd out-of-the-way places. Both the police and the port captain politely suggested I should bribe them—one called it "an optional gift," the other "transportation money"—and my sense was their demands might have been less polite and less moderate had Abdul not been with me. Clearly, he was well known to both of them.

The sums involved, in any event, were utterly insignificant. The port captain wanted a pack of cigarettes, and the police officer who handed me immigration forms to fill out wanted 500 West African francs (called CFA, or "*say-fa*"), which amounted to all of $1 US. I had no cigarettes and no CFA, as I hadn't yet changed any money, but both officials accepted my solemn promise that I would return and pay them the next day.

It was late by the time I returned to the boat, and we had little choice but to spend the night on the wall. It was, I think, the worst night I have ever spent on a boat that was tied up somewhere. The yellow glare of the sodium lights on the mole cast ghastly shadows that twisted around the cabin as *Crazy Horse* tossed and turned like a sleepless child, yanking hard on her dock lines. I tossed and turned with her, listening to her fenders grind against her hull just inches from my head. Twice I heard one pop out of place, and I instantly jumped out on deck to replace it—a very dirty job, as the fenders by now were coated in black, sticky oil, as was a large section of the hull.

Peering up over the edge of that foul wall through the glare of the lights, I could just make out the form of first Willy, then later Abdul, silently watching over us. Both times I waved, but they did not wave back. I remembered the fishermen we had seen earlier that day and felt conflicted. On the one hand I resented that we were dependent on these men; on the other I was grateful for their presence.

Late the next morning, after I changed some money and hustled around paying off minuscule bribes, Abdul directed us to a more comfortable location. The local yacht club, Cercle de la Voile de Dakar (or CVD, pronounced "*say vay day*"), lay a couple of miles north of the main port, at Hann beach, where the local fleet of fishing pirogues was based. There was a busy market here, and incessant activity around the many pirogues, but the club's stretch of beachfront was inviolate and seemed an oasis of calm after the dirt and clamor of the harbor. Poking out from the beach into an open anchorage inhabited by about 20 well-worn yachts was a spindly wooden pier. Off to one side was a crude slipway—a large rusty boat cradle that could be winched up and down the beach. Behind the beach, through a thin screen of trees, was a funky clubhouse with a bar trimmed in bright blue paint.

Modest as it seemed, this I soon learned was the epicenter of the yachting scene in West Africa from Spanish Morocco as far south as the Ivory Coast. Besides being headquarters for any local expatriates keeping boats here, CVD was also a staging base for the few foreign cruisers who came each year to explore the Casamance and Gambia river systems and the more challenging waters of Guinea-Bissau a bit further south. Almost all of these cruisers were European, and during our brief tenure there *Crazy Horse* was the only American-flagged boat in the anchorage.

The sailors I met at CVD, French and English for the most part, were quiet and reserved, but there was one, a German who called himself Robert, who was very outspoken. I spent part of an afternoon buying him beer while trying to extract useful information from him.

Robert was not fond of Americans and did not mind telling me so. He chastised me at once for being so foolish as to hire Abdul and complained that the few Americans who did cruise in West Africa spoiled it for everyone else "by leaving too much money behind."

"America is a very racist country," he proclaimed. "The Americans who come here feel guilty about that and try to make up for it by being too generous with the people in Africa. This makes it very hard for other white people who come here. Everyone thinks all whites should give as much as the Americans."

I could only laugh in response to this. "Americans are generous people," I said. "I have never heard any Europeans complaining about all the money we have left behind in Europe."

"That is different," objected Robert. "In Europe we have a great culture, and America needs our culture to be civilized." And from there he launched into a soliloquy about his travels in America and the great cultural desert he had found there. "There is nothing beautiful there," he complained. "There is nothing worth saving."

I tried initially to argue with him about this, pointing out that certain aspects of American culture—American films, for example, and jazz and rock music, which, ironically, were first created by African-Americans—seemed to be quite popular in Europe. But he kept talking over me, so I kept quiet and waited for a lull before trying to turn the conversation back to West Africans and how best to deal with them.

"They are monkeys!" he hissed. His tone was just as bitter and angry as that displayed by Jean, the disappointed job applicant I had met in the main harbor. Only Robert wasn't acting. "They are greedy, grasping, disgusting monkeys. You must give them as little as possible, or they will only get worse."

I WAS PUT OFF by Robert's bigotry, and by his hypocrisy, but on venturing into the city I understood better how he got that way. Everywhere we went the tourist touts were relentless. It seemed every single person on the street had something to sell us, something they would like to do for us, some place they would like to take us, someone they would like us to meet, or some very good reason why we should just plain give them some money. *Non, merci. Non, merci. Non, merci.* Every time we left the confines of the CVD compound, we had to utter this ceaseless mantra to keep the hordes at bay.

Finally, I learned the secret. If I marched around like I belonged there, with my best New York City don't-fuck-with-me-motherfucker-or-I'll-fuck-you-up scowl on my face, kept my eyes always focused straight ahead, never made eye contact, and never looked around at anything, people left me alone. It was that, or only go out on Friday afternoons, when everyone everywhere was down on their knees on little prayer carpets, facing east, praying to Allah. Then, at last, you could enjoy some peace and quiet and think a bit while gazing around at the sights.

By West African standards, Dakar is a rather large cosmopolitan city. Back in colonial times it was the administrative capital of all of French West Africa, a vast swath of the continent that encompassed what is now Mauritania, Senegal, Mali, Guinea, Ivory Coast, Burkina Faso, Benin, and Niger. Culturally, it is still the predominant metropolis in the region. But Carie and I were there mostly on business. We needed visas to enter Gambia, our true destination, and I needed a new passport, as my current one was due to expire. I also wanted desperately to get some idea of what we could expect sailing up the Gambia River. Beyond that, we agreed, we weren't interested in staying in the city any longer than was necessary.

We made the rounds at the Gambian embassy, again paying tiny bribes to get otherwise somnolent bureaucrats interested in their jobs, and I made two trips to the American embassy. It was, by comparison, a fount of efficiency and integrity, but ironically, even without the bribes, was a much more expensive place to do business. If nothing else, it made me value my citizenship. Both times I visited the line of Senegalese seeking to enter the embassy to apply for visas to visit the U.S. stretched down the street for several blocks. All I had to do was flash my passport, that magic little blue book, and I was instantly admitted. Rarely had I ever felt so important.

Meanwhile, back at the bar at the CVD clubhouse, I kept trolling for local knowledge. Finally, I hit paydirt. A young British sailor, Brian, who appeared one afternoon aboard a scraggly looking boat that had a galvanized-wire rig and was badly in need of painting, turned out to be both knowledgeable and loquacious. He had been cruising the coast, from Dakar to Liberia, for several years and had helped research an unpublished cruising guide of Senegal and Gambia that had been written by a friend of his. Like an apostle bestowing the gospel upon an acolyte, he loaned me a copy of the manuscript so that I could photocopy it.

"Don't let Dakar put you off," he declared. "The touts here are worse than anywhere else. It's much nicer away from the city."

"Out in the bush, though, you do need to watch for bugs," he warned. "Especially the mossies. The French never really care if they get malaria, but you'd be crazy not to take something for it. Once you're in fresh water, you'll also find the tsetse flies are fierce, but you don't have to worry about getting sick from them…" He paused, and the weary look in his eye suggested this was something he had learned the hard way. "Unless you stay too long."

THE ONE PLACE I MOST WANTED to visit while in Dakar was Gorée, the small island we had slipped past on our way into the harbor. I thought at first we should go on *Crazy Horse*, but after studying Brian's guide I concluded this might not be wise. There is a small harbor there, but it is not secure and is open to wakes from the main port. Instead, just two days before we left the city, we went out on the ferry, which ran every hour.

Gorée is the hard fortified seed from which the rest of the city sprouted. One of the first places in Africa to be settled by Europeans, the island was initially claimed by the Portuguese in 1444 and was subsequently held by the Dutch, the Portuguese again, the Dutch again, and then the British, and finally the French. Prior to the founding of the city on the mainland in the mid-19th century, Gorée was an important trading post and transshipment point for slaves, beeswax, hides, and ivory. After the slave trade waned in the late 18th century, its commerce was dominated by Franco-African Creole women, known as *signares*, who were renowned on the coast for their sense of fashion and sharp dealing.

What struck me most was how quiet it was. Unlike the city, whose architecture is dominated by the high-rise buildings that have sprung up since Senegal achieved independence in 1960, Gorée is covered by much older colonial structures that have been carefully maintained and preserved. We found a community there—various dwellings, a small hotel or two, and some other businesses—and though the island is hailed as Dakar's most popular tourist attraction, we also found no tourist touts. The void created by their absence was filled with a devout, delicious hush, as though the island were a monastery whose inhabitants had all taken vows of silence.

Carie and I wandered the cobblestone streets unmolested, toured the great fort at the island's southern end, inspected a church, a mosque, and the infamous Maison des Eclaves, with its cells, chains, and implements of servitude. Circling north again, we finally heard a great noise coming from the harbor. Children were laughing and playing on a small beach, splashing each other and jumping off a wall into the water.

There was a restaurant on a terrace nearby, and we took a table there. We sat for what seemed an eternity—watching the children, sipping tea, eating pastry—and for the first time since arriving in West Africa, I felt at peace and content.

FINDING MY TOMA

Banjul to Mandori Creek
November–December 1996

WHEN IT CAME TIME to leave Dakar, I found we were, almost literally, hanging by a thread. We had anchored on about 100 feet of three-strand nylon rope, plus there was a 30-foot chain leader. On hauling back all the rope I discovered the rode, just a few feet back from the chain, had almost chafed right through. Two strands were severed entirely; the third was cut in half.

On making this discovery I was, of course, both shocked and relieved. Something down there clearly liked to chew on rope, and I reckoned in only a few more hours it would have been done chewing on mine. At best we would have lost the anchor; at worst we might have lost the boat. I also couldn't help laughing, for it seemed appropriate that we should escape the city by the skin of our teeth.

The run down to Banjul, at the mouth of the Gambia River, was just 90 miles. Geographically this was a very short passage, but to me it seemed a quantum leap. In my mind, the distance between Dakar, where I felt incessantly anxious and ignorant, and Banjul, where I hoped I could again at least pretend I knew what I was doing, was very large.

We left late in the afternoon so as to arrive in daylight the next morning. We were sailing just 15 miles offshore, give or take, and through much of the night were surrounded by local fishing pirogues. Most, fortunately, were showing lights of some kind. These bobbed and weaved over the black ocean swells, scribbling short tendrils of yellow and white across the water. None of the pirogues were showing red and green side-lights, so it took some vigilance to avoid them. I was up all night monitoring their movements and by daybreak was fuzzy-headed from lack of sleep.

By 0900 hours we were just 10 miles from Banjul, heading up the fairway into the river through a maze of pirogues and unmarked drift nets. I was determined to sail up to town, though both the wind and tide were against us, and it wasn't until mid-afternoon that we were finally in the river mouth proper with Banjul directly abeam of us. It was a drab low-lying place, a thin scrum of nondescript brown and gray buildings punctuated with an occasional minaret. At last I relented, started the engine, stowed the sails, and turned toward the harbor. Soon I noticed a group of men standing on a large wharf, waving and shouting at me to come land the boat there.

Thanks to our experience in Dakar, I was wise to this game. Rule No. 1 when cruising in West Africa: never come alongside anywhere. I cheerfully waved back at the men, then trotted up to the bow to get the anchor ready to launch.

Aha! I had forgotten about the anchor rode. I whipped my rigging knife out of my pocket and at once started cutting out the damaged section. It was a very sharp knife, with a cruel serrated edge, and in my haste I slashed open my thumb on my right hand. Cursing, I ignored the wound. I finished trimming the rode, then worked feverishly to re-splice the rope around its thimble while simultaneously waving some more at the men on shore. By the time I was done, the foredeck was covered with vivid red parabolas of blood.

We anchored amid a collection of half-submerged wrecks that jutted out of the oily brown water at calamitous angles. Though I was by now thoroughly exhausted, I quickly taped up my thumb, inflated the dinghy, hoisted it overboard, mounted my trusty Yamaha outboard on its transom, and then motored to shore to confront the authorities, leaving Carie to mind *Crazy Horse*.

The men who had been waving at me now gathered at the small dock where I landed.

"No, thank you," I told them. "I do not need any guides."

"Fine, fine," they insisted. "We will help you anyway."

With entourage in tow, I wandered a short distance inland and soon found a guard shack with a guard inside. He immediately phoned the immigration officer, who presently arrived wearing a small cap like a yarmulke and a long white robe.

"I have come from prayers," he announced. "I do not normally work on Fridays."

Of course, I could see where this was going.

The immigration man led me to his office, which was in a small trailer nearby, and handed me forms to fill out. He inspected our visas, stamped our two passports, and then proclaimed: "Come! We must inspect your yacht."

We stopped at another trailer to pick up the customs officer, who was wearing a trim blue uniform and looked rather pleased when he learned there was a yacht to inspect. As we clambered down into the dinghy and headed out to *Crazy Horse*, the two men explained it was customary to present gifts to government officials who worked on Fridays.

As soon as we arrived at the boat Carie offered our guests tea, but they declined and at once started roaming the deck. I could tell from their eyes that what they were looking for were things that might make good gifts.

"What has happened here?" asked the immigration officer, eyebrows raised as he pointed at the blood stains on the foredeck.

I held up my bandaged thumb and smiled sheepishly. "I had a little trouble anchoring," I explained.

The customs officer, who seemed to know a bit about boats, looked mildly disturbed. "Please," he said. "Can you give us a tour of the cabin?"

I led the men below and could tell they were disheartened by the boat's shabby interior. They poked into a few lockers and cabinets in a desultory manner, finding mostly corroded tools and unmarked cans of food. They did perk up briefly when they came upon my portable tape player, which was lying in a pile of dirty laundry on the V-berth up forward.

"This is nice," said the immigration officer as he carefully extracted the tape player from a tangle of underwear. "Can you plug it into a wall?"

"Yes, of course," I answered and cheerfully produced the AC power cord. "It runs on batteries or on 110-volt current."

The officer carefully inspected the cord, saw that the tape player would not plug into his wall, and set it aside with a sigh of disappointment.

"You have passed inspection," announced the customs officer, who now seemed bored. "Can you please take us back now?"

We quickly climbed back into the dinghy and were headed back to shore when the outboard suddenly seized up and stopped running. I put the engine in neutral and at once restarted it, but it stalled again as soon as I popped it back into gear.

"It is the head-rope," said the customs officer, his voice dripping with disdain. "The head-rope is in the propeller."

Sure enough, I saw I had forgotten to pull the dinghy's painter all the way inboard before setting off from the boat. It had streamed aft under the dinghy and was now so firmly caught in the prop I could not raise the engine to free it.

"Not to worry," I announced. "I can row us in."

I pulled out the oars, awkwardly rearranged my guests on the dinghy's sponsons, parked myself on the thwart seat, and started pulling hard for the dock. The river current was strong, however, and there wasn't room enough to row properly, so we made little progress.

"Here, give those to us," said the customs officer.

And the men took the oars from me and began paddling toward shore with grim looks on their faces. By now it was clear they were wondering how I ever managed to pilot my grubby little sailboat all the way from America to Africa.

My entourage, which still waited patiently on shore, murmured in wonder when they saw me sitting idle while two government officials labored to paddle my dinghy back to the dock. As soon as we landed, the men quickly clambered up the ladder and ran off for their trailers. The crowd then watched expectantly as I spent several minutes fishing around the outboard's propeller with my uninjured hand.

Eventually, I managed to free the painter. I then restarted the engine and motored slowly back out to *Crazy Horse*. The sun by now was hanging low in the sky, and the water had turned the color of bronze. The dark silhouettes of the several wrecks in the harbor seemed much more ominous than before. I was bleary-eyed with fatigue, my thumb throbbed with pain, but still I felt triumphant and proud.

BANJUL, WHICH IS THE CAPITAL of Gambia, is not a very salubrious place. Situated on a low island, surrounded by a vast mangrove swamp, it seemed little more than an open sewer festooned with corrugated tin, palm fronds, and decayed colonial architecture. Historically, it has suffered unduly from flooding and pestilence. Case in point: the neighborhood off which we anchored on arrival, the most ramshackle part of the whole ramshackle town, was called Half Die, after a cholera epidemic that once wiped out half the city's population.

No one who visits Gambia by yacht stays here for very long. Instead they wend their way through the serpentine maze of pencil-thin mangrove creeks west of the city and arrive at a much larger creek, where there is a well-protected anchorage just below a low bridge over which runs the only road into town. The cruising sailors who come here call this place Oyster Creek;

the locals call it Denton Bridge.

Unlike the anchorage off the CVD yacht club in Dakar, where we'd been warned never to leave anything on deck lest it be stolen, Oyster Creek was very secure. Whoever controlled Denton Bridge controlled the nation's capital, and it was therefore heavily guarded. Just a short distance from the anchorage on the far side of the road leading up to the bridge there was a large police station. On the road itself overlooking the anchorage was a military checkpoint, which was manned around the clock.

Just below the checkpoint, off the west end of the bridge, was a small beach covered with makeshift huts dressed with hand-lettered signs: Art Center, Warrior Sportfishing, Pleasure Boats For Hire. The huts were mostly empty and idle, but there was one very active business here, Baba's Harbour Café, which was deployed around a more substantial steel shipping container.

Baba was a serious young man, a devout Muslim who nonetheless was happy to serve large quantities of alcohol and food to the visiting sailors, European expats, and less devout locals who gathered here. He worked hard and kept his café neat and tidy. Out front there was a small verandah, diplomatically decorated with an official portrait of Gambia's new president. Behind the container, which housed the café's crude kitchen, was a larger area with several more tables and chairs. Sprouting from the top was a wind generator, the café's sole course of electrical power, which Baba had salvaged from an abandoned sailboat.

CVD might have been the logistical focal point of West African cruising—the best place to haul out, order in parts, and get work done on your boat—but Oyster Creek was by far the best place to just hang out. Indeed, it was so comfortable we soon learned that some of our fellow cruisers had been hanging out there for years. The reigning king and queen, Kase and Anika, a middle-aged Dutch couple living aboard a well-maintained steel boat, were now into their third winter. They occasionally wandered upriver, or to the nearby Siné-Saloum just north of the river in Senegal, and sometimes left the boat to fly back to Europe, but they considered the creek home and were not shy about singing its praises.

Most of the others were more transient. There was a French family, all of whom had malaria, who had roamed both the Gambia and the Casamance River in southern Senegal ever since the previous winter and planned soon to leave for Brazil. There was a dour German singlehander who stopped in briefly most years on his way to the Grenadines. There was an Englishman, a retired electrician with two young Swedes as crew, sailing an amazing miniature wooden barkentine, all finished bright, who had no idea what he was doing next.

There was also another younger couple—Marco, from Spain, and Nadine, from France—who lived on two separate boats and were entering their second winter on the creek. Carie and I had them for dinner one evening aboard *Crazy Horse*, and I was amazed to learn that Nadine, in spite of having been in Gambia for over 15 months, had never even left the anchorage to cruise upriver.

"I do not like to sail in places where the water is not clear," she explained.

"Why then did you ever come to West Africa?" I asked.

"This creek, just here," she said. "I had heard about it." She sipped at her wine, then took a languid pull on her cigarette. She pointed toward a gorgeous purple heron that was creeping along the creek bank with its neck arched, hunting for fish. "It is convenient, but also very magical, don't you think?"

I did think so, but I was also determined to go upriver. Carie and I spent a week decompressing, recovering from the intensity of Dakar, drinking beer and chatting with our new friends at Baba's, and then we prepared to move on.

In terms of provisioning, Oyster Creek was reasonably well situated. On the east side of the anchorage, outside a mysterious facility called the Lyefish

Factory, there was an open standpipe with a tap from which flowed clean fresh water. Nearby there was a gas station fronting the road just off the bridge, where it was easy to land a dinghy and load jerry jugs of fuel. Just down the road west of the bridge, in the sprawling suburbs of Bakau and Serekunda, there were surprisingly modern supermarkets. We took two separate trips by bush taxi, carrying maximum baggage each time, and managed to bring back enough food and drink to last six weeks or more.

On the third trip we played tourist and spent a morning on the beach at Fajara. As beaches go, it was quite nice, a broad strand studded with majestic palm trees and fancy hotels. For most tubabs visiting Gambia ("tubab" being the local term for white people) this was the only part of the country they ever saw. It was particularly popular with sun-worshipping Germans, Swedes, and the British, of course, all of whom came in droves each winter to lie on the flawless white sand wearing as little clothing as possible.

Such a large concentration of tubabs was, of course, highly attractive to touts, and this was the only place in Gambia we visited where they were nearly as prevalent as in Dakar. They roamed the beach like locusts, pitching cold drinks, food, marijuana, souvenirs, package tours, and hard-luck stories to any and all persons with pale complexions. The most exalted members of this tribe were the ambitious Don Juans, known as bumpsters, who relentlessly romanced single females in hopes of forging a relationship that might somehow take them to Europe.

We'd heard about bumpsters at Baba's, from a young expatriate Dutchman, a friend of Kase and Anika's, who had recently lost his German girlfriend to one. He of course despised them, but the local Gambians who also hung out at Denton Bridge obviously admired them. Later, after we traveled inland, we learned how the lure of bumpsterism had ruined many rural families. Parents, we were told, would often sell their cattle to raise money to send a favored son to the beaches outside Banjul. Usually they returned empty-handed, with a larger wardrobe and perhaps a watch, but with no hope of otherwise improving their circumstances.

We had lunch on the beach, fending off touts all the while, and then went to Serekunda to see the Sacred Crocodile Pool. Baba and several of his friends had insisted we should go there.

"You must see," they urged me. "There you will find your *toma*."

I asked for, but did not receive, an intelligible explanation of what this meant. I gathered it was a Mandinka word and translated to something like "soulmate."

The pool itself certainly did not look sacred. "Murky pond" would be a more apt description. Next to it was a cinder-block hut, painted pale green, with a big sign and a man inside wearing sunglasses and a bright red Chicago Bulls T-shirt. Inside the pool was a group of about a dozen Nile crocodiles, a species indigenous to Gambia, that were so lethargic and inactive I thought at first they might be fiberglass statues.

"I have come to meet my toma," I announced after we paid the entrance fee.

The thin man took off his sunglasses and studied me carefully. "What is your name?" he asked.

I told him, and he nodded gravely: "Yes, your toma is here."

He led us down to the far side of the pool, where he crouched next to a large croc that lay motionless in the dried-out mud.

"This is the oldest, biggest crocodile," he said. "He is very tame. You can pat his head, give him a big slap on the back, even shake his hand. He will not mind."

I did these things, and the crocodile did not flinch or in any way acknowledge my existence.

The thin man, now squinting in the sunlight, slipped his sunglasses on again and gave me a broad smile. "His name is Charlie," he told me. "Just like you."

AT THE U.S. EMBASSY in Dakar, where I had renewed my passport, they had urged me to check in at the embassy in Gambia before sailing up the river. I duly presented myself and was ushered into a small office inhabited by a bald man with a nicely trimmed mustache who told me that, due to the current political situation, American citizens were being asked not to travel inland.

I was somewhat familiar with the political situation. I knew that Gambia, the smallest country in Africa, normally had a stable government, but that just two years earlier President Dawda Jawara, who had ruled for three decades, had been overthrown in a military coup led by Yahya Jammeh, commander of the presidential bodyguard. Jammeh, so I'd heard at Baba's, had launched his coup shortly after receiving special military training in the United States. He had also been confirmed as president in an election held a few months before our arrival; another parliamentary election was due to be held soon.

What I didn't know was that very recently there had been another coup attempt upriver at a town called Farafenni. Evidently, eight rebels with pistols had stormed the police barracks there; five had been killed, and three others had escaped.

Having once lived in a bad neighborhood in Brooklyn, this didn't sound too serious to me. I asked the man with the mustache if I was in fact prohibited from sailing upriver, and he said no, he was just warning me not to go. I told him I thought I'd go anyway.

We left on a Saturday. After carefully picking our way through the narrow creeks southwest of the city, we emerged in the river proper and started beating our way east into a firm 20-knot breeze. We had the flood tide behind us, and the thick brown water had been kicked up into a short, steep chop. The river here seemed almost as wide as the sky overhead, with only a hint of a thin gray shoreline in the distance. The sky itself was overcast, and there were no other vessels in sight.

By late afternoon the sun was out, the wind had died, and we had reached James Island, a lonely lump of a place covered with ruined fortifications and baobab trees. For centuries, before Banjul (originally Bathurst) was established in 1816, this had been a key focal point in the European conflicts that punctuated the slave trade. First discovered by the Portuguese, this islet had belonged variously to Polish Lithuanians, the Dutch, and primarily the French and British, who quarreled persistently over control of the river. Though the island was ultimately indefensible, as it has no fresh water, the British in the end prevailed and established the Gambia as a distinct political entity, a narrow sliver of English sovereignty jammed up the bunghole of French West Africa.

We anchored *Crazy Horse* off the island's west end and went ashore shortly before sunset. It was the first time since arriving in West Africa that we had been anchored out anywhere on our own, and the feeling of serenity, of at last being self-contained again, was sublime. We silently wandered the empty island for a while, then returned to the boat, where I sat in the cockpit for some time, feeling palpably relieved as I watched the derelict silhouette of this Gibraltar of the Gambia fade into the plush-pile night sky.

Moving east from James Island in the days that followed, we found sailing the river to be frustrating. Each morning we waited patiently for the incoming tide, then hoisted sail and tried hard to make progress inland. The wind, however, was maddeningly fickle, and usually by lunch we'd given up and started motoring. Here on the Gambia's lower reaches, the scenery was also monotonous. The river was still quite wide, and all along its banks there was nothing but low-lying thickets of mangrove.

Much later in the day, after the tide turned, we anchored off one of the villages on shore, or in one of the capillary creeks, called bolons, that sprouted off the main artery of the river. Visiting the villages was fascinating, but exhausting. As soon as we landed in the dinghy a cry of "Tubab! Tubab!"

would split the air, and in an instant we were lost in a horde of children, all of them clinging to us like we were life-sized Sesame Street characters. Soon we were joined by adults, who were also extremely hospitable. We'd be given a grand tour of the village, our crowd of hosts growing ever larger as the tour progressed, were introduced to village elders and other important persons, and invariably were asked if we'd like to drink China green tea.

This was always time-consuming. First a child was sent to buy some tea (often we were asked to provide the money for this) and meanwhile a fire was built. The fuel was always raw charcoal, which, we'd learned, was the main power source throughout rural West Africa. Once the fire was hot enough, a small tin kettle of water was boiled, the tea was steeped in it for many minutes, then was strained out, a great deal of sugar was added, and the resulting beverage was poured back and forth, back and forth, between kettle and cup, from a great height, for an amazingly long period of time. This, we were told, was the most important part of the process, as it brought out the full flavor of the tea.

Eventually, two small demitasses of tea were served. We were always served first, as we were the guests, and then the process was repeated, with much pouring back and forth, until everyone in attendance had been served, or until the tea leaves had entirely lost their potency. In most cases, we found, it was impossible to visit a village without spending at least two or three hours socializing and drinking tea on shore.

Anchoring in the bolons, on the other hand, was an exercise in intense isolation. The entrances were normally narrow, with a shoal at the creek mouth so that we had to fret about running aground. Once over the bar, however, it seemed we had entered an alternate reality. The soundings would suddenly increase again, so much so we sometimes had to hunt for spots shallow enough to anchor, and the absence of humans, the complete lack of any evidence of their existence, became nearly tangible, a non-presence that haunted the dense walls of mangrove lining the creek bank.

What there were instead of people were birds. So many, and of such variety and color, that it seemed we were watching tropical fish upside down in the air.

Picture this: the most intense dinghy ride of my life. We had anchored in a place called Mandori Creek, some distance west of a village called Tendaba. The sun was just beginning to set, the colors around us growing richer with each passing moment, and from the impenetrable growth on shore a finely blended medley of hoots, squawks, and trills rose up around us. As soon as the hook was set, I jumped in the tender, yanked on the outboard's starting cord, and was away up the creek in a mad rush of internal combustion. The engine carved a long, clean scar on the creek's shiny copper surface, its roar flushing great flights of birds as I passed. A fleet of white egrets, an exaltation of brilliant blue kingfishers, frenzied masses of emerald green parrots, screeching like a nation of cranky old ladies as they swirled in clouds around my head.

On and on for a mile or more, until I reached a spot where suddenly the tall mangrove forest was broken by an open glade of bright green turf. Startled by this unexpected variation in landscape, I at once throttled down and stopped the boat, my cloud of parrots skittering away across the creek like brilliant marbles dumped loose on a plate of glass. The glade was studded with naked dead trees, and in their midst stood one burning dead tree with fingers of red flame flickering along its trunk and lower branches. I sat for several minutes, studying this apocalyptic scene, then turned back down the creek and puttered slowly back to *Crazy Horse* through the gathering darkness.

What, I wondered, had started this fire? Was it spontaneous combustion? A lightning strike? Some eco-voodoo phenomenon?

That night, as on any night when we anchored in a creek, insects descended en masse and we had to shroud every aperture in the boat with netting to keep them out. After dinner, as we lay in our berths, we could hear bats banging off the standing rigging as they wheeled about trying to eat them.

Hours later Carie shook me awake from a deep sleep.

"There is a light," she said. "Someone is coming."

This simple statement, affirming that we were now suddenly not alone in what seemed the loneliest of places, in the middle of the night no less, instantly put me on alert.

I quickly pulled on a pair of shorts and pushed my way through the companionway netting into the cockpit. Downstream in the inky darkness I could see a thick yellow beam of light poking at the mangroves on either side of the creek. I jumped below, turned on the masthead light and all the cabin lights, then came back out into the cockpit with a flashlight, which I waved back and forth through the black void surrounding the boat. Whoever was down there, I wanted them to know that I knew they were there.

The light downstream suddenly went out, then after many minutes just as suddenly came on again. A man in a small pirogue with a lantern strapped to his head calmly paddled past *Crazy Horse* without a word, resolutely ignoring our presence. I stood watching for a while until the light disappeared around the next turn in the creek. Then I went below, shut off everything but the masthead light, and lay in my berth unable to sleep.

Who was this guy? What was he doing here in the middle of the nowhere in the middle of the night? Was he a threat?

Then finally it dawned on me: he was going to the burning tree, to collect charcoal. He was the one who set the fire.

AFRICA DANCES

Farafenni to Georgetown
December 1996

IT IS AN UNWRITTEN RULE that every cruise up an African river must have some Greater Purpose—some guy named Kurtz to chase after, a lost explorer to rescue, a legendary city of gold to loot, some palpable goal to lure you onward into regions where you might not otherwise venture. After two weeks on the river, Carie and I decided finally we had two: we wanted to see a hippopotamus and we wanted to attend a dance.

Our desire to see a hippopotamus was, of course, quite facile, merely a box to check off on a bucket list. Hippos were the local megafauna, the largest creatures indigenous to the river, and it was only natural we should want to clap eyes on one. Seeing a dance, on the other hand, we hoped might yield some significant insight into the soul of the continent. I had long admired Isak Dinesen's famous memoir, *Out of Africa*, and recalled in particular her description of the great dances, called *ngomas*, that were held on her property in Kenya.

"The real performers," she wrote, "the indefatigable young dancers, brought the glory and luxury of the festivity with them, they were immune to foreign influence, and concentrated upon the sweetness and fire within themselves. One thing only did they demand from the outside world: a space of level ground to dance on."

More recently I had discovered a lesser-known work, *Africa Dances*, by Geoffrey Gorer, an anthropologist who traveled throughout West Africa in the early 1930s studying traditional African dance. He considered it the continent's most important art form:

> *Africans dance. They dance for joy, and they dance for grief; they dance for love and they dance for hate; they dance to bring prosperity and they dance to avert calamity; they dance for religion and they dance to pass the time. Far more exotic than their skin and their features is this characteristic of dancing; the West African negro expresses every emotion with rhythmical bodily movement. Dancing [for them] has always held first place.*

But first, we realized, we needed more fuel. Thanks to the tide, river current, and wind, all of which flowed against us more than we would have liked, we were doing more motoring than anticipated. Between her small fuel tank and the one jerry jug on deck *Crazy Horse* carried just 35 gallons of diesel, and already we'd used up nearly 20 of those. I did expect we'd do much more sailing after we finally turned around and came back downriver, but still it seemed prudent to increase our supply. The best place to do this, I guessed, would be at the ferry crossing at Farafenni, which was the first place east of Banjul where motor vehicles could cross the river.

I had expected to see some evidence of the ferry landings from a distance. But as we motored past the ominous-looking wreck of the *Lady Chilel*, a Swedish tourist boat that sank back in the 1980s, then through a sweeping bend in the river at Devil's Point immediately west of Farafenni, we spied only unbroken walls of mangrove and no hint of human infrastructure. I was just beginning to wonder if this ferry was a myth, when an ungainly yellow blob of a motor vessel suddenly sprang out of the trees off our port bow and trundled across the river blaring BBC news and Western pop music through its loudspeaker.

We didn't see the landings themselves until they were almost directly abeam. The one on the north side, to port, looked much more substantial, so we anchored there and went ashore in the dinghy to investigate. There was a narrow cut through the foliage leading down to the ferry dock and a crude road, the sides of which, for a short distance, were jammed with small tin-roofed shops. Unlike every other place where we'd landed on the river, no one here paid us any attention. It seemed a very Wild West sort of atmosphere. Off to one side a small group of black-winged vultures with pink bubble-gum heads picked over the carcass of a large dead animal. In the middle of the road, roaming through the cars and trucks that stood waiting for the ferry, various police and military types with guns swaggered about in their own vulture-like manner, asking questions and looking at papers.

This presumably had something to do with the coup attempt I'd learned about at the embassy. The police, fortunately, were not interested in us, though all the shopkeepers were, once they realized we actually wanted to buy something. Unfortunately, they had no diesel fuel; for that we had to take our one empty jerry jug a few miles up the road by taxi to a service station in the main town. One enterprising fellow did, however, convince us to buy an empty 5-gallon cooking-oil jug so we could augment our carrying capacity.

Past Farafenni the river quickly became much narrower, with deep water close to the banks on both sides, and the water itself became brackish. We soon came to Elephant Island, the first of the large upriver islands marked out on our chart. Directly opposite, on the north bank, was a village called Bambale, with a substantial wooden wharf. We anchored the boat and went ashore here and, as always happened when we visited a village, were quickly lost in a swarm of children.

The first adult to spot us was a middle-aged woman who at once pulled us into her hut to show us a younger woman, heavily pregnant, who was feverish and lay on a bed wrapped in blankets. On the dirt floor beside her a charcoal fire was blazing away in a tin brazier. The older woman spoke anxiously in Mandinka, pointing alternately at the sick woman in bed and at us. Our herd of children, meanwhile, all of them yammering at each other, packed themselves into the tiny mud dwelling behind us so that they could see what was happening.

The crowd in the hut grew larger and larger, and louder and louder, and just when it seemed we might be suffocated by all the confusion, a young man in a long blue robe suddenly appeared, parting the crowd before him like a prophet.

"This woman's daughter has been very sick for five days," he announced in perfect English. "She wants to know if you have medicine to help her."

This was in keeping with the pattern we'd noted as we traveled up the river. Close to the coast, near Banjul, people always asked for money; further on they had asked for books; more recently they'd been asking for medical supplies. This woman with the fever, I guessed, probably had malaria, and I did have some antimalarial drugs onboard, but I had no idea if they would help her, or if they were safe for pregnant women.

"We are not doctors," I said. "She needs to see a doctor. Is that possible?"

The young man explained that there was a clinic in Farafenni, but that to take her daughter there this woman would need money to pay for a donkey cart ride out to the main road, then money to pay for a bush taxi, and more money still to pay the doctor at the clinic. All these things, he said, would cost 45 dalasi.

Carie gave me a worried look. "Shall we give her 35?"

What she was worried about, I knew, was that these people were somehow swindling us.

"Let's make it 50," I answered.

Which was all of $5 US, a very small price to pay, I figured, to know we had done what we could to help. I took out my wallet and extracted from it five 10 dalasi notes, an act that made me feel quite omnipotent. But it also made me self-conscious, and I was careful to make sure no one could see how many more notes I had.

"Please take this," I said to the woman as I held out the money. "Please take your daughter to a doctor as soon as possible."

Her reaction was everything a budding philanthropist might hope for. She gave out a great howl of surprise and glee, dropped to her knees, literally groveled at my feet, clasped one ankle with both her hands, and promised she would for the rest of her life pray to Allah on our behalf.

HAVING FOUND US, the young man in blue, whose name was Ebrahim, seized on us like a terrier with a bone. He was the only person in the village who could speak fluent English, as he had spent four years at a secondary school downriver. This had been paid for, we learned, by a generous Irish couple who, like us, had met Ebrahim while cruising up the river. Ever since then Ebrahim had zealously befriended the crews of every foreign yacht that stopped at Bambale. He remembered the names and nationalities of every sailor he'd met and could describe in great detail everything they'd said and done while visiting.

We hadn't intended to stop here long, but Ebrahim convinced us we should stay at least two days, until Sunday, when the villagers would perform a calabash dance.

"The Swedish tourist boat will come," he explained, eyes bright, as though he had guessed what our ambition must be. "It is a very important ceremony."

Meanwhile, he worked hard to monopolize our time. The morning after our arrival, the very instant I stuck my head out the companionway at the crack of dawn, there he was standing on the wharf waving his arms.

"Hello, hello," he cried. "Please come ashore. We have many things to do today."

We spent most of the morning with Ebrahim touring the village in detail. We met women grinding meal with huge wooden pestles in great wooden bowls; we met women doing laundry; we met women hauling water on their heads from the village well. We also met many men—the village elders taking their ease under a baobab tree, a group of holy marabouts who sat on benches and copied out long reels of Arabic onto gray chalkboards, a group of men putting a new thatched roof on a hut. It seemed as if we were introduced to most everyone in town, and during our procession many people complained at length about their health. One man claimed he'd been kicked in the head by a donkey when he was a boy and had never been the same since.

"It is true," said Ebrahim sadly. "This man, he is always very confused."

Carie poked me in the ribs. "You see," she hissed. "They all think you will give them dalasi, like the woman from yesterday."

I listened to all these complaints and took notes on a piece of paper, nodding my head gravely, but otherwise said nothing.

That afternoon Ebrahim took us over to Elephant Island in a dugout pirogue to show us the bush pigs that lived there. We had heard about these animals, wild warthogs that often made pests of themselves by decimating rice fields, and were happy to have a chance to meet some.

"Sometimes we must hunt them and kill them," explained Ebrahim. "It can be very hard. They are dangerous when they are trapped."

"Are they good to eat?" I asked, as I assumed they must be a valuable source of protein.

"No, no!" exclaimed Ebrahim. "We are Muslims. We cannot eat the filthy meat of pigs."

Unfortunately, Carie and I made a great deal of noise mucking through the dense mangrove roots on the shore of the island in our big rubber boots. Ebrahim, meanwhile, who was barefoot, slipped like a silent wraith through the muddy tangle. When finally we reached high ground, Ebrahim pointed out several monkey tracks, but we found the bush-pig dens—holes dug in the ground between the roots of baobab trees, neatly carpeted with dry grass—

were all empty.

"This is too bad. Very too bad," said Ebrahim. "Normally the bush pigs will sleep here all day and only go at night to look for food."

"They heard us," I replied. "They heard the clumsy tubabs coming ashore with you, and they have all run away."

Ebrahim said nothing, but smiled shyly in agreement.

That evening he had us to his hut for dinner, a meal of fish and rice, which had been prepared by his sister. The three of us ate with spoons from a single steel bowl while the inevitable horde of children, who were very curious to see if we would eat Gambian food, watched from the open doorway and window. Afterwards we were joined by these children, and by many adults, who all crammed into the hut to drink China green tea with us. While the tea was prepared and served, always a laborious process, there was a great deal of lively conversation.

Like all villages we had visited, Bambale had no electricity, and the only light in Ebrahim's hut came from a single candle. There was also an old flashlight that clearly needed new batteries. Amazingly, it seemed to be the only one in town, as people often stopped by to borrow it. There was no moon that night, and the world outside the hut was as black as ink. Never before had I been in any human community that was so devoid of illumination.

Our tea party went on for hours, and when I eventually checked the time, I was surprised to see it was almost one in the morning.

"Is this normal?" I asked Ebrahim, pointing at my watch.

"What do you mean?" he replied.

"Do people here always stay up this late? Or is tonight different, because you have tubabs in your house?"

"Oh, no," he laughed. "This is what we always do. We are often awake late at night, laughing and talking with each other."

I was astonished by this and immediately envied these people. They had so little, but it seemed they always had food to eat, and they had each other. Did they really need much more than that? I wondered: if they became wealthier, would they do what we had done? Would they segregate themselves into hermetic homes filled with electric light and material objects, lock their doors, and become lonely? Was this the price of prosperity?

The next morning, again, Ebrahim waved to me eagerly from the wharf. I waved back, but we did not immediately go ashore. As much as I appreciated the intense sense of community we'd experienced the night before, this relentless companionship, so freighted with expectation and desire, felt burdensome. Visiting villages on the Gambia, especially this one, had given me a good idea of what it's like to be a Very Famous Person, and I wasn't too sure I enjoyed it. Having the boat to retreat to, with its portable moat to protect us, was a blessing I greatly appreciated.

We spent most that day on the boat, hiding from the people in the village. In the late afternoon we finally went ashore to fill our water jug and invited Ebrahim to join us for dinner aboard that evening. He was thrilled and insisted on bringing the food, a spicy peanut soup with rice, which again was prepared by his sister. While we were eating together, Carie remarked on this and belabored Ebrahim about the unequal division of labor in Gambian villages.

"I see the women, they are always working," she insisted. "And the men, they do nothing! I do not think this is right."

Ebrahim was flabbergasted and could not utter a word in response. I actually agreed with Carie; it did seem the men were mostly idle in every village we visited. But out of loyalty to my gender, I came to Ebrahim's rescue and listed the few jobs I knew of that the men did: building and repairing huts, tending the vegetable gardens (as opposed to the rice fields, a much more labor-intensive chore that fell to the women), and killing bush pigs. I hoped Ebrahim might add to this list, but he simply nodded.

"Yes, yes," he said, greatly relieved. "The men also do work."

Afterwards we presented him with gifts, a moment that inevitably felt awkward. For Ebrahim there was a pair of sunglasses and some books and magazines. For the village as a whole I had prepared a bag of medical supplies, along with some general instructions on how to use them and a list of what could be used specifically to treat the people who had complained to us of their maladies. There were also two packs of fresh D-sized batteries for the communal flashlight.

Ebrahim was effusively grateful, but still I felt embarrassed that our gifts were not more lavish. Ebrahim had made it very clear he hoped we, like our Irish predecessors, might pay for more schooling, and in fact this was, by our standards, entirely affordable. A year in school here cost little more than $100. But Ebrahim's fervent desire couldn't help but taint his hospitality and made it seem something like extortion. This, I think, now haunted all his relationships with visitors.

The following morning we went ashore—at last!—to see about the calabash dance. I had assumed the tourist boat was coming on this day because this was when the dance was taking place, but in fact it was the other way around. The owners of the boat, explained Ebrahim, regularly paid the villagers to perform the dance and had also promised to someday build a small medical dispensary here.

And the boat, unfortunately, was running late. While standing on the wharf with the rest of the villagers waiting for it to appear, I noticed there was a marked change in the behavior of the children who always followed us around. Before they were always trying to hold our hands and constantly asked: "What is your name? What is your name?" But now, for the first time, as if caught in some Pavlovian reaction, they became much more aggressive and asked if we would give them candy and money.

Eventually the boat did come, two hours later than expected. It was a dilapidated steel thing, perhaps 70 feet long, and looked like it might have been a gunboat in some previous existence. On board were 10 German tourists, plump and prosperous, festooned with cameras, all of whom looked horrified when they stepped ashore and were mobbed by the locust children, who grabbed at them, demanding candy and money. I noticed one man in particular, heavy-set with jowls in a brightly colored shirt, who was especially vicious and slapped hard at his tormentors as he barked at them to stay away.

Because the boat was running so late, it turned out the calabash dance was cancelled. The tourists only had time to rush into the village for a quick 15-minute tour, and then immediately came trundling back down the trail toward the wharf. The man with the jowls, I noticed, had resigned himself to his fate and was now holding hands with two children, whom he lectured quietly in German.

Finally, once all the tourists had gathered again on the wharf, the skipper of the boat gave a great happy shout and hurled handfuls of candy in all directions. With an ear-piercing squeal, the children all chased after it, and the tourists quickly scrambled aboard the boat and escaped downriver.

JUST A FEW MILES UPRIVER from Bambale we came to Sea Horse Island, so named because this supposedly was where European explorers first discovered the species hippopotamus back in the early 15th century. From here the water in the river became fresh and the scenery on shore was transformed. Instead of the endless unbroken walls of mangrove, we now saw open marshes and rice fields, nipa palm trees, and enormous termite mounds that looked like wax drippings from giant red candles. In the distance in a few places we saw low hills, bright red knolls standing proud over the landscape, and sometimes low cliffs that crowded up to the riverbank.

We also now were tormented by new sorts of insects. At night, as before, we had to defend ourselves against mosquitoes, but now during the day we were also assaulted by tsetse flies, which had an almost supernatural ability to evade detection. You'd see nothing, hear nothing, then suddenly you were bitten and felt a sharp stab of pain. Only then would you notice a rather large noisy fly that seemed to have materialized out of nowhere. They liked me much better than Carie, and every bite I received swelled up into an itchy red welt that took days to subside.

There were other types I could not identify, including one species that looked like a cross between a centipede and a Star Wars satellite. I found the first one under the floor in our inflatable dinghy and thought little of it as I flipped it overboard with an oar blade. Just two days later, however, I found nearly a hundred of these "dinghy bugs," as I now called them, swarming under the teak grate in the cockpit on *Crazy Horse*. Yelping in surprise, I grabbed a can of insecticide and sprayed and sprayed, screaming like a victim in a zombie movie, until finally the can was empty and all the bugs were dead.

The dragonflies, at least, were both harmless and beautiful. I noticed them often as they perched in the early morning like iridescent gems on our anchor rode, just a fraction of an inch above the surface of the water, with their wings quivering gently in the weak breeze.

Searching for hippos now became an important priority. An old man in Bambale had told me that he remembered when there were so many of them you could walk across the river on their backs. An apocryphal statement, no doubt, but I had no reason not to believe him when he also told me they were now hard to find. In the past, I'd heard, hippos had been hunted, as they are destructive, with enormous appetites, and are capable of devouring most of a rice field in one night. Now they were protected by law, which meant you could only kill one if you caught it actually eating your rice. Supposedly there were less than a hundred left living in the navigable portion of the river below the falls at Fatoto.

Between Sea Horse Island and Kuntaur, once an important river port, there was a long series of islands stretching along the south bank of the stream. Between and behind these islands was a network of small creeks, and I was hopeful we could find hippos here if we tried hard enough. To increase our chances, we set out in the dinghy in the mornings and early evenings to look for them.

One morning while we were out creek-crawling, the dinghy's outboard got tangled up in a crude unmarked fish net that stretched clear across the creek we were exploring. Unfortunately, I had to cut the net with a knife to get free of it. Further up we found more nets, which we successfully evaded, and then the fisherman who had set them, who was paddling along in a dugout pirogue.

I hailed the man and led him back to the net we had damaged, showed him where I had cut it, and offered him 10 dalasi in reparations. He was clearly angry and at first rejected my offer, out of pride it seemed, but then thought better of it and accepted. After I actually paid him, he became much friendlier, and I was emboldened to ask if he knew where we could find some hippos. He pointed in the direction of the next creek upriver and nodded his head vigorously.

We could not be certain, of course, whether the fisherman had sent us to this creek because there really were hippos there, or whether he simply wanted us well away from his nets, but this did not dampen our enthusiasm. The further up the creek we went, the more wildlife we found—first an otter swimming deftly through the water, then numerous monkeys racing through the trees on shore—and with each sighting our hopes soared higher. The creek became ever narrower and more twisted, and soon we spotted big mudslide breaks in the foliage on shore where very large animals had obviously entered the water.

"This is it," I told Carie, and I shut down the engine, pulled out the oars, and started rowing so that we wouldn't frighten our hippo once we found it.

The creek became narrower still, such that there was barely room to swing the oars, and finally it dawned on me that meeting a hippo at such close quarters could very well be dangerous. But still we pressed on. Just one more bend in the creek, I told myself, and then we'll turn back. And so it went, through bend after bend, until finally we reached an open pool ringed with tall grass.

We paused a moment here, as we could go no further, and then, as I was struggling to turn the dinghy around, we heard a rustling noise in the grass on the creek bank above us. The noise grew louder… and louder… and we held our breath, bracing for the impact of a one-ton hippo swan-diving down into our tiny inflatable boat.

Then, at last, we caught a glimpse of the beast. Not a hippo (fortunately), but an old bush pig, which poked its head through the grass, inspected us briefly, flashed a curved tusk in our direction, and then stomped off inland away from us.

COINCIDENTALLY, OUR HIPPO MANIA was assuaged the very next day. While motoring on to Kuntaur aboard *Crazy Horse* in the late morning, we spotted two at a distance on the open river. They looked like slim gray lozenges floating on the surface of the water—a mother and calf, presumably, as one was much smaller than the other.

"Shall we go closer?" asked Carie.

"No," I answered morosely. "I think it's best we just leave them alone."

We stopped two days at Kuntaur, to search (unsuccessfully) for more diesel fuel and to see the famous stone circles at Wassu, just two miles inland. We marched over in the early morning, before the sun rose too high, and inevitably collected an entourage of people, mostly children, along the way. It was startling how quickly the green foliage along the river gave way to dry barren savannah and surprising, too, how little the people who lived here knew about these mysterious stone monuments.

"These once were houses," proclaimed one man who had repeatedly offered to be our guide.

But this, I knew, was patently false. The red laterite cylinders, which had been carbon-dated to about 750 AD, were arranged in neat circles around grave sites that were considerably older. Similar sites have been found through out West Africa, from the Sahara as far south as Guinea, but the largest concentration by far was right here, on the north side of the Gambia. Aside from the great pyramids in Egypt, they are the only evidence of megalithic culture on the continent, and no one knew for sure who erected them.

Past Kuntaur the river turned back on itself and flowed west for some distance through a small archipelago, the Baboon Islands, which were part of the River Gambia National Park, a nature preserve that was strictly off limits to visitors. The vegetation on shore grew even more lush and jungle-like, and while passing by in the boat we strained to catch a glimpse of chimpanzees in the trees, as we'd been told there was a troop that lived here. We had no luck, but we did see river eagles soaring high overhead and various smaller birds, clothed in shocking iridescent plumage, that skittered along the shore.

Soon the river turned east again, passed through another lush archipelago, the Kai-ai Islands, and arrived at MacCarthy Island and the old provincial capital of Georgetown. From the river it seemed a bedraggled place, but it was much larger than a village, and that in itself made it seem an important destination. The most startling thing about it was the black steel schooner we spotted anchored off its southern end, the first foreign yacht we'd seen since leaving Oyster Creek outside Banjul. A tattered Australian flag flew from its backstay and on its transom was a hand-carved board that had the name *Black Pic* inscribed upon it.

We circled the schooner hopefully, and almost immediately a head popped out the companionway—a bearded face topped with a long tangle of blond hair.

"Meet you for drinks at sunset," shouted the cheerful man who belonged to the face. "At the tourist camp across the river." And he pointed to a small pier directly opposite the town.

We anchored *Crazy Horse* about a half mile further on and dinghied over to the pier at the appointed time. The tourist camp, which was run by Monica, a German woman, and her Gambian consort Modu, was like something out of the Swiss Family Robinson—a series of elevated platforms and dwellings hanging among the trees, illuminated by burning torches, with gangs of monkeys filtering through the surrounding foliage like a raucous wind of laughter.

We were still on the Gambia, but it seemed now we had been transported into an alternative dimension, into some ideal travel-magazine version of the river. We savored cocktails, nibbled on delicious hors d'oeuvres, and talked for hours—with Monica and Modu, the professional hostess and host; with one of their guests, a bizarre Italian woman with an intense gleam in her eye who was traveling alone across the breadth of West Africa on a three-week holiday; but mostly with Colin, our fellow sailor, master and commander of *Black Pic*, who had recently returned to the river after a two-year absence.

"It has infected me," he admitted with a broad grin. "Africa is in me now, and I had to come back here."

During his last visit, he explained, he had been overwhelmed by the simple desire to help people. He had a spare pump aboard his boat, a big gasoline-driven trash pump, and had given it to some rice farmers he met on the north bank of the river near the Kai-ai Islands.

"I showed them how to run it and how they could use it to grow twice as much rice each year by pumping river water up into their fields during the dry season."

Colin poured himself another vodka tonic, took a long sip, and settled back in his chair.

"I tell you I felt like Prometheus, like I'd fucking changed everything for these people. But you can guess what happened. They had one year with two good harvests, and now I come back and everything's gone to shit. Pump's busted, ruined for good, and everything's exactly the same as before."

Now Colin had decided to do good by helping himself. "It's so obvious!" he exclaimed. "They kill bush pigs here all the time and waste the meat, because they're Muslims. I reckon I can buy dead pigs dead cheap, smoke the meat, pack it aboard, and sail out to the Cape Verdes to sell it. It's an easy reach, three days or so, and they're all Christians out there, just dying to taste some pork."

Next morning we were awakened early by the haunting wail of a muezzin calling the devout to prayer at the mosque in town. After breakfast we went ashore, eager to explore, and were amazed. Georgetown, in spite of its dowdy appearance, seemed a fount of modern civilization. There were powerlines hanging from poles, electricity everywhere, and even a public telephone outside the marketplace, where women in brightly colored shawls and robes hovered over small piles of fresh food and other commodities they offered for sale.

We soon ran into Colin, who greeted us with a great shout. "Come!" he declared. "I've just the lad for you to meet."

And he led us a short distance down the waterfront to a small café and "galary" run by a young man named Yahya. He seemed a bit bashful, with a wry smile on his face, but perked up instantly when he noticed the large plastic water jug dangling from my hand, which I'd brought along in hopes of getting it filled.

"I see there," he said hopefully. "That looks like a very useful container. Would you like to sell it to me?"

I cannot describe what a relief it was to hear those words. We had been months now in West Africa and had met many people who wanted things from us. Not once, until now, had anyone offered to buy something from us, rather than just suggesting, or demanding, that we simply give it to them. I felt a rush of gratitude and was immediately chagrined that I could not agree to this request.

"I'm very sorry," I explained. "But this is the only one we have, and we really need it."

"Yes, yes, I understand," said Yahya. "But perhaps you can lend it to me for a short time, so I can fetch some water with it."

I said I'd be happy to, if only Yahya would show me where I could get some water myself. And from that moment on, at least as far as I was concerned, we were fast friends. Carie and I spent several hours that day talking with Yahya in his little shop and returned again the next day to talk some more. He was unlike anyone else we'd met thus far on the river—first because he was a member of the Fula tribe, rather than Mandinka or Wolof, and also because he was not at all Muslim.

He never declared this to us, but it soon became evident from his conversation. I remarked to him, for example, remembering my friend Charlie the crocodile back in Serekunda on the coast, that Yahya was the toma of Gambia's new president, Yahya Jammeh.

"Yes, that is true," he smiled. "I know very well I am the toma of the president, but alas he does not know he is the toma of me. But perhaps, if I am lucky, the spirits will tell him so."

Yahya was also the first Gambian to offer us marijuana, rolled up in a nice fat joint, or "wrap," as he called it. The marijuana, he explained, was grown in the Casamance in southern Senegal and was brought across the border by men who were protected by the spirits, as they carried special amulets given to them by a famous fortune-teller.

"You have met the husband of Monica, Modu, from across the river," he explained. "He also carries such an amulet, so the spirits can protect him from being caught by Monica when he goes with other women."

THAT EVENING YAHYA INVITED US to have dinner with him, a meal of cous-cous he served al fresco at a small table he set up outside on the old ferry pier near his shop. After the meal he passed around a wrap, and as the pungent fumes of Casamance homegrown oozed through my consciousness, he looked at me quite intently and asked, "How is it that you find your way at sea? How do you know where to go?"

"There are satellites in the sky that tell me where I am," I explained. "And if the satellites are broken, I can look at the sun and the stars. I have a tool I can use to measure exactly how high in the sky they are. Once I know that, I can always figure out where I am."

Yahya nodded his head carefully. "There is another way," he announced and proceeded to tell a long involved story about a bush-pig hunt.

It seems Yahya and several other men had tracked the pig in question far out into the bush, far from the river, until they were surrounded by hills that they did not recognize. Finally, they succeeded in cornering the pig in a den at the foot of one of the hills. For a long time they threw rocks into the den, until eventually the pig came out, and they surrounded it. It was Yahya himself who administered the death blow, as he struck the beast in the head with a large stone.

Yahya then suggested, to the amazement of his companions, that they take the pig back to town to sell it. Most of the men believed the pig had no value, but Yahya insisted he knew people who would pay good money for it. After some debate, the men all agreed to this plan and skewered the pig on a long pole they cut from a tree so they could carry it more easily. The only problem was they now had no idea where they were and did not know in which direction the town lay.

"Fortunately, there was one man with us who was a soothsayer," explained Yahya. "He said he could find the way. He took a leaf from a special tree he found and folded the leaf four times, so that one end was longer than the others. He then put a small stone inside the leaf and threw it into the air. When it fell back to the earth the man examined it to see which way the leaf was pointing, and he said this is the direction we must go. We all followed him, and he led us straight back to town!"

Yahya now had a self-satisfied look on his face, as though he had demonstrated to me an important scientific proof.

"What became of the pig?" I asked. "Were you able to sell it?"

Yahya laughed out loud. "That is the best part of the story. The soothsayer and I took the pig and left all the other men to wait for us. We brought the pig to our friends and together we cooked it and feasted on it and drank palm wine together all night long. The next day I told the other men that they were right, no one would buy the pig, and that we had thrown it into the river."

And as soon as he'd finished this story, Yahya then asked, out of the blue, if we would like to attend a dance.

"What sort of a dance?" I asked, a bit suspiciously, remembering the bogus calabash dance for tourists we had failed to witness in Bambale.

"It is given by the ruling government party," explained Yahya. "To announce the nomination of the party's candidate from Georgetown in the elections to parliament next month."

"You mean it's a political dance?"

"Yes, yes. It is very political. It is starting just now."

In the distance we could hear the faint sound of a drum, interspersed with blasts from a whistle. Together the three of us walked away from the river, toward the sound, and soon found the dancing ground, in the middle of an unpaved street, beneath a single naked lightbulb dangling from a wire overhead. A single row of wooden benches had been set out in a large square around the ground, and already these were packed with people, with still more people standing behind them, all swaying in time to the music. The band consisted of just one man, a slender crooked-looking fellow with odd tufts of hair sprouting from his head, who capered about beating on a single drum hanging from a cord around his neck while simultaneously blowing on a shiny tin police whistle.

The music, which was remarkably rich and complex given its source, continued for a short time, with no one dancing to it, until suddenly there appeared a spotless white Mitsubishi pickup truck. In the back of the truck, sitting in a large upholstered armchair, was a young man wearing fancy basketball shoes, a red satin track suit, a baseball cap, mirrored sunglasses, and several gold necklaces.

As soon as the truck stopped, several other men came forward, picked up the armchair out of the truck bed, and carried it and its inhabitant to a prominent space at one end of the dancing ground. As soon as they set the chair down, the music stopped. The man in the chair rose up, and the crowd cheered. The man smiled, his teeth glistening in the thin electric light, and waved grandiosely in all directions.

"This is the district commissioner," whispered Yahya. "He is also a major in the army. He is very popular here, but the law prohibits him from speaking at political events."

The commissioner continued waving for perhaps half a minute, while the crowd continued cheering, and then he sat down and the music at once started up again. In between beating on his drum and blowing his whistle, the one-man band started chanting a refrain. Something to the effect, as Yahya translated it, of what a great and glorious man the president was. Soon all the crowd took up the chant and the dancing started, but it wasn't the sort of dancing I expected. There were no traditional costumes and no ceremony or ritual of discernible sort. Instead it was very much like any Western disco or school dance, where anyone could get up and dance however they wanted.

I started swaying a bit in time to the music and in just a moment heard the familiar cry of "Tubab! Tubab!" coming from somewhere nearby. A strange woman suddenly appeared in front of me, grabbed me by the hand, and pulled me out into the dancing ground. My head still thick with the fumes of Casamance homegrown, I threw myself into the music for all I was worth. Arms and legs akimbo, I flailed about in comic style, then threw myself on the ground and wriggled madly like a fish out of water. The crowd ate it up and gave me a huge cheer and a laugh as I retreated again to the sidelines.

In between the spates of dancing, like commercials on TV, there were political speeches. Instead of a PA system, there was the one-man band, who stood beside whoever was talking and repeated everything they said, only louder. The most important speech was by the woman who would be running as the ruling party's local member of parliament. This was a huge triumph for her, Yahya explained, as she had long been the town's most outspoken opponent of the old president and his government.

Most of the other speeches were fairly anodyne, the sort of clap-trap you'd hear from politicians anywhere, except for one old man who got up and told an old folktale about farm animals who failed to tell the farmer about the rat and the lizard who were quarreling in the ceiling of the farmer's house. The rat and the lizard fought and fought, until they had destroyed the roof of the house, and it collapsed upon the farmer's head. The moral being (again per Yahya's translation) that the people of Georgetown should "keep it all in the family."

"Don't let your troubles take you to the opposition," warned the old man. "Talk to us, and we will help you."

The people of Georgetown endured all this rhetoric patiently, but no one cheered the speakers too loudly, and it seemed clear the dancing was all anyone really cared about. Once the speeches were finished, it continued unabated and the energy of the dancers grew ever more intense.

And again I started swaying a bit in time to the music, and soon another woman appeared in front of me and took my hand. In her other free hand she held a white shawl. I resisted at first, but Yahya laughed loudly and pushed me forward. The woman carefully tied the shawl around my waist, and we then we started dancing.

Once again, I gave it my best, dancing wildly in all directions, though this time I did not fall on the ground and wriggle like a fish, as I suspected something important was happening. When we were done, the woman darted at me, grabbed her shawl from my waist, seized it to her breast, and scampered off into the crowd like a scared rabbit.

The crowd laughed and cheered loudly and pointed at me.

"What the hell is going on?" I asked as I returned panting to the sidelines.

Yahya was grinning like the Cheshire cat.

"You have just performed a fertility dance," he explained. "It is very powerful magic. The woman you just danced with has been trying to have a baby for 10 years. She is hoping now you have broken her curse."

I stood for a while catching my breath and felt the music, the improbably powerful music, flowing through me. I felt the rhythm of it relentlessly bearing down on me, the living pulse of this place and these people. I felt my body wanting to move again, but this time I marshaled my willpower and consciously controlled the urge. I needed to savor what had just happened.

And in my stifling of my body, my refusal to let it succumb to the rhythm of the music, I felt something else unlocking within me. I felt myself carried away down the river, merging with the water in it, the water that had carried us into this continent. Down the river and all the way out to the ocean, where at last the pulse of the music was merged with the scend of the sea and the ceaseless rhythm of the waves.

Then finally I relented, let my legs start moving with the music again, and in an instant I was pulled back into myself, into this ring of people dancing in the light cast by one lonely lightbulb. I looked up at the sky then, at the stars shining brightly overhead, and prayed to the spirits that soon I might have another toma in these parts.

Scott Kennedy

PART IV

SHIPMATES

There are no passengers on Spaceship Earth. We are all crew.

—Marshall McLuhan

MAURI CULLEN
Until the End of His Days

OF ALL THOSE WHO WERE SHIPWRECKED in Spain in that summer of 1992 after we lost *Constellation* in the Rio Odiel, only Dave Lankshear and I were determined to return to North America the same way we had come. While the others soon took to airplanes and flew back across the Atlantic Ocean, Dave and I rode a bus back to Puerto de Santa Maria and walked out the beach toward the Puerto Sherry Marina with our seabags slung over our backs. We crashed a few days aboard a teak-bespangled Cheoy Lee ketch called *Rangoon Lady*, one of many America 500 boats that were waiting with caretaker crews for the next rally start, then moved on to Gibraltar, where we heard there was one rally boat with an owner who desperately needed crew.

We found the boat, *Goatlocker III*, a doughty aft-cockpit Westsail 43 with red tanbark sails, strapped into a slip at Sheppard's Marina in a dusty corner of the waterfront. Aboard we found a retired U.S. Navy chief master petty officer, one Maurice Cullen, who at once assured us he was bound and determined to sail around the world, with or without crew. Mauri, as he called himself, was shaped something like a small bull trained to walk erect, with a bald cue-ball head, heavy-framed eyeglasses, and a trim goatee. He was lively and outspoken, running on in a gravel-toned voice, often rude and crude, but always funny, and politically somewhere to the right of Genghis Khan.

Dave, who had less education and thus more sense than me, and also more sailing experience, quickly perceived that it might be a bad idea to sail with Mauri. I on the other hand, blinded as ever by my attraction to interesting and amusing people, quickly agreed to sign on as crew.

I suppose I just assumed that anyone with 30 years in the Navy must know something of seafaring. Mauri at least had indeed spent much time working aboard ships as an electrical engineer, but in fact, I soon learned, knew little of sailing or boat-handling. The first hint of this came a week before our departure from Gibraltar for Puerto Sherry, where we were to rejoin the rally fleet, when I asked him to explain to me how *Goatlocker*'s running rigging worked. Mauri assured me everything was fine and all had worked perfectly last time he sailed the boat (several months earlier), but he could not for the life of him tell me which line was which and what was supposed to go where.

I also learned early on—the first time we tried to leave Gibraltar, but failed due to an overheating engine—that Mauri was much more humanitarian than me. We spent that day adrift in Algeciras Bay fuming over the engine and eventually, at my insistence, tried to sail out the bay when the wind came up. I almost lost a finger as I fiddled with the frozen headsail roller-furling drum, which suddenly became functional again with a great out-flowing rush of sail, but soon enough the wind died again anyway. As the sun went down and the bay went dark we found ourselves motoring slowly back toward Gib with eyes glued to the engine's temperature gauge.

All around us we could hear the insistent whine of speedboats shooting back and forth between Gibraltar and the city of Algeciras across the bay. These were smugglers bringing cases of tax-free cigarettes to the heavily taxed smokers of Spain. During the many days I'd spent alone aboard *Goatlocker* at Sheppard's waiting for Mauri to return from a trip home to the States, I'd watched these men. They were out all night long running the bay in high-powered ski boats painted flat black showing no lights at all. I'd seen them load their boats in the marina, then tear out through the anchorage with engines screaming, and sometimes return with Spanish helicopters in hot pursuit. I'd heard about how much money they made, and how ruthless they could be.

Suddenly, as we approached the anchorage, we heard one boat close by tearing through the black void directly ahead. Then we heard what sounded like a crash, muffled in the night, followed by an eerie silence. I went forward to the bow and leaned out over the pulpit peering into the gloom as Mauri circled the anchorage's outer edge. We went around once, twice, and on the third pass I thought I saw something in the water dead ahead. Floating wreckage, cardboard cartons, figures waving their arms.

"People in the water here!" I shouted back to the helm, and Mauri immediately throttled down into neutral.

"I guess we should get ready to pick them up," he called, his tone implying this might be more a question than a command.

And I immediately countermanded him: "I think we should just stay out of this."

And my instinct did prove correct. Our help was not needed, and might well not have been appreciated, as two police boats from Gib immediately shot out of the marina with searchlights blazing to recover the survivors. But still ever since in remembering that night I've always regretted that Mauri's gut response was so much more appropriate than mine.

It was one of many things I came to regret about Mauri. In Navy vernacular, a "goatlocker" is what you call the quarters of a chief petty officer, and Mauri thus was proud of the term, but it was also an apt physical description of both the boat itself and its chief inhabitant. Mauri was, with all apologies to his memory, a monumental slob, and his vessel and equipment reflected this. He liked making impromptu repairs on his boat—nigger-rigging he called it—much more than he liked sailing it, and often it seemed he kept everything in a state of slovenly disrepair simply to increase his chances of needing to do so.

He was himself a walking catalogue of ailments. He suffered, among other things, from vascular disease, diabetes, emphysema, and gout, which had led to all but three of his toes being amputated. He laughingly called all the pills he had to take "rat poison" and was otherwise cheerful about his ills. "Keep your toes crossed, because I can't!" was his signature salutation, and he seemed perfectly sanguine about his possibly imminent demise.

In *Goatlocker*'s saloon, screwed to the main bulkhead, there was an official framed certificate from the Vatican that read: *The Holy Father John Paul II Paternally Imparts His Apostolic Blessing As A Pledge Of Heavenly Favors To Mr. Maurice Cullen Skipper of Goatlocker III.*

Above that was a plaque commemorating Mauri's military career, topped in turn by the official U.S. Navy American flag he'd been given on his retirement to be buried with, folded into a neat triangle and encased in glass.

If ever he did die at sea, Mauri explained to me several times with some relish, I was to break that glass, wrap him in that flag, tuck the Pope's certificate in next to his chest, and push him overboard. Then, he said, I could go on any sort of a cruise I wanted, so long as at the end of it I sailed the boat to Key West and gave it to a man named Joe Osterman.

WE DID FINALLY MAKE IT to Puerto Sherry, in spite of the fact the engine was constantly breaking down and spewing water and oil all over itself. We made repairs there, but it broke down once more, its cooling system again suffering a major hemorrhage somewhere, when we were in the Bay of Cadiz. This just after we left Puerto Sherry with a group of other rally boats that were headed up the coast to Huelva, close to where *Constellation* died, to attend Jimmy Cornell's second re-creation of the departure of Columbus.

We had left in the evening, so as to arrive at Huelva in daylight, and the sun was just setting when we discovered the leak and shut down the engine. There was a steady 15-knot breeze blowing into the bay from the west, and Mauri, who was on the wheel, at once ordered me to unfurl the jib. Given the breeze, we should have been able to more or less keep up with the other boats sailing a closehauled course on port tack, but it soon became apparent we could not sail to windward under a headsail alone.

Mauri was quickly reduced to a state of irate frustration, unable to get any feel for the helm, unable even to tell which way the wind was coming from, so that he repeatedly stalled the boat in irons, or worse, backwinded the sail altogether. Meanwhile I kept leaping back and forth across the cockpit, madly grinding on winches, dragging the jib back and forth across the rig's foretriangle, trying to keep up with Mauri's wild gyrations on the wheel.

After more than half an hour of this, I convinced him to let me try steering for a while. I soon had the boat settled out on a beam reach and explained we needed the mainsail to steer closer to the wind. Mauri went forward to the mast to raise the sail and for some reason took an awfully long time doing it. Back in the cockpit I could hear him cursing and grumbling and groaning, but couldn't tell what the problem was. Finally the sail went rattling up the track and Mauri returned to the cockpit, completely exhausted, looking as though he was on the verge of a nervous breakdown.

"I've got to sleep," he gasped and immediately disappeared below.

I was stunned and came within a hair's breadth of calling him back on deck to chew him out. He was the captain, this was his boat, and he had to decide what to do, where he wanted to go. But I bit my tongue and grimly assessed the situation.

The boat was already on starboard tack heading southwest, and after I got her sails balanced out so she could steer herself for a bit, I jumped down to the nav station to check the chart. I saw there was no immediate cause for alarm and if we kept sailing closehauled we should be able to keep clear of both a shoal patch in the middle of the bay and the Cadiz light.

A couple of hours later, Mauri emerged from his stateroom and pronounced himself restored by his nap.

"I've been thinking we should just sail straight to Madeira," he said.

My answer was taut with resentment: "Well, that's where we're headed right now."

The only alternative, as Mauri saw it, was to sail back to Puerto Sherry and fix the engine again, but if we did that he figured we'd fall behind the rally fleet and never catch up again. I suggested we might sail to Huelva and join the fleet there, as originally planned (thinking to myself, I must confess, that I might jump ship and join another boat there), but Mauri said this was out of the question. To get to Huelva without an engine we'd probably need a tow up the river, and this was something Mauri's enlarged sense of nautical pride could not countenance.

So Madeira it was. All through the night we sailed on to the southwest and in the morning, like a turtle trying to crawl across a freeway, had to stand on and off for an hour before lumbering through a long line of freighters stalking down the shipping lane into Gibraltar. The voyage ahead of us, which normally should have taken three to five days, in fact went on for nine, with the two of us standing alternate six-hour shifts.

I protested early on that six hours was much too long for a solo watch, but Mauri insisted he really needed that much off-time for sleeping. Indeed, it turned out he needed more, as I ended up on several nights having to stand parts of his watch after he reprised his act of the first night.

On our third night out, in the dark pit of the earliest morning when we had to jibe over after a big easterly wind shift, Mauri, who was on the wheel at the time, almost killed me when he backwinded the main the very instant after I released the boom preventer. As the boom snapped over with a thunderous crash, I slithered down the deck toward the cockpit with my head as low as possible and my heart pounding like a jackhammer.

"That is *not* the proper way to jibe a boat!" barked Mauri, as though this had somehow been my fault.

Whereupon he immediately backwinded the main again, and the boom crashed back across the boat as we once again power-jibed. Mauri said nothing and smiled sheepishly, like a kid caught with his hand in a cookie jar.

Just a few hours earlier during the afternoon I'd seen that same weak smile after he confronted me and asked in a querulous tone why it was our position plots on the chart never matched.

I told him I had been wondering that too and led him down to the nav desk to demonstrate how I plotted mine. And he showed me how he did his, and I learned he did not know there were just 60 minutes in one degree of latitude or longitude and not 100.

And now, after we finally managed a controlled jibe with me on the wheel and Mauri on mainsheet following my direction, I sent him down to get some sleep and pondered our position on the chart. It had become painfully clear that it was up to me to somehow get us to Madeira, and this knowledge electrified me.

For the first time since I'd started sailing offshore the fact of being on the ocean in a small sailboat, far from the sight of land, failed to stir the romantic optimist in my soul and instead inspired a vague sense of dread and hideous expectation. But buried not far below that anxiety there was also a deep well of empowerment, confidence, and satisfaction. I knew I could do this. I could get us from this point in the chart's white void off the coast of Morocco to this tiny island here labeled Madeira, way off in the middle of nowhere, come what may. And never before had I felt so alive and so alert to the adventure of voyaging.

ONE REASON WE WERE SO SLOW on this passage of course had to do with breakage. Primarily, we suffered much damage to our threadbare sails. The foot of the mainsail was torn on our second power-jibe during that electric night of mine, and from that point forward we always had to keep two reefs in it to cover the damage. Likewise the jib later tore right near its luff, and we had to keep it perpetually roller-reefed. Later still we also lost the staysail, as it was blown to bits in a squall. Meanwhile, both our autopilots failed, so that we always had to hand-steer the boat, and whenever Mauri was driving it seemed we wandered far off our course.

We had another excuse, too, in that we were becalmed for a full day in the middle of the passage, which at least gave us an opportunity to try and fix the engine. Here Mauri was relieved to find himself in his element and did a superb job jury-rigging a repair of the ruptured hose we found running between the heat exchanger and the exhaust manifold. When he was finished and had reinstalled the hose, we found what had been a catastrophic waterfall of a leak was now a mere trickle of escaped exhaust water. This didn't seem like a big problem to me, and I was eager to get the boat moving again. But Mauri decreed we should only run our semi-rehabilitated engine in an emergency, so we continued to drift until the wind returned.

We were becalmed again for most of a day when we at last had Madeira and its sister island of Porto Santo within sight. It was maddening to have to sit motionless with the mainsail down and our mast swaying back and forth like a mother's shame-on-you-boy fingertip with our destination so nearby. I pleaded with Mauri again and again that the leak wasn't bad and that we should just start the engine and motor into port, but he steadfastly refused.

Finally the wind returned again, and we enjoyed a few hours of sailing in the right direction before it suddenly shifted in the middle of the night and came on a full gale, blowing 35–40 knots from precisely the wrong direction.

With our misshapen sail plan, no staysail and just a baggy roller-reefed jib up forward, we could not sail on the wind and had to start reaching away east of the islands. Mauri however could not abide this and after a couple of hours ordered we should come about and reach back in the other direction. This I saw would eventually put us in the channel between the two islands with Porto Santo to leeward, and I was worried we might lose more sails and get blown down on to it. I argued we should instead heave-to where we were, in open water clear of both islands, but Mauri would have none of it and insisted we tack.

Twice we tried, but could not get *Goatlocker*'s bow through the high wind and steep seas, so were forced to jibe around, which we fortunately managed without mishap. Soon we were headed right back where we came from, with the gale-force wind roaring in our ears.

By sunrise we were again in the channel. Much to my relief the wind suddenly disappeared as we passed in front of Porto Santo, dropping from 40 knots to nearly nothing in just a few minutes, as if some mighty finger somewhere had punched a button marked OFF. Now we were becalmed again, powerless as we wallowed in the heaving swell left over from the night before. We tried to keep moving as best we could but had little luck, as the sails were banging back and forth too much to hold any air for very long.

Even worse, it soon became obvious some current had grabbed us and was dragging us toward the southwest shore of Porto Santo. This was a very forbidding coast with large rocks scattered before it like giant dice in the sea. Where before I'd feared we might be driven ashore by high wind, now it seemed we'd land there through a lack of wind, and I couldn't help but laugh out loud.

But Mauri was not amused and began cursing, complaining he was too tired to think and had to sleep. Once again he tried to pull off his disappearing act, but I grabbed him by the shoulder this time and cut him off.

"What exactly do you want me to do while you're napping?"

"Well, what do *you* think we should do?" he countered defensively.

"I told you yesterday. We should motor into Madeira."

He again refused, but at least abandoned his plan to take a nap.

For the next two hours, as Mauri resumed cursing, we continued our fruitless effort to somehow sail the boat out of danger in the nonexistent wind. Finally, when we had drifted to within half a mile of the rocks off the coast, I was allowed to start the engine, but Mauri decreed we must run it only at slow speed so as not to stress the jury-rigged hose.

I rolled up the jib, sheeted the main flat, and had Mauri steer us toward Funchal, Madeira's main port. Every few minutes I checked the hose, and though it was still leaking slowly, it did not seem to be getting worse. Soon we felt confident it would hold up long enough to get us into port.

We both began to relax a bit, exulting in the prospect of our passage finally ending, when the wind came back. Not as strong as before, but still a very stiff breeze, 20–25 knots, blowing again from the wrong direction.

"We have to tough this out and leave the engine running," I bellowed at Mauri over the wind. "Otherwise we'll never get there."

And thankfully Mauri agreed with me. But even with the engine running at higher revs he could not steer a course to windward through the steepening seas and was perpetually luffing the mainsail and stalling the boat, killing all our forward momentum.

I took the wheel from him, quickly got a feel for the waves, and soon we were moving forward again. Our progress was painfully slow, with the boat crawling along at just over 2 knots, but at least it was progress. I now swore to myself I would not leave the wheel until we reached Funchal and told Mauri he might as well go below and get some sleep. He insisted however he wanted to stay on deck and help me out.

Slowly we crawled to the southwest, motor-sailing closehauled on starboard tack, until at last we reached the east end of Madeira and passed north of a string of barren islets known as Ilhas Desertas. Here the steep mountains of Madeira briefly sheltered us from the wind and our progress increased, but as soon as we emerged in open water on the island's south side the wind was in our teeth again blowing as hard as ever. Slowly we labored forward through the late afternoon, through a dull copper sunset, and into the evening, bringing to a close a second full day spent within sight of our destination.

Finally, as we were approaching Punta do Garajau, the island's southernmost headland, just four miles past which lay Funchal, we saw an enormous wall of awful-looking weather coming in fast from the west. Not so much a front as a positive vacuum, a jet-black curtain of evil that ate up the sky, the moon, the clouds, and the stars and turned them all into angry fingers of lightning.

"Look at that," I murmured. "I bet there's a lot of wind in there."

And together our hearts sank as we imagined ourselves swept away again by another gale. Even worse, I thought, we have those bloody Ilhas Desertas behind us now waiting to catch us and smash us to bits.

"It's up to you," declared Mauri. "Whatever you think is best."

And so in an instant that which to me had seemed implicit since that night off Morocco, and to Mauri presumably since I had taken the wheel from him that afternoon, now became explicit. I was the one in charge.

So I laid out a plan: we would crawl in as close to shore as we dared, well into the lee of Punta do Garajou, move up the coast to the end of the point, then shoot out past it into the anticipated gale, open up the engine's throttle as far as we dared, and hope to God we could tack, clear the point, and make it into Funchal in one go. If not, depending on how bad the gale seemed, we would have to think seriously about bearing away again to the southeast to gain sea room to leeward of the Desertas.

We moved in close to shore and turned for the end of the point as the black wall swept toward us. Closer and closer, until finally Mauri muttered to me: "Aren't you nervous? My sphincter is wound up so tight I can hardly breathe."

I had been on the helm now for nearly 12 hours. I was feeling dizzy, and my hands and arms ached from wrestling with the wheel and the waves all day.

"Don't worry," I told him. "We'll be fine."

And then, as we shot out past the end of the point, it was upon us. First a light rain shower, then fierce bolts of lightning stabbing at the horizon, and thunder rolling like artillery fire in the distance. But no wind, not a breath of it. What breeze there was died away to nothing, and we quietly cleared the point, dropped our mainsail, and motored through the rain into Funchal.

EN ROUTE TO MADEIRA Mauri had told me a story from his days in the Navy, about how one of his jobs at sea was to conduct a monthly man-overboard drill. To do this he would first select a crew member at random to play the victim, would hide this person away somewhere, and then take the ship's life-sized man-overboard dummy, which was always referred to as Oscar, and throw it overboard. He would sound the man-overboard alarm, and the rest of the crew would leap into action to stop the ship, identify the missing victim, locate Oscar, and lower a boat to recover him.

Mauri had always thought this a realistic simulation, until he was sent to serve as a special liaison officer aboard a West German ship, where as a formal courtesy he was asked to conduct a man-overboard drill. He launched into his familiar routine, selected a victim and hid him away, but could not find the ship's man-overboard dummy. He could not ask a crew member, as this would destroy the requisite element of surprise, so he went straight to the ship's first officer and asked where Oscar was stowed.

"What do you mean?" asked the officer. "Who is this Oscar?

And when Mauri told him he laughed: "It is me. I am the one you call Oscar!"

I remembered this story on our next leg to the Canary Islands, during which we had many of the same problems as before. I had by now lost all respect for Mauri, and various aspects of his personality I once found amusing, or at least could tolerate, had become supremely annoying. I was worried also about his basic fitness. His weird fits of manic exhaustion were almost pathological, and increasingly it seemed hard for him to move around the boat. What with his frequent jokes about dying at sea, and his repeated instructions as to what to do with his American flag and papal certificate, I couldn't help but wonder if he was on a suicide mission.

Certainly I could appreciate the sentiment. Though utterly incompetent on a sailboat, Mauri had a great deal of U.S. Navy pride, and it made perfect sense he'd want to end his days on the water, aboard a boat of his own, before any doctors had a chance to shelve him. I did not however want to become a footnote in his obituary, and eventually my annoyance with him morphed into something like loathing.

I found myself late one night—as we were running off on a broad reach toward the island of Gran Canaria before a firm breeze, overtired as always, because the autopilots were broken again and I again had to stand part of Mauri's watch—indulging in a wild fantasy.

"This is it," I would tell him. "Time for the man-overboard drill."

"What are you talking about?" he would ask with that hapless look on his face.

"And you!" I would declare in triumph. "You are the one they call Oscar!"

So, no, it didn't take me very long after we reached the Canaries to work up the nerve to tell Mauri I was leaving the boat. He was incredibly magnanimous about it, and at once my loathing was dissolved by his generous spirit. He laid all the blame for our differences on himself, thanked me for all he claimed I had taught him about sailing (though he also confessed he was likely to soon forget it), and insisted I stay aboard *Goatlocker* while looking for a berth on another boat.

I soon found one, on another America 500 rally boat, a sleek well-financed yacht named *Antipodes*, but still I kept a careful eye on Mauri and helped him work on *Goatlocker* whenever I could. He made a lot of blustery noise about not needing crew, boasting that he was perfectly willing to sail singlehanded across the Atlantic Ocean, but I knew—and I think he did too—that he was not capable of this.

Fortunately, anyone with a sailboat, even Mauri, can find crew in Las Palmas de Gran Canaria in November, and soon he was blessed with two new volunteers. The first (thankfully) was young, a strong Swiss sailor named Mark. The other was an older American, Ralph, who looked as pale as Bartleby the Scrivener and was keenly interested in navigation, but admitted to having no practical experience.

I had a fantastic passage on *Antipodes* sailing west from Las Palmas to the Bahamas with the rest of the rally fleet. We finished first in our class, and I became good friends with both the skipper and the Australian owner and sailed with them again in later years, in the Sydney–Hobart Race and at Antigua Race Week.

After our arrival that December at Georgetown on Great Exuma, Geoff, the owner, threw a grand party for the whole America 500 fleet, and in the middle of it I encountered Mark. He looked thinner than before, but had a smile on his face. He was very tired and had just told Mauri he was leaving the boat. Ralph, he confided, had been seasick during most of their passage and had often missed his watches, as had Mauri.

A few days after the party I ran into Mauri on the beach carrying a load of provisions back to his dinghy. Yes, he told me, he was alone again, but that was no problem. He planned soon to sail to the U.S. Navy base at Roosevelt Roads in Puerto Rico, with or without crew. Once there he could use his veteran status to refit *Goatlocker* and stock up on everything real cheap before setting off for Panama and the Pacific beyond it.

I gave him a few suggestions on what needed doing on the boat and warned him he definitely needed crew and new sails. He thanked me for the advice, then described in some detail a scheme he had devised to coat all his sails in contact cement to make them last longer.

It was the last time I ever saw him, and I knew even then what his fate would be: he would sail west until he expired from either mishap or disease.

I FOUND OUT JUST HOW FAR he got almost 10 years later. Geoff Hill, owner of *Antipodes*, made a point of asking me to join him again when in 2002 he sailed his last passage on the boat from Fort Lauderdale to Annapolis, where he proposed to sell her. And within moments of boarding the boat in a Fort Lauderdale marina, fresh off a late-afternoon flight from Boston, I found a bedraggled Westsail 43 just four slips down that looked strangely familiar. There was no name or homeport inscribed on her canoe transom, but as I studied her flanks closely in the fading evening light I could just make out the ghosts of letters that had been removed. They read: *Goatlocker III.*

I felt at that moment a sensation nearly as intense as the one I'd experienced a decade earlier while sitting at this boat's nav station not many miles off the coast of Morocco. First, of course, there was the fantastic coincidence. I had long since learned that in the world of bluewater sailing one often encounters familiar boats and people in disparate locations, but this was something else. To join *Antipodes* for the last time and accidentally encounter the boat I'd left to join her for the very first time—nearly 10 years after the fact, practically right next door—seemed almost supernatural.

Mostly though I was deeply grateful and just wanted to thank this vessel and the man who sailed her. This was the boat that had taught me a very important lesson, that I was perfectly capable of sailing a boat of my own offshore, and Mauri, perversely, had been the anti-matter mentor who helped lead me to that realization.

"Ahoy, *Goatlocker*!" I called from the dock, not knowing what else to call her.

Instantly there appeared in the companionway a leather-skinned, white-haired old man with a warm smile. He told me his name was Joe Osterman.

We didn't have too long to talk just then, but I got the essential facts: he was the one who sold Mauri the boat—at a very favorable price with no-interest term payments—on the condition that he get the boat back when Mauri died. This had happened late the previous year, after Mauri sailed into Antigua, just 300 miles shy of officially closing the loop on his circumnavigation at Roosevelt Roads. He had to leave the boat there and flew back to the States for emergency surgery, but did not survive the operation. Joe now had a crew of family members onboard—I could see and hear them through the companionway just below him—and together they had just finished sailing the boat back from Antigua.

I took down Joe's phone number and went to visit him a month later at his home on Boca Chica, just a couple of islands up from Key West. He had a big yard with a concrete wall all the way around, and inside there was a nice collection of Harley-Davidson motorcycles and a huge black pig living in a pen in a carport. Joe lived in a small house just over the pen with his young wife, infant daughter, and a 21-year-old stepson. The stepson was very protective and insisted on coming along when I took Joe out to lunch, but didn't join us afterward when Joe took me down to the local marina to show me all the work he was doing on the boat.

He talked proudly of the great success he'd had racing the boat, which he called *Guiseppe*, before he sold her to Mauri, his old Navy buddy. In a heavy full-keeled cruising boat with 15-year-old factory sails, he had in fact put up an amazing record: 17 top-three finishes in Florida Keys regattas over a six-year period, 10 of them first-place finishes, including a course record in the Naples-Key West Race. His secret weapon, he confided, was a well-patched 110-percent genoa staysail his wife had made for him.

"It added a lot of power without heeling the boat," he explained.

Joe had followed Mauri's trip around the globe, helping when he could by sending on parts he needed. Mauri, he said, had simply lurched from crisis to crisis, always relying on crew to get him to his next port, and often had to fly back from remote destinations on military planes to get medical treatment.

"When I sold him this boat it was in perfect condition," he said sadly as he showed me the interior, which was a confused jumble of unfinished repair projects. "He sailed it 10 years without doing a lick of maintenance. If it hadn't been top-drawer when he got it, and if he hadn't had the good Lord looking out for him, he never would have gone 100 miles on it."

When Joe finally got to the boat in Antigua after Mauri died he found it in a terrible state. The master stateroom, he said, was filled to the overhead with dirty laundry, and there was rotting food and cockroaches everywhere.

"I went down below, and the damn roaches threw me right back out. I ended up puking all over the deck."

In the end he and his stepson took 65 bags of garbage and debris off the boat, and it took them six weeks of nonstop work to get the boat ready to leave Antigua.

The question I most wanted to ask, of course, was whether Joe had ever sailed with Mauri. I needed to know if he knew what that felt like, if we shared that bond.

Joe explained that he had originally agreed to sail across the Atlantic in the America 500 with Mauri, but first tried a short passage with him across the Gulf of Mexico from Mobile, Alabama, to Key West.

"I truly did love the man," he said with a smile. "But you know what it was like. No one ever sailed with him twice."

Westsail 43: Big Sister to a Seminal Cruising Boat

That *Goatlocker III* (hull no. 23) was able to carry a sailor of Mauri's caliber all the way around the world is ample testament to the seaworthiness of the Westsail 43. The boat was designed by Bill Crealock, was first produced in 1975, and was the last of the Westsail line. As such, it was the high-water mark in the company's brief career.

When they first started their business in 1971, young Snider Vick and his wife Lynne had nothing but a few thousand dollars and a used boat mold they'd just bought at a bankruptcy sale. Within a couple of years, thanks mostly to Lynne's marketing acumen, they managed to turn the Westsail 32s they built with that mold (the boat was originally built, and failed, as the Kendall 32) into a cultural phenomenon. Sailors who came of age in the mid-1970s will always remember the company's seductive advertising slogan—Westsail the World—which peppered the pages of sailing magazines. Others may remember that the boat was also featured in *Time* magazine, and even for the public at large it became the physical personification of the dream of bluewater sailing.

By 1978, however, after building more than a thousand boats in less than seven years, Westsail itself was bankrupt, a victim of too many orders and too little capital. In spite of this, the great success of the Westsail 32 launched a great wave of imitation heavyweight double-ended cruising boats from other builders. To this day some die-hards still insist that these sorts of boats are the only proper small yachts to cross oceans in.

The mold for the aft-cockpit 43 was originally used to produce a center-cockpit boat, marketed as the Westsail 42, of which 117 were built. Though not as popular with the public as the 42, the 43 (a total of 71 were built) was a huge hit with the sales staff, who felt strongly it was the best boat the company produced. (There was one other smaller boat, the Westsail 28, that was also built.)

The hull lines of the Westsail 32 were thoroughly archaic, drawn by William Atkin, and only its interior and sail plan were designed by Crealock. The 42 and 43, by comparison, were Crealock conceptions from stem to stern, hence more sophisticated, with proportionately less beam and better-shaped keels. One can see at a glance that they are in fact the very direct ancestors of the several successful and very attractive designs Crealock later drew for Pacific Seacraft.

SPECIFICATIONS

LOA	42′11″
LWL	33′4″
Beam	13′
Draft	5′8″
Displacement	31,500 lbs.
Ballast	11,000 lbs.
Sail area	968 sq.ft. (cutter); 990 sq.ft. (ketch)

DON STREET

A Fastnet Mutiny

I CANNOT HONESTLY SAY when it was that the concept of Donald M. Street, Jr., was first imprinted upon my mind. During the time when I was coming of age he was a seemingly ubiquitous authority on the subject of bluewater cruising, and in certain circles to ask when you first became aware of him would be like asking when you first learned of Christopher Columbus, or Isaac Newton, or the Easter Bunny.

Back in the day both Don and his engineless red yawl *Iolaire* were near-legendary fixtures in the sailing community. His byline often appeared on feature stories in the top sailing magazines. Nautical sections of bookstores and libraries were certain to carry books with his name inscribed on their spines. His great two-volume reference work, *The Ocean Sailing Yacht*, was in its time one of the most popular sailing tomes ever published, and his well-wrought cruising guides to the West Indies, as well as his meticulously surveyed charts, played an important role in opening the great playground of the Caribbean to yachtspeople on both sides of the Atlantic.

I do remember that the first book of Don's that I ever studied in detail was *Street's Transatlantic Crossing Guide*, on which I relied a great deal as I voyaged back and forth across the North Atlantic on *Crazy Horse*. So it was only fitting that my first live encounter with the man came toward the end of that cruise, in a very proper way, in a Caribbean anchorage after many days at sea.

My crossing from the Cape Verdes in company with Carie and an old sailing buddy, Michael, who joined us at Praia on the island of Santiago just before we set out, was ideal in almost every respect. We were in all 17 days in transit, all of it spent on one tack, with strong tradewinds blowing up our quarter and stern the whole way over. It wasn't until the very last day that we finally had to jibe over to lay the south end of Antigua, and this unfortunately caused my well-worn mainsail to split into two pieces.

Shortly afterward, with the remains of my mainsail neatly stowed away, we arrived in English Harbour on a bright March morning with a proud mustache of gooseneck barnacles dangling from our transom. It was the height of the season, and the anchorage was so crowded we could find only one conceivable place to lay a hook, which was perhaps a few yards too close to a small yawl that looked nearly as disreputable as my own. Heading ashore in my hastily assembled dinghy, I saw the name inscribed upon the transom of the tiny red boat was *L'il Iolaire.*

What's this? I gawked. Could it be some pathetic groupie masquerading as Don Street in this Lilliputian knock-off of a sailboat?

But then a grizzled elf with a white beard appeared in the companionway, clad in a Tilley hat and the tattered remains of a button-down Oxford shirt, and I gawked a bit more. It was—it had to be—the master himself. So I gunned my outboard, the better to clear customs and immigration as quickly as possible, so I could come back and have a chat with the man.

The clearance formalities, as conducted in the Antiguan fashion, were unfortunately painfully slow. They were administered by an immense bowl of a man who looked very much like Jabba the Hutt and was just as disagreeable. I behaved very meekly while in Jabba's presence, so as not to anger him, and when finally he was done with me I quickly hopped into my dinghy and rushed back down the harbor. I was very disappointed to find the elf in the red yawl had hoisted up his anchor and was just raising sail.

I waved eagerly, but Don only frowned in return, and I dope-slapped myself, thinking he must have left because of how close I had anchored.

I NEXT ENCOUNTERED DON STREET professionally, through the knotted ganglia of his unfinished prose, when I became his editor at *SAIL* magazine just a few years later.

Don often likes to tell the story of how he decided to become a writer—of how he once had John Steinbeck as a guest aboard *Iolaire* during a charter, and how Steinbeck had proclaimed to him that to be a writer all you really had to do was "put your ass on a hard wooden chair and look at a goddamn typewriter six hours a day, six days a week, and then you become a writer." Don had protested that he could not spell or punctuate and knew nothing about grammar, but Steinbeck assured him he needn't worry about any of those things, because that's what editors are for.

I can assure you Don took the man at his word. Preparing his copy for print was always rewarding, as he is extremely knowledgeable and has a strong, distinctive voice as a writer, but it was also challenging, as he cannot organize a sentence, much less a paragraph, to save his life. When unraveling his anarchic stream-of-consciousness pronouncements, I always felt like a cryptographer trying to decipher deviously concocted military codes.

It was during this time when I was struggling to interpret Don to the world that he asked one fall if I wouldn't like to come crew for him down in the West Indies aboard *L'il Iolaire*. I had by then learned a bit more about this boat that had so mystified me when I first saw her at Antigua. Built of plywood in 1964 in Northern Ireland by an amateur shipwright, she was just under 28 feet long and had been adopted by Don as his Caribbean survey vessel of choice after he decided he was getting too old to handle *Iolaire*, which he still owned but was trying to sell. He had made several modifications so as to elevate *L'il Iolaire* to his own eccentric notions of perfection. Most notably, he'd added a mizzenmast to make her a yawl and removed her engine so as to have more room to store cold beer. He also liked to brag about how fast he could sail her.

I eagerly accepted Don's invitation, as I was excited to have a chance to sail with him. But by now I knew him well enough that I was also worried about what it might be like being cooped up with him on such a small boat. He has a rather high-pitched voice, which is why his oldest friends have always called him Squeaky, and when you are in his presence he likes very much to exercise it and will dispense anecdotes and odd nuggets of nautical wisdom at a machine-gun pace.

Unfortunately, just a few hours before I planned to commit myself to whatever fate awaited me aboard *L'il Iolaire* by actually buying a plane ticket down to the islands, Don called to share some terrible news.

The boat was gone! Hurricane Ivan—the very first hurricane to hit Grenada in living memory—had swept her off her mooring and had blown her out to sea, where presumably she had sunk.

Which in fact was only the latest in a series of misfortunes Don had suffered on Grenada. The first having come way back in the 1950s, when his first wife Marilyn was murdered by burglars who broke into a house they kept together on the island. Many years later it was the real estate itself that was victimized, as the People's Revolutionary Army seized five acres of land and two houses Don owned when they took control of Grenada in 1979. Then finally, as if to rub salt in this wound, both houses were destroyed by helicopter gunships four years later when the United States invaded and liberated the island.

"I've always been a tough old goat," Don Street once told me. "Even before I got old. Whenever I get knocked down, I just get back up again and get on with it."

So I wasn't too surprised when he called me the following summer and asked again if I wanted to go sailing with him.

"*Iolaire* will be 100 this year!" he crowed to me over a bad cellphone connection. "I'm turning 75. I'm going to celebrate by doing the Fastnet Race again! You want to come along?"

The story of Don and *Iolaire* being yet another example of his ability to get up and go again after suffering a setback. He first acquired the boat in 1957 from H. R. "Bobby" Somerset, a founding member of the Royal Ocean Racing Club (RORC), but after just one year in the charter trade under Don's command she was wrecked on a beach in St. Thomas when her anchor shackle broke in a mean onshore swell. Her insurers declared her a total loss, paid off the claim, and Don immediately bought back the wreck for just $100. He then gutted the old girl right there on the beach, somehow got her patched and upright again, and floated her off. Within 14 weeks she was out on charter again—with many new planks, several new frames, a new rudder, and a whole new interior. This in an age when there were no real yard facilities for yachts anywhere in the West Indies.

What struck me immediately about the boat when I arrived at Cowes, on the Isle of Wight, two days before the race start was that her topsides were painted white. It was almost like a slap in the face. Since well before I was born *Iolaire* had always been painted bright red, and to see her in any other color seemed an unsettling confirmation of the existence of parallel but wildly various alternate universes.

"The reason *Iolaire* is painted red," Don had always proclaimed, "is so that she matches the color of the ink on my bank statement."

So why the big change now? I wondered. Had Don suddenly struck it rich?

As always, he had an elaborate explanation.

"Iolaire," it turned out, was actually a Gaelic term that translated into English as something like "white-tailed sea eagle." Don's second wife Patricia, who was Irish, had therefore always argued over the course of their nearly 40-year marriage that the boat itself should also be white. Now finally, in honor of *Iolaire*'s centennial, Don had succumbed to her reasoning.

I was also struck by how disheveled the boat seemed, which was a trait she shared with her owner. Her hull seemed firm and fair, her decks well laid, but all the hardware and gear attached to her was old and tarnished, eccentrically mismatched, and in some cases entirely dysfunctional. Wandering her deck was very much like perusing the aisles of a marine salvage jumble. Likewise, Don's wardrobe—a torn pair of corduroy trousers, the frayed remains of an Oxford dress shirt, and an old Navy pea-coat that was missing two buttons—appeared to have been pilfered from a Salvation Army dumpster. Glued to his hand was his favorite coffee cup, a plastic foam-insulated mug that had one corner melted away in a broad smear of blackened foam and dried blood.

As dissolute as they appeared, I soon learned that both Don and his boat were highly organized. Within moments of my stepping aboard he handed me a five-page single-spaced typed document, written in his rambling prose, that he urged me to study and memorize. It contained detailed instructions on every aspect of life onboard: when to eat, when to sleep, how to change watch, who would serve what food when, how to wash pots and pans, how to use the head, where to stow your gear and boots, and so forth, ad infinitum.

Most important of all were the directions on sail and line handling, which were illustrated with detailed diagrams of all the officially sanctioned knots to be used onboard. The most important and representative of these, I soon divined, was the towboat hitch. This being an elaborate and arcane knot I had no experience with, which was used to tie off the headsail sheets on the antique primary winches, which had no regular fixed cleats beside them and were instead equipped with primitive cam cleats that had long since fallen apart.

Though superficially Don and *Iolaire* may have seemed decrepit, they were both in fact inherently robust. As Don described it to me with respect to himself: "My doctor tells me everything I do is unhealthy. But I'm in perfect health, so he says I shouldn't change a thing."

This reflected Don's own philosophy with respect to the boat. It was as if his imperfect human tendency to somehow organize things was working in perfect harmony with the natural entropic tendencies of decay and deterioration to create the unique phenomenon that was *Iolaire*, this immortal century-old boat of his.

THE MORNING OF THE RACE Don was awake well before sunrise, rattling pans in the galley as loud as he could as he prepared to serve us an enormous breakfast of pancakes and bacon. Quite clearly he was anxious to get going.

This was to be his fifth Fastnet Race. His first had been exactly 50 years earlier, in 1955, when in a fit of pique he'd quit his job as skipper aboard Huey Long's famous 53-foot yawl *Ondine*. Just an hour before the start of the race he made a pier-head leap on to another boat, *Lutine*, a 57-foot Laurent Giles yawl owned by Sandy Harworth, who was then a leading marine underwriter, the commodore of Lloyds Yacht Club, and rear commodore of the RORC.

Halfway down the Solent, as Don remembers it, Harworth turned to him and demanded: "Young man, who the hell are you and where did you come from?"

It was for Don an auspicious encounter. Harworth soon became a mentor to him and within a year had helped him gain membership in the RORC and also got him started in a sideline career as a marine insurance broker.

And now, because he had been a member for so long, and because of his reputation, the RORC had this year decided to allow Don to race *Iolaire* in a special "demonstration class." She had previously raced in the Fastnet under Don's command in 1975 and 1995, and once under Bobby Somerset in 1953, but these days could no longer meet the more modern and more stringent race qualifications. So the club instead was allowing her to sail as an unofficial entrant, starting alone 10 minutes before the rest of the fleet.

Though we were not rated and could not possibly win anything, Don was nonetheless taking the race quite seriously. As soon as he finished stuffing us full of food, he bustled us up on deck for some last-minute preparations. All told, including Don, we were six, and it seemed he'd assembled his crew to reflect various aspects of his life afloat. There was Quentin, age 27, our youngest mate, and Rod, age 46, both from Besso Ltd., the marine underwriter with which he had done much business over the years. There was his old mate Barney, age 69, who many years ago had managed *Iolaire* in charter service on Don's behalf, and of course myself, representing his persona as a writer. Finally, as evidence of his ruthless intentions, there was Bruce, age 40, an Aussie foredeck jock who normally crewed for Giovanni Agnelli on a hot black maxi-racer named *Stealth*.

On our way up to the deck Don pulled me aside to the chart table and handed me a tiny yellow plastic lozenge. It was a cheap handheld GPS receiver, the sort used by casual recreational hikers.

"I'm putting you in charge of this," he said in a grave voice and explained it was the only piece of modern electronic gear he had onboard. "You'll be backing me up as navigator."

"You have any instructions for it?" I asked as I studied the device's tiny display screen and its two control buttons.

He shook his head.

"You ever use it yourself?"

"No," he answered. "But I'm sure you can figure it out."

Once on deck Don immediately declared that Bruce and I should haul him up the mainmast, as there was a spare headsail halyard stranded at the masthead that needed retrieving. He insisted we take him up on the mainsail halyard, which was all wire instead of rope, as was standard on sophisticated racing boats in the early half of the previous century. The halyard was controlled by an antique wire-reel winch that had only a friction brake for making things fast, a type of contraption long ago abandoned by most sailors as unreliable.

To both Bruce and me it seemed almost suicidal for someone to go aloft on a halyard like this, as there was no other way to secure the wire should the brake on the reel let go.

"Don," I insisted, "this isn't safe. There must be a better way."

Bruce nodded in assent and was about say something along similar lines, but Don immediately cut him off.

"It is perfectly safe!" he proclaimed. "I've been doing it this way for over 40 years."

Soon afterward he descended to the deck again with the missing halyard in hand—perfectly safely, as he'd predicted. He next ordered Quentin and me to take the anchor off the bow and stow it below. The ground tackle, we found, was like the rest of the gear aboard, well used with a patina of corrosion, except for the anchor-rode shackle, which was very fancy, all bright stainless steel, and was closed with an exotic Allen screw instead of a simple flange-headed screw.

"An Allen key!" called Quentin. "We need an Allen key."

Instantly Don's bony hand emerged from the foc'sle hatch holding aloft the foulest, most rusted conglomeration of Allen keys I had ever seen.

Like Arthur receiving Excalibur from the Lady of the Lake, Quentin was awestruck. "They're not metric or imperial," he exclaimed. "They're prehistoric!"

But they worked well enough, and in just a few moments we had the anchor stowed safely below and were sailing off our mooring.

The harbor at Cowes, which spans the mouth of the Medina River on the north shore of the Isle of Wight, is normally one of the biggest yacht magnets in all of Great Britain. On this morning—one day after the end of Cowes Week, one of the largest regattas in sailing, an hour or so before the start of the Fastnet Race, one of the oldest and most popular ocean races—it was positively thick with sailboats. Never had I seen so many masts jabbing skyward from one enclosed body of water.

It seemed daunting we should have to sail through this maze with no engine to aid us, all to windward no less, but I needn't have worried. To Don this was old hat. He steered us expertly through the vast jumble of moorings and boats, calmly calling for us to tack every few minutes, until at last we reached the main channel leading out to the Solent, the open strait that separates the Isle of Wight from the south coast of England. Only then, as we suddenly noticed an enormous ferry inbound from Southampton bearing down on us at high speed, did Don raise even a mild note of concern.

"Oh, damn," he muttered as we tacked across the great vessel's bow. "This is going to be tight."

And it was, but he betrayed no serious alarm. Just the bemused world-weary crankiness of a canny old salt who'd spent more time than most maneuvering under sail in close quarters.

THANKS LARGELY TO THE INFAMOUS RACE of 1979, during which 15 sailors lost their lives in an unexpected storm, the Fastnet has a reputation for strong weather. Often, however, conditions during the race are quite moderate, and so it was this year. The wind was very light and variable, and so we meandered oh-so-slowly west down the coast toward the Celtic Sea that separates England from Ireland. In all it took us most of three days to pass by the celebrated landmarks that span the shore from the Solent to the southwest corner of Cornwall—the Needles, Portland Bill, Start Point, the Lizard, and Land's End.

Don thus had plenty of time to warm up his pontification gland and shared with us many snippets of nautical esoterica, of which he had a large supply. On shore, I'd noticed, listening to Don go on about things could sometimes be taxing. Aboard *Iolaire*, however, everything he had to say seemed important and relevant.

Among various lectures we received were the following:

Sheeting Headsails to the Main Boom. Don is very big on this. Whenever we were sailing on a reach he had us run the sheet for the genoa or yankee jib out the end of the boom, which greatly widened the sheeting angle. This kept the headsails properly shaped, eased the helm, and helped the boat sail faster. To capture the sheet on the high-cut yankee we ran a clever tag-line, which Don claimed to have invented, from the boom out to a stopper knot tied into the sheet that was low enough to reach from the deck.

Reefing the Mainsail. Raise the boom, boys! Don taught us we should use the topping lift to hoist the back end of the boom several feet into the air before reefing the mainsail. This effectively scandalizes the sail by dumping all the air out of it and keeps the boom from banging around while you are easing the main halyard and tightening up the reef lines. Believe me, it is very effective!

To facilitate the maneuver on *Iolaire*, Don had rerigged the topping lift so that it ran to the end of the boom from up one of the twin backstays. This way one crew member could take up the topping lift and raise up the boom from the back of the boat while someone else went forward to the mast to deal with the reef lines.

What To Do When Not On Watch. Words of wisdom from Don to Ron after he found him loitering on deck while off duty: "Get to sleep, man! The only reason you should ever leave your berth is if you're called on deck or if someone tells you that food is being served."

Becue Your Anchor. If you need to drop anchor in very deep water in the middle of nowhere to keep from being swept backward by the tide when there is absolutely no wind to speak of (as almost happened to us when we were well off the Lizard), this is what you should do to be sure of getting your anchor back. Shackle the bitter end of the anchor rode to the head of the anchor, then lash the rode with light line back along the length of the anchor's stock. If the hook gets stuck down on the bottom, some strenuous heaving on the rode should break the lashing and allow you to pull the anchor up more easily by its head.

(I asked Don if he had ever actually saved an otherwise irretrievable anchor by using this trick, and he confessed he hadn't. He admitted also he'd learned the trick from a book by Uffa Fox, but still was very proud of it.)

The Glorious Multi-Purpose Genoa (or MPG). The poor man's asymmetric sail is what Don called it. It was a huge flat-cut loose-luffed reaching sail that could take the boat to windward when its Kevlar luff was set up bar-taut. Or we could use it as a spinnaker of sorts by throwing some slack into the luff and setting the tack on either the bowsprit or out to windward on a regular spinnaker pole. These days many people would call this a Code Zero sail. This was Don's secret weapon in light air, hence was the most popular sail in our inventory during our slow crawl to Ireland.

ONE OF THE OTHER THINGS I learned during this race, though Don did not lecture on it directly, is that the key to sailing well in light air is to stay extremely focused.

In the competitive sense, time and the march of modern yacht design had not been kind to *Iolaire*. In the 1975 Fastnet, Don recalled, she rated at the bottom of Class I, the biggest and presumably fastest group of boats. Now he figured a modern IRC rating would put her in the middle of the smallest class. Plus, of course, her hull form, which was very narrow with a long full keel, was utterly archaic, and compared to contemporary boats of the same size she was also very heavy. Still, as we drifted at last past Land's End and out into the Celtic Sea toward Fastnet Rock at the start of our fourth day offshore, we couldn't help noticing that when the wind was at its lightest the boats behind us seemed to get smaller. Only when the wind increased did they get larger and pass us by.

This was due entirely to Bruce, who really was a superb racing sailor. He had remarkable powers of concentration, was a wizard when it came to reading the wind on the water, and had an uncanny ability to trim sails to their most efficient shape, even when they were banging around all over the place in near-calm conditions. Though he was not sailing on a fast boat, these attributes gave him, and therefore us, a real advantage in light conditions. The only problem was the rest of us did not share his magic powers. Bruce paid ceaseless attention to our sails, complained that no one else was doing the same, and constantly harangued whoever was on the helm, urging them to steer up or down one or two degrees. As the race wore on, it was clear he was growing increasingly frustrated with us.

The breaking point came late on that fourth morning when Don, like Ahab, suddenly appeared on deck with a mad look in his eye. In his hand he held an old book he'd been studying below, *On the Wind's Way*, by one William Snaith, from which he recited an imprecation to the stingy wind gods of the British Isles:

Oh great gods of the Western Approaches to the British Isles, we on the yawl Figaro *racing to Sweden salute you.*

Oh hear us, you gracious ones, hear your people on Figaro*! We offer this libation to you. We ask that you look kindly upon us, your servants who have been put to sore trial on your heaving bosom. We know that it is the way of Olympians to put to the greatest trial those whom they love best, a kind of chosen people syndrome that you godhead folks swap around. But, as your omnipotences must know, we are in a race and time is running short; it is time for you to make your move.*

We ask that you stop crapping around and provide us and us alone with one of your finest breezes to take us all the way to the finish. We ask this in view of our long and loving acknowledgement of your existence when other people thrash around in Zen Buddhism and other apostasies of faith.

If you do as we ask, oh great earth shakers, we will raise our children to recognize your names, and on coming in victoriously we will make proper celebrations. We will pour champagne into you until you are as drunk as we are.

But mind you, our patience wears thin. We are fed up with the way we are being treated. All day we have been putting up with your shit and we are tired of it. It is now 2200 hours. Now hear this, you meatheads. We give you until 2300 hours to come up with a favorable wind. If you deliver, we in turn will do what we can to preserve your everlasting glory. But if you don't, we will join in the calumny on your names.

After reading this aloud, Don, over the strong objections of Bruce, who as always wanted us to concentrate very hard on sailing very slowly in almost no wind, declared it was time for all of us to enjoy a morning dose of Heineken. He disappeared below and soon returned with several bottles of beer that he handed round to everyone on deck. And then, before taking a swig himself, he poured about half of his overboard.

THE FIRST SEEDS OF MUTINY were sown later that same afternoon. It began as an idle joke that Bruce bandied about the deck while Don was below—that perhaps instead of sailing direct to Fastnet Rock, then sailing back across the Celtic Sea to the finish line in Plymouth, we should stop off first in Glandore, where Don had a home, and have a few pints in the local pub. He didn't say as much, but the implication was that if we weren't going to take the race seriously, we might as well take a break and do some proper drinking.

As the afternoon wore on, meanwhile, it seemed that Don's little ceremony had had some effect. The wind started slowly growing stronger, and by sunset, for the first time during the race, it was clear *Iolaire* was carrying too much sail. We at first resisted this conclusion, feeling convinced the wind would soon die away again, and so reduced canvas only grudgingly.

In the end we had a very long night and were led on a grueling tour of the boat's sail inventory as the wind varied from Force 0 all the way up to Force 6 and back again. The hardest spot came in the smallest hours of the morning, when it was all hands on deck to strike the mizzen, double-reef the mainsail, and roller-reef the yankee jib. We were closehauled, barely maintaining a reasonable course, pounding into an oppressive sea, drenched in spray, when suddenly we were blinded by a bright spotlight that stabbed at us through the darkness from not very far away. A great bolt of adrenaline ran through us as a loud voice came crackling over the VHF radio.

It was an Irish Navy vessel demanding particulars. Who were we? What nationality? Why were we in Irish waters? What was our destination? Young Quentin grabbed the microphone and tried his best to propitiate them while the rest of us struggled with the sails.

Just an hour and a half later, Bruce, Barney, and I were not feeling at all rested when we hauled ourselves back up on deck at 0400 hours to start our sunrise watch together. The wind by now was slowly tailing off again and in between more sail changes—shaking out reefs, rehoisting our light-air sails—Bruce once again broached the subject of that pub in Glandore. Except this time he was dead serious.

"Enter Glandore as a waypoint in the GPS," he ordered. "See how far away it is."

I retrieved the yellow puck from the nav desk and started fumbling with the buttons.

"It's just 20 miles away," I answered. "Ten miles closer than Fastnet Rock."

Together the three of us developed a plan. Because the race had been going so slowly, I actually did have a serious scheduling problem. My wife and infant daughter were waiting for me at my in-laws' home in County Kerry, not too far from Glandore, and if I didn't return in time we'd all miss our return flight to the United States. So at the change of the watch when Don came back on deck at 0800 hours we decided I would pitch him first, pleading to be put ashore, then Bruce would have a go, and finally Barney.

It worked like a charm. I was on the helm when Don came up, and after some conversation about the need to get more sail up, I asked casually: "What are the chances of us putting into Glandore?"

"Very slim," answered Don grimly and immediately went below again.

Soon afterwards, as Bruce served up pancakes for breakfast in the saloon, I gave Don the full pitch about missing my flight and was sure to emphasize the infant daughter.

Then came Bruce in his broad Aussie brogue: "Just check the GPS, mate. We're much closer to Glandore than Fastnet Rock. Besides, it's not like we're really racing, is it?"

On checking the GPS, Don was chagrined to find I had already entered Glandore as our destination.

"Okay, okay," he grumbled. "I'll think about it."

Not long after breakfast, Barney, in his capacity as first mate and oldest friend aboard, took Don aside below and mentioned there'd been talk in the wee hours of his being put adrift in the dinghy if he didn't cooperate.

"He'll go for it!" announced Barney with a great smile as he emerged on deck, and there was general jubilation onboard. Even those fickle wind gods whom Don had courted so assiduously the day before seemed to approve the decision, as the breeze now shifted, lifting us into Glandore Bay and away from Fastnet Rock.

But then the dull gray form of a military vessel appeared on the horizon behind us. It was the Irish Navy again, and they were headed straight for us. Soon they hailed us on the radio. In an instant it seemed likely our carefully crafted victory would be wrenched away from us, for surely the Navy would not approve of us putting into the little village of Glandore without first clearing customs and immigration in some larger port.

"Give me that microphone," muttered Don.

I wondered: would he seize this opportunity to scuttle our plan?

But no, he was too mad at the Navy to take advantage of their presence and proceeded to give them an earful. First he berated them for the unseamanlike manner in which they'd approached us during the night. Then he chastised them for not receiving competitors in the world-renowned Fastnet Race in a more courteous manner.

The poor radio operator on the patrol boat offered abject apologies, but Don was on a roll now and could not be placated. He demanded to speak with the captain, identified himself as the famous Donald M. Street, Jr., and started listing all his accomplishments. Finally, he recited the address of his website. Whereupon the Irish Navy stopped answering their radio, turned tail, and steamed away from us as fast as possible.

Less than two hours later, as the last of the late morning breeze died away, we were gliding into the flat water of Glandore Bay. As soon as the anchor was down, we saw a skiff put out from shore. In it was a young man pulling as hard as he could at his oars, and in just a moment he was alongside. It was Don's son Don (or D-3, as Don likes to call him) with a huge smile on his face and an ice-cold glass of Heineken for his dad.

Soon enough D-3 had rowed us all to shore and we found ourselves in paradise, seated outside Don's favorite waterfront pub, all of us with dark pints of Guinness in our hands. In the bright sunlit bay below us, *Iolaire* rested on her anchor with her bright red battle flag hanging limp from her forestay. Don, like an all-powerful Mafia boss, received effusive greetings and salutations from all members of the community who strolled by.

"Whatever are you doing here?" they asked in amazement.

"Can't you see?" we replied, pointing proudly at our pints and at the boat in the windless bay below. "We're in the middle of a sailboat race!"

Iolaire: The Immortal Sea Eagle

Don Street has always liked to brag about *Iolaire*'s pedigree—about how she was owned by, among others, two different founding members of the Royal Ocean Racing Club (Major T. P. Rose-Richards and R. H. Somerset), etc.—but in fact it was under Don's ownership that *Iolaire* achieved her greatest notoriety. Don has estimated that she has sailed in the neighborhood of 350,000 miles during her lifetime, which includes some 200,000 miles sailed since he purchased her in 1957. In addition to extensive cruises in the Caribbean, Baltic, and Mediterranean seas, she has crossed the Atlantic Ocean 12 different times, including seven crossings under Don's command.

Iolaire was built in 1905 at the Harris Brothers boatyard in Netherton. Originally rigged as a gaff cutter with a very long bowsprit, she has carried several different sail plans over the years. Currently she is rigged as a "double-headsail yawl," as Don likes to put it, with aluminum masts and wooden booms and a short bowsprit. The main boom, which is spruce, may be original to the boat. The two working headsails are a high-cut yankee jib flying forward of an overlapping genoa staysail. The mizzen can be used as an "air rudder" (another Streetism) to enhance maneuverability under sail in close quarters.

As originally conceived, *Iolaire* was built of teak on grown oak frames. Her original deck was kauri pine. Her original teak planks are still in place down to the waterline, below which they've been replaced with pitch pine, except for the bottom four planks, which are elm. Over the years any broken frames needing attention have been replaced with laminated iroko. The original bronze spike fasteners have all been replaced with silicon-bronze screws. The deck, meanwhile, is now teak over two layers of epoxied half-inch marine plywood. The original non-structural bulkheads have been replaced with structural pieces made up of 3/4-inch marine plywood that are bolted to the frames and deck beams.

Though Don famously removed *Iolaire*'s last engine and dropped it overboard in 1972 (replacing it with a chart table that produced nine books and 150 magazine articles), he did install a new power-plant just three years before he finally sold the boat in 2010. This consists of a 48-volt diesel generator, which was installed in the forepeak, and an electric motor and battery bank, which were installed aft. The motor drives an offset feathering propeller and is used primarily to get the boat in and out of harbors.

SPECIFICATIONS

LOA	46′
LWL	35′
Beam	10′6″
Draft	7′3″
Displacement	42,000 lbs.
Ballast	15,000 lbs.
Sail area	1,020 sq.ft.

REID STOWE
The Longest Voyage

WE ARRIVED AT THE NORTH END of Sandy Hook, that long tendril of barrier beach that juts out from the Jersey shore like an erect member, not long after sunrise on a clear morning in mid-June. All through the night we'd traveled first west along the north shore of Long Island, then south through Hell Gate, down the East River between Manhattan and Queens, and across the Upper Bay past Staten Island to get here. All told we were six aboard *Avocation*, a sleek Swan 48: myself, my old friend Hank Schmitt, and a mutual friend, Tania Aebi, the once-renowned teen circumnavigator, who was all grown up now and had brought along her own teenage son, Sam, and two of his friends.

Dead ahead we could see the vessel we had come to greet—a large schooner, gaff-rigged, its eccentric superstructure, once painted white, now thoroughly streaked with rust, its black hull mottled with a vast array of ugly blemishes. In her cockpit stood a lean man wearing dark trousers and a rumpled white shirt that billowed gently about his torso in the rising breeze. This was Reid Stowe, who had anchored here alone on this great hulk two days earlier, thus ending a nonstop ocean voyage that had consumed more than three years of his life.

The total tally of days Reid had spent at sea without once touching land or casting anchor was 1,152. This almost certainly was a new world record, though it was a record of such obscure provenance no one could say for sure what the old one had been. It might have been 658 days, which was how long Australian yachtsman Jon Sanders had spent sailing three times around the world without stopping in 1986–88. Or some had argued it was 1,067 days, which is how long the Norwegian explorer Fridtjof Nansen and his crew had spent frozen into the Arctic ice while trying to drift to the North Pole during the years 1893–96. Or it might have been some higher number achieved in some other unlikely and unheralded voyage, of which there was no record and that no one alive now remembered.

Whatever the scope of his achievement, Reid now intended to celebrate it. Having made arrangements with his shore team, who had faithfully documented his voyage online and had confronted his rabid detractors while he was away, he would now sail just a few miles north to the city he'd departed from over three years earlier. He would be received, he hoped, by a great fleet of vessels and a crowd onshore, which was why we were here, to follow him in and join the throng that awaited him.

We circled the schooner—named *Anne*, after Reid's mother—waving and shouting back and forth, and then Reid turned to the job of raising anchor and getting underway. The wind had been southerly when he first anchored here, and now it was westerly, blowing about 15 knots. Before he had all of the Lower Bay behind him to leeward, with lots of room to pick up his anchor and raise sail. But now he was just a few hundred yards to windward of the beach.

"You want some help?" I shouted.

Reid glanced around the immense 50-ton vessel he'd been sailing single-handed for so long on the open ocean, without any sort of self-steering mechanism to assist him, and then peered to windward. It seemed clear the wind was growing stronger.

"Yes!" he shouted back.

Hank started working the throttle and wheel on *Avocation* and in just a moment had her bow close enough for me to hop over onto *Anne*'s transom.

I was struck immediately by how exhausted she seemed. Never mind the wasted paint and varnish; all of her gear and rigging was now badly worn and corroded. Once-beefy clevis pins under turnbuckles carrying major shrouds had chafed almost clean through, with only micro-thin strips of metal holding them together. Her steering wheel was falling apart, held together by tight rounds of whipped-on twine; her running rigging was a maze of make-do knots and splices. Her sails, even when furled down, were obviously heavily patched.

But to Reid all this now seemed normal and acceptable. We hugged each other, and then, like a proud father, he swept an appreciative hand about the one solid bit of reality that had sustained him for so long in the void of the sea.

"She looks rough," he admitted. "But I could keep going if I wanted. Everything works, and I still have plenty of food."

I wasn't about to argue with him, and we turned instead to the business at hand. *Anne* did have an engine, an old 140-horsepower Detroit Diesel, but she didn't have any sort of a windlass. To pick up her anchor, Reid had to bend a working line on to the rode with a rolling hitch, then run the line aft to a big sheet winch, where he could cinch it up along most of the length of *Anne*'s deck, whereupon he had to rebend the line on the rode forward and do it all over again. Several times. What he wanted me to do was act as a smart autopilot and work the helm and throttle to keep the boat's nose to the wind while he hauled back on the rode and hoisted sails.

When finally Reid broke out the anchor, which took nearly half an hour, he had the full main and foresail flying, the wind had piped up to 20 knots, and I was wondering, thinking of those clevis pins, if we shouldn't take in a reef. Reid, however, was determined to fly as much canvas as possible. As soon as he had strained to pull the anchor home, he hoisted the working jib and shouted to me to bear away north toward the Verrazano Narrows.

In just a moment *Anne* was bowling along on a fine power reach. With her sails properly trimmed we could make better than seven knots, but the helm then was very heavy, thanks to *Anne*'s missing bowsprit, which had been lost in a collision with a freighter just 15 days into Reid's voyage. To balance the sails and ease the load on the rudder, Reid kept the mainsail loosely trimmed, so that it was often luffing a bit, but the helm still needed a firm hand and the jury-rigged wheel did not inspire confidence. Every time I leaned hard on it to keep the boat from rounding up in the breeze, it creaked and groaned and felt as though it might at any moment splinter into pieces.

It was understood when I came aboard that I wouldn't stay long. Reid only really needed help getting underway, and it was important to him that he manage the boat on his own during his approach to Manhattan. So the plan was once we got most of the way up the Lower Bay, we'd rendezvous again with *Avocation*, and I would hop off. But the breeze shifted northward and continued to build as we approached the big bridge spanning the wind funnel that is the Narrows. Soon the waves were a good bit steeper, with whitecaps glistening here and there, and the prospect of another boat-on-boat encounter began to seem questionable.

Eventually Tania's voice came crackling over the handheld radio that lay on the coachroof before me: "Schooner *Anne*, Schooner *Anne*."

I picked it up: "Schooner *Anne* here." And I glanced over at *Avocation* as she motored along about a quarter mile off our starboard quarter.

"We think it might be getting too rough for another transfer. What do you guys think?"

I looked to Reid, who stood calmly surveying the scene on the side deck nearby, and he nodded his head.

"Affirmative," I answered. "We agree. I'll stay aboard for the duration."

I FIRST STARTED STUDYING REID during the late 1990s while working as an editor at *Cruising World* magazine. The magazine then was running some short pieces on an earlier voyage of Reid's that was underway, a precursor to his Thousand Day Voyage, that he called the Odyssey of the Sea Turtle. This had consisted of him and his newlywed wife, a much younger Frenchwoman named Laurence Guillem, sailing together aboard *Anne* for 194 days nonstop as they traced out the form of a giant sea turtle with their wake in the middle of the South Atlantic Ocean.

Examining the photographs of Reid that ran with these stories, I couldn't help but think that he seemed affected and even silly. He wore a navy blue blazer and a classic yachtsman skipper's hat, and carried on his face a posed, obviously insincere smile. He looked like some cartoon parody of a sailor and reminded me of Daryl Dragon from the old pop duo Captain and Tenille.

Reid, always striving for superlatives, had hailed the Odyssey of the Sea Turtle as "the longest honeymoon in history" and the turtle itself as "the largest work of art ever created." The success of the voyage convinced him that a Thousand Day Voyage was perfectly feasible, but it also convinced his bride that maybe she didn't want to go along. They divorced a little over a year later, after she injured her jaw in a knockdown off Bermuda during an aborted midwinter passage to Trinidad.

"I love Reid," she announced after the split. "But he is a fish, and I am not."

I first wrote about Reid in early 2002, a couple of years after I moved from *Cruising World* to *SAIL* magazine, in a short sidebar to a longer story on sailing records. I briefly described the turtle voyage and Reid's plan for a 1,000-day voyage, and in what I considered a throw-away line characterized what he did as "defining and conquering new realms of sailing achievement."

A few months later I decided to write a full profile and went to the Chelsea piers on the West Side of Manhattan to meet him aboard *Anne* for the first time. There was no sign of the cartoon sailor from the magazine photos. Instead I was confronted by a warm, affable man, not unlike many other cruising sailors I'd met over the years, who swarmed up the gangway of a floating dock with a smile on his face and a pair of empty propane bottles swinging from either hand. He quickly inserted the propane bottles and myself into a battered Jeep Cherokee that soon was rattling angrily over the cobblestone streets of the old meat-packing district.

"I have to thank you," he exclaimed over the din of truck and street. "People everywhere, my family in particular, they've always have a hard time understanding what I do. But now I know exactly what to say to them. I just tell them I'm 'defining and conquering new realms of sailing achievement,' like it says in *SAIL* magazine, and that does it."

I couldn't help but laugh. "You mean it works? That's what shuts them up?"

"It works!" he crowed. "Everywhere, for everyone."

For the next hour, as we roamed lower Manhattan filling propane bottles and purchasing bright pink sheets of foam to insulate *Anne*'s interior against the bitter cold of another Northeast winter, Reid poured his vision into my head.

The idea first came to him, he explained, back in the mid-1980s as he was preparing *Anne* for an earlier voyage he titled the First Arts and Cultural Expedition to the Seventh Continent. This was an extended Southern Ocean cruise, a challenging undertaking in itself, during which Reid and a group of artists and performers, only one of whom had been to sea before, toured Antarctic research bases putting on shows for base personnel. On the way back, during an incredible one-month run in which Reid and company sailed nonstop from the Falkland Islands to the West Indies while barely having to touch the wheel or any lines, this notion of an open-ended infinite-seeming voyage infested his mind.

"I didn't pose it to myself in terms of a challenge," he told me. "What I asked myself was: what can I do to evolve? I decided I didn't want to just sail from point A to point B anymore. That shouldn't be the point of sailing; it should be about something larger than a destination."

Originally his scheme was rather grandiose. After meeting Dr. Albert Harrison, a space psychologist at the University of California, Reid cast his voyage as a "Mars Odyssey" and with Harrison published an article in *Ad Astra*, the journal of the National Space Society, arguing that a 1,000-day ocean voyage was a useful precedent for a very long manned space flight. Reid's proposal called for a crew of six to eight persons, substantive funding, a full course of environmental and psychological research, and a rigorous route that led mostly through the Southern Ocean, where the planet's waves and winds were strongest.

Neither the funding nor the crew ever materialized, but Reid's fervor never waned. He was determined to be the first human being to spend 1,000 days at sea without stopping. And he would go alone if necessary, on a shoestring budget, but really, he confessed, he would much rather at least have a woman along to keep him company.

"I really like women," he assured me with a smile.

Reid's boat, I learned after we returned from our errands, was a countercultural wonderland. On the aft deck there was a gimbaled yoga platform that blended in nicely with the traditional rigging. Down below there was a maze of sculptured hand-carved joinery that flowed through the boat's interior on panels of tropical hardwood. The galley was filled with potted plants and tiny sprout gardens nourished by honey-thick light that flowed through small blurry-paned windows that seemed almost medieval, like embrasures in the dark wall of a fortress.

On deck there was a group of people waiting for Reid to feed them lunch—volunteer workers, an ever-evolving flock of young Bohemians, most of them half Reid's age, who were drawn to him and his dream like moths to a flame.

Two of these current volunteers, Reid explained, had brought with them some important synergistic energy. One was a young Estonian, Ivo (pronounced *Ee-vo*), who correlated to another Ivo Reid had known when he was young, a Dutchman he met in the Pacific and later sailed across the Atlantic with. The other was Stephan Moitessier, a young photographer who correlated to his famous father, Bernard Moitessier, who Reid claimed had introduced him to Tibetan Buddhism by giving him a copy of the *Book of the Dead* when they met in California over 30 years earlier.

"I never would have gone on my first ocean voyage if it wasn't for Ivo," he told me. "And Stephan's father, of course, was a huge influence. To have them with me in spirit again is a very positive thing."

After feeding everyone lunch below, Reid handed out white Tyvek jumpsuits and sent his crew up topside into the cold October breeze with scrapers, brushes, fiberglass cloth, and pots of epoxy resin. Supervising them through a series of deck and cockpit repairs, he calmly hopped back and forth between each location and the schooner's pilothouse, where he mixed up fresh batches of epoxy in front of a big space heater while describing to me some of the voyage's logistical requirements. How much water he could carry, how much he must catch from the sky, how much propane and fuel he could carry, how much food he would need. The boat itself needed new sails, new running and standing rigging, and at least one large self-tailing winch.

Anne had never carried any winches before, he explained. He had always sailed with crew and never needed them. But if he had just one he now figured he could handle the boat on his own without any crew at all.

I asked him bottom line what was the minimum amount of money he needed to do the voyage, and he answered instantly: "Twenty thousand. I'd like to get more, of course, but I'm sure I could do it with just that much."

Later as the sun sank into the Jersey shore and painted the river behind us in copper light, the crew on deck started cleaning up for the night. Down below in the saloon a bottle of wine was uncorked, candles were lit, and people slowly poured like syrup down the companionway on to the cushioned settees.

I talked to Stephan Moitessier, told him how much I admired his father, and he rolled his eyes and quickly changed the subject. Meanwhile, some of the others discussed a prospective mate for Reid, a woman plumber who had worked on the boat recently.

"Even better than a plumber!" exclaimed Ivo. "I think she is Estonian, too."

Overhearing my conversation with Stephan, another crew member interrupted us. "Aren't you that writer?" he asked. "The one who wrote that thing he's always saying?"

"I guess," I answered. "But I thought he was pulling my leg about that."

"Oh no, man. We are *so sick* of hearing about defining and conquering new realms. He talks about it all the time."

I SOON REALIZED, just like all those young volunteers, that I was emotionally invested in Reid's dream. I really wanted him to do the voyage. I wasn't about to give him $20,000, but I figured I could at least find him a winch. I scoured a couple of marine consignment stores, found a big old Lewmar winch that cost me only a few hundred dollars, and dutifully delivered it to the Chelsea piers. When I handed it to him, I told Reid this meant he had one less excuse not to go.

By the time he finally did leave I had learned a great deal more about him. He'd given me an unpublished manuscript of his to study, a memoir of his early life entitled *The Voyage of the Lightship Tantra* that told of his adventures sailing a small plywood catamaran with his old friend Ivo van Laake. Comparing this document with Bernard Moitessier's published work, I soon realized that he and Moitessier had probably never met.

In fact it was Ivo who met Moitessier, in Tahiti not long after the iconoclastic Frenchman landed there at the conclusion his famous Golden Globe voyage in 1969. Ivo had sailed out into the Pacific from California on his own on a tiny 19-foot plywood sloop named *Vlaag*. After leaving Tahiti and Moitessier behind him, he then met Reid first in Fiji and later again in New Zealand, where the two of them bunked together aboard *Vlaag* for three months. During this time Reid wrote in his memoir, "I received a series of spiritual illuminations that opened my mind and gave me guidance in my search for the great common mind of man."

Much later, in an e-mail he wrote to me during the Thousand Day Voyage, he gave Ivo more direct credit for his enlightenment: "It was Ivo who brought the Bernard influence into my life. I did some yoga before I met him, but I had never read. Ivo had onboard the *Tibetan Book of the Dead* and Carl Jung's autobiography, which became the two most influential books in my life. The spiritual connection is what brought us together."

Reid himself had ventured out into the Pacific by other means. He'd been a young surf bum who dropped out of the University of Arizona and flew to Hawaii to chase big waves. There he met another teenage surfer, Craige Fosveldt, who had sailed out from California on a 35-foot teak Cheoy Lee sloop named *Moondance*. Reid joined Craige as crew on *Moondance* and with one other teenage crew member struck out west across the Pacific.

They stopped at Fanning Island and sailed on to Samoa, Tonga, and Fiji, where Reid and Ivo first met. Eventually they landed in New Zealand, where Craige announced he planned to marry and settle down. Reid moved in with Ivo on his tiny boat, and during this time met another young man, Klaus Alverman, who had built his own tiny boat, a flush-deck 26-foot double-ender named *Plumbelly*, on a beach in Bequia. Like Ivo, Klaus had recently spent time in Tahiti with Bernard Moitessier and no doubt he too helped pass the gospel on to Reid.

But what most impressed Reid about Klaus was *Plumbelly* herself. Reid had mentioned her during our conversation in the Jeep.

"*Plumbelly* had a huge influence on me," he told me. "Her beautiful hardwood, the curves, the gracefulness of her. I decided then I had to build my own boat too. I could see what my path was, and it wasn't the path being followed by other people on their boats."

Reid returned to the United States determined to build his own boat so he too could set out on "an enlightening ocean voyage." In October 1972, at age 20, he set up shop in the backyard of his family's beach house in North Carolina and started work on a 27-foot catamaran he ultimately named *Tantra*. The original design, which Reid pirated, was by James Wharram, who was himself a great proponent of alternative sailing and had spent time with Moitessier many years earlier, in the late 1950s, when they were both shipwrecked in Trinidad.

Tantra was built of 3/8-inch plywood sheathed in fiberglass. Her cross-beams and spars were of Sitka spruce. She had one single berth in each of her 3-foot-wide hulls, no standing headroom, no electricity, and no engine. Her standing rigging consisted of 1/4-inch galvanized wire set up on deadeyes and lanyards. Reid installed a simple two-burner gas cooktop down below; water he planned to carry loose in 40 one-gallon jugs distributed throughout the two hulls.

It was in building *Tantra* that Reid discovered his talent for assembling and effectively supervising large volunteer work crews. At times he had as many as 10 friends on site helping build the boat. These included a young woman named Iris, who later became his first wife, and also Ivo, who came from the Pacific in early 1973.

Reid and Ivo both developed a romantic interest in Iris, and Reid was surprised when Iris proposed marriage to Ivo. But this never inhibited his relationship with either party. Just one day after the wedding, on June 15, 1973, Reid and Ivo set out together on *Tantra* bound for Europe.

"[Ivo] said Iris is my wife, and I said okay, she's my cosmic lover," wrote

Reid. "But we both went to sea without a lady and our fantasy lovers existed only in our minds."

Sailing on *Tantra* was often cold, wet, and very uncomfortable. Space inside the hulls was extremely limited, there was little freeboard, and the boat leaked a good deal. At one point Reid likened being on deck in strong weather to standing waist-deep in breaking waves on a beach. But little of his memoir dwells on this; instead he focused much more on the ecstasy of the experience.

The endless movement has opened up new channels of feeling and a psychic world of motion brings on a series of unique illuminations. Wave after wave I ride, relaxing, feeling the roll forward, then backwards. There is no pause. Endless water rushes down the full length of each hull. Tantra *gives with the movement, contracting and expanding, bending from one plane to the next. Wave after wave thumps against the cabins, and with each wave-bang colors explode before my eyes.* Tantra *is in tune with nature, dancing and singing in a musical concert.*

Reid and Ivo relentlessly practiced yoga and made mountains of art while sailing together. It took them about 30 days to reach the Azores, then another week or so to reach Portugal. Here Ivo left the boat to visit Holland while Reid continued south to Morocco on his own, his first experience as a single-hander.

Ivo rejoined the boat in Morocco, and the two of them then voyaged on to the Canary Islands. They sailed into the dirty industrial harbor at Arrecife, on Lanzarote, and were so disgusted by it they at once sailed out again and continued on to the south. They set course for Mauritania in West Africa, a very challenging destination, but were thwarted by bad weather and continued instead to São Vicente in the Cape Verde Islands, where they landed 17 days after leaving Morocco. After a brief stay they struck out west back across the Atlantic bound for Brazil, where they landed at Salvador after a 26-day passage.

It was in Brazil that Reid's relationship with Ivo at last began to unravel. They brought *Tantra* north from Salvador to the Amazon and settled down with some locals at a riverside farm outside Belem. Then Iris suddenly arrived from the United States and proclaimed her love for both of them. In the end she chose Reid over Ivo, and the two sailed off together on a river cruise aboard *Tantra*. Ivo meanwhile consoled himself by inviting another girlfriend, Moea, to come from Tahiti to join him.

After they finished their cruise Reid and Iris decided to join another boat sailed by a Belgian couple, Peter and Zaza, who were heading north to the Caribbean. Reid left *Tantra* locked up on a mooring in front of the farm outside Belem and asked Ivo to keep an eye on her. Their very first night aboard with the Belgians, however, Reid, Iris, and their hosts were all taken prisoner by a band of pirates. These were led by an ex-mercenary named Horst, who had been stalking Peter and Zaza for some time and hoped to take their boat for his own. After holding the two couples at gunpoint for two days, Horst at last relented and merely plundered the boat, warning his victims he would kill them if they ever returned to the river. Reid in his memoir described the denouement of this ordeal:

[The pirates] planned to leave when darkness fell, but the weather was too rough for them to leave in their fully loaded open motorboat. So they had Peter motor the sailboat into a protected river mouth at the very entrance to the Amazon. When they were ready to depart, [one] young pirate came inside, grabbed the sextant, and started to climb out the hatch. I shouted in Portuguese: "You leave that sextant. We need it to leave Brazil." He put the sextant back without looking at me and climbed outside. As the pirates left, we loosened our bonds and quickly hoisted anchor and motored away. The water was shallow and we passed rows of

fish trap poles. Alive and free! We weren't enthusiastically overjoyed. Our hands and arms hurt and we still had to navigate past big sand bars to get out to sea. It began to rain heavily and we motor-sailed out. Peter used his lead line, and when it suddenly got shallower we tacked the other way. We did this for hours until we reached the safety of the open ocean.

The next morning was Thanksgiving and we were thankful. We were lucky to have a good Thanksgiving dinner of fresh Spanish mackerel. The fish jumped aboard, clanged the ship's bell, and fell into the cockpit. The water was already getting clearer. How nice it was to leave that muddy brown water. We wondered how Ivo and everybody was doing back on the farm and wondered how they could live there so close to our place of calamity. That experience muddied our vision of the Amazon River.

Fourteen days later the two couples reached Martinique, where Reid soon took a job teaching yoga at the local Club Med. Later, after contracting hepatitis, he flew home to North Carolina to recuperate. Once there he received word from the farm in Brazil that Moea had arrived from Tahiti and that she and Ivo had left for Bolivia, leaving *Tantra* untended.

Agonizing over all he had invested in *Tantra*, and all the original artwork and the journals he had stored aboard her, Reid concluded he had no choice but to return to the Amazon to retrieve her. His Belgian friends, Peter and Zaza, warned him by letter of the danger. Horst, who had informants in the area, would likely know of his return to the river. *Tantra* probably wouldn't be ready to head immediately out to sea, and it would be very difficult, during the windless Brazilian rainy season, to get the little catamaran out of the river without an engine.

Reid nevertheless flew to Belem and returned to the farm, where he found *Tantra* in a sorry state. He quickly prepared her as best he could and with two other volunteers who'd been staying at the farm, after many consultations with the Tarot and I Ching, set out again for the open ocean. It took several days to escape the clutches of the river mouth. Next came a passage up the coast to Parimaribo in Suriname, then on to Barbados and Martinique, where Reid's crew left him.

Reid sailed on to the Grenadines on his own and after cruising for a while there stopped in Carriacou, where he hauled *Tantra* on to a beach for a thorough refit. After again assembling a large volunteer work crew, Reid rebuilt the boat in just a month. He was then joined by his brother, Bobby, who helped him sail *Tantra* back to North Carolina. Prior to leaving, however, as they sat together on a hilltop tripping their brains out on psychedelic mushrooms, Bobby and Reid made an important decision: "We will sail home, and in our front yard we will build a big schooner for our family to go sailing on all together."

And that is precisely what they did. Just as they envisioned, the schooner—first called *Tantra*, then later *Anne*—was built in front of the family house in North Carolina, without any plans, in less than two years and was first launched in March 1978.

ULTIMATELY REID NEVER SECURED any major funding for his Thousand Day Mars Odyssey, though he did scrabble together a good collection of modest in-kind sponsorhips involving donations of food and other necessities. He was never able to replace *Anne*'s sails or rigging, but he did get another winch, an electric one, which helped a lot when handling the mainsail halyards, particularly the one for the heavy throat of the sail.

And he did find someone to go with him. Soanya Ahmad, age 23, a first-generation Guyanese-American woman from Queens who had studied photography at City College, first met Reid while wandering the West Side piers. She asked if she could take pictures of his boat and ended up joining *Anne*'s ever-evolving volunteer shore crew. Eventually she also volunteered to join Reid on his voyage, though she had zero sailing experience. She seemed anxious to find a life different from the one she'd been born to, and when I last saw them a week before they set out from the Hoboken piers in April 2007, she seemed as excited as Reid was to be going to sea.

The voyage itself, given its great duration, proved remarkably uneventful, at least with respect to the sailing and seamanship involved. The collision with the freighter just two weeks in was almost its only emergency, and Reid coped with it admirably. He was very aware that his hero and role-model Moitessier had suffered a similar accident early in his great voyage of the Long Way, when he hit a freighter and bent his long steel bowsprit close to the coast of South Africa.

Moitessier had been able to solve his problem with a block and tackle, a gin-pole, and a sheet winch. Reid, however, wasn't quite so lucky. His bowsprit wasn't just bent, it was broken. But just like Moitessier, be it intentionally or instinctively, his immediate response was to stop the boat and rest while thinking deeply about what to do next. Ultimately, to resume sailing he had to cut away most of his bowsprit, thus greatly reducing the size of his rig. He shortened the headstay and moved it aft to the stem of the bow, which cost him his forward-most headsail, which in turn limited his ability to balance the boat's sail plan. Since he carried no self-steering mechanism, relying instead on the boat to mind herself under a balanced rig, this reduced his speed potential, as he normally had to reduce sail aft to compensate for the missing sail area forward.

Other than that the biggest technical problem was the sails themselves, as they repeatedly blew out and had to be repeatedly sewn together again. All by hand, as Reid had not thought to bring a sewing machine, which was probably the only major mistake he made in preparing for and executing his remarkable voyage.

Burdened with a compromised vessel, Reid, as would any competent seaman, focused on accomplishing his goal, which was to safely move *Anne* from Point A to Point B not in space, but in time. To do that he had little choice but to baby his rig and sails. He had once hoped to sail multiple circumnavigations while completing this voyage, but in the end he limited himself to just one and spent much of his time at sea drifting around the South Atlantic off Africa, in the calmest, most boring stretch of ocean on the planet's surface.

Emotionally and psychically, the voyage posed more of a challenge. Soanya early on was plagued with chronic seasickness, which never went away, and eventually she told Reid she had get off the boat. She was evacuated just out of sight of land off the coast of western Australia, where *Anne* rendezvoused with a launch sent out by a local yacht club. Soanya soon learned she was in fact pregnant, which she'd guessed had been the case.

After that Reid was all on his own, alone, just as he claimed he was always willing to be in order to do this. And he didn't like it much. He badly missed Soanya and wondered about the child she was now carrying. It was harder working the boat without her, and he began to think the voyage might be hopeless. The pain in his arms from working the boat's heavy rig sometimes woke him up at night, and he prayed to God to send Jesus and Buddha to heal them. He had a waking vision in which said deities and prophets did appear to him, intermixed with some barbecued spare ribs, and they all bumped their heads together when the boat suddenly lurched beneath them.

Not long after this, while drifting aimlessly between the Galapagos Islands and South America, Reid rediscovered his purpose after a friend e-mailed him and pointed out that his GPS transponder track as displayed on his website looked something like a whale. Energized by this revelation, Reid spent nearly a month working to finish the whale, first drawing in a side fin, then sailing many miles out of his way to a precise point so as to complete the figure. He then carefully sailed out of the area on a course perfectly reciprocal to the one he'd sailed in on so as not to mess up his picture.

From there Reid sailed on around Cape Horn, the most daunting headland in all the seven seas, and soon after suffered the voyage's only other emergency-type situation, when a rogue wave rolled *Anne* upside down and briefly knocked him unconsciousness. He recovered from this and sailed on into the South Atlantic. Surveying his chart, he saw he could combine his current course track with his earlier track in the South Atlantic to create the form of a giant oceanic heart. He dutifully worked to complete this next piece of GPS art, right in the middle of the ocean between Africa and South America. Then he moved in closer to Africa, where he played rope-a-dope with the sea for many months, laying low and saving his ship and strength until it was time to sail back to New York.

IT COULD BE SAID the most dramatic aspect of Reid's voyage actually took place on shore, on the Internet, in an obscure forum discussion on a racing sailor's website called Sailing Anarchy. The forum thread, entitled Couple Cruise for 1,000 Days, ran on for more than 1,200 pages over some five years, contained over 30,000 posts and ultimately registered well over a million hits. One of the leaders of the rather small group of manic racing sailors who generated all this content was a middle-aged Melges 32 crewman who sailed mostly on Long Island Sound and called himself Regatta Dog.

Regatta Dog became obsessed with Reid. He created two different websites devoted to denigrating and humiliating him and with the help of his Sailing Anarchy buddies decorated these sites and the forum thread with photo-shopped images of Soanya in chains in the nude, of Soanya shooting Reid in the head in the streets of Saigon, of a badly scourged Reid being staple-gunned to a cross, and of Reid's new son Darshen in humiliating poses, to name but a few. The result was a long cyber-war with Reid's shore team.

Regatta Dog was blatantly aggressive. He hacked into the shore team's internal e-mail, made FOIA requests, searched public archives, and teamed up with a disgruntled ex-girlfriend of Reid's. With her guidance he learned that Reid had never had a holding tank for *Anne*'s toilet while docked in New York, that Reid had once been $11,000 in arrears on child-support payments pertaining to a daughter (now an adult attorney) he had with Iris, and that Reid had once served nine months in federal prison for smuggling pot. And he broadcast all this information online, denounced Reid for committing such heinous crimes, and ridiculed his voyage and all it pretended to stand for.

He also stalked Soanya. He tried to meet her plane at JFK airport when she flew back to New York City from Australia, succeeded in attending her welcome-home party, and posted videos of his misadventures online. Reid's shore team, which until then had done little more than shout back at Regatta Dog and his followers online, responded in kind and published Regatta Dog's real name in the forum thread and let him know they also knew the identities of his ex-wife and his children.

All of this was alarming, but I did understand why Reid inspired such fervent animosity. I think his shore team did too, though they, as did I, always stayed loyal to his cause.

One thing that made Reid such an easy target was his tendency to exaggerate and hyperbolize when promoting himself and his exploits. At times he even lied, as I found with his claim of having met Bernard Moitessier. He also, for example, often claimed his voyage to Antarctica had been the first by an American yachtsman, when it was very easy to discover online that in fact it had been the second. For Reid never misrepresented anything in a very deliberate or calculated manner; it was always perfectly thoughtless, and it was never hard to find him out. Sometimes he'd produce the contradictory evidence himself without even realizing it.

It was also easy to mock Reid's intense spirituality and his new-age view of the world, particularly as his shameless self-promotion seemed to fly in the face of it. In this secular age direct assertions of spiritual connections can seem very artless, especially to those who have no spiritual existence of their own. But no one who ever met and knew Reid could ever deny that he was sincere in his beliefs. They truly do animate and inform everything he does.

Most damning of all, perhaps, was Reid's inability to accurately perceive himself as others do. It was almost contradictory—he was very self-aware, but not at all self-perceiving, and this gave him an uncanny ability to parody himself without meaning to. (Take, for example, his Captain and Tenille phase during the Odyssey of the Sea Turtle.) Which of course made it painfully easy for others to parody him as well.

I ALWAYS REMEMBERED WHAT REID had told me in the Jeep that day we first met, about evolving, and I wondered as his voyage neared its end if in fact it had changed him. I discussed this in an e-mail exchange with his friend Dr. Harrison, with whom he'd co-authored the Mars Odyssey article in *Ad Astra*, and the good doctor thought it unlikely.

"I think he was already about as spiritually evolved as he could be when he left," he wrote me.

I was thinking of this as we sailed together that bright morning up toward the Verrazano Narrows aboard *Anne*. There was a potentially dangerous shoal, Reid remembered, somewhere off to the west, south of Staten Island, that we needed to be aware of as we beat our way up toward the bridge.

"Let me see a chart," I called.

And Reid handed up a much-crumpled chart of New York Harbor and the Upper and Lower Bays. It was covered in abstract hand-painted watercolor images, and right below Staten Island there was an especially florid burst of form and color that made it hard to read the water depths in the west part of the Lower Bay.

I was hardly surprised and tapped my finger on the shoal we were worried about in a mute accusation.

"I've always incorporated art into my navigation and navigation into my art," explained Reid without a hint of embarrassment. "I was trying to improve the chart's appearance."

"Yeah, but it would work better as a chart if you just left it alone," I replied, and couldn't help but smile. This was the same Reid, exactly the same guy I'd known three years earlier.

Studying the chart closely we at last divined the controlling depth on the shoal in question. It would be best, we decided, to tack away, and soon we were rewarded for our trouble. Sailing on port tack up toward the eastern end of the bridge in Brooklyn, we enjoyed a great lift that allowed us to carry on much further than we expected. We tacked back toward the west when we at last closed the shore, but soon had to tack right back again to avoid a hard-charging tug and barge that were steaming north into the harbor.

At the end of that very short board, as we again closed the Brooklyn shore, this time on the north side of the bridge, we found a car full of Reid's family waving at us. They somehow had managed to drive down the south-bound side of the busy Belt Parkway, found a spot to pull over and park the car that just happened to be at the exact spot we had reached in the boat, and timed it all so they could arrive just before we did. Yet another synchronistically choreographed magic moment in Reid's life story.

We waved back, joyfully, but Reid was only momentarily distracted from the job at hand. By the time we beat all the way up to the Statue of Liberty, the wind was gusting to well over 25 knots. We hove-to to wait for a press boat to come out and meanwhile studied the other vessels that had come to greet us: two big schooners, *Pioneer* and *Adirondack*, plus one fireboat that filled the sky with rainbows from its water-cannon.

Reid looked at me thoughtfully: "I suppose this is something we'll always have, the two of us sailing in here today, finishing my voyage together."

Soon the press boat appeared just as the wind, fortunately, died down to below 20 knots.

"I need you to stay below now," said Reid.

And I knew then for sure he hadn't changed. I knew in the not-too-distant future in describing this day to some future audience he would thoughtlessly boast of how he had sailed up the harbor on his own, and it didn't bother me in the least. He wanted to bask alone in the glare of what publicity he'd managed to attract after many years of effort, and I believed he had earned that right.

I knew one part of Reid would be disappointed by this reception he was about to enjoy. He had sometimes complained about how little attention his voyage had received, both while he was planning it and while he was sailing it, and I knew he once had high expectations of this moment. Maybe the President of the United States would be here to greet him; at a minimum he hoped at least the mayor might show up.

But in this here and now there could be no disappointment. It was a very odd interlude, waiting inside the pilothouse well out of sight as Reid sailed those last few miles up to pier at the end of 42nd Street. There was a fast close reach over to the Battery, where he tacked one last time, and then a tight closehauled board up the West Side. I heard the engine come on, and then felt *Anne* shivering as Reid brought her nose to the wind and dropped her sails to the deck. A pause while he deployed some old truck tires as fenders. Then the chunk of the transmission as he put the engine in gear and—finally, after so many years at sea—brought the boat to a dock.

I watched through one corner of the pilothouse window as Reid stood a moment poised at the gunwale before stepping ashore. His voice cracked as he gazed out at the crowd of friends and family who had gathered to greet him: "I see a lot of people here I love!"

In his first moment ashore he was greeted almost shyly by Soanya, who was holding his two-year-old son Darshen, whom he had never seen before, and also more effusively by his grown-up daughter Viva, who held his three-year-old granddaughter Lucy, whom he had also never met. I saw my chance and slipped ashore when no one was looking and in instant was standing in the middle of the crowd, just another member of the press gathered to witness this curious ceremony.

Finally, as Reid took up a microphone he started to cry.

"This is a new human experience," he declared. "No one understands what I did, spiritually, physically, or mentally. I definitely want to share it, but it is something no one understands."

Anne: Schooner of the Thousand Days

Reid Stowe built *Anne* without any plan or design and simply eyeballed her form and dimensions from the roof of a neighbor's house on the North Carolina shore. Her "ferro-lite" construction is very similar to that of a ferrocement boat. She has a metal mesh frame composed of rebar and high-tensile spring steel, and this was filled out with a putty-like mash of chopped-up wet-out fiberglass fabric instead of concrete.

Construction of the hull, deck, and original rig took nearly two years. She was launched in March 1978, whereupon Reid immediately sailed her to the West Indies with a load of cargo. Her interior, which Reid has estimated is composed of at least 20 different kinds of tropical hardwood, is filled with elaborate hand-carved joinery.

Over the years, *Anne* helped support Reid, working both as a cargo and charter boat in the West Indies at various points in her career. Her enormous capacity as a load carrier, most particularly, made her an ideal platform for a low-tech voyage of 1,000 days duration. As Reid once put it to me: "No matter what I want to carry, there's no way I can overload this boat."

During her historic voyage *Anne* carried 400 gallons of fuel, plus 1,500 gallons of water in three different tanks. Though he had a desalination system onboard, Reid never had to use it, as he was always able to refresh his water supply with rainfall. He loaded on six tons of imperishable food—Parmesan cheese, peanut butter, lentils, rice, and pasta—a diet he augmented with sprouts he grew onboard and fish he caught while sailing. For heat and cooking, he carried 3,000 pounds of coal and wood, plus 25 bottles of propane gas. To generate electricity, the boat had a shaft alternator, a towed water generator, plus four solar panels.

Anne's standing rigging consists of heavy galvanized steel wire secured over thimbles with bulldog clamps. This held up well during the voyage, with the exception, as noted, of the clevis pins that secured the shrouds to their chainplates. The Dacron sails, which were already old when Reid started, needed many repairs en route. Otherwise the rig performed well, and even without the bowsprit Reid was always able to balance the sails so the boat could steer herself.

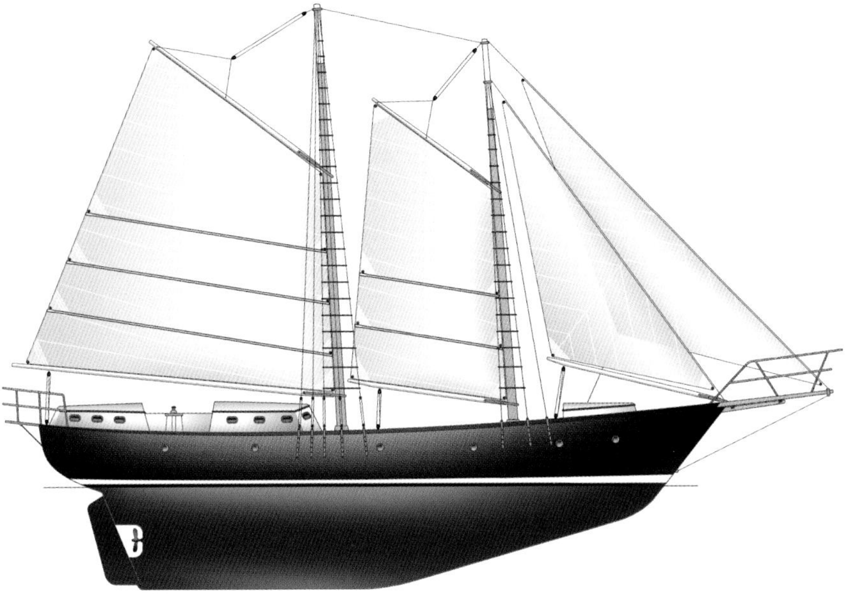

SPECIFICATIONS

LOA	85′ (approx.)
LOD	70′
Beam	16′6″
Draft	9′6″
Displacement	50 tons (approx.)
Ballast	22 tons
Sail area	2,000 sq.ft. (approx.)
Power	Detroit Diesel 453 (140 hp)

JIMMY CORNELL

The Dark Prince of Bluewater Cruising

I SPENT MOST OF THE YEAR 1992, during which I completed my first two transoceanic voyages, dwelling in a realm ruled by an energetic Romanian emigrant who called himself Jimmy Cornell. In those days I was a mere peasant in Jimmy's kingdom, and to me his regime seemed a bit overbearing. On *Constellation*, in that frantic week in May before we set out east from St. Augustine in Jimmy's Europe-bound TransARC rally, it was Jimmy's minions who descended on us and declared us unfit to go to sea. For three days afterward, we scrambled like ants with a stick stuck in our hill conforming the boat to his requirements. And later, after *Constellation* was lost in the Rio Odiel chasing the coat-tails of Jimmy's America 500 fleet, it was Jimmy's minions who glared at me in the Puerto Sherry marina in Spain (or so I imagined) and willed me (unsuccessfully) not to report to other sailors in the fleet just what had happened in the anchorage that night at Huelva, when we all tried to moor exactly in line as they had demanded.

In all I crewed aboard three different boats in Jimmy's rallies that year: on *Constellation*, until she was abandoned in August; on *Goatlocker*, during my eccentric run with Mauri from Spain to the Canary Islands in October; and lastly on the Australian boat *Antipodes*, which in November sailed with the whole body of the America 500 fleet from Las Palmas de Gran Canaria to first San Salvador and then Great Exuma in the Bahamas.

I heard the story, shared amongst us peasants, of how Jimmy summarily exiled from the fleet one young crew member who'd been caught stealing a banner after a rally party in Madeira. And I heard other complaints from sailors throughout the fleet, particularly about the top-secret rating rule Jimmy had devised to gauge our performance against each other. The ones who complained the loudest were usually Americans, who chafed at Jimmy's insistence on protocol. The Brits and Europeans in the fleet didn't seem to mind the protocol so much, and the Brits in particular were already inclined to regard Jimmy, a naturalized Brit himself, as an ocean-sailing demigod. But there was also a strong herd mentality that colored everyone's perception of Jimmy. The herd was made stronger and more cohesive, more loyal to itself, by sharing him as a nemesis of sorts, and even then I wondered if he had not intended this.

The definitive moment, when the group's loyalty to Jimmy was most severely tested, came at the final pre-departure skipper's meeting in Las Palmas. As a lowly crew member, I wasn't allowed to attend this gathering, but I heard a lot about it afterwards.

There were by then several boats gathered at Las Palmas that had not joined our rally, filled with sailors who wished to honor Columbus nonetheless. Many of these people intended to shadow our fleet on its voyage to the Bahamas, and it was widely known that Jimmy resented this. The most extreme of these hangers-on were an Italian man, Federico di Benedetto, and his son Alessandro, who proposed to follow us on a tiny Hobie 18 beach cat, just two slim hulls and an open trampoline, that they called *United States of the World*. Known to us all simply as "those crazy Italian guys," they'd been wandering the marina for more than a week handing out photocopied statements of their views on the global economy and the environment.

Our skipper on *Antipodes*, an American, and her owner, an Australian, came back from the skipper's meeting outraged at Jimmy's just-announced proscriptions against all of these people. According to them, Jimmy had ordered that rally boats should not share any rally radio frequencies, nor should they answer any distress calls from boats not enrolled in the fleet.

"It's a violation of international law!" fumed skipper Glenn, an unreconstructed rebel from South Carolina. "We are absolutely required to answer any distress call. From anyone!"

This did seem draconian, so I asked other skippers what they thought they'd had been told. One good friend, an American, assured me that was exactly what Jimmy had ordered: rally boats should answer no calls, not even distress calls, from boats outside the fleet. But another, a Brit, was more circumspect.

"Well," he intoned in a cautious voice, drawing out the syllable so as to underline his diplomatic tendencies. "I can see how some people might have interpreted it that way."

I finally got to meet the man myself and shake his hand not long after we arrived at Great Exuma in December of that year. Geoff, the owner of *Antipodes*, had shipped in many cases of Australian beer and wanted to throw a party for everyone. He put me in charge of creating and awarding joke trophies, and insisted there be one in particular, a Jimmy Who Award, which should be awarded, he urged, to Jimmy Cornell.

The afternoon of the party, after a good bit of Australian beer had flowed through a large number of sailors gathered on a lawn in the Exumian hamlet of Georgetown, Jimmy got up and made a fine speech in his heavily accented English. He spoke about the rally and the party and the great camaraderie we enjoyed, sounding very much like the man who'd organized and paid for the party himself. Which, in fact, was one thing many of us had noted about Jimmy—that he had a tendency to commandeer and take credit for social events he had not engineered.

In this case he was followed immediately by Geoff, who ambled up to the microphone, still glaring at Jimmy, and pronounced: "I want to thank you all very much for coming to drink my free beer."

The awards ceremony followed immediately afterwards and was well received, thanks mostly to the beer. I had created prizes for various categories of achievement: the Watchdog of the Sea Award for a crew that had stopped their boat in mid-passage after mistaking a shooting star for a distress flare, a Party Animal Award for the most gregarious crew, a Golden Microphone Award for the fleet's radio-net moderator, and so on. In presenting the final award, which consisted of a custom-made "Jimmy Who?" T-shirt Geoff had had sent from Australia, I cast the winning criteria as "the person who looks most like Jimmy Cornell." To go with the T-shirt there was a cheap plastic glasses-nose-and-mustache disguise.

There was a huge roar of approval as I announced Jimmy's name. He had until that moment always struck me as a stern and humorless man, dark and handsome, but with a perpetually glowering brow, the very antithesis of a carefree cruising sailor. But his reaction to winning this deprecatory award totally belied all this. Grinning like a mindlessly happy child, he danced up to the front of the crowd, shook my hand eagerly, immediately pulled on the T-shirt, and donned the ridiculous disguise. He then capered through the drunken crowd, dancing a merry jig with one hand held oddly to the side of his head to keep his disguise from falling off, as everyone laughed and pointed at him.

HE HAD BEEN BORN with a very different name, Dragos Corneliu Cismasu, in a very different place, in a Transylvanian village in landlocked central Romania at the very start of World War II. One of his formative childhood memories was of his father being arrested and taken away in the middle of the night by Communist secret police not long after the war ended. His father, a loyal retainer of the Romanian royal family, had passed up a chance to flee Romania with the royals and their retinue, and ultimately died in a Communist prison in 1959.

Dragos was proud of his father, but he swore he would not follow his example and throughout his life always chose pragmatism over principle. He remembered some very nautical advice he received from his uncle: never piss against the wind. And as he later wrote in his autobiography, *A Passion for the Sea*: "I have followed that simple advice all my life, trying to navigate the best course through life and, later, across the oceans."

As a young man he picked up a job as a go-fer for a British film company shooting an epic sword-and-sandal movie inside Romania. With his boundless energy and persistence, and his knowledge of various languages, he had little trouble solving seemingly insoluble logistical problems for the actors and film crew and quickly earned a reputation as "Jimmy the Fixer." Meanwhile, he also became romantically involved with a British tourist, Gwenda, who ultimately became his wife.

It took years of waiting and bureaucratic wrangling, but Jimmy née Dragos (he ultimately also took an Anglicized corruption of his middle name as a last name) was finally allowed to emigrate to the United Kingdom in 1969. The same night he finally departed Romania, he told his bride he had a terrible confession to make.

Gwenda expected the worst, the inevitable admission that Jimmy did not really love her and had only used her to escape west across the Iron Curtain. But instead he blurted out: "I want to go to sea. I want to see the world."

Though his only meaningful exposure to boating had been one camp-cruise he made on the Danube River in an inflatable kayak, this oldest of human dreams had somehow infected Jimmy's mind. He worked in London broadcasting Romanian language radio into Eastern Europe for the BBC World Service and in his spare time took sailing lessons in 14-foot dinghies on the Thames River. In just a few years he'd acquired the first of four cruising sailboats named *Aventura* and had taken Gwenda and their children, Doina and Ivan, on his first of three circumnavigations.

Jimmy's great notoriety within the sailing community was earned first through the application of skills he learned as a BBC journalist. Where most cruising authors simply wrote tales of their own adventures, Jimmy instead interviewed other sailors on the gear and tactics they employed. He also compiled mountains of information on the routes they followed. The impressive compendium of very useful reference books he published made him one of the best-selling sailing authors of his generation.

More importantly, utilizing skills he'd honed as Jimmy the Fixer, he figured out a way to commercialize bluewater cruising when he organized the first Atlantic Rally for Cruisers in 1986. It was a brilliant, but obvious idea. Every fall a thousand or more yachts move through the Canary Islands on a well-established annual seasonal migration from Europe to the Caribbean. Why not give them a chance to sail in an organized group? Jimmy vetted boats, organized dock space, smoothed transactions with government officials, created a semi-competitive racing format, and staged big parties to forge camaraderie amongst his customers, who paid fees to join the rally on both a per-boat and per-person basis. His very first ARC was a smash success, with well over 200 yachts enrolled. It was immediately the biggest transoceanic sailing event ever run, and to this day it is still the largest such event and still attracts over 200 boats a year.

Jimmy quickly grew the business, and by the time I first encountered him in 1992 he was running a series of rallies in addition to the ARC: the TransARC for boats sailing from the U.S. to Europe, the one-off America 500 to commemorate Columbus' great voyage, and a World ARC that had sailors voyaging in company on a two-year cruise around the world.

When I next encountered him some 20 years later, at a private party in a penthouse apartment overlooking the Miami International Boat Show, he'd retired from all this, having sold his business many years earlier. He was now in his 70s. His jet-black hair had turned gun-metal gray, his once-strong physique was now a bit stooped over, but his eyes still burned with energy.

He had spent much of his retirement sailing his third *Aventura*, a French-built aluminum Ovni 43, all over the world, including to Antarctica. Now he told me he was starting a new round-the-world rally, the Blue Planet Odyssey, and would lead a fleet of boats through the Northwest Passage to raise public consciousness about global warming.

We met again the following year at the Annapolis boat show aboard a new 45-foot "exploration" craft that had just been built to Jimmy's specifications. Both he and the builder, Garcia Yachts, were hailing it as "Jimmy Cornell's dream boat." It too was aluminum, with a centerboard like his Ovni, but with collision bulkheads fore and aft and other rugged features that made it very suitable for cruising the Arctic and other extreme locales. Just a few months after this, much to my surprise, Jimmy sent me an e-mail and invited me to sail with him on this boat from Florida down to the Panama Canal.

I ARRIVED IN FORT LAUDERDALE on a hot Tuesday afternoon in March and was picked up at the airport by a young South African, Dunbar, who had a shaved head and wore a flat deadpan expression on his face. He had once been an accountant, but now was working as the mate on Jimmy's boat, which had been based in south Florida since January and had just appeared in the Miami show.

Jimmy had already briefed me on his mind-boggling itinerary. Even before he'd displayed his new boat at Annapolis six months earlier, he'd already sailed her with a small squadron of Blue Planet Odyssey boats north into the Arctic in what proved to be an unsuccessful attempt to transit the Northwest Passage from east to west. The route had been clear enough for yachts to get through during previous summers, but this past summer the ice had been thicker. The only way to get through was to winter over, which for Jimmy was out of the question.

Now, after this hiatus in Florida, he was rushing to catch up with the main body of the Odyssey fleet. These boats had elected not to try the Northwest Passage and had already reached the Galápagos Islands in the Pacific. Jimmy's plan was to get his boat south to Panama and through the canal as quickly as possible. Then he would strike out nonstop to Tahiti, a distance of over 5,000 miles, and join the fleet there.

We arrived at the boat, tied to a dock in the labyrinth of Lauderdale's canals, and I was introduced to Dave, our other crew member. He was American, even younger than Dunbar, a ski bum who had only recently fallen into the world of ocean sailing. I instantly took a liking to him, and we were a having a fun getting-to-know-you conversation on the foredeck, when Jimmy suddenly came marching up to us.

"You'll have plenty of time for that," he exclaimed, waving his arms. "I really want to leave as soon as possible."

A few moments later he called all three of us to the cockpit and issued a warning: "I will not be easy the first three days, until you are used to the boat. Then I will stop being Captain Bligh."

We cast off our lines that same afternoon, extricated ourselves from the labyrinth, and struck out east across the Gulf Stream, motor-sailing with just the mainsail up in a desultory northeast breeze.

I couldn't help but be impressed with the route Jimmy had plotted out for us. Having studied the charts myself, I'd concluded there were just two options, neither of which seemed too palatable. The shortest route by distance, I figured, was west around Cuba, but this would set us up for a long slog southeast to Panama across the heart of the western Caribbean, sailing right into the teeth of the prevailing easterly tradewinds. Or we could go east-around through the Old Bahama Channel, close to the north coast of Cuba, struggling, although for a shorter time, against both the prevailing wind and a strong westerly current.

But Jimmy now had us heading straight east through the northern

Bahamas well north of Cuba, where the tradewinds do not blow. Once clear of the main body of the Bahamian archipelago, we would then sail southeast down its Atlantic side, passing between Great Exuma and San Salvador, where the America 500 rally had landed all those years ago. We wouldn't turn straight south until we reached the Turks and Caicos and had all the easting we needed to clear Cuba. This was longer than the routes I'd considered, but much easier to follow. Ultimately, I was sure, it would also be quicker.

The weather through the first part our passage was benign, with a mix of light and moderate wind, and we quickly fell into a comfortable routine. In all it took us three days to transit the Bahamas and reach the Windward Passage, the broad channel that separates Cuba and Haiti. I noticed that each time he mentioned this significant waypoint in our voyage, the door that would lead us from the Atlantic into the Caribbean, Jimmy mistakenly referred to it as the Northwest Passage.

"You seem to be obsessed with the Northwest Passage," I declared.

"Oh no, no," he insisted. "I would like to do it, but I am not obsessed. Going to Antarctica, that was an obsession."

One thing Jimmy obviously obsessed about was food and clearly was penurious in this regard. He gave strict instructions for boiling water for coffee or tea, insisting we measure by the cup the amount of water going into the kettle, so as not to waste propane gas heating more water than was necessary. And each day he set out just four pieces of fruit in a basket—bananas or oranges, and always the most overripe examples—one for each of us to snack upon. I noticed also the refrigerator smelled overripe and soon discerned that the odor emanated from our supply of milk. Studying the labels on the UHT cartons, I saw they were all well past their sell-by dates.

"Yes, yes," Jimmy explained. "We got that milk in Greenland last year on our way to the Northwest Passage. It is good for at least six months after the date. Do not worry."

He also had an old-world attitude about meals. As the weather was fine, these were all served in the cockpit, thrice daily with all of us seated round the cockpit table together, always in the same positions, with proper placemats and cloth napkins laid out in personalized napkin rings. On our second night out we learned how important this was, after Dave failed to set out knives and forks at each place-setting and instead left them in a heap in the middle of the table.

"This is not proper," declared Jimmy. "You really need to be more proactive about doing jobs on the boat." Then he smiled: "I am sorry, but I have to get these things off my chest before my three days is up."

The following evening Jimmy was fast asleep in his berth when dinnertime rolled around.

"You think I should start fixing something?" I asked Dave.

"He did say we should be proactive," he replied.

And so I set to work, setting some rice to simmer while stir-frying some sausage, peppers, and onions in a pan. As soon as the odor from this permeated the boat, Jimmy emerged from his stateroom and was immediately waving his arms again, his voice squealing in a high-pitched panic.

"You are using the good olive oil! You should be using sunflower oil instead!"

"You have not covered the pot properly!"

And my most mortal sin: "You are stirring the food with a metal spoon... in a Teflon pan!!!"

There were other outbursts of this sort, over matters just as picayune, but Jimmy later always apologized for them quite graciously. During the meals themselves, as we bathed in the al fresco warmth of the tropics, he was loquacious and told stories of his life and career. This was the best time to ask him questions, and I took full advantage of it. I queried him on the details of his current rally, on his selling his old rally business, on his relationship with two former employees, whom he'd once fired, but who now were running that business, and finally I screwed up my courage and asked him the question that had gnawed on me for two decades: what exactly had he said at that skipper's meeting in Las Palmas?

A small cloud of concern passed over Jimmy's face as he pondered this, then his brow quickly settled into a frown.

"It was many years ago," he said dismissively. "I cannot remember now exactly what I said, but I would never tell anyone not to answer a distress call. There is an obligation. You must *always* answer a distress call."

He held forth at some length on his father, and told one story over lunch that was very moving. About how his father, as a teenager serving in the Austro-Hungarian army during World War I, had had to ford a river with his unit after they suffered heavy losses on the Italian front. His father was in the water clinging to the side of a boat when a wounded comrade grabbed hold of him for support. To save himself from drowning, he grabbed the wounded man by his face and pushed him away to a certain death.

"He always felt guilty about that and afterwards became a very religious man," Jimmy concluded. "He prayed every morning and evening and always prayed at any church he passed."

"You think maybe that's why he was unwilling to save himself when the Communists came?" I asked. "Because he felt guilty about saving himself before?"

And I was surprised by Jimmy's response to this. His eyes lit up for a moment, as though this might be an important idea, but then came the same frown that had crossed his brow when I asked about the skipper's meeting.

"I have never thought about that," he said. "It is interesting, but I am not sure it explains anything."

THOUGH HE DID FRET ABOUT FOOD, Jimmy seemed less anxious when it came to sailing the boat. It helped, of course, that conditions remained moderate throughout our passage, even after we ventured into waters normally roiled by strong tradewinds, and that we all knew what we were doing. Dave had the least experience, but made up for this with his boundless energy and enthusiasm. He was extremely fit and practiced yoga for an hour each evening on the foredeck before dinner. He was also eager to climb the mast while underway—an ideal attribute in any crew member—and twice volunteered to go to the masthead to inspect chafed halyards and take photos for Jimmy's website.

Because conditions were so moderate, we spent much time working with our light-air headsails. We had a Parasailor spinnaker, with a special slot in the middle, to fly when the wind was abaft the beam. We also had what many people now describe as a Code Zero sail, essentially a large lightweight genoa that furled on its own luff, to fly when the wind was forward of the beam.

Jimmy explained he'd been skeptical of this sail, but that the people at Garcia had talked him into adding it to his inventory. Now he was quite pleased with it. He was even more pleased when I pointed out we could fly it together with the staysail, and he thanked me effusively for sharing this idea with him.

We sat talking together in the cockpit one afternoon while sailing on a close reach with the Code Zero flying in an apparent breeze that sometimes touched 14 knots.

"I really think this must be the upper limit for this sail," remarked Jimmy. "If it stays like this, we must take it down."

Just a moment later we heard a loud pop at the masthead as a halyard let go. The Code Zero sail came fluttering down and in an instant was trailing in the water alongside the boat.

"Aha! I am psychic!" keened Jimmy. He jumped up with a child-like enthusiasm that at once reminded me of his accepting the award I gave him all those years before. Together then we rushed to the foredeck and cheerfully hauled the sail back aboard.

Three days later, as we eased across the heart of the Caribbean basin in the weak tradewinds, we had another minor problem, and again Jimmy's spider-sense started tingling. We were flying the spinnaker this time on a broad reach, but the steering was strange and fluttery. I guessed we had Sargasso weed on our rudders, as the Caribbean was thick with it that season and I'd had the same problem on an earlier passage in the fall. Dunbar at once leaped up, grabbed a GoPro video camera, and held it underwater off the transom facing forward. He pulled it out and showed us the feed. Sure enough, both rudders had big clumps of weed caught on them.

I suggested we drop the spinnaker, round up and stall the boat, and let the weed fall off. Dunbar, meanwhile, wanted to drop everything so he could dive on the rudders and remove the weed by hand.

But Jimmy would have none of it. His intuition told him we should just leave the weed alone. He didn't want to douse the spinnaker, and he certainly didn't want Dunbar in the water.

"I really do feel I have some sort of psychic sense," he told me later. "When I get a feeling I should or should not do something, I have learned it is best to respect it."

In the end it took us seven days to sail from the Windward Passage down to Panama, and during most of that time I felt we worked well together as a crew. But then came another big eruption about food. Dave was particular about his diet and would not eat processed food, and though he claimed he told Jimmy this before the passage, Jimmy increasingly seemed to resent the fact that Dave's meals were not the same as ours. Dave also had a large appetite, to go with his strapping physique, and had taken to grazing for snacks among the ship's stores after our daily fruit ration was consumed.

The showdown came one evening when Jimmy was preparing dinner and left eight hard-boiled eggs on the galley counter to cool. Dave, ever on the prowl for something to nibble on, thoughtlessly helped himself to two of these, and when Jimmy found out he exploded.

"You have no respect for me!" he shouted. "You have no respect for anything!"

And Dave was just as angry.

"Why are you such a freak about food?" he shouted back. "I'm just trying to feed myself!"

The next morning Dave went to Jimmy and apologized, but the writing was on the wall. We pulled into Panama a day later, and just moments after we arrived in the Shelter Bay marina where yachts gather to await their canal transits, Dave was on deck with his bag packed. He and Jimmy shook hands amicably before he stepped off the boat, but it was clear Jimmy had no regrets.

Jimmy and I later had a quiet dinner together in the marina hotel, and when the conversation turned to Dave he became animated.

"He was stealing food!" he exclaimed with a hiss. He rolled his eyes in disbelief. "Why would he do that? When my father was in prison they killed people they caught stealing food!"

He took a sip of wine and composed himself. Then he waved a finger at me.

"But really that is not what bothers me about Dave. What I really have trouble with is this spiritual interest of his. The meditation and the yoga. People who do these things I think are interested only in themselves, and in staring at their own navels."

"You yourself are not a religious person, are you?" I asked.

Jimmy considered this for just a second, then shrugged.

"No," he replied. "I really am not."

WHEN JIMMY HAD ASKED if I'd like to sail to Panama, he assured me there'd be plenty of time for me to stay aboard and transit the canal. I was skeptical, though, as I'd heard what a hassle it can be for yachts to get through.

The business of the Panama Canal Authority, of course, is mostly concerned with large commercial vessels, and bluewater sailboats are by comparison only a nuisance. Typically, therefore, sailors on yachts must wait two to six weeks before being allowed to lock through from the Caribbean and the Pacific.

But Jimmy had Panama wired. He not only expected to be assigned a transit date within hours of our arrival in Shelter Bay, he also wanted to get the boat hauled and have our bottom painted before we started our transit. I'd been impressed by the route he plotted to take us to Panama, but now I was amazed at how much he accomplished during our brief stay in Panama.

Even before we arrived at Shelter Bay, Jimmy had been working his connections from the boat via satellite e-mail. This was to be his fourth transit on a boat of his own, plus he'd personally shepherded six different rally fleets through the canal. He was acquainted with the president of Panama and was also good friends with the administrator of the Canal Authority. For this transit he'd already posted the necessary bond and had arranged for the boat to be measured the same morning we arrived at Shelter Bay.

Sure enough, the Canal Authority's launch was in the marina when we appeared, and as soon as we bid farewell to Dave, Jimmy marched down the pontoon to have a word with the admeasurer. A moment later he returned in a huff, as he'd been told we wouldn't be measured until the following day.

Jimmy turned to me and pointed at the launch, which was now underway, heading out of the marina.

"I asked him: do you know who I am? And I told him: you will be back. And he glared at me." Jimmy smiled proudly. "I am sure he hates me now."

Jimmy fired off an e-mail and the launch returned, as he expected, just two hours later. Fortunately, there was a different admeasurer aboard. He pulled out a pile of forms and a tape measure and went about the chore of measuring *Aventura IV*, from her aft-most to forward-most extremity, and when he was finished announced we were 50.3 feet long.

"No, no!" exclaimed Jimmy, waving his arms. "You must do it again!"

That extra third of foot meant we would be charged double the rate of a boat measuring less than 50 feet long.

"Quick, quick!" he ordered me and Dunbar. And we ran around the boat together doing everything we could think of to make it shorter: pulled the anchor into the bow-roller as tight as it would go, tilted the solar panels on the aft arch as far forward as they would go, and threw an extra line around our dinghy, hanging on davits under the arch, and tied it in as tight as we could.

The admeasurer obligingly deployed his tape again, and this time we came in at 49.8 feet.

By the end of that day the marina's yard had also hauled the boat and had applied one fresh coat of bottom paint. The following morning I supervised the application of another coat while Jimmy and Dunbar went off in a taxi to buy provisions. By the time they returned the boat was ready to be launched again.

Remarkably, by the afternoon of our second full day in Panama, we had completed all formalities, had hired two local line-handlers to temporarily augment our crew, and were motoring out of Shelter Bay. Soon we were anchored with four other yachts out on the Flats below the city of Colón waiting for a pilot to come aboard.

IN THE LORE OF BLUEWATER CRUISING, the Panama Canal has long enjoyed almost mythical status. It is the Charybdis to the Scylla of Cape Horn. Yachts wandering into it, so the stories go, are tossed about like flotsam in the roiling waters of its locks. They may be crushed against the towering lock walls, or smashed against the giant steel freighters right next to them.

But in fact the whole business is rather prosaic, like any other canal transit, only on a larger scale. Inevitably, we suffered some delay. Our pilot was late coming to us, it took longer than expected for the ships ahead of us to clear the lock entrance, and by the time we finally got to the entrance ourselves it was well after dark. Workers clad in overalls, standing like sentinels on the walls overhead under glaring yellow arc lights, bombarded us with monkey-fists trailing messenger lines. Our line-handlers bent these on to our lines, which were then dragged to the top of the wall and secured.

The water around us boiled a bit as it filled the lock, but the turbulence was not extreme. We were tied up with two other yachts, beam abreast of each other in a raft of three, and just ahead of us the other yachts we'd waited with on the Flats were lashed together in a raft of two. It seemed almost preposterous that all this infrastructure might be exercised on behalf of such insignificant vessels.

What is physically impressive about the locks is not so much their size but their altitude. Because there are three locks in a row one right after another on the canal's Atlantic side, you can both feel and see your ascent from sea level. Once you are in the top lock, the descending steps of the locks behind and beneath you make it clear that you have climbed a very large hill.

What is even more impressive is the lake on which you emerge. This is Gatun Lake, once the largest manmade body of water in the world, covering 164 square miles and contained by what was once the world's largest earthen dam. We could not see it in the black of midnight, as our pilot led us to giant steel mooring barrels he ordered us raft against, but in the morning, after we woke to a bright red tropical sunrise, I sat on deck and studied it intently. The cries of birds and howler monkeys drifted out to us from the shore, and all around us a sea of molten orange water reached on and on through a wilderness of dense rainforest.

Jimmy served us breakfast (he later privately voiced some complaints about the table manners of our line-handlers), we received a new pilot, and by 0730 hours we'd cast off from our barrel and were motoring south in the gathering heat with the other yachts in our flotilla. It took most of the day to cross the lake to the Pedro Miguel and Miraflores locks on the other side, and by the time we'd locked down and were at sea level again it was late in the afternoon. In all it had taken us 82 hours since our arrival in Panama to get from the Atlantic to the Pacific, which I suspected must be a world-record total transit time for a private yacht.

Jimmy was hell-bent on getting to Tahiti as quickly as possible and had no intention of stopping at Balboa on the Pacific side of the canal. By the time we'd cleared the last lock and were motoring toward the Bridge of the Americas, I had my bag packed and was on deck shaking hands with him once again. He seemed distracted, and I assumed he was focused instead on the broad Pacific before him.

He took the helm from Dunbar and brought us alongside one of the other of the yachts from our flotilla, which now was heading to shore in search of a fuel dock and a mooring for the night. I threw my bag across, then climbed aboard myself and stood for a while watching *Aventura IV* advance into the distance. She first rounded up, and I saw her mainsail crawl up her mast. Then she turned again, bearing away before the wind with her one wing spread, passed under the bridge, and headed out to sea.

I wasn't too surprised, however, when just five days later I received a cryptic e-mail from Jimmy in London:

On March 31, while sailing en route to Tahiti, an unexpected matter requiring my presence forced me to make a drastic change to my long-term plans. So I have decided to abandon my plan to sail to Tahiti and have turned around. We changed course for Golfito in Costa Rica, from where Aventura *will be shipped to Vancouver, BC. Another attempt on the Northwest Passage will be made this summer.*

I assure you that it is nothing serious, just an unforeseen change of plan... it happens when you are sailing!

This is in fact a better solution for me. Everyone is happy with it, Gwenda most of all.

That same summer, as promised, having abandoned the notion of joining his rally fleet, Jimmy Cornell completed a transit of the Northwest Passage aboard *Aventura IV* from west to east. With Dunbar and two other crew members he sailed more than 3,700 miles across the top of North America in little more than a month, battering his way through the ice-choked channels of the Canadian Arctic with *Aventura IV*'s stout aluminum hull.

Less than a year later I received yet another e-mail, with a very long distribution list, in which Jimmy announced he was selling his new boat, which was now back in France where she'd first been born. In the short time he'd owned her, Jimmy had sailed the boat some 25,000 miles, had circumnavigated North America, and had twice crossed the Atlantic.

I had sensed during the time I sailed with him that this might be how this would play out. Jimmy all along had had his eye on that one goal, completing what he felt was the most difficult passage a sailor could make, in that last place on Earth he felt he needed to sail to. Now at last he had fulfilled all of the youthful ambition that burned in him when he left Romania and could withdraw from the sea in peace.

Garcia Exploration 45: Jimmy's Fourth and Last *Aventura*

Jimmy Cornell's first two cruising boats were built of fiberglass and steel respectively. By the time he came to his third *Aventura*, an Alubat Ovni 435, he had settled on aluminum as his preferred hull material. His fourth boat, like his third, also had internal ballast and an integral centerboard, features that are common on French-built alloy cruisers. Boats like this are quite versatile, as they are strong enough and stable enough to take to sea, but can also easily take the ground and dry out on a beach or mudflat.

Unlike the Ovni, the Garcia Exploration 45 is not entirely aluminum and has a cored fiberglass superstructure, which both saves weight and allows the design of the cabinhouse to involve more complex shapes. It also has twin rudders, dual helms in the cockpit, and an anchor locker in the middle of the boat, just in front of the mast, rather than all the way forward in the bow.

In ordering the boat Jimmy made concessions to contemporary trends he had not made on his previous boats. He accepted that the boat could not carry a self-steering windvane, as the air flowing over its stern is too dirty for these to work properly. He also resigned himself to carrying a large tender in stern davits under the boat's radar arch, a practice he had not approved of in the past. He splurged on some fancy faux-teak decking material, precisely because, as he explained to me during our passage, he knew this would make the boat more attractive to future owners.

In other particulars Jimmy adhered to certain pragmatic principles he'd developed over the years. Most particularly, over the objections of Garcia, he insisted that the boat have partial skegs in front of the two rudders and that all fuel flowing to the engine come via gravity feed from a translucent day-tank that allows one to easily monitor fuel quality. The boat also has a dedicated line-reel locker in the transom, raised standpipe through-hull fittings, and a bulletproof companionway door.

Test-sailing the boat off Annapolis, I found she was reasonably closewinded, thanks to her foil-shaped centerboard (a feature not enjoyed by the Ovni), and during our Caribbean passage it seemed to me she is also easily driven. One of the boat's best features, shared with others of this type, is that her motion in a seaway is remarkably smooth for a monohull.

SPECIFICATIONS

LOA	45′10″
LWL	40′6″
Beam	14′6″
Draft	9′2″ (board down)
	3′5″ (board up)
Displacement	31,085 lbs.
Ballast	9,480 lbs.
Sail area	979 sq.ft.

POPPA NEUTRINO
The Random Particle Man

I NEVER ACTUALLY SAILED ANYWHERE with Poppa Neutrino, though when I first met him I very much wanted to. This in spite of the fact that he had, as far as I knew, almost no experience as a sailor, much less as a seafarer, and was voyaging (or trying to voyage) on an absurd vessel that even from a distance looked, as the U.S. Coast Guard might put it, manifestly unsafe.

I was aboard *Crazy Horse*, sailing from Oyster Bay, on Long Island's north shore, to nearby Huntington Bay when I first spotted it.

"Over there!" I exclaimed as I pointed at a large indistinct object in the distance. "That thing that looks like a pile of floating garbage with lawn chairs on top. What is that?"

My companion Nim Marsh, who was aboard as crew, at once scrambled down the companionway to fetch the binoculars and after a moment's scrutiny made a positive identification.

"It is," he declared, "a pile of floating garbage with lawn chairs on top."

So I changed course and we sidled over for a closer look. The boat, if you could call it that, was entirely amorphous in appearance, with no discernible bow or stern, and seemed to be constructed of dock pilings, odd lengths of garden hose, stray bits of block styrofoam, and large sheets of waterlogged plywood. We waved at the crew, who were sprawled about the roof of the vessel's superstructure in the aforementioned lawn chairs, and they all waved back. After we passed them we noticed they had evidently set sail—or were attempting to capture birds—as they'd hoisted a large net up a long pole that jutted skyward from one end of the boat.

Soon the Thing, as we called it, was far behind us, a speck on the horizon, and we were opening Huntington Bay. This was in the early summer of 1995, and at this point I'd been afloat on *Crazy Horse* for less than two weeks. Already, like birds lost in a gale, Nim and I had been swept up in a vortex of boat preparation. It truly is a gruesome process, fitting out a boat for sea. Every decision made, every chore checked off the list, every dollar spent or not spent, seems to involve the most dire consequences. This is particularly true for dilettantes like me. At the time I really had no idea what I was doing and was only learning about boat maintenance and repair as I went along.

Fortunately, there is something about boats and being on the water that makes people want to help each other. It is commonly said that we project human qualities upon our vessels, but really I think it works the other way around. Even more fortunately, it seems the more ludicrous and ambitious a mariner's proposed voyage, the more willing are other mariners to help him or her embark upon it.

Already, during our stay in Oyster Bay, Nim and I had been the recipients of extreme generosity. Howard and Debbie Wiggins, who ran the Oyster Bay Sailing School, had given us dock space and the free run of their workshop, and there, amidst the faded grandeur of the old Jakobsen Shipyard, we had taken our first faltering steps toward converting *Crazy Horse* from a weekend coastal cruiser to a live-aboard bluewater boat. Now in Huntington we planned to hook up with our mutual friend Hank Schmitt, who was working then as a rigger and had promised to help us work on the boat.

We arrived in Huntington in the late afternoon. As soon as we found Hank, he at once thrust cold beers into our hands, lured us aboard his boat, a Tayana 37 aptly named *Hunk-a-Schmitt*, and soon had us out on the bay again sailing in the local Thursday night beer-can race. It was dark by the time we finished racing, and as we motored through the gloom up toward the head of Huntington Harbor, Nim and I suddenly recognized the black form of the Thing. It seemed to be drifting aimlessly through the crowded mooring field.

Hank pulled alongside in *Hunk-a-Schmitt.*

"Where you headed?" he shouted.

"Newfoundland!" shouted back a stout man with a white beard, who stood atop the superstructure of the Thing peering ahead into the night.

"No, I mean now," called Hank.

"Oh," said the man, as though taken aback at the thought that we might be interested in his immediate predicament. "We're looking for a place to tie up."

Hank shouted out directions to the town dock and suggested as a last resort they might also try the dock at the public trailer ramp.

"Thanks," waved the man.

We headed on up the harbor and Hank landed on a dock in front of a waterfront dance club. He insisted we join him inside, and when finally we emerged hours later after some energetic drinking and dancing, Nim and I were exhausted. Hank, however, wasn't quite ready to call it a night.

"C'mon," he said as he jumped first down on to the dock and then behind the wheel of *Hunk-a-Schmitt.* "Let's go find those guys."

A few minutes later we were landing at the trailer-ramp dock alongside the Thing. Now, in the darkness and at such close range, its construction seemed even more improbable than before. Through one of the holes in the boat—a window, or a porthole perhaps—we saw a dim light and so were emboldened to call out.

After a pregnant pause, long enough for a man to don a pair of trousers, there appeared the bearded one. Up close it was hard not to notice that he was missing several teeth. He seemed very disheveled, almost like a homeless person, and smelled heavily of perfume. I wondered if, like aristocrats of old, he was wearing this in lieu of bathing. He introduced himself as Poppa

Neutrino, the leader of a traveling jazz band known as the Flying Neutrinos. Fortunately, as would be expected among sailors, he was not at all put out at having been called out of bed at one in the morning to describe his vessel to perfect strangers.

The name of the Thing, we now learned, was *Son of Town Hall*. She was the successor, we were told, to an earlier vessel named *Town Hall*, another raft-like conglomeration of this-and-that built on similar lines, but with paddlewheels. This craft, unfortunately, had been accidentally destroyed in some vaguely described and glossed-over imbroglio involving the U.S. Coast Guard.

This new vessel, Poppa explained, was built entirely out of debris and scrap he'd scrounged up on the West Side of Manhattan. Aboard her, in company with the Flying Neutrinos, who were ensconced belowdeck with one or more dogs we could hear snuffling about, he now planned to sail first to Newfoundland and then across the Atlantic Ocean to England.

Surprisingly, Poppa had developed some rather abstract theories of naval architecture while building *Son of Town Hall* and these, viewed objectively, seemed almost sane and rational.

"The last thing you want is a watertight integrity hull," he advised in a stern tone. "They sink right to the bottom as soon as you put holes in them. It's much better to have holes like you have here on my boat."

Poppa pointed to a gaping fissure close to the waterline on what we now knew was the bow of his vessel, then to another slightly larger one several feet behind it.

"See here. All kinds of water goes in that hole there, but then it all comes right out this next one here."

To achieve this miraculous effect, Poppa had built the main body of his raft out of 40-foot dock pilings, all of which were buoyant when soaking wet. He had lashed these together with strong rope, then added some outriggers and large blocks of Styrofoam to improve the raft's stability. On top of it all he'd constructed the haphazard superstructure. For a power-plant he mounted a 4-horsepower Yamaha outboard motor on a tangle of two-by-fours hanging off the stern. This, Poppa boasted, was capable of pushing *Son of Town Hall* at speeds of up to two knots. In a good breeze with the sail hoisted—which was in fact, we learned, a golf course driving-range net Poppa had scrounged up somewhere—this velocity could be increased by a knot or more.

"It's a fantastic sail," proclaimed Poppa. "No matter how hard the wind blows, I almost never have to worry about reefing it."

It was a great deal to take in all at once, this contrarian approach to yachting. Perversely, I found myself wishing I could somehow get rid of my boat and join Poppa on his. What I wanted most, of course—my primary purpose in buying a boat in the first place—was to be free and to embark upon fabulous adventures. Comparing my boat now to Poppa's, it seemed obvious he not only was much freer than me, but was also more likely to have adventures. My act of nonconformity, my carefully nurtured and overthought rebellion against the mediocrity and complacency of modern life, seemed very mild compared to his.

We continued staring at *Son of Town Hall*—in amazement, and with some longing, at least on my part—for some moments after our conversation died away. Finally then we excused ourselves and let Poppa return to his bed.

We undid our lines and scrambled back aboard *Hunk-a-Schmitt*. Then, as we motored slowly away from the trailer ramp, Hank muttered to us both in a low voice, only half in jest: "I think they're all going to die."

BY 6:30 THE NEXT MORNING, Hank was in his dinghy alongside *Crazy Horse*, banging on her hull, urging us to wake up. Half an hour later he and I were roaming the town in his car, fetching bagels and coffee and searching for an odd bit of stainless-steel hardware I needed for some boat project I was working on. Hank's old Mustang rattled like spoons on a washboard, and a loose piece of ceiling liner lay draped across my head like a monk's cowl.

"Over there!" cried Hank suddenly. "We have to help them!"

He twisted the wheel and the car lurched abruptly to the right. Amid a squeal of underinflated tires, we landed alongside a pair of uniformed police officers who were leading Poppa Neutrino and two sullen crew members across a waterfront parking lot toward the harbormaster's office. Hank was out of the car like a paramedic at a crash site, talking a blue streak.

"I know these guys," he assured the two officers. "We'll find a place for them to put their boat, then I'll take them to the harbormaster, I promise."

We stuffed Poppa and crew in the back of the car and at once drove down harbor to a marina run by a friend of Hank's. Here Hank arranged for a mooring for *Son of Town Hall*, then we all drove back to the harbormaster, another friend of Hank's, who was happy to hear that the floating pile of garbage tied up at the trailer-ramp dock would soon be tied up somewhere else.

"Anything else you need?" Hank asked Poppa when we were done.

"I was hoping I could find another small outboard for a good price," said Poppa. "I was thinking the boat might do real well with twin engines."

Hank pondered a moment, then scrawled a phone number on a scrap of paper. As Poppa took it from him he asked if there was anything he could for us.

"I'd really like to see the inside of your boat," I said with a quick gleam in my eye.

"Sure, anytime," said Poppa as he waved goodbye.

Unfortunately, I never did get to see the inside of *Son of Town Hall.* All the rest of that day Nim and I were lost in a tornado of boat chores, and when we woke the following morning Poppa and his raft were gone, having drifted out the harbor, we guessed, with the first of the ebb tide.

A week later we were ready to leave too. With Hank's help we had fixed several problems with the rig, sorted out some wiring, installed a self-steering windvane, and acquired some rope and rigging hardware at wholesale prices. *Crazy Horse* was ready to move on. We'd spend another week or two at a yard in Rhode Island attending to a few more details, then we planned to set off across the Atlantic.

The night before we left Hank treated us to Chinese take-out on board *Hunk-a-Schmitt*. We waxed philosophic over the fortune cookies, and Nim, who had the charming habit of falling in love with any town he visited by boat, went on at some length about how friendly everyone in Huntington had been.

Hank frowned and waved his chopsticks dismissively.

"Don't be fooled," he growled. "It's like anywhere else in the world. You go two blocks inland and everyone turns into assholes again."

THE NEXT TIME I SAW POPPA was almost exactly two years later, in the early summer of 1997. I was still aboard *Crazy Horse*, but by then I had completed my circuit of the North Atlantic, and Carie and I were bringing the boat up the Kennebec River to Bath, where my parents now lived.

For me this was the closing of a circle, not only geographically, but karmically. Here I was bringing a boat I had sailed all the way to West Africa and back past the island and old Civil War fort at the river mouth where I'd first learned to handle boats as a boy. Up the tide-wracked estuary where I'd first intuited basic concepts of navigation while trying to find my way in the fog. Through the dog-leg turn in the river at Fiddler Reach and Doubling Point just below the city that had served as an ultimate limit of my aquatic wanderings when I was young. And just there, parked in a salt marsh at the mouth of Winnegance Creek about a mile below the bustling shipyard of the Bath Ironworks, I spied from a distance an ungainly looking dark blob of a vessel.

We negotiated a transit of the Carlton lift bridge just above the shipyard, where my grandparents back in the 1930s had enjoyed counting the cars they held up on the road as they passed through in their schooner. And on landing at the city dock just above the bridge, whom did I find loading groceries and crew into a homemade plywood skiff but Poppa Neutrino.

In that instant I understood that the blob I'd spotted in the creek was *Son of Town Hall.* Her profile had changed a great deal, but she was still, undeniably, nothing more than a pile of floating garbage. Though I recognized Poppa, I'm sure he did not recognize me. So I introduced myself, reminded him of our encounter in Huntington, and pointed at *Crazy Horse.*

"That's the boat I was on," I bragged. "I've just finished bringing her back across the Atlantic. All the way from West Africa."

Poppa at once looked crestfallen. In the time it had taken me to sail across the Atlantic and back, he'd only gone from Long Island to Maine. Though he was quick to point out he had in fact set out from Maine to cross the Atlantic. Unfortunately, however, he and his crew hadn't gotten very far. Their first night out, he explained, when they were just 30 miles offshore, the wind came on blowing 20 knots from behind the raft, a theoretically ideal angle. Despite all their best efforts, however, he and the Floating Neutrinos (as they now styled themselves) couldn't get the raft to do anything but lay broadside to the breeze and the waves it created.

Once the wind died down they put into Portland, where they suffered first a stroke of very bad luck and then a stroke of good luck. The bad luck being that Poppa had a heart attack and had to spend two weeks in intensive care. The good luck was that while he was in the hospital, a ship spilled oil in the harbor. The Neutrinos got an insurance pay-off of over $5,000, as the oil had saturated the foam blocks in the hull of *Son of Town Hall.* With that money in hand, Poppa totally redesigned and rebuilt his raft, and one of his most important improvements was the addition of some daggerboards.

"We've tested them," he explained. I detected a hint of pride in his voice, but only a hint. "Now we can sail directly downwind."

We didn't spend too much time talking on the dock that afternoon, as this was only a casual encounter, but I did remind Poppa that he'd promised to give me a tour of his boat's interior.

He said the same thing he'd said before: "Sure, anytime."

Except this time we shook hands, and I said: "Good luck, and I hope you don't need it."

Two days later I hopped in my dinghy and puttered down the river to the mouth of Winnegance Creek in hopes of getting that tour I'd been promised, but once again *Son of Town Hall* had disappeared.

I HAD TOTALLY FORGOTTEN about Poppa Neutrino when suddenly, over a year later, in the late summer of 1998, the international wire services announced that he'd arrived in Castletownbere, Ireland, after spending 60 days at sea. He and his crew had drifted over from Newfoundland, and their approach to Ireland was so slow people in Castletownbere saw them coming and had plenty of time to prepare. Journalists appeared, every hotel room in town was booked full, and the harbor walls were lined with people.

In the end *Son of Town Hall* was towed into port, while Poppa and the other Neutrinos sat in their lawn chairs on top gaping at the great crowd they had attracted.

"We have broken the scrap barrier," announced Poppa to the press as he stepped ashore.

This was in fact the culmination of his third attempt to cross the ocean, for he'd set out again not long after I spoke with him on the dock in Bath. After spending some 40 days drifting from Maine that summer out toward the Grand Banks—during which time food supplies ran low and Poppa suffered another cardiac event that left him unconscious for more than a day—the

Neutrinos admitted defeat and called for a tow into Newfoundland.

Son of Town Hall spent 10 months there, in a town called Fermeuse, before Poppa and company set out once again the following summer. It was by no means an easy voyage. The raft now had an inboard engine, a 19-horsepower diesel considerably larger than the little outboard she carried when I first met her, but it was not reliable and broke down just a few days into the passage. The Neutrinos were stuck for several days on the Grand Banks, literally drifting in circles, before they finally caught some current that sent them out to join the main body of the Gulf Stream headed east toward Europe.

The ship's navigator, Poppa's wife, Momma Neutrino, as she introduced herself back on the dock in Bath, later calculated that their average speed between Newfoundland and Ireland was less than two knots.

"You can walk to Europe faster than that," she pointed out.

The biggest problem, again, was food. Supplies kept running low, particularly for the three dogs onboard, but fortunately the Neutrinos were reprovisioned three different times by ships they met. Their next biggest problem, ironically, was almost getting run down by ships, which happened twice, as far as they knew. They also encountered one iceberg, which proved more than a transitory hazard. They were themselves traveling so slowly the iceberg had no trouble keeping up and stayed alongside, matching their speed and course, for over a day.

The most frightening bits, of course, were the gales. During the worst one Poppa saw seas he estimated were over 20 feet high. The waves loomed over the raft like giant walls, and the raft went nearly vertical each time one passed beneath it.

"I was absolutely stone terrified," Poppa confessed in a video they made during the voyage.

Calm weather, however, was much more common than bad weather, and for much of their crossing, when they weren't fretting about food or collision threats, the Neutrinos led a relatively benign existence.

"When you're on this vessel, most of the time everything seems so calm and peaceful," explained Momma Neutrino. "But when you step off and look at it from the outside, that's when it seems really scary."

THE MOST IMMEDIATE EFFECT of Poppa's having at last completed his voyage was that he became famous. First came a rash of common news stories, both in print and on television, that heralded his achievement. Soon afterward there appeared a three-page spread in *Life* magazine, which described *Son of Town Hall* as "a tribute to the Huck Finn spirit of adventure and an artist's monument to man's wasteful ways."

"The design is absolutely flawless," boasted Poppa to *Life*'s correspondent. "You could blow it up and it would survive."

This initial burst of media attention quickly and predictably subsided, but it never subsided entirely. There was something compelling about Poppa's story—not just his voyage, but the whole of his life—and in the years that followed he was the subject of a National Geographic television documentary, a long feature story in the *New Yorker* magazine, a book-length biography, and a documentary film. Through these I learned much more about the happy, nearly toothless man I'd once met on Long Island.

His given name was William David Pearlman, and he was born in Fresno, California, in 1933. His father, Louis Pearlman, was serving in the U.S. Navy when he was conceived and disappeared, never to be heard from again, long before he emerged from his mother's womb. The womb in question belonged to one Vilma McDaniel, an inveterate gambler who liked to shoot dice and play low-ball poker. She moved her son from one cheap hotel to another throughout his childhood, and by the time he was 15 he later estimated he'd attended over 40 different schools.

"I was always being shifted around," Poppa told his biographer, Alec

Wilkinson. "And for some reason I loved this. If I ever wanted a more stable life as a child, I've repressed it."

When he was 12 years old young Bill Pearlman happened to wander into a cinema screening a documentary film about Australian aborigines. These people, he learned, periodically burned down their dwellings and walked away naked with no possessions, and to him they seemed like role models.

"The idea of freedom became paramount to me," he told Wilkinson. "Remaining free to move, free to plan or not plan, free to have an adventure, free to explore an idea or an intuition, free to make my own choices and determine my future drove my life from that day forward."

His life and career as a result were absolutely peripatetic, and he very rarely had any fixed address. He enlisted briefly in the Army, spent time hanging out with Jack Kerouac and company in San Francisco, worked as a preacher, a sign painter, and a war correspondent in Vietnam, and when he wasn't working, which was much of the time, wandered the country in what one writer termed "a state of exuberant homelessness." He also married four times (the Momma Neutrino I met, one Betsy Terrell, was his last wife) and raised four of his own children, a stepdaughter, and two adopted children.

His alternative identity emerged in 1984, when he was traveling with a Mexican circus and suddenly recovered from a long illness he believed had been caused by a dog bite. He had thought he would surely die from this illness and to commemorate his rebirth renamed himself after the neutrino, a tiny subatomic particle that behaves unpredictably and is always in motion. As Poppa Neutrino he organized his family and other hangers-on he'd attracted into a traveling Dixieland jazz band, the Flying Neutrinos, that performed on the streets of New Orleans, New York, Atlantic City, and Provincetown.

Poppa's interest in boats developed early in his life. His first attempt to build one, a canoe he framed up in the basement of a New York apartment building, was not successful. He'd hoped to sail his canoe to Cuba so as to meet Fidel Castro and personally shake his hand, but on finishing it he realized it was too big to fit out the basement door. Later he turned to building scrap rafts, first as a simple means of providing shelter for his tribe of Neutrinos, but then ultimately as vehicles for voyaging.

Son of Town Hall was by far Poppa's most successful creation. After reaching Ireland he ultimately sailed her to France, then through the French canals to the Mediterranean, where he eventually abandoned her before returning to the United States, where he constructed other voyaging rafts. In terms of size his most ambitious project was a scrap raft he named *Vilma B*, which he envisioned as a 120-foot floating orphanage in which he would wander the world taking in homeless children. *Vilma B* was constructed in early 2000 in Minneapolis, and though she never became as large as Poppa hoped, he did succeed in piloting her down the Mississippi River and out into the Gulf of Mexico to Texas.

Just a couple of years later, according to some press reports, Poppa also succeeded in sailing from Mexico to Cuba on a small scrap raft with one companion. There is no record, however, of his ever getting to meet and shake hands with Castro. His next project, a 12-foot raft named *Island Rooster*, enjoyed much better publicity, as it was featured in Alec Wilkinson's *New Yorker* feature on Poppa and also in the biography of Poppa he wrote, *The Happiest Man Alive*. According to Wilkinson, Poppa built *Island Rooster* in southern California in just four hours and proposed to sail her singlehanded first across the Pacific and then around the world.

As Wilkinson described her: "[I]t was a scrappy, scuffed-up, bummy-looking, broken-down wreck of a doghouse on a bed of plywood. It looked like something a child had made."

Though he did trailer this contraption down to Baja and sailed it along the shores of the Sea of Cortez, Poppa soon abandoned it there.

Poppa's very last scrap raft adventure began and ended on Lake Champlain in 2010. As I understand it, he called his final creation *Grace the Dancing Dandelion*, though in some accounts I've seen she was named *Sea Owl*, after a political party Poppa had formed, the Owl Party, which espoused three basic principles: eye contact, courtesy, and due process. Whatever her name, she was built in Burlington, Vermont, and aboard her Poppa and two crew members proposed to sail south down the lake into the Hudson River and from there around the world. Poppa, who'd just been fitted with a pacemaker, had been warned by his doctors that he shouldn't embark on this voyage, but he was determined to ignore their advice.

"I told them my destiny was waiting for me," he announced to the local press before leaving.

Unfortunately, Poppa didn't have too much destiny left in him. He and his crew set out from the Burlington town dock on a Tuesday afternoon in early November and later anchored for the night off Thompsons Point, just a few miles down the lake near Charlotte, Vermont. During the night their anchor rode parted, and the raft was blown into a rocky cliff base on shore. Elements of five local fire departments, the U.S. Coast Guard, and a helicopter from the U.S. Border Patrol all participated in a hair-raising rescue that saw firefighters rappelling down the face of a 30-foot cliff to pluck Poppa and crew from a lakeside cave.

I followed news coverage of this exploit with a smile on my face, as I figured Poppa would soon be afloat again, challenging the gods to smite him down again. But no, the next story I read about Poppa Neutrino, less than three months later, was that he had died of heart failure in a hospital in New Orleans at age 77.

His daughter, Jessica Terrell, a newspaper reporter, concluded his obituary with the following words:

He died like he lived: Plans in the works for a boat trip to Cuba the following week, a novel in progress, and $4.44 in his bank account.

His family asks that in lieu of flowers those who wish to honor his life do so with an action. That mourners go and do something they were always afraid of, meditate on their dreams and pursue them with reckless abandon, or perhaps hold a wild party and toast to Poppa, who has now embarked on what he would consider his ultimate adventure.

It was, I thought, a very fitting epitaph for a man who might well be described as the ultimate ocean voyager.

Son of Town Hall: Breaking the Scrap Barrier

The first modern mariner to cross an ocean on a raft, or most of an ocean, was Thor Heyerdahl, who in 1947 gained much notoriety when he sailed with five crew on his balsa raft, *Kon-Tiki*, some 4,300 miles across the Pacific from Peru to Polynesia. A less well-known imitator, William Willis, followed in his wake soon afterward and in 1954 sailed another balsa raft singlehanded from Peru to Samoa, a distance of 6,700 miles. Nine years later Willis struck out again on his own from Peru, this time on a raft he called *Age Unlimited*, which was constructed of steel pontoons and pipes filled with foam. In this contraption Willis sailed (and drifted) all the way to Australia, a distance of almost 10,000 miles, in 210 days.

Poppa Neutrino was aware of these precedents and William Willis in particular was a great hero of his. He was inherently attracted to the concept of a raft. These were vessels that could be constructed very cheaply of various buoyant components, and as long as enough components somehow stayed connected to each other, the vessel's integrity was assured. As had been the case with *Kon-Tiki* and William Willis's first raft, *Son of Town Hall* was composed mostly of wood and was lashed together, primarily with electrical cordage discarded by New York City's telephone company. This made her quite flexible, so that she could twist and bend as waves passed beneath her.

The *Son of Town Hall* I first met in Huntington in 1995 was very different from the vessel on which Poppa crossed the Atlantic in 1998. The raft I knew had a higher superstructure with exposed outriggers and a very exposed frame-like structure on the transom from which outboard engines could be hung. The raft I saw photos of in *Life* magazine had a lower profile and was much more streamlined. The tangled frame on the stern was gone, as the engine had been brought inboard, and the outriggers were better incorporated into the main body of the raft and looked much more like sponsons.

The biggest difference was in the rig. In 1995 *Son of Town Hall* carried but one mast, positioned well forward, from which Poppa had flown his unique never-needed-reefing net sail. The vessel that reached Ireland carried three masts, the tallest of which, perhaps 20 feet high, was amidships. The sails were more conventional than before, composed of a patchwork of opaque fabrics borrowed from parachutes, bed-sheets, and circus tents.

SPECIFICATIONS

LOA	50′
LWL	50′
Beam	12′
Draft	1′8″ (boards up)
	6′ (boards down)
Displacement	18 tons (approx.)
Sail area	unknown
Power	Lister diesel (19 hp)

AFTERMATH: A Flight Back West

Approx. 300NM East of Cape Hatteras

January 2014

THE ENDLESS PARADE OF WAVES, many of them hissing as they break around us, keeps on coming. For the first half-hour or so, as I sit inside the saloon watching them march up to the boat, I am anxious, half expecting at any moment that disaster may strike. But as I study how well *Be Good Too* lies to the seas, this feeling is transformed into amazement. She is a good bit wider than most catamarans of her size and type and also taller, with more clearance between the water and the underside of her bridgedeck. Both these factors seem to help her cope with the turbulence that surrounds her.

Indeed, we are now much more comfortable lying ahull than we were dogging into the teeth of this gale just a few hours ago. Yes, the boat is rolling and lurching dramatically as the waves pass beneath her, but the motion is not too abrupt or pronounced, and the sharp, jerky blows of seas slapping hard against us have mostly stopped. Very few of these waves are coming aboard, and the deck, once drenched in driven spray, has almost dried out.

We are biding our time—eating, sleeping, reading books, taking turns standing watch in the comfort of the saloon. Outwardly we all seem relaxed and are grateful for this relatively quiet respite, but inwardly we feel tense and vulnerable. I am sure Gunther and Doris, who have less experience in bad weather and are the owners of this crippled boat, must be particularly worried.

Come afternoon Hank switches on a portable satellite phone and dials the number of our weather advisor, Ken, who lives in Maine, far to the north of us. He informs us we are now just south of the main body of the Gulf

Stream, which is good news in itself, but his weather forecast is not propitious. He expects the wind where we are will keep blowing hard from the south, the direction we need to go, all through the night to come. Even worse, it will get stronger, increasing to 45 knots with frequent gusts over 50, before shifting to the west and subsiding sometime tomorrow afternoon.

Meanwhile, though we are grateful for *Be Good*'s uncanny ability to lie beam-on to waves, we are increasingly concerned about her build quality. It is one thing to endure weather like this in a boat you have great faith in, in a boat you believe is much stronger than you. It is another to do it in a boat you fear may be fundamentally flawed.

Water from outside the boat is now appearing everywhere, though we're not sure where or how it is coming aboard. The problem seems most pronounced in the starboard hull, where the engine compartment aft and the main bilge amidships are slowly but continually being flooded. As with the port hull earlier, we find outlet plumbing running overboard without check valves or siphon loops and try to remedy this as best we can, pulling slack out of the hose runs and building up loops wherever possible. But still the water keeps creeping in.

Later, during the darkest part of the night, when the wind is blowing its hardest (Gunther later will claim he saw gusts to over 60 during his watch), I am wakened in my berth in the forward part of the starboard hull by the sound of water splashing around inside the boat. It sounds like a great deal of water.

In an instant my nervous system goes on high alert, and I struggle to extract myself from my cocoon of blankets. I pull on my boots and stalk down the hull looking for the source.

Sticking my head through the open door of the head compartment, I can hear the sound of splashing water is louder there. My flashlight beam roams the space. It crawls down the wall of the shower stall to the right, where I am shocked to find the shower pan is full of seawater that has slopped aboard through an escape hatch that has somehow sprung open. The light stabs through the open aperture and shows me the black waves just outside waiting to come in.

Hatches like this are always very close to the waterline and are designed so people can safely exit the boat should it get turned upside down. Normally they are built as strongly as possible with heavy-duty locking latches that prevent them from opening accidentally. Inspecting this open hatch, however, I see it is rather flimsy with a weak plastic latch that has little purchase on the hatch frame when closed. As I close it up again, I find there is no way to lock it shut. We'll have to check it frequently, I realize, to make sure the hatch stays closed and does not swamp us.

I notice also with a perverse sense of wonderment that the cabin sole, both in the head and in the main part of the hull, is delaminating. It is skinned with a thin veneer of some synthetic material with a faux-finish wood grain, and this veneer is now coming loose. I can easily peel up large sections of it with my fingertips, and underneath I find a thin film of water that seems to be flowing, as though it is coming from somewhere, though I have no idea where.

At 0400 hours I go up to relieve Hank and find him sitting in a pitch-black saloon, with no light showing anywhere. His voice is a bit grim as he explains there is now no more electrical power. The house batteries are dead. The generator won't start, he says, and though he had the port engine running earlier, he couldn't get its alternator to charge the battery bank.

I describe to him what I've just found in the starboard hull, and he shakes his head: "This is just going from bad to worse."

And I am surprised to hear him say it, for he is normally fervently optimistic, one of his best traits as a skipper.

The good news is the wind has already shifted west, much earlier than expected, and hopefully will soon diminish.

Most likely it is the electric bilge pumps that have run our batteries flat. They were running more and more often to pump water out of the boat, and then would just keep on running after the water was gone, thanks to the defective switches that have prevented them from shutting down on their own. Now they are permanently shut down, and we must use our one manual pump to clear the entire boat of seawater. This is mounted under a cockpit seat outside and has one very long mobile intake hose, made of light plastic with a strum-box filter on the end, that can reach every compartment in the boat.

And this is how I spend my watch: scuttling about like a bilge rat with a penlight between my teeth, shifting the intake hose and strum box from one compartment to the next, counting the strokes as I pump each one dry.

COME DAYLIGHT THE WIND SPEED has decreased to around 25 knots and the seas have eased proportionately. Hank, Gunther, and I all turn out simultaneously to see what we can do to get the boat moving again. We are anxious to be anywhere but here, and the morning light and more moderate conditions have fueled our optimism.

Though our big battery bank is flat, the smaller starting batteries for the engines still have juice, so first we try these. Both the generator and the port engine, however, refuse to turn over. The starboard engine will start, but again its alternator isn't sending power to the batteries. Climbing around in the two engine compartments, we find the systems are all damp and are now visibly corroding, with beads of saltwater everywhere dripping from wires and components.

So we turn to the sails. We rig one new sheet for the jib on centerline, lead barber-haulers to the rails on either side to control the trim angle, and then unfurl about half the sail. With the wind now blowing from the west, this large fraction of a headsail should be all we need to start sailing southeast toward Bermuda, 300 miles away, which we now figure is our best destination.

But we can't get the boat to turn downwind, even with the starboard engine in gear to help provide forward momentum. We try everything we can think of. We find we can easily turn the boat with the engine in reverse, but once we get her lined up in the direction we want and shift into forward gear and sheet home the sail, the boat just rounds up into the wind. The best we can do is effectively heave-to, with the bow cocked up pointing southwest into the wind at an angle while the boat drifts slowly southeast.

We wonder if the mainsail might help us, but decide against trying to raise it. The wind is still strong, and we are worried about the damaged full battens at the head of the sail. Rationally, too, we know the mainsail most likely will only increase the boat's tendency to round up to windward.

Later in the morning the wind increases again to about 30 knots, and now, curiously, we have much better luck sailing under the jib alone. First we can manage a close reach, with the boat sailing almost due south, then later as the wind builds to 35 knots we find we can turn downwind on to a broad reach, sailing southeast more or less straight toward Bermuda.

Our optimism is rising again, but still we have trouble controlling the boat. Every once in a while, for no apparent reason, she suddenly spins around in a circle. Sometimes she bears away, sometimes she rounds up, jibing or tacking as she turns through 360 degrees, and then inexplicably she settles down again and resumes sailing southeast.

By late afternoon the wind is decreasing again, and the boat starts spinning around more frequently. We fight to sail southeast for as long as we can and take turns hand-steering all through the evening and the early part of the night. First Gunther, then Hank, and then me, coming on shortly after midnight. By the dark part of the morning I have no control at all and the boat is doing nothing but spinning out doughnuts in the water. So I reluctantly furl the jib and once again let her drift to the seas.

We have now been at sea for more than five days and for going on two days have been mostly unable to steer. For more than one day we've had no house power. We are still taking on water at a steady rate and every hour or so must pump out the boat by hand. It is also still midwinter in the North Atlantic, and it is certain another gale will come—probably sooner rather than later.

BY NOW, OF COURSE, it is clear there must be something wrong with the boat's steering system. Ever since that big wave hit us something hasn't been working right, and we've discussed at some length what it might be. Given the boat's behavior, however, we can't come up with any rational theories. There's no unusual friction when the wheel is turned, so the rudder stocks can't have been bent off their vertical axes. And it doesn't seem either rudder has broken away. If both were gone we wouldn't be able to steer at all; if just one was gone we should still be able to steer with the other.

By sunrise the wind is in the south again and has gone light for the first time, blowing only about 10 knots. There is still a lot of swell running, but there are no breaking waves. The sun is bright and the air feels nourishingly warm: the calmest, most pleasant conditions we've experienced since leaving New York.

Full of hope again we fire up the starboard engine, which thankfully still starts reliably, and throw it into gear. Immediately, however, the boat starts spinning to port, even with the wheel hard over all the way to starboard.

We shut down the engine, and Hank swarms through the mechanical spaces at the aft end of each hull, carefully inspecting all visible components of the steering system. Soon we hear his voice chirping cheerfully out the open hatch on the port side.

"I found the problem... and I think we can fix it!"

After so many hours of uncertainty and bad weather, it is an enormous relief now to be able to try to repair something that is obviously broken.

What has happened is the port-side tiller arm, which ties the port rudder into the rest of the steering system, is no longer connected to its rudder stock, which is the spine of the rudder blade. We are amazed to discover that the only thing that was securing the tiller to the stock was a tiny set-screw, but are not at all amazed to find that it has broken in two.

With the set-screw gone the tiller, a flat steel bar that fits around the head of the rudder stock, has slumped down on top of the rudder bearing beneath it. Its motion now is only vaguely correlated to that of the rudder stock. Sometimes the tiller has enough grip on the stock that it can turn the stock a short distance, but mostly the stock, driven by the force of the swells passing beneath us, is twisting back and forth much more than the tiller is turning. The mostly random relationship between the two parts seems a likely explanation for the boat's unpredictable steering.

We can see the tiller and stock have been drilled out to receive a large retaining pin, which if installed would have passed all the way through both parts to join them firmly together. Pushing the tiller up off the rudder bearing to where its through-pin hole is in the same horizontal plane as the hole through the stock, we can also see what probably happened when the rudder was installed.

When the holes are horizontally aligned, the tiller rides about an inch down from the top of the stock, just low enough that the long bar connecting it to the starboard tiller drags back and forth across a large section of the interior bridgedeck laminate. Push the tiller up to the top of the stock, and the tiller bar just barely clears the laminate.

Once they figured this out, we reckon the building crew was confronted with a choice. They could do a cheap fix and set the tillers on both sides at the right height with just a couple of set-screws. Or they could do the right thing, which would be much more expensive and time-consuming: build two new rudders and rudder stocks with their through-pin holes drilled out at the right height.

Fortunately, the fact of the empty through-pin holes now gives us an easy road to follow in improvising a repair. Indeed, Hank has done this before on another delivery when he lost steering while underway. All we have to do is line up the holes on the tiller and rudder stock, both horizontally and rotationally, and drive in an Allen key to serve as a through-pin.

This is easier said than done, but in the end doesn't prove too difficult. First we disconnect the tiller bar and the autopilot's rudder-angle sensor, then I hold the tiller up to the right height while Hank probes with a proper-sized Allen key, waiting for the hole through the rudder stock to twist into line with the one in the tiller. Once he gets the key partway in, I grasp the tiller as firmly as I dare. I struggle to keep it from swinging with the stock as Hank pounds on the Allen key with a hammer, driving it millimeter by millimeter deeper into the hole. The tiller meanwhile is trying to smash my hand into a nearby bulkhead as the swell outside grabs the rudder and twists it back and forth.

Soon we're finished and after reconnecting the tiller bar and the rudder-angle sensor are suffused with a sense of accomplishment. With this problem now solved, there should be nothing to stop us from motoring or sailing to Bermuda, where hopefully we will quickly solve all our other problems.

But when we start up our one engine and put it in gear, we once again find we cannot steer the boat. No matter what we do with the wheel, all the boat will do is drive in circles to port, and very quickly our wild extrapolations of success are collapsed like a telescope.

"We have to get in the water," declares Hank. "We have to see what the rudders are doing." And he at once starts pulling off his sweatshirt.

"No," answers Gunther. "Not you. I should do it."

And in just a few moments he has changed into swim shorts and has pulled on a mask and snorkel. He slips quietly into the water down the port-side transom swim ladder and disappears beneath a trail of bubbles. Periodically he reappears and asks that we turn the steering wheel this way or that. Then he swims over to the starboard transom and disappears again. Soon afterward he is clambering back up the swim ladder, describing what he has found.

As we surmised, both rudder stocks are still lined up in their bearings and have not been bent off their turning axes. But the rudder on the starboard side is no longer connected to its stock and is spinning freely around it, like a wheel around an axle, so we have no way to control it. The only explanation we can think of is that all the welds inside the rudder blade that connect its steel armature to the steel stock must have broken together when the big wave slapped the boat and pushed it backwards.

On the port side, meanwhile, the rudder blade is still connected to its stock, hence will turn when the stock is turned by the steering wheel, but the blade is pitched way off the port hull's centerline, canted always to starboard even when the wheel is turned hard to port, so that it is always steering to starboard to either a lesser or greater degree.

All of which seems incomprehensible. On the starboard side the force of the wave backing up the boat was sufficient to break all the internal rudder armature welds without breaking the set-screw that secured the rudder stock to its tiller. And on the port side it would seem the welds all held, but the armature as a whole was bent to starboard, perfectly symmetrically, without bending the rudder stock itself off its axis, while simultaneously the set-screw securing the stock to its tiller snapped in two.

How could the tiny rudder stock set-screw on the starboard side have been stronger than multiple armature welds? Why didn't the broken set-screw on the port side act like a fuse and save that rudder's armature from being

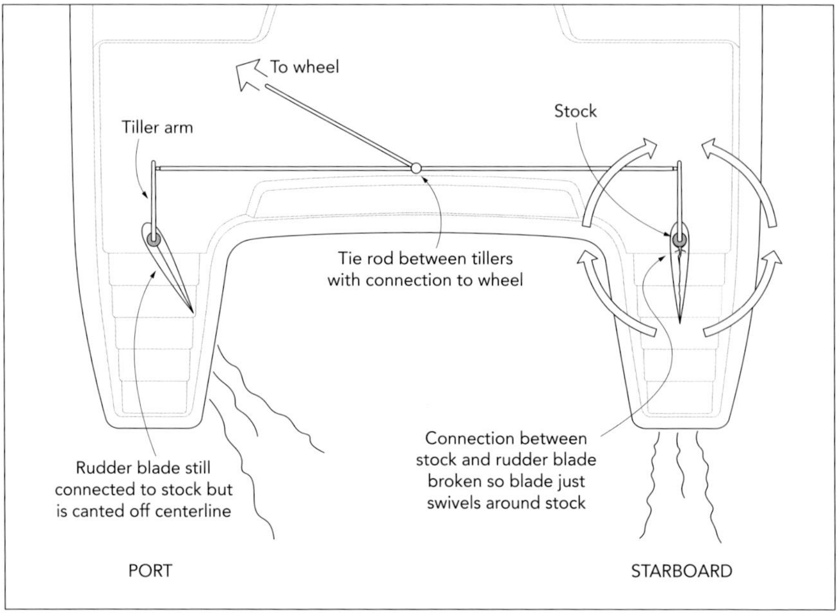

The starboard rudder was useless and was just spinning around its stock like a windmill. The port rudder was perfectly intact, but was pitched to starboard, so that it was always steering to the right.

bent? How the hell could the armature have been bent so symmetrically? And how could the stock not have been bent at all?

We don't spend too much time puzzling over these bizarre questions. Instead we focus on the functional hydrodynamics of our crippled steering system. Effectively we have no rudder on the starboard side, as that rudder blade will just line up with the water flowing past it. So with just the starboard propeller turning it must be the asymmetrical propeller thrust alone that is turning the boat to port. The port rudder, though canted to starboard, has no effect, because that side of the boat is not moving forward and its rudder has no water flowing over it.

We wonder: what if we had the port engine running too? So we turn our attention here, try to start this engine again, and smell burning wiring when we turn the ignition key. We follow the main lead into the engine and quickly realize its starter has shorted out.

What about the two sails? In these much calmer conditions we are confident we can raise the mainsail with the two top battens loose, and with both the main and the jib, plus the starboard engine running, maybe we can achieve a balance that allows us to control the boat.

So up go the sails, and over the next few hours, as the sun reaches its zenith and then starts descending again, we work through every combination we can think of. But no matter what we do, even with sails backed and the starboard engine running hard to maximize turning momentum to port, the boat will now only turn to starboard. Turning the wheel, we can affect the rate of turn, but we cannot stop it, as it would seem once the boat is moving forward there is no force—either from the sails on whichever tack, or from the starboard propeller—that is sufficient to counteract the turning momentum created by the bent rudder.

So we drop the sails again and begin debating what to do next.

Hank, who handled the hammer that drove in the Allen key that rejoined the tiller to the port rudder stock, who remembers clearly just how hard he was hitting that key, doesn't believe it will be possible for us to extract it again and so undo our seemingly unhelpful repair. Whatever happens, whatever we think up, it seems we are stuck with our port rudder blade fixed at an offset angle to starboard.

Gunther fixes on the notion of somehow starting the port engine again, though it's not clear this will solve anything. He opines that perhaps we can remove the starboard engine's starter while that engine is running, then install it on the port engine to get that one started too.

But both Hank and I think that sounds crazy, and Hank asks instead whether it might be possible to get someone to come out and tow us back to shore. According to our handheld GPS receiver, which runs on AA flashlight batteries, we are now 300 miles from anywhere, poised almost equidistantly between New York, Bermuda, and the mouth of Chesapeake Bay. Hank, who once worked on commercial fishing boats, says he still knows guys on Long Island with boats big enough to come out this far. And the more he talks about it, the more he warms to this idea.

"They can't make much money fishing anymore," he explains. "I bet one of them might be happy to make some doing this."

But we don't have any way to recharge our two satellite phones, thus cannot communicate promiscuously with shore. We can't be dialing multiple numbers, leaving messages, waiting for calls to come back, but we can call Gregor and ask him to do all that for us.

Gunther turns on his phone and makes the call, only to find Gregor is not available. Instead he gets Marco, Gregor's partner, the man with the hands-on experience who actually constructed this brand-new boat that seems to be disintegrating around us. He is very upset with us, that we have broken the boat he built, but takes some names that Hank has provided and agrees we can call again later to see if he has found anyone to help us.

By now the afternoon is well advanced, and the sun is slumping toward the horizon. Gunther wants to understand how a tow back to shore is likely to proceed, and I am happy to tell him what I think, for I am not nearly as optimistic as Hank.

Even if we can find an appropriate vessel to come to us, I posit, it will be at least two days before it can reach us. Once we rendezvous, the tow back to shore will then have to proceed very slowly, due to the bent rudder. Figure a towing speed of three knots maximum, which means, if we're lucky, a four- to five-day trip back to shore. In the meanwhile, however, there will certainly be at least one more routine winter gale, perhaps more, just like the one we just went through. During any gale the tow line most likely will have to be dropped, and the two vessels will have to lie ahull separately, waiting for the wind and seas to subside before proceeding onward.

Hank agrees with all of this, but does not seem daunted by it. Gunther, who also has Doris to think about, seems somewhat more daunted. When he dials up Marco again an hour later, the point seems moot in any event, at least for the time being, as Marco has found no one who is willing to come to us.

WE HAD IN FACT previously discussed the notion of abandoning the boat. At least Hank and I had, mostly as a joke, in the dark morning after the batteries went dead. This damn boat has so many things wrong with it, we declared, it would probably be easiest for everyone if we just left it out here.

But now this seems a more realistic prospect, and finally as the sun starts setting, bringing to a close our third day adrift, Gunther reluctantly announces this is what he thinks we should do. He immediately calls the Coast Guard on his sat phone to make arrangements, and when he is finished the feeling of relief aboard is palpable.

"Maybe we should open a bottle of wine," says Gunther hopefully, looking to Doris, who thus far has forbidden any drinking during our passage.

"Yes, just one," she answers with a smile, and Gunther quickly uncorks a bottle.

Hank and I by now know the story of these people and understand the contours of their dream. They're not at all unusual. Gunther has only recently retired after a long and successful career, and both he and Doris have long been looking forward to being able to spend a whole winter together exploring the Caribbean. After years of cruising a monohull for just one or two weeks at a time, they'd wanted a larger more comfortable boat, a catamaran, so they'd have enough space to make a proper home and could invite family and friends to join them.

Gunther, however, had very specific requirements and hadn't found any production boats that satisfied them. Until he found Gregor, who was himself searching for a buyer for hull number one of his new line of boats. Gunther had read Gregor's book on catamarans, which advises that you should never buy a prototype boat, and yet he bought this prototype first boat from Gregor, because it was exactly what he thought he wanted.

Now all these dreams—both Gunther's and Gregor's—are dead in the water. Gunther and Doris waited patiently for two years to take possession of this boat, have spent barely a week aboard, and now will leave it behind them. Throughout our long trial they've been remarkably calm and collected, and now they tell us they feel mostly grateful, for we are all safe and there are no lives at stake.

This is just a boat, after all. Just a huge piece of plastic cast in the shape of a hull with some sails and engines attached to it.

And together we laugh a bit about all the problems we've had as we each savor our one glass of wine in the gathering darkness.

"Well, this is a first for me," says Hank and turns to me. "But for you this will be the second time."

And I can't help but smile. For the first time I ever met Hank was 22 years earlier at the Puerto Sherry marina in Spain, just days before we abandoned *Constellation* in the Rio Odiel.

"Yes," I answer. "But last time all I had to do was get in a dinghy and drive a few hundred yards to shore."

This time, for sure, it will be more complicated.

Because we are so far from shore, beyond the normal range of any helicopter, we had assumed the Coast Guard would divert a freighter to retrieve us, and this in fact is what Gunther was told: a westbound commercial ship will rendezvous with us at 0800 hours in the morning.

After we finish our wine we resume our watch rotation and all through the night take turns sitting in the pitch-black saloon. We keep an eye on the boat and the outside world; we pump the bilges by hand every hour. The weather is still settled and calm and all is quiet, but during my off-time I find I cannot sleep. My mind is running hard—imagining what it will be like to have a huge steel ship come alongside us, wondering how hard it will be to climb up its side, figuring out what I can fit in the one small bag I'm allowed to bring with me.

Throughout the night we are also in regular contact with the Coast Guard, checking in with them by sat phone every few hours, and when I come back on at 0300 hours to relieve Gunther I learn there's been a change in plan. The U.S. Navy, it turns out, has vessels in the area looking for a helicopter they lost in the gale, and apparently the Coast Guard wants to take advantage of this. They've decided to send a helicopter from shore, due to arrive at 0900 hours, which will land and refuel on a Navy missile destroyer en route to us, then do the same on the way back.

At 0900 sharp we spot a C-130 Hercules search plane coming straight at us over the western horizon at low altitude, followed five minutes later by a MH-60 Jayhawk helicopter. The sound of their engines, after so many hours of hearing only the lullaby of waves moving past us, is a welcome intrusion. Conditions are still relatively calm, though the wind has been increasing steadily since sunrise. By early afternoon, we've been told, it will most likely increase again to near gale force.

The Jayhawk hovers just 50 feet over the water a short distance astern of us, the blast from its rotors flattening the waves beneath it. We watch as an orange figure descends at the end of a cable. In just a moment the figure is swarming up the swim ladder on our port transom and cheerfully introduces himself as John, our rescue swimmer.

He explains how this works. We go one at a time. Jump in the water, swim away from the boat, then we get hauled up to the chopper. Just one bag each.

Hank has already told us the order he wants us to go in, and now he reiterates: me first, so Doris and Gunther can see what will happen to them, then Doris, then Gunther, and lastly Hank, because he's the skipper.

But Gunther, as owner, again decides to pull rank. "No," he says. "I will be the one to go last."

I jump face forward off the port transom, turn my body as I fall, and hit the water back first. I am dressed in full foul-weather gear, wearing a cheap coastal life-vest, with one small canvas bag slung over my shoulder.

The water feels warmer than I expected. Deliciously so. In the midst of this very unfamiliar procedure, the sensation of being immersed in it is reassuringly familiar. Though my rational mind knows we are yet a long ways from safety, my body, now that it is soaking wet, already feels safe. My muscles relax instinctively, commune with the giant bath that surrounds me, and in an instant it feels as if I have arrived in a place that might be called home.

John, who is wearing mammoth swim fins, grabs me by my life-vest and pulls me easily away from the boat. The waves hadn't looked very big from the boat, but down here they're more imposing. Some of them, I note, are topped with small white-caps. I kick with my feet a bit to help keep my head well clear.

John shouts at me: "You're going up in a basket. Wait for it to settle in the water, climb in, keep your hands inside going up."

The steel-framed basket is rectangular, with deeper sides than I expect, large flotation sponsons at either end, and a solid four-legged steel bridle overhead. Entering from the water is awkward, but somehow I manage to slither in. I am immediately swamped by a wave, and the basket lists precipitously to one side. Then suddenly it is airborne, and I watch fascinated as everything beneath me gets smaller. I shout and wave eagerly at the others down on the boat below.

At the top of the hoist there is another orange figure wearing a flight helmet leaning out the chopper's open side door. He pulls the basket aboard and I slither out again like an eel. He gives me a wave with one gloved hand, points at a jump seat in the corner, unclips the basket, and shoves it aside.

Looking forward I can see the backs of two pilots through thin tendrils of steamy vapor that are exhaled through vents overhead. They ignore me and stay focused on the multicolored array of electronic displays in front of them.

The figure at the door likewise stays focused on his job, keeps a heavily gloved hand on the wire cable in front of him, and in a few moments Doris appears, strapped to John's chest. She is released and crawls up off the floor into another jump seat, while John disappears out the door again.

The crew member stays focused on the cable as it winds out the winch above him, but then after a moment he turns to check on us.

I raise my hand and shout over the din of the engine and rotors: "What about the basket?"

He spins his finger clockwise around the top of his wrist, and I hear him shout in return: "Not enough time!"

Next comes Hank and finally Gunther, who carries beneath him a large ice-chest, crammed full of personal belongings, which John has graciously allowed him to bring along. The side door slams shut, and as I feel the helicopter first turning and then moving forward it occurs to me that I will be sitting here in these soaking wet clothes for some time to come.

I crane my head and peer out the window beside me. Far below I can see the angular white form of *Be Good Too*, bobbing in the waves, growing ever smaller as we fly west toward the continent.

POST MORTEM
Could We Have Saved the Boat?

THIS IS THE QUESTION that raged across a few obscure Internet sailing forums in the days after the crew of *Be Good Too* returned to shore.

The fact is, in more than a few cases over the past several years, bluewater sailors have abandoned their boats in rather dubious circumstances. The story of *Circe* from the 1998 Caribbean 1500 rally, where the crew abandoned a sound boat due to a weather forecast, is not as unusual as you'd think, and many critics, myself among them, have warned that modern communications make it all too easy for sailors to call for help before it is needed.

One of the best-known, yet unheralded examples of how a vessel can be evacuated unnecessarily was that of the Westsail 32 *Satori* in the so-called Perfect Storm of 1991 that Sebastian Junger so profitably memorialized in his famous bestseller. In Junger's book Ray Leonard, the skipper of *Satori*, was depicted as a sullen introvert who ignored the reality of the storm and was sneaking sips from a bottle while his brave, yet inexperienced crew put out the Mayday call that got them all rescued. Not surprisingly, this was the crew's version of the story.

In fact Leonard, whom Junger never interviewed, was a very seasoned bluewater sailor who was confident his boat would weather the storm. Nothing had gone wrong aboard, and he never believed he or his crew were in immediate danger. He never authorized any Mayday call and was not at all happy when the Coast Guard came and compelled him to leave his boat. He did not drop to his knees in gratitude on reaching shore, but instead, with a deliberate calmness worthy of his vessel's name, pulled out a chart, calculated her drift, and later recovered her unharmed from a beach in Maryland.

In our case perhaps a quarter of those making comments online thought we were justified in leaving *Be Good Too*, but a much larger contingent rose up to berate us and offered many opinions on how we might have saved the boat. Some of these focused on Gunther's idea of swapping engine starters with the engine running, and a few experienced diesel mechanics insisted they had actually done this themselves. None of us on *Be Good Too*, however, were very good mechanics, and even if we had both engines running I still do not believe we would have been able to steer. As we proved trying to sail the boat, once we got both hulls moving forward the bent port-side rudder inexorably turned the boat to starboard. Adding more thrust on the port side, all of it coursing over the affected rudder, could only have greatly increased this tendency.

Many more people insisted we first should have "dropped" the bent rudder and then should have jury-rigged an alternative steering system. Many of the suggested rudder-removal techniques were patently absurd or impossible, usually involving large power tools no one is ever likely to carry on a boat. Many also failed to comprehend that because we couldn't get the tiller off the top of the rudder stock, we couldn't simply "release" it. Also, even if we could let the rudder stock go, the rudder itself was buoyant and would not have simply dropped out of the hull. (Though as one commentator cleverly pointed out, we could have solved this problem by tying off our anchor to the rudder and then letting it go overboard.)

Pondering all this in retrospect I have realized first that the port rudder was very likely installed wrong and was offset to starboard before we ever left New York Harbor. As noted, it seems impossible that it could have been bent so perfectly symmetrically along its turning axis by the force of a wave, or that it could have been significantly bent in any way once the set-screw securing the rudder stock broke away. Also, as described in the prelude, the boat always seemed slower than it should have been and the helm was always canting to port to go straight. Both effects are perfectly consistent with one rudder being pitched off centerline to starboard, as one offset rudder in a dual-rudder system should both increase drag and require over-steering to compensate for it.

I have also realized something else that seems blindingly obvious to me now, but which never occurred to any of us aboard *Be Good Too* at the time, nor to any of the dozens of armchair admirals who criticized us from behind their computer screens after the fact.

All we had to do to neutralize the effect of the offset rudder was simply remove the tiller bar that joined its tiller to the other tiller and the rest of the steering system. We in fact removed this bar and then replaced it while solving the problem of the broken set-screw and could easily have removed it again. With the tiller bar off, the port rudder could then have swung freely, lining up with the water flow beneath the boat so that, just like the already free-swinging starboard rudder, it would have no effect on the boat's steering.

Could we then have managed to somehow steer the boat without the rudders? The most likely method, as several of our armchair admirals pointed out, would have been by towing a drogue through the water behind the boat on a bridle spanning the boat's transom. By canting the bridle one way or the other the drag created by the drogue turns the boat accordingly, and as long as you are carrying enough forward momentum to overcome the drag you can make controlled progress in any direction you choose. It is a crude technique, but has proven effective in several loss-of-steering emergencies and should be particularly effective on a catamaran, as a very wide transom only increases the leverage of the steering bridle.

It is arguable, however, whether this technique would have worked on *Be Good Too*. We had no commercially produced drogue on board (though we probably should have) and I can't say now whether we could have improvised one. Like most brand-new boats that have just been delivered to their owners, *Be Good Too* carried very few of the more specialized tools and other spare bits of this-and-that that inevitably find their way on to more seasoned bluewater boats. We didn't have too much to work with, but we might have been able to come up with something workable had we tried.

We might also have had a problem with the tiller swinging around inside the hull after we released it. As it was offset in relation to the rudder, the tiller might easily have been slamming into the starboard side of the hull's interior at certain common steering angles, as there were no proper tiller stops to prevent this. Having not tried to steer the boat in this way, I can't say now whether this would have hampered us.

My ultimate conclusion, I am embarrassed to say, is that we certainly should have tried all this before calling the Coast Guard for an evacuation. More than anything, I believe our unfortunate situation aboard *Be Good Too* illustrates just how subtly corrupting and seductive the convenience and certainty of modern offshore communications can be. We never panicked and never believed we were in immediate danger, but we did believe we'd exhausted our options in trying to steer the boat. If it hadn't been so easy to communicate with shore, I'm sure we would have resisted this conclusion more tenaciously. I can only hope we then might have eventually come up with the idea of releasing the tiller bar.

This is one of the more prosaic lessons Bernard Moitessier teaches us in his book *The Long Way*. His solving the problem of *Joshua*'s bent bowsprit after her freighter collision is properly hailed as one of the great moments in his sailing career, and the key to that success was how he approached the problem. Though he at first despaired of being able to fix the bowsprit while alone at sea, he carefully pondered his dilemma over two full nights and one full day. It was important, he felt, not to "crystallize my thinking prematurely," and to get his creative juices flowing he imagined himself chewing on the problem with an old cruising buddy, Henry Wakelam.

When Henry and I had had to work out a really sticky problem together, neither of us was allowed to mention it. No bursting out with 'Say, I've got an idea! What do you think of this?...' It was not allowed, because the thing had not matured enough, and putting forth an idea that was not worked out in detail wasted the other's time and kept him from letting it 'ripen'. Only that evening or the next morning would we talk about possible solutions.

The point being that Moitessier's elegant solution to his seemingly intractable conundrum required a full and proper gestation period. In our case, though we did spend three days adrift on *Be Good Too* before deciding to abandon her, we spent less than a full day and not a single night thinking about how to solve our problem once we properly understood it. Perhaps if, like Moitessier, we had slept on the problem for a night or two and had let it percolate in our minds for a while, *Be Good Too* would still be sailing today.

Aside from the problem of how to fix the boat, there was one other very pertinent question some of our online critics raised. What the hell were we doing out there in the first place? Several people insisted it was blatantly irresponsible of us to take a yacht, particularly a new untested one, offshore in the middle of winter. On the one hand this is a hard argument to counter, and of all the critiques we endured it was the one I thought was most valid. On the other hand, it is a question you can easily raise about many other voyages.

Was it irresponsible for all of us on *Constellation* to try and sail her across the Atlantic Ocean in spite of her age and uncertain health? Certainly our friends the Dons at Rybovich-Spencer believed it was. Shouldn't Mauri Cullen, as incompetent as he was, have been prevented from sailing anywhere on *Goatlocker III*? Should I have sailed up the Gambia River after being told by the U.S. government not to? Shouldn't someone have stopped Poppa Neutrino from embarking on his crazy raft voyages? Or to ask the largest possible question: were the first humans who ever ventured out on to the ocean and out of sight of land justified in doing so?

This book, you may have noticed, is filled with misadventures that can be described as foolish or ill-advised. If you spend much time in a sailor's bar anywhere on this planet, you will hear many similar stories. It is a fine line that separates those exploits that are worthy of admiration from those that should be condemned as foolhardy, and often no one can be certain where that line should be drawn until well after the fact. One thing I do know for sure is that it is a line we must each draw for ourselves.

Another question raised whenever a yacht is abandoned at sea is what becomes of it. In the case of *Be Good Too*, I wasn't at all sure she would stay afloat after we left her. Though, as a catamaran, she was unballasted with no "lead mine" aboard to assuredly drag her under, her fiberglass hull was not fully cored with buoyant foam. Below her waterline she was all solid laminate, and what with the weight of all her machinery, etc., I knew there was a good chance she might sink once she filled with water, as was sure to happen without us aboard to man her bilge pump and keep her insecure escape hatches closed.

As the number of yacht abandonments have increased, so has the number of sightings of abandoned yachts, particularly in the North Atlantic, which is heavily trafficked by both commercial vessels and yachts spinning out wakes back and forth between Europe and North America. So after several months passed with no reported sightings of *Be Good Too*, I was certain she must have foundered and gone under. When I thought of her, I thought of her then only in the past tense.

But I was wrong. Almost three years to the day after we abandoned *Be Good Too*, much to my amazement, I received an e-mail advising she'd been found on a beach in the Outer Hebrides off the west coast of Scotland. She was upside down, covered from bow to stern with long, well-developed gooseneck barnacles, and bits of her cabinhouse lay strewn all about her, as evidently this had been stripped off her as she dragged across a reef in being driven ashore. I can only assume she was dismasted and flipped over rather early in her drift across the ocean, or else she would have been spotted much earlier.

In the flurry of communication that followed this discovery, I also learned that my old shipmate Gunther had not survived to hear the news. He and Doris had taken the insurance money they collected after losing their boat and immediately bought another catamaran they had delivered directly to the Caribbean. In 2016, while sailing this vessel through the West Indies, so Doris informed me, Gunther developed a serious foot infection and was hospitalized on the island of Antigua, where he suddenly died of a heart attack while being treated.

All of which, to my mind, proves just one thing: it is never too soon to start making your own dream a reality.

Portsmouth, New Hampshire
February 2017

ACKNOWLEDGMENTS

I CANNOT PRETEND that all the text you find in this book has never before been published. Various bits, sometimes in very different forms, have appeared in various magazines over the years, including primarily *SAIL*, but also *Ocean Navigator*, *Blue Water Sailing*, and the now sadly defunct regional monthly *New England Offshore*. Some bits have come from a previous unpublished book manuscript and others first appeared in my online blog WaveTrain (wavetrain.net). All these components have been torn apart and stitched back together, along with a great deal of new material, in such a complex quilt that it would be tedious and perhaps even impossible to detail exactly which parts came from where. Though I do feel the eggs have been so thoroughly scrambled that this can count as a fresh omelette, I still must thank the editorial staffs of the abovementioned magazines for whatever prose-polishing they've done on my behalf over the years.

I must also thank Lin Pardey, Tim Murphy, Jenny Marshall, and Clare O'Brien, who all read an early version of the manuscript and provided much useful guidance.

As far as production of the book goes, I am indebted to Spencer Smith, as light-footed a publisher as one could hope for; Jane Crosen, for her deft copyediting; Claire MacMaster, for this volume's elegant design; my old friend Kim Downing from *SAIL*, for his incisive boat profiles and technical illustrations; and my new friend Scott Kennedy, for his evocative watercolors.

All these people have helped make this book as wonderful as it is. Only I am responsible for whatever is less than wonderful.